# COERCIVE COOPERATION

# COERCIVE COOPERATION

## EXPLAINING MULTILATERAL ECONOMIC SANCTIONS

*Lisa L. Martin*

PRINCETON UNIVERSITY PRESS   PRINCETON, NEW JERSEY

**Copyright © 1992 by Princeton University Press**
Published by Princeton University Press, 41 William Street,
Princeton, New Jersey 08540
In the United Kingdom: Princeton University Press, Oxford

*Library of Congress Cataloging-in-Publication Data*
Martin, Lisa L., 1961–
Coercive Cooperation : explaining multilateral economic sanctions /
Lisa L. Martin.
   p.  cm.
Includes bibliographical references and index.
ISBN 0-691-08624-9 (alk. paper)
1. Economic sanctions.  2. Economic sanctions—Case studies.
3. International economic relations.  4. International
cooperation.  5. World politics.  I. Title.
HF1413.5.M37 1992
337--dc20    91-40190

This book has been composed in Linotron Sabon

Princeton University Press books are printed
on acid-free paper and meet the guidelines
for permanence and durability of the Committee
on Production Guidelines for Book Longevity
of the Council on Library Resources

Printed in the United States of America

10  9  8  7  6  5  4  3  2  1

# Contents

# *Figures*

# Tables

# Preface

THIS PROJECT developed from discussions about two theoretical and substantive puzzles in international politics: the conditions for international cooperation and the uses of issue linkage. An interest in these two subjects made a study of international cooperation on economic sanctions an obvious choice. Economic sanctions are a common example of issue linkage in international politics, as states attempt to use economic levers to achieve political gains. While the secondary literature on cases of sanctions is extensive, few authors have focused on the problem of cooperation among those states interested in seeing sanctions imposed. Likewise, although theories and individual case studies of international cooperation proliferated during the 1980s, few authors have applied these theories to the problem of economic sanctions or attempted to test them across a large number of cases. Gary Clyde Hufbauer, Jeffrey J. Schott, and Kimberly Ann Elliott of the Institute for International Economics recently collected an invaluable data set on most twentieth-century cases of economic sanctions. Therefore, the time seems appropriate for a study of international cooperation in this area. The centrality of economic sanctions in the first major post–Cold War international conflict, Iraq's invasion of Kuwait, seems to have justified this choice.

This study should contribute to a number of ongoing research programs. Substantively, it is an empirical study of economic sanctions, and it should be of interest to academics and others attempting to understand and utilize this foreign-policy tool. By building on evidence from a relatively large number of cases, this study attempts to avoid some of the bias evident in studies of sanctions that emphasize just a few major cases. While many authors have noted the need for cooperation if sanctions are to be effective, few have attempted to specify the conditions under which such cooperation is possible. Thus, this book fills a substantive gap in the literature on economic sanctions.

The second body of work to which this book is relevant is the study of international cooperation. Like studies of sanctions, this literature has tended to focus on a fairly small set of cases, thus inhibiting development and testing of generalizations. The approach adopted here, which combines game theory, statistical analysis, and case studies, moves in the direction of developing generalizations while at the same time establishing causal relationships through process tracing. While the empirical work here is only on economic sanctions, some of the conclusions may indicate problems or new directions for research in other areas of international cooperation. For example, this study finds no support for theories of declining hegemony, but extensive support for the causal role of international institutions. Hegemony and institutions are two of the key factors in many theories of international cooperation, so this evidence suggests that future research could fruitfully ask whether these results hold up in other issue areas. This study also finds that considerations of credibility are central in most cooperation problems; this possible unifying theme for the study of international cooperation suggests that both realist and neoliberal theories have important insights and that a creative synthesis of the two could yield high payoffs in enhancing our understanding of international politics.

A third major body of literature to which this book may have relevance is the study of bandwagoning and balancing behavior in international politics. This line of theorizing comes primarily from the realist tradition and has been applied largely to military alliances. In this tradition, theory and evidence have led researchers to conclude that states practice primarily balancing behavior. However, the evidence here suggests that in cases of economic sanctions, bandwagoning behavior predominates. This empirical finding is consistent with a strategic model of mixed-motive rather than zero-sum games. It suggests the need for further work on the conditions under which states will choose to balance or bandwagon, as well as the need for more-careful definition and operationalization of these two concepts.

Many individuals and organizations have contributed to the development of this book. I would like first to gratefully acknowledge the intellectual and personal debt I owe to Robert O. Keohane. He guided me through the treacherous waters of graduate school in the Harvard government department, making the journey stimulating and rewarding. He patiently read innumerable drafts of this work, providing direction and insight along the way. My other dissertation advisers, James E. Alt and Gary King, likewise devoted an immense amount of time and energy to reading and advising, keeping me from taking many egregious wrong turns. My thanks to all of them for their time and effort, and my apologies if the finished product falls short of the quality of their input.

I would particularly like to thank Michael Mastanduno, Kimberly Ann Elliott, Duncan Snidal, and one anonymous reviewer for their valuable comments on the manuscript; and Malcolm DeBevoise and Nancy Trotic, whose editing I greatly appreciate. Others who contributed to the development of this book include Henry Brady, Peter Cowhey, Stephen Krasner, Joseph Nye, Richard Rosecrance, and Peter Yu. My thinking about international politics, institutions, and cooperation owes a great deal to participation in Harvard's Seminar on International Institutions. Financial support from the MacArthur Program on International Peace and Security, the Center for Science and International Affairs at the Kennedy School of Government, and a Social Science Dissertation Fellowship allowed me to pursue the research for this project.

La Jolla, California

# COERCIVE COOPERATION

# 1

## Introduction

WHEN Saddam Hussein's Iraqi army invaded Kuwait on 2 August 1990, nearly every state in the United Nations was outraged. Beyond posing a severe economic challenge by consolidating control over vast oil reserves, Iraq's action violated one of the entrenched norms of the international community—a norm against forcible acquisition of disputed territory. While neither concern taken in isolation would likely have been sufficient to prompt a vigorous response, the two taken together created widespread interest in finding a way to strip Saddam Hussein of his newly acquired territory. The United States took the lead in organizing an international response, which initially took the form of stringent economic sanctions against Iraq. In spite of the widespread common interest in responding to Saddam's aggression, the United States found that organizing support for sanctions required some effort. States faced a collective-action problem, since the potential economic and, in some cases, domestic political costs to potential sanctioners from joint action were high. However, after establishing a firm commitment to act against Iraq by sending hundreds of thousands of troops to Saudi Arabia, the United States successfully maintained broad international support for sanctions. Manipulation of issue linkages (debt, trade, protection, and so on) and of international institutions contributed to this success. This book studies the dynamics of such international cooperation on economic sanctions.

Economic sanctions occupy a central position in the foreign-policy repertoire of most states. Because economic sanctions can impose costs (both on the states that employ them and on their targets) without carrying the degree of risk attached to military actions, governments use them to signal resolve and exert pressure for policy changes. Sanctions straddle the line between the issue areas of national security and international economics, giving rise to unique theoretical and policy puzzles. In particular, although the goals of sanctions are highly political, states' ability to use sanctions is subject to the rules of economic exchange. This means that unilateral sanctions—those undertaken by just one government—usually fail because the target can find alternative markets or suppliers for the sanctioned goods.

Thus, states with an interest in using economic sanctions face the problem of gaining the cooperation of others. Without such cooperation, their efforts probably will be futile. The problem of cooperation motivates this book, which examines the conditions under which two or more states will jointly impose economic sanctions against a third. The modes of analysis I use are game-theoretic, statistical, and historical; together they allow both generalization and explanation of the circumstances that have proven conducive to cooperation. As a study of economic sanctions and of international cooperation, this work lies at the interface of two active and important research problems. Thus, it generates insights into two significant problems in international politics. By providing an understanding of the conditions for multilateral economic sanctions, it clarifies the role and significance of sanctions as a tool of modern statecraft. Furthermore, it applies theories of cooperation to cases of sanctions in order to refine, test, and modify these theories.

The title of this book, *Coercive Cooperation*, has a double meaning. Multilateral sanctions are coercive in two ways. First, their purpose is coercive—to pressure the target of sanctions to adjust internal or external policies. Second, as the cases in this study show, multilateral sanctions frequently are achieved through coercive policies, as one state with a strong interest in sanctions attempts to convince others to cooperate through persuasion, threats, and promises.

## The Study of Economic Sanctions

The study of economic sanctions provides one part of the theoretical underpinning for this book. The literature on sanctions encompasses basically three types of studies. A large number of authors have undertaken single-case studies, most of which focus on the impact of sanctions on the policies of their targets. A second set of studies also emphasizes the success of sanctions but broadens the definition of success and draws on comparative case studies to ask about the conditions under which sanctions are most effective. Finally, a small group of works focuses on dimensions of economic sanctions other than their success, such as international cooperation.

Individual case studies primarily ask whether sanctions work, in the sense of causing policy change in the target.[1] Typically, the answer is no.[2] While this type of work suffers from the usual methodological problems inherent in single-case-study designs, intensive study of particular cases has yielded some interesting insights into the purposes and effects of sanctions.

The drawback of single-case studies, of course, is that we have no way of knowing whether an instance of sanctions resembles in any way a "typical" sanctions episode, or whether the results of any study can be generalized across a wider range of cases. In addition, this type of work has been dominated by study of just a few cases, many of which are conspicuous examples of failure. For example, a number of authors have written on League of Nations sanctions against Italy in 1935–36, which not only failed to restrain Italy's actions against Abyssinia but may have backfired and increased Italian aggressiveness.[3] Sanctions against Rhodesia (1965–79) and South Africa (since 1962) have also received a great deal of attention.[4] Johan Galtung, for example, uses the Rhodesian case to develop a model of societies' responses to sanctions, discussing how these responses can undermine the impact of negative economic sanctions and even cause them to backfire.[5] The U.S. grain embargo against the Soviet Union in 1980 also generated a number of case studies, which typically argued that the embargo could never work and was far too costly for the United States.[6] As I argue in chapter 3 of this book, the emphasis on just a few major cases has distorted analysts' view of the dynamics and characteristics of economic sanctions. Nevertheless, these case studies have provided some important insights into some dilemmas and puzzles about economic sanctions.

A second stage of research responds to the first in a number of ways. These studies argue that earlier work did not define the concept of success carefully and that sanctions' effectiveness varies across cases. Two influential books in this category are *Economic Sanctions Reconsidered* by Gary Hufbauer, Jeffrey Schott, and Kimberly Elliott and *Economic Statecraft* by David Baldwin. These studies directly address questions of the definition and determinants of success, and they go beyond individual case studies. Thus, they allow the authors to make conditional generalizations about when and how sanctions might succeed. Hufbauer, Schott, and Elliott have collected data on most twentieth-century cases of sanctions, and they use statistical analysis to identify factors that tend to increase or decrease sanctions' effectiveness (defined as their contribution to desired policy change in the target).

Baldwin, on the other hand, contributes to a body of literature that assumes that sanctions usually have only minimal impact on the targets' policies and that looks for other purposes states might have in imposing them.[7] Baldwin argues that economic sanctions cannot be analyzed in isolation but must be compared to the costs and benefits of other potential state actions. From this perspective, sanctions appear to be a relatively attractive foreign-policy tool in spite of their questionable impact on the target. Sanctions, precisely because they can be costly for the state imposing them, allow governments to demonstrate resolve and to send signals to others about their policy preferences and intentions. When these purposes are taken into account, sanctions appear to have more usefulness than is commonly attributed to them.

Yet even these sophisticated studies of sanctions' effects leave numerous questions untouched. Because sanctions are a common element of state behavior in the twentieth century, they present a wide range of puzzles for those who wish to understand international politics. A third stage of the sanctions literature has begun to ask questions that go beyond the issue of effectiveness. Political scientists who write on issues such as compliance with extraterritorial sanctions constitute part of the latest development in the field of economic sanctions.[8]

Some economists, particularly public-choice theorists, have turned their attention to economic sanctions. These scholars look closely at the interests of particular groups in imposing sanctions and at their differential effects on sectors in target countries.[9] Like Baldwin, these authors suggest that states impose sanctions for reasons other than the hope of inducing policy change in the target. However, rather than focusing on signaling and reputation effects, they emphasize the economic benefits of particular sanctions for domestic interest groups.

Another of the "new issues" is the question of cooperation among states to impose economic sanctions. In one sense, this focus follows directly from a concern about success, as analysts frequently have noted that sanctions cannot succeed if they are unilateral (unless the sanctioning state is in the rare position of having monopoly power over some valuable good).[10] Thus, countries attempting to use sanctions as a tool of statecraft are confronted with the problem of convincing alternative suppliers to refrain from undermining the effectiveness of sanctions by selling goods to the target or acting as a point of transshipment for embargoed goods. The topic of international cooperation recently has engaged the attention of theorists of international politics, and applying theories of international cooperation to the issue of economic sanctions should provide both a test of such theories and insights into the substantive question of economic statecraft.

Although this study does not address directly the question of whether or when sanctions work, the issue of cooperation has two links to the question of success. First, as just noted, a successful sanctions effort usually requires cooperation among the target state's trading partners. Thus, cooperation is one step removed from success, a necessary if not sufficient precondition for it. Second, I argue that governments take into account the probability that sanctions will be effective when deciding whether to impose them. Thus, we may find greater willingness to cooperate in situations where sanctions will most likely succeed. This study of cooperation builds on the existing literature on economic sanctions by focusing on one dimension of the "sanctions problem" that numerous authors have mentioned in a normative context but that has not yet received sustained attention as an empirical question: when do states cooperate to impose economic sanctions?

## The Study of International Cooperation

This book also builds on a second body of theoretical literature, one that develops general models of international cooperation. In the last decade, spurred by concepts such as international regimes and game-theoretic models such as the Prisoners' Dilemma, political scientists have drawn generalizations about factors and strategies that facilitate cooperation among states. Authors have applied these models to a wide range of issue areas, including international financial and commercial affairs, national security, the environment, and health policy. However, this work has not been applied to the topic of economic sanctions.

Most of the literature on international cooperation draws on understandings of collective-goods problems. One prevalent theory of international cooperation, hegemonic-stability theory, argues that cooperation is a public good that can be produced only when a single dominant state is able and willing to provide it.[11] While general patterns in world politics, such as the decline of the Bretton Woods system, lend support to some versions of hegemonic-stability theory, numerous studies have challenged its empirical and logical basis. Empirically, some works question whether U.S. hegemony actually has declined significantly, or whether the pattern of international cooperation has changed much over time.[12] On the theoretical level, some authors question the collective-goods model underlying hegemonic-stability theory and suggest that a better understanding of strategic interaction in the face of changing power relationships provides an explanation for cooperation.[13] Robert Axelrod's work on the dynamics of repeated Prisoners' Dilemmas has suggested another path to cooperation without the influence of a hegemon—cooperation through strategies of reciprocity.[14]

One response to the weaknesses of hegemonic-stability theory focuses on the role of formal or informal institutions and regimes in facilitating cooperation. Rejecting the limitation of the notion of international institutions to formal, treaty-bound organizations, regime theorists examine the constraints that rules and norms can impose on state behavior within particular issue areas.[15] Through the interests built up by regimes and the information they provide about other states' preferences and actions, these institutions can help states overcome collective-action problems. Robert Keohane explicitly argues that international institutions, through the functions they perform in helping states overcome market failure, can provide a mechanism for maintaining cooperation in the face of declining hegemony.[16]

The cases in this book take seriously the proposition that institutions constrain state decisions. By looking for a correlation between institutional actions and cooperation and by exploring the basis of any correlation in detailed case studies, I ask about the ways in which institutions can contribute to cooperative outcomes. The primary problem is to show that institutions actually have an impact on state decisions, that they are not epiphenomenal. Finding a correlation between institutions and cooperation is not sufficient to demonstrate this effect. In two of the case studies in this book, the Falkland Islands episode and technology sanctions against the Soviet Union, formal international organizations play an important role. In the other two cases, institutions did not become as deeply involved, and the level of cooperation among states was lower. I argue that institutional factors did influence state actions in a number of ways and that organizations' calls for sanctions did not simply reflect prior government decisions about sanctions. Instead, some governments made their decisions contingent on institutional approval or rejection of economic sanctions.

In these cases, it appears that institutions worked, for the most part, through the linkages they created among issues and the information they provided to members about other members' preferences and actions. In the Falklands case, Britain used the European Community to coordinate sanctions. This allowed other European states to ask for British concessions on other issues in exchange for their assistance on sanctions and enhanced the credibility of this tactical linkage. In the high-technology case, CoCom (Coordinating Committee for Export Controls) allowed the United States to link the foreign-policy problem of responding to the Soviet invasion of Afghanistan to broader national-security issues. In both cases, the leading sender—Britain or the United States—would have faced credibility problems and much higher transaction costs if it had attempted to forge similar linkages outside the context of existing institutions. In addition, institutions gave governments information about what actions other governments were willing to take, thus alleviating fear that they could be stuck taking costly actions on their own.

Institutions are just one of the mechanisms that international-relations theorists have identified that increase cooperation among states.[17] However, in these cases of economic sanctions, they seem to be one of the most powerful mechanisms for overcoming collective-action problems. In spite of this finding of institutional effects, these cases differ in one important respect from the models political scientists have used in much recent work on cooperation. The difference has to do with the configuration of state preferences.

Neoliberal institutionalists, or neoliberals, have developed theories of cooperation by the study of symmetric collective-action problems, for the most part. These models, such as the Prisoners' Dilemma or coordination games, assume that all actors have similar patterns of preferences, that they have symmetric ordinal preference rankings. Economic sanctions commonly deviate from this model in that one state, the leading sender, has a much more intense interest in seeing sanctions imposed than others. This asymmetry suggests that the explanation of cooperation in cases of sanctions might diverge from hypotheses developed from examining models of symmetrical preferences. For example, if all potential sanctioners had similar preferences, we might expect to find that they tended to cooperate more when sanctions would not be very costly. However, when one state has an intense interest in fostering multilateral sanctions, costly actions on its part can actually increase the level of cooperation by sending important signals about credibility and intentionality. Because different patterns of preferences lead to different expectations about the factors that can facilitate cooperation, I argue that we need to analyze different types of "cooperation problems," and I develop a typology of such problems in chapter 2.

At first glance, the problem of coordinating economic sanctions seems isomorphic to that of forming and maintaining a cartel. In both cases, actors collude to restrict the flow of goods, and they face economic incentives to defect. Thus, the economic literature on cartels could be useful in analyzing this cooperation problem.[18] However, multilateral sanctions differ from cartels in one crucial respect: sanctions are discriminatory. As modeled by economists, cartels wish only to restrict the supply of goods, without regard to who buys the restricted supply. Countries imposing sanctions, on the other hand, direct their restrictions against one specific country. If possible, they would prefer to avoid cutting their overall exports of sanctioned goods, by increasing sales to other markets. Thus, the sanctions problem is fundamentally different from the cartel problem, requiring different strategies to maintain cooperation. While the cartel literature is useful in directing our attention to problems of monitoring, it cannot provide direct hypotheses about factors that lead to cooperation in economic sanctions. Instead, I develop a game-theoretic model of the sanctions problem as a starting point for theory building.

In common with much of the political-science work on cooperation, I begin by assuming that the state is a unitary, rational actor. This assumption allows me to work with game-theoretic models and develop hypotheses that apply across countries and throughout the period between 1945 and 1989. In some of the case studies, however, I find that describing the state with a single utility function would obscure some of the most important dimensions of the cooperation problem. For example, in the 1982 gas-pipeline case, divisions within the U.S. government undermined the credibility of its threats and so contributed significantly to the failure of cooperation. These cases force me to weaken the assumption that the state acts as a single unit. However, throughout the cases, I continue to assume that states are goal-driven and that factors such as anger or frustration cannot explain their decisions on whether or not to cooperate. Since some explanations of U.S. failures, in particular, tend to rely on such nonrational factors at work in other governments, this study challenges the conventional wisdom by looking for more goal-oriented explanations of state behavior.

## Methodology

In this book I examine the conditions under which states cooperate to impose economic sanctions. The analysis is organized into two parts. First I develop a model, drawing on game theory, of the sanctions problem. This model suggests that numerous "cooperation problems" may characterize situations involving economic sanctions. I develop a typology of problems based on this model and use this typology to formulate hypotheses about factors that may facilitate cooperation. These hypotheses are subjected to a preliminary test using ninety-nine cases of economic sanctions—drawn from the post–World War II period—identified and coded in Hufbauer, Schott, and Elliott. I investigate and evaluate the hypotheses using three different statistical approaches, since cooperation can be measured only with proxies that require different methods of analysis.

I cannot, however, fully address many of the most interesting questions about cooperation through statistical analysis alone. For example, we can understand the role of international institutions only through careful process tracing, focusing on how institutions constrain and influence states' decision-making processes.[19] Thus, while looking at the statistics gives us some confidence about generalizability, explanation of how and why certain results appear requires careful case studies. Therefore, to complement the quantitative work, I examine four cases of economic sanctions in more depth. These cases have been chosen to highlight the effects of three factors: institutions, costs, and bipolarity.

In this study, I will define *cooperation* in a loose sense, to refer to any joint activity among states. Using this broad definition allows me to make distinctions among different types of cooperation problems. Employing terminology developed by Hufbauer, Schott, and Elliott, I call countries imposing economic sanctions *senders* and those they are directed against *targets*. In each case of sanctions, I have identified one country as taking an entrepreneurial or leadership role among the senders; I call this country the *major sender* or the *leading sender*.

My work proceeds in nine chapters. Chapter 2 develops a game-theoretic model of the decision to impose sanctions and uses this model to refine theories of cooperation among states. I argue that authors frequently have conflated different cooperation problems, leading to narrow perspectives about the conditions under which joint actions will occur. By distinguishing among different types of cooperation problems, I develop a set of testable hypotheses about the factors likely to increase or decrease the level of cooperation found in sanctions episodes. The problem of credibility and of ways for states to establish credible commitments underlies several of these hypotheses.

Although many authors study cooperation, few have considered how to operationalize the concept in any kind of generalizable manner. Chapter 3 therefore develops measures for the independent variables specified in chapter 2 and for the dependent variable, cooperation. Chapter 4 subjects my hypotheses about cooperation to a preliminary test by examining their performance in ninety-nine cases of sanctions in the postwar period. This quantitative work allows me to further refine the hypotheses and provides a framework for the case studies that follow in chapters 5 through 8.

These case studies include U.S. sanctions against Latin American countries over human-rights issues in the 1970s; U.K. sanctions against Argentina during the 1982 Falklands War; Western controls on high-technology exports to the Soviet Union implemented through CoCom, with a focus on the 1980 "no-exceptions" policy and the 1978 sanctions in response to dissident trials; and 1982 sanctions against the Soviet Union and Poland. In the case studies, I look for evidence to support the causal relationships underlying the aggregate results of chapter 4. Chapter 9 summarizes my findings about the causes of cooperation. Taken together, theory, data, and case studies provide strong evidence for the impact of international institutions and self-imposed costs on cooperation. Both are mechanisms that allow states to signal credible commitments. Beyond providing support for the hypotheses put forward in chapter 2, the cases demonstrate the utility of the general framework of this book for providing insight into actual cooperation problems.

The results of this study should be of interest from a number of different perspectives. First, as an empirical study of economic sanctions, it enhances our understanding of this common foreign-policy tool. Second, from a methodological perspective, it demonstrates the utility of adopting a multimethod approach to allow both generalization and the establishment of causal relationships. However, its major contribution may be to the literature on international cooperation. One weakness in this literature has been an emphasis on theory development and the relative neglect of empirical testing and application. I draw on this theoretical work to develop testable hypotheses about a specific class of cooperation problems, and I subject these propositions to empirical analysis.

The major finding of this study is that considerations of credibility provide the most explanatory leverage. In nearly every case of sanctions, one state acts as the leading sender. This state needs to establish a credible commitment to sanctions in order to convince others to cooperate. In many cases, other potential sanctioners prefer to free-ride on the leading sender's efforts. In this situation, the leading sender must use tactical issue linkage—either threats of countersanctions or promises of side payments—to convince other states to cooperate. If the leading sender does not attempt to make such linkages, or to establish a credible commitment to them, little cooperation emerges.

Thus, credibility assumes center stage. I find, in both the aggregate analysis and the case studies, that two factors in particular—self-imposed costs and international institutions—are useful commitment mechanisms and are positively associated with the level of cooperation achieved. Contrary to the conventional wisdom, in many cases the costs of economic sanctions to the major sender are negligible or even negative (for example, when sanctions mean just cutting foreign aid). This typically signals either that sanctions are a low priority for the leading sender or that significant domestic opposition to them exists. In either case, other potential sanctioners will question the commitment to sanctions and the associated issue linkages. Wanting to avoid imposing sanctions in isolation, or not believing the leading sender's threats and promises, they will refrain from cooperating.

International institutions similarly allow the leading sender to establish credible commitments. Institutions tie together a number of issues, providing diffuse (and sometimes very specific) benefits to their members. Therefore, they facilitate the leading sender's construction of tactical issue linkages. Once an institution's members have agreed to impose sanctions, reneging on the agreement threatens the other benefits the institution provides. Likewise, the leading sender's reputation is at stake in any threats or promises made within the institution. For these reasons, organizing cooperative efforts within such frameworks increases both the leading sender's credibility and the incentives for others to cooperate.

Beyond these findings about costs and institutions, the third major conclusion of this study is that potential sanctioners bandwagon. The cooperation problems that characterize economic sanctions are ones in which states want to avoid acting in isolation. For this reason, their decisions to sanction are not made independently, but are contingent on one another. Only when states (other than the leading sender) are assured that others will act will they impose sanctions. This constitutes bandwagoning behavior, and I find extensive evidence of it in both the statistical analysis and case studies. This work therefore poses a challenge to traditional realist thinking, which has consistently emphasized the importance of balancing behavior—the opposite of bandwagoning—in international politics.

# Part One

THEORY AND DATA

# 2

## Model and Hypotheses

THIS CHAPTER develops a game-theoretic model of the decision to impose economic sanctions and uses this model to generate a set of hypotheses about the conditions under which states will cooperate on sanctions. I begin by considering a situation in which two states are confronted with a decision about imposing sanctions against a third. The two potential sanctioners can choose to sanction at a level between zero (i.e., no sanctions) and full capacity (completely severing economic ties with the target). The strategic interaction between potential sanctioners gives rise to a number of plausible games, each with its own equilibrium pattern of cooperation or noncooperation.

To use these games to develop hypotheses about the conditions under which states might cooperate, I group the games into three categories according to the equilibrium outcome.[1] These categories, which are exhaustive and mutually exclusive for the games considered here, are *coincidence*, *coercion*, and *coadjustment*. The third section of this chapter discusses these cooperation problems, relating them to various paradigms for the study of cooperation in international relations. I argue that these cooperation problems are best thought of as ideal types and that real-world cooperation dilemmas generally combine the dynamics of two or even all three types of games, since they usually involve more than two players.

In spite of this empirical difficulty, we can generate hypotheses applicable to actual cases of economic sanctions by considering factors that will encourage cooperation in coincidence, coercion, or coadjustment games. Coincidence leads us to consider factors that promote common interests in seeing sanctions imposed, while coercion games suggest that variables that increase the coercive power of the leading sender should increase the observed level of cooperation. Coadjustment suggests factors that can help overcome dilemmas between conflicting and common interests. Cases of sanctions are messy, combining elements of these three ideal types; but the relationships the games suggest should hold in the aggregate, even if we cannot neatly categorize most actual cases.

The rest of the chapter focuses on developing specific hypotheses about when cooperation will be most likely to occur. The next chapter will take up the task of operationalizing both the concepts used in these hypotheses and the dependent variable of cooperation.

## A Model of Economic Sanctions

To begin sorting out the factors that might be conducive to cooperation
in cases of economic sanctions, I develop a general model of the decision
to impose sanctions. This game-theoretic model considers the situation of
two states deciding whether to impose sanctions against some other country. For simplicity, the model does not consider explicitly the potential
target of sanctions. Instead, I assume that information about the characteristics of the target is included in the utility functions of the potential
sanctioners.

This model includes two other important simplifications of actual decisions to impose economic sanctions. First, it is a single-period model, in
which both states decide simultaneously at what level to sanction. Second, the model includes just two states. While a model allowing for repeated interaction and more than two actors would capture more of the
complexities of actual sanctions decisions, it would also give rise to a
plethora of equilibria. Even the simple situation considered here will result in at least ten distinct types of interaction and multiple equilibria. A
model that appeared to be a closer approximation of reality because it did
not simplify as drastically might provide better insight into particular
cases, but it would not prove very useful in developing hypotheses about
sanctions in general. Since the purpose of the modeling exercise is to develop testable hypotheses and generalizations across a wide range of
cases, the simple two-player, single-period situation seems an appropriate
starting point.

In order to move from this simple model to these hypotheses—about
the factors that should influence the level of cooperation between states—
I categorize the games derived from the model into three types of cooperation problems. The first type, coincidence, has equilibria in which both
countries impose high levels of sanctions. The second type, coercion, has
equilibria in which only one country imposes sanctions. This country then
faces the problem of using issue linkages to gain the cooperation of the
other. Finally, the third type of game, coadjustment, has equilibria in
which both countries sanction at something less than full capacity, but in
which this equilibrium is suboptimal and both would prefer full mutual
sanctions.[2] After showing that this typology exhausts the range of possible outcomes, given the assumptions of my model, I discuss factors that
should lead to cooperation in each of these games.

Consider two countries, both of whom are deciding whether to impose
sanctions against a third. Typically, this third state has become the object
of sanctions by engaging in domestic or foreign acts that others find
threatening or morally unacceptable. Figure 2.1 shows the game the two

Player 2

|  | $y=0$ | $y=1$ |
|---|---|---|
| $x=0$ | $n, n$ | $f, u$ |
| $x=1$ | $u, f$ | $m, m$ |

Player 1 (at left, between $x=0$ and $x=1$ rows)

2.1. General Payoffs in a Bilateral Sanctions Game

potential sanctioners are playing between themselves. Player 1 decides on her level of sanctions, $x$, where $x = 0$ means that she imposes no sanctions and $x = 1$ means that she sanctions at maximum capacity by cutting all economic ties with the target. Likewise, Player 2 decides on her level of sanctions, $y$. Player 1 receives payoff $n_1$ (for no sanctions) and Player 2 receives $n_2$, if neither imposes any sanctions; if both sanction at full capacity, they receive payoffs $m_1$ and $m_2$ (for mutual sanctions), respectively. Unilateral sanctions receive payoff $u$, while free-riding on the other's sanctions results in payoff $f$. It is important to note that although only two alternatives are shown in the figure—full sanctions and no sanctions—each player in fact decides on a value bounded by 0 and 1. The two-by-two matrix does not show the full game, only the boundary payoffs.

In general, Let $p_1$ be Player 1's payoff and $p_2$ be Player 2's payoff. The respective utility functions have certain restrictions. Specifically, they must fit the payoffs of figure 2.1, so that when $x = 0$ and $y = 0$, for example, $p_1 = n_1$ and $p_2 = n_2$. Assuming linearity in $x$ and $y$, for simplicity, there is only one utility function for each player that yields the correct payoffs for the boundary conditions on $x$ and $y$. These functions are

$$p_1 = (n_1 - f_1 + m_1 - u_1)xy + (f_1 - n_1)y + (u_1 - n_1)x + n_1$$
$$p_2 = (n_2 - f_2 + m_2 - u_2)xy + (f_2 - n_2)x + (u_2 - n_2)y + n_2.\,[3]$$

We can impose some reasonable restrictions on the ordering of payoffs in this sanctions game. First, I assume that if a state is going to impose sanctions, it prefers that the other state do so as well. Unilateral sanctions are costly to the country imposing them and are bound to be less effective than bilateral sanctions. Thus, both states should prefer bilateral to unilateral sanctions, so that $m>u$.

Second, I assume that even if a state doesn't impose sanctions, it prefers that the other side impose them, implying that $f>n$.[4] This restriction is not quite as obvious as the first. It means that in this game, both countries have some interest in seeing sanctions imposed, for either economic or political reasons. Even if a state has no political interest in sanctions, it can profit if the other side imposes them—by charging increased prices for its exports, for example. Therefore, this game does not apply to cases where one player is an ally of the target country, since the target's allies receive disutility from any imposition of sanctions. It applies only to potential sanctioners and neutrals with an economic interest in the target state. For both these groups of states, it seems reasonable to assume that they prefer that the other player sanction, regardless of their own decision. Together, the first and second assumptions rule out pure coordination games, since the assumptions imply that each player has an unconditional preference for seeing the other act. Regardless of her own decision, Player 1 prefers that Player 2 sanction, and vice versa. This condition cannot hold in problems of pure coordination, which are defined by players' preferring that they both adopt the same strategy and where no equilibrium is preferred over another by both players.

Third, I assume that at least one of the two states is a *leader*. A leader is a state that prefers bilateral sanctions to no sanctions at all. Player 1 will always be a leader, so this restriction implies that $m_1 > n_1$. It is possible, but not necessary, for both states to be leaders in this game. Finally, I distinguish between a *weak leader* and a *strong leader*. A weak leader, while preferring bilateral sanctions to no action at all, is not willing to impose unilateral sanctions: $n_1 > u_1$. A strong leader, conversely, is willing to go it alone: $u_1 > n_1$. The question of whether the leader is willing to impose unilateral sanctions becomes crucial in some of the cases in this study, as such willingness relates to central issues of credibility.

Thus, I can divide sanctions episodes into two initial cases: those with a strong leader and those with a weak leader. For a strong leader, the following relationships hold: $m_1 > u_1 > n_1, f_1 > n_1$. A strong leader prefers bilateral sanctions to unilateral, and her own unilateral action to none at all, although she would prefer free-riding over no sanctions. Therefore, there are three possible configurations of preferences for a strong leader, which I call cases S1, S2, and S3. In case S1, $f_1 > m_1 > u_1 > n_1$. Here, the leader's highest payoff comes from seeing the other state impose unilateral sanctions. Case S2 occurs when $m_1 > f_1 > u_1 > n_1$; the leader's highest payoff comes from multilateral sanctions, which are now preferred to free-riding. In case S3, the leader has a strong interest in imposing sanctions, so that she even prefers engaging in unilateral sanctions to allowing the other state to go it alone. This yields $m_1 > u_1 > f_1 > n_1$, with mutual sanctions still giving the highest payoff. Although case S3 may appear an unlikely preference ordering, strong domestic pressure to respond to a crisis, for example, could lead the government to this kind of utility function, where $u > f$. In S1, the strong leader has no dominant strategy.[5] In S2 and

Player 2

|          | $y=0$ | $y=1$ |
|----------|-------|-------|
| $x=0$    | 1, 1  | 3, 2  |
| $x=1$    | 2, 4  | 4, 3  |

Player 1

2.2. Player 1 Has Dominant Strategy;
Player 2 Does Not

S3, on the other hand, Player 1 does have a dominant strategy—to sanction at maximum capacity regardless of the other state's decision. Therefore, I collapse cases S2 and S3 into one, as the behavioral outcomes are identical.

A weak leader has the following restrictions on preferences: $m_1 > n_1 > u_1$, $f_1 > n_1$. This kind of leader is more reluctant to act alone and prefers no action at all to being stuck with unilateral sanctions. Therefore, a weak leader has two possible configurations of preferences. In case W1, $f_1 > m_1 > n_1 > u_1$, so bilateral sanctions have a lower payoff than allowing the other state to act alone; the weak leader wants a free ride. Case W2 reverses the payoffs for bilateral sanctions and free-riding, so $m_1 > f_1 > n_1 > u_1$. In case W1, even though she prefers bilateral sanctions to none at all, the weak leader's dominant strategy is to impose no sanctions. These preferences are those found in a Prisoners' Dilemma.[6] In case W2 the leader does not have a dominant strategy either to impose or refrain from sanctions, but gets her highest payoff from bilateral sanctions.

To find the equilibria of this game, we need to consider two situations: one in which one or both of the players have a dominant strategy, and one in which neither does. If one state has a dominant strategy, it will play according to this strategy. The other player will recognize this and determine her best response. For example, consider figure 2.2, where 4 is the highest payoff and 1 the lowest. Player 1 has a dominant strategy to sanction at full capacity. Player 2 has no dominant strategy, but she will recognize that Player 1 is going to choose $x = 1$ and will respond with $y = 0$. Because both utility functions are linear, dominant strategies imply the choice of either no sanctions or full sanctions. The best response to a choice will also be a boundary condition, i.e., a choice of 0 or 1—not something in between. Sanctioning at less than full capacity in equilibrium results only from games where neither state has a dominant pure strategy.

a.  Coincidence Problem #1                    b. Coercion Problem #1

Player 2                                         Player 2

|  | $y=0$ | $y=1$ |
|---|---|---|
| $x=0$ | 1, 1 | 3, 2 |
| $x=1$ | 2, 3 | 4, 4 |

|  | $y=0$ | $y=1$ |
|---|---|---|
| $x=0$ | 1, 1 | 3, 2 |
| $x=1$ | 2, 4 | 4, 3 |

Player 1 (left table), Player 1 (right table)

### 2.3. Strong Leader with Dominant Strategy

What happens when neither player has a dominant strategy? In this case, the equilibrium can be found by maximizing each player's utility function: taking its derivative and setting this equal to 0. We then find the following equilibrium strategies:

$$x^* = (n_2 - u_2)/[(n_2 - f_2) + (m_2 - u_2)]$$
$$y^* = (n_1 - u_1)/[(n_1 - f_1) + (m_1 - u_1)].^7$$

Putting together these equilibrium strategies with the four cases outlined above (S2 and S3—strong leader, dominant strategy; S1—strong leader, no dominant strategy; W1—weak leader, dominant strategy; and W2—weak leader, no dominant strategy), we find that there are four basic types of sanctioning episodes, based on Player 1's type.

(1) If *Player 1 is a strong leader and has a dominant strategy to impose sanctions*, Player 2's response will depend on whether she, too, is a strong leader with a dominant strategy. Only if she is will she impose sanctions; otherwise, Player 1 will be stuck with unilateral sanctions. These two situations are shown in figure 2.3. In the first game, both players are strong leaders with dominant strategies. This is a harmony game, where the best outcome for both is bilateral sanctions.[8] Neither state has any incentive to deviate from the two-player, full-sanction outcome.

In the second game, Player 2 does not have a dominant strategy. However, knowing that Player 1 is going to sanction no matter what, she is able to get her best payoff by not imposing any sanctions—i.e., by free-riding. In general, when Player 1 has a dominant sanctioning strategy, Player 2's best response will be either full sanctions or none at all. If we observe in a situation like this that Player 2 actually does impose some sanctions, this is evidence that Player 1 has used some kind of threat or linkage, or that there are effects of repeat play or institutional factors not being captured by this simple game. In other words, cooperation is the result of coercion or persuasion by Player 1.

a. Coercion Problem #2                        b. Coercion Problem #3

Player 2                                      Player 2

|        | $y=0$ | $y=1$ |
|--------|-------|-------|
| $x=0$  | 1, 2  | 4, 1  |
| $x=1$  | 2, 4  | 3, 3  |

Player 1 (left of the table)

|        | $y=0$ | $y=1$ |
|--------|-------|-------|
| $x=0$  | 1, 1  | 4, 2  |
| $x=1$  | 2, 3  | 3, 4  |

Player 1 (left of the table)

c.   Coadjustment Problem #1

Player 2

|        | $y=0$ | $y=1$ |
|--------|-------|-------|
| $x=0$  | 1, 1  | 4, 2  |
| $x=1$  | 2, 4  | 3, 3  |

Player 1 (left of the table)

## 2.4. Strong Leader without Dominant Strategy

(2) If *Player 1 is a strong leader without a dominant strategy*, the outcome depends on whether Player 2 has a dominant strategy. This case encompasses three possibilities: Player 2 may have a dominant strategy not to sanction at all; she may have a dominant strategy to sanction fully; or she may not have a dominant strategy. Figure 2.4 shows examples of these three situations. In the first two, Player 1 responds to Player 2's dominant strategy, so that the result is unilateral sanctions by one of the two sides; which side imposes them depends on Player 2's payoff structure. In figure 2.4a, Player 2 will not impose sanctions, so Player 1 does so in order to avoid her worst outcome—no sanctions. In figure 2.4b, Player 2 always benefits from imposing sanctions. Player 1, even though a strong leader, benefits in this case from allowing the other to act unilaterally.

In the third game, neither has a dominant strategy. $X^*$ and $y^*$, described above, give the equilibrium here, which is suboptimal. When neither player has a dominant strategy, $y^* = (n_1 - u_1)/[(n_1 - f_1) + (m_1 - u_1)]$. $Y^*$, the equilibrium sanctions imposed by Player 2, are

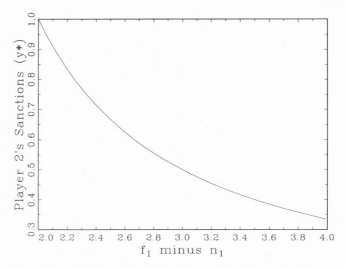

2.5. Player 2's Sanctions When Player 1 Is a Strong Leader

greatest when $f_1 = m_1$, i.e., when Player 1 is indifferent to whether she lets Player 2 sanction alone or joins her. As $f_1$ (Player 1's payoff for free-riding) grows relative to $m_1$ (the payoff for mutual sanctions), Player 2's equilibrium level of sanctions decreases. In other words, as the strong leader values bilateral sanctions less highly, Player 2 responds by decreasing the intensity of her sanctions, in equilibrium. In figure 2.5, $y^*$ is drawn as a function of $(f_1 - n_1)$, or the amount by which Player 1 prefers free-riding over having no sanctions imposed at all. The more highly Player 1 values free-riding, the less willing Player 2 is to impose stringent sanctions. Player 1's equilibrium strategy would depend in a similar way on Player 2's payoffs. This leads to the outcome that if both players value free-riding highly, both will sanction at low intensity in equilibrium. When neither state has a dominant strategy, both sanction at less than full capacity. When $f_1 < m_1$, so that Player 1 prefers mutual sanctions to free-riding, she has a dominant strategy and we are in case 1.

(3) When *Player 1 is a weak leader with a dominant strategy not to sanction*, Player 2's response will depend on the relationship between $n_2$ and $u_2$. If $u_2 > n_2$, meaning that Player 2 prefers imposing unilateral sanctions to seeing none imposed at all, only she will impose sanctions in equilibrium. If, alternatively, $n_2 > u_2$ and Player 2 is not willing to impose unilateral sanctions, $x^* = 0$ and $y^* = 0$; neither state sanctions. This result—a Prisoners' Dilemma—occurs if both players are weak leaders with a dominant strategy not to sanction. Examples of games leading to these two outcomes—unilateral sanctions by Player 2 and no sanctions— are shown in figure 2.6.

a. Coercion Problem #4

Player 2

| | | y=0 | y=1 |
|---|---|---|---|
| Player 1 | x=0 | 2, 1 | 4, 2 |
| | x=1 | 1, 4 | 3, 3 |

b. Coadjustment Problem #2

Player 2

| | | y=0 | y=1 |
|---|---|---|---|
| Player 1 | x=0 | 2, 2 | 4, 1 |
| | x=1 | 1, 4 | 3, 3 |

2.6. Weak Leader with Dominant Strategy

(4) If *Player 1 is a weak leader without a dominant strategy*, we need to ask whether Player 2 has a dominant strategy. Figure 2.7 shows three games exemplifying the possible cases. In the first game, Player 2 has a dominant strategy to impose no sanctions. Player 1 responds by also refraining from sanctions—although this is a Pareto-inferior outcome, as

a. Coadjustment Problem #3

Player 2

| | | y=0 | y=1 |
|---|---|---|---|
| Player 1 | x=0 | 2, 2 | 3, 1 |
| | x=1 | 1, 4 | 4, 3 |

b. Coincidence Problem #2

Player 2

| | | y=0 | y=1 |
|---|---|---|---|
| Player 1 | x=0 | 2, 1 | 3, 2 |
| | x=1 | 1, 3 | 4, 4 |

c. Coadjustment Problem #4

Player 2

| | | y=0 | y=1 |
|---|---|---|---|
| Player 1 | x=0 | 2, 1 | 3, 2 |
| | x=1 | 1, 4 | 4, 3 |

2.7. Weak Leader without Dominant Strategy

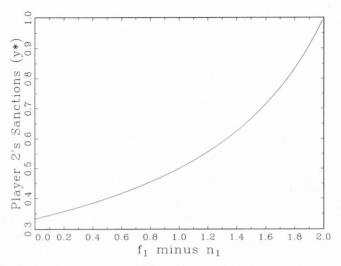

2.8.  Player 2's Sanctions When Player 1 Is a Weak Leader

both would prefer mutual sanctions. However, neither player has an incentive to move from this point. Both states would benefit from bilateral
sanctions, but Player 2 would have an incentive to deviate from this outcome. In the second game, Player 2 has a dominant strategy to sanction.
Player 1's best response now is to sanction as well, leading to bilateral
sanctions. It is interesting to compare this outcome to case 2 when Player
2 had a dominant strategy (figs. 2.4a and 2.4b). There, we saw unilateral
sanctions by one of the two players in equilibrium. Now, when we have
a weak leader instead of a strong one, we don't find unilateral sanctions
in equilibrium, but only bilateral activity or none at all. Although the
game shown in figure 2.7a is not a Prisoners' Dilemma, it does exhibit
some of the same obstacles to cooperation.

   If neither player in this situation has a dominant strategy, the equilibrium is that given by the equations above for $x^*$ and $y^*$. $Y^*$ is equal to 1
when $f_1 = m_1$, i.e., when Player 1 is indifferent to whether unilateral
sanctions (by Player 2) or bilateral sanctions are imposed. As $f_1$ grows
relative to $m_1$—that is, as Player 1 becomes more willing to free-ride—
Player 2 will increase the level of sanctions she is willing to impose. $Y^*$ is
shown as a function of $(f_1 - n_1)$ in figure 2.8. In contrast to the situation
with a strong leader shown in figure 2.5, sanctions now increase as free-
riding becomes more attractive. In this situation—where Player 1 is not
willing to impose unilateral sanctions, as she was in cases 1 and 2—we
find that if both value free-riding highly, both will sanction at a relatively
high level. This is a counterintuitive proposition. However, as long as the
ordinal payoffs remain as shown in figure 2.7c, this is the behavior we

should expect. When $f_1 > m_1$, so that Player 1 prefers free-riding to mutual sanctions, she has a dominant strategy to impose no sanctions, and we are in case 3.

To summarize this model of bilateral decisions about imposing economic sanctions, we begin in each case by asking whether either player has a dominant strategy. If so, the equilibrium outcome is a boundary solution, in the sense that $x^*$ (Player 1's level of sanctions) is either 0 or 1, as is $y^*$ (Player 2's level of sanctions). If neither player has a dominant strategy, different outcomes result; both players will sanction at less than maximum capacity, with the equilibrium given by the relative values of each player's payoffs. Even with the restrictions I have imposed on the two states' utility functions, we find a full range of equilibrium outcomes. In equilibrium, we might find no sanctions, unilateral sanctions by either side, maximum bilateral sanctions, or bilateral sanctions at something less than full capacity. The next section organizes this array of outcomes into three types of cooperation problems, as the labels on the games discussed here have suggested.

## Identifying Cooperation Problems

The bilateral sanctions games that follow from this game-theoretic analysis can be split into three exhaustive and mutually exclusive groups of cooperation problems: *coincidence, coercion,* and *coadjustment.* Many authors writing about cooperation among states tend to assume that only one model of cooperation is correct for understanding its emergence. It is the thesis of this study that such an assumption is incorrect. In fact, there is a wide range of alternative cooperation problems, even when our focus is narrowed from international politics in general to economic sanctions in particular. Only by understanding the nature of strategic interaction in specific cooperation problems can we understand the factors that encourage or inhibit cooperation.

### Categorizing Sanctions Games

The first group of games includes cases where both states impose sanctions in equilibrium, either at full capacity or using some kind of mixed strategy. In these situations, we should expect cooperation to follow directly from the nature of state interests. Neither player has an incentive to defect from bilateral sanctions. These cases include the games shown in figures 2.3a and 2.7b; they fit into the *coincidence* category, since both states choose to impose sanctions in equilibrium. These are games of harmony, where the players face relatively few conflicts of interest. Coincidence games can also result when one player is a strong leader with a dominant strategy to impose sanctions, as in figure 2.3a, if the other player also has a strong interest in sanctions.

One coincidence game deserves further comment. In the game represented in figure 2.7b, Player 1 is a weak leader without a dominant strategy, while Player 2 has a dominant strategy to impose sanctions. Under these conditions, both states sanction at full capacity in equilibrium, as long as both are acting rationally. However, if Player 1 suspects that Player 2 may defect for some reason, she may be reluctant to impose sanctions. This situation is an assurance game, similar in dynamics to the Stag Hunt analyzed by Robert Jervis, although it has an asymmetry not present in that game.[9] As long as both players are capable of acting rationally, they face no problem in reaching the mutually beneficial bilateral-sanctions outcome, which gives both their highest possible payoff. However, if Player 2 is somehow prevented from following this course—for example, by domestic political upheaval—Player 1 faces the possibility of being stuck with her least-favorable outcome, unilateral sanctions. This game does by definition fit in the coincidence, or harmony, category, since mutual sanctions are an equilibrium outcome; but a state facing such a situation may be reluctant to trust the other, perhaps fearing involuntary defection from the other side.[10]

A second group of sanctions games has unilateral sanctions as an equilibrium outcome. Examples of such games are found in figures 2.3b, 2.4a, 2.4b, and 2.6a. They involve situations where one of the players is a strong leader who prefers to undertake unilateral sanctions rather than to see the no-sanctions outcome. This strong leader, however, always prefers bilateral actions, so she faces the problem of convincing the other state to impose sanctions. These are *coercion* games.

In equilibrium, the other player has nothing to gain from cooperating with the strong leader in a coercion game. Thus, the leader has to find some way of coercing the other into sanctions, through linkage to other issues and using threats or promises. These threats and promises have to be credible to the other state; this requirement introduces problems of signaling that are not captured by this simple, single-play model of the decision whether to sanction. In the following case studies, issue linkage, threats, side payments, and credibility (or lack thereof) play central roles.[11]

A final group of games is characterized by suboptimal equilibrium outcomes. In the games shown in figures 2.4c, 2.6b, 2.7a, and 2.7c, neither state imposes full sanctions in equilibrium. However, both would benefit from stringent bilateral sanctions. The game in figure 2.6b is a classic Prisoners' Dilemma, while the one in figure 2.7a is a variation where Player 1 benefits even more from bilateral sanctions. Player 1 thus has no incentive to defect from the cooperative outcome in figure 2.7a, but

Player 2 does; knowing this, Player 1 does not impose sanctions. In figure 2.4c, both players impose some sanctions, but at a level that is suboptimal. In this case, both players will impose some sanctions in equilibrium but will stop short of completely breaking economic ties with the target state. The two states may not impose equivalent levels of sanctions. Under these conditions, states face the problem of jointly moving away from an equilibrium that leaves both dissatisfied. Later in this chapter, I focus on the role of international institutions as I discuss factors that might facilitate this kind of mutual policy adjustment. When neither player has a dominant strategy, *coadjustment* games result.

To summarize this typology of cooperation problems, *coincidence* refers to a situation where the equilibrium outcome is for both states to impose sanctions. In the literature on cooperation, coincidence of interests is usually called *harmony*. Calling such a situation a "cooperation problem" is something of a misnomer because, given harmonious interests, the emergence of cooperation actually is not a problem at all. However, conflicts may remain over the relative costs to be borne by the parties, what kind of sanctions to impose, and so on. In addition, assurance games are a subcategory of coincidence, one in which states need reassurance that the other will behave rationally. *Coercion* can occur when states have asymmetrical interests. In the bilateral sanctions model, it becomes a possibility when the equilibrium outcome is for only one state to impose sanctions. Under these conditions, it will be in that state's interest to attempt to get cooperation from the other through promises, threats, linkage, or whatever techniques are available and cost-effective.

Finally, we have found games where cooperation comes about through *coadjustment* of policies. In these situations, the equilibrium outcome of a single-play game is for neither state to impose sanctions. However, this outcome may be suboptimal. While neither player has an interest in unilaterally imposing sanctions, both would find themselves better off with bilateral sanctions than with none. Maintenance of such an optimal non-equilibrium is difficult, giving a special character to this kind of sanctioning dilemma.[12]

### Cooperation Problems and International-Relations Theory

Students of international relations often fail to distinguish among these three variations on the theme of cooperation. This situation has generated substantial confusion, especially when scholars attempt to cross paradigm boundaries. Traditional realists would contend that state behavior that appears cooperative is, in fact, usually the result of coercion by a major power.[13] A clear example of such an argument is found in the "malevolent" version of hegemonic-stability theory, in which the order that prevails under a system dominated by a single hegemon is explained by this state's manipulation of the structures and processes of the international system to benefit itself.

Robert Gilpin, for example, contends that hegemons use their power to force other states to behave cooperatively. Because the hegemon has control over vital resources, it can forge linkages that increase the penalties attached to noncooperation or the benefits others derive from cooperating. For example, hegemons often run a "security racket," linking protection to economic issues. In addition, hegemonic control over the rules of the international system provides a lever with which to gain compliance from other members of the system.[14] Even if the hegemon does not rely on explicit threats and linkages, it can manipulate institutions and economic conditions to change the costs and benefits associated with certain courses of action. Thus, we might expect that when the United States, for example, decides to impose sanctions against some country, its allies might feel compelled to cooperate in this effort. Hegemonic-stability arguments as explanations of cooperation receive more attention later in this study.

We can find coercion situations in a number of the bilateral sanctions games developed above. In these cases, one state (Player 1) has a strong interest in imposing sanctions, while the other (Player 2) is content to free-ride on Player 1's efforts. Nevertheless, Player 1 would prefer Player 2's assistance in imposing sanctions. If Player 2 refuses to comply, Player 1's efforts to deny the target certain goods could quickly become irrelevant if the target finds new sources of supply or if Player 2 serves as a point of transshipment for Player 1's exports, redirecting them to the target.

Thus, if Player 1 feels that Player 2 is indeed a threat to the success of sanctions, she has an incentive to convince Player 2 to cooperate with the effort. This kind of persuasion may take a number of forms. Through either positive linkages (side payments) or negative ones (threats), Player 1 can tie the sanctions issue to other issues in which Player 2's interests are affected by Player 1's actions. Under conditions of interdependence, Player 1 can search for actions that may lead Player 2 to reconsider her decision to free-ride in a particular sanctions case. Player 1 could use either public or private, or even implicit, threats and promises. If Player 2 is highly dependent on Player 1 or expects that she will need Player 1's help on some issue in the future, a simple request from Player 1 for Player 2's cooperation may be sufficient to activate tacit linkages. In any case, Player 1 faces the problem of credibly linking the sanctions issue to other issues.[15] Since in many cases of economic sanctions one state has a stronger interest in sanctions than other potential sanctioners, coercion games are common.

A typical coercion game could take the form shown in figure 2.3b. In this game, only Player 1, the strong leader, will impose sanctions in equilibrium. At this point, Player 2 receives her highest possible payoff by free-riding; within the context of this simplified, single-play situation, she will refuse to join in the sanctions effort. However, Player 1 may have resources that she can use to convince Player 2 to cooperate. If Player 1's incentives to coerce, whether employed through public or quiet diplomacy, are strong enough and if she can effectively use appropriate tools to influence Player 2, the actual sanctions outcome will not be the equilibrium of the simplified game. Instead of unilateral sanctions, we may observe cooperation, i.e., joint activity by Players 1 and 2.

If coercion can be called the realist explanation of cooperation, coincidence is the liberal explanation. Cooperation results, some liberals would argue, simply because states have an interest in cooperating. There are many areas—the environment, free trade, avoidance of war—in which states have a coincidence of interests, according to liberal theory. Such situations of harmony mean that, while international relations are not free of conflict, the emergence of cooperation in some issue areas should come as no surprise.[16]

In the bilateral sanctions case, a typical game of harmony could take the form shown in figure 2.3a, where both players have dominant strategies to impose sanctions. In this game, both states have a strong interest in seeing sanctions imposed—strong enough that they derive the highest payoff from bilateral activity. Here, it would be unexpected to see a state hold back from the sanctions effort rather than cooperate. A situation of harmony does not, theoretically, require that states be anything other than self-interested and myopic, although harmony might occur more frequently in a world of altruistic states. All it requires is that both believe that some action of the target requires their response and that economic sanctions are an appropriate reaction. Given the alternatives to sanctions—risky military or covert action on the one hand and the less-forceful course of diplomatic protests on the other—governments could find economic statecraft the best response in many circumstances.[17] The analytical problem in such a game is understanding not how states resolve a cooperation dilemma, but why they have a common interest in economic sanctions.

Many students of international relations, especially realists, find the liberal explanation of cooperation unsatisfactory. They argue that while situations in which states have extensive common interests may occasionally occur, they are rare, and the explanatory power of the liberal paradigm is thus quite limited. A more interesting and relevant problem might be to explain cooperation in cases where states have conflicts of interest.[18] This is the challenge taken up by the neoliberal institutionalists.[19] These theorists begin from realist assumptions about the nature of state interests but show that cooperation in the form of mutual policy adjustment can nevertheless emerge. For these authors, the cooperation problem is essentially a problem of mutual policy adjustment to reach Pareto-superior outcomes.

This school of thought frequently begins with consideration of the Prisoners' Dilemma. As shown in figure 2.6b, the bilateral sanctions case can take the form of a Prisoners' Dilemma. Here, both states have a dominant strategy to refuse to impose sanctions. Thus, the equilibrium outcome is no sanctions, although both states find this outcome inferior to bilateral sanctions; both would be better off with joint activity than with none. In order to get away from this inefficient equilibrium, states must mutually adjust their policies. A number of authors have pointed to conditions that might help nations escape Prisoners' Dilemmas; I discuss these conditions later in this chapter.

The realist, liberal, and neoliberal-institutionalist logics about the causes of cooperation are all correct, given certain configurations of state interests. Thus, debates among them about the "truth" of their theories are misdirected. Since each group of theorists has a different set of referents, each properly believes itself to have the "correct" explanation of cooperation. More fruitful would be empirical questions: what configurations of state interests are most commonly found in certain situations? One approach to sorting out these various explanations of cooperation involves analysis of a relatively large number of cases. In order to understand the problem of cooperation among states, we have to acknowledge that international politics creates a wide range of cooperation problems and that explanations of how states cooperate will vary, depending on specific sets of interests.

Recognition of the distinctions among coercion, coincidence, and coadjustment is vital if we are to gain insight into how and why states cooperate to impose economic sanctions. Misconstruing the cooperation problem could lead to incorrect assumptions about how states arrive at the decision to cooperate. For example, in the case of coincidence of interests, the decision to impose sanctions does not require a process of negotiation between two potential sanctioners, consideration of tacit or explicit linkage to other issues, or careful calculation of what international institutions are available to coordinate the sanctions process. Instead, the process may be characterized by more-independent decision making, since both states have a strong interest in sanctions and each recognizes that the other does, too. Potential sanctioners will probably communicate to simplify implementation and management. However, they will not make their initial decisions to impose sanctions dependent on complex negotiations with one another, because each has an unconditional preference for sanctions.

In contrast, a coadjustment problem will involve very different decision-making processes within each state. Here, each has good reason to expect the other to be reluctant to impose sanctions, and each wants to avoid acting alone. Thus, we should expect a complex process to precede the decision of each potential sanctioner. This process could take a number of forms—actual bargaining between states, decisions to submit to the demands of an international institution on a contingent basis, careful consideration of other issues on which cooperation with the other state will be desired, the potential future payoffs from taking the risk of imposing unilateral sanctions now, and so on. The key point is that in each of the two idealized cases—pure coincidence of interests and a Prisoners' Dilemma—the decision-making processes leading to cooperative outcomes will bear only a weak resemblance to one another. Distinguishing among the ideal types of cooperation allows us to anticipate different paths to cooperation.

## What Explains Cooperation?

Under what conditions will states cooperate to impose economic sanctions? We can begin to answer this central question by breaking the general cooperation problem down into the three situations described above—coincidence, coercion, and coadjustment. This section develops hypotheses about variables that will prove useful for explaining cooperation in each of these three circumstances. Later chapters test these hypotheses through analysis of ninety-nine cases of post-1945 economic sanctions, using appropriate statistical techniques, and through detailed case studies.

According to the logic of the previous section, there is more than one path to cooperation. I have specified three: coincidence of interests, coercion, and coadjustment. Different structures of state interests give rise to different expectations about the factors that will be conducive to cooperation. Thus, in the case of economic sanctions, we should distinguish among the three types of cooperation problems and search for factors that will allow states to arrive at a cooperative outcome in each circumstance. Although actual sanctions cases conflate these three ideal types because such cases involve many states, distinguishing among the three types is a useful analytical tool for developing testable hypotheses.

The following discussion requires clarification of the concept of success in cases of sanctions. There is an ongoing debate in the economic-sanctions literature about how to measure the success of economic sanctions. Gary Hufbauer, Jeffrey Schott, and Kimberly Elliott adopt the traditional position. In their view, states use sanctions "to coerce target governments into particular avenues of response."[20] Thus, success is measured by changes in the target's behavior that analysts can attribute to economic sanctions. While Hufbauer, Schott, and Elliott concede that governments may have additional motives for imposing sanctions, such as to show resolve, sender governments invariably call for policy change in the target country.

David Baldwin expresses an alternative viewpoint. In his social-power framework, economic sanctions have multiple objectives. In fact, he argues, the major audience for sanctions may not be the "target" country at all. Instead, states may impose sanctions in response to domestic demands to "do something" or in order to send a signal to third countries. If governments do indeed have this range of objectives, measuring success solely by policy change is misleading and will cause the success of sanctions to be underestimated.[21]

Baldwin's arguments are a useful corrective to the traditional observation that "sanctions never work." However, his framework so expands the definition of success that success becomes impossible to measure. In Baldwin's terms, any imposition of sanctions in response to domestic pressures is necessarily "successful," because the sending government has shown its willingness to take action. This overinclusive definition of success, while allowing for the possibility that governments may sometimes impose sanctions that have a low probability of causing policy change in the target country, provides us with little guidance as to the criteria we should use to evaluate governments' sanctions decisions.

Beyond the conceptual weakness of a broad definition of success, it is difficult to imagine that governments would not feel that their sanctions had been "successful" if they caused policy change in the target state. Even if states consider policy change more of a hope than an expectation, surely they would be pleased if their sanctions did lead to compliance with their stated goals. For example, although the United States may have had motives in imposing a grain embargo against the Soviet Union in 1980 that went beyond encouraging the Soviets to withdraw from Afghanistan, it certainly would not have been disappointed if the sanctions had had such an effect.[22] Thus, I would argue that Baldwin is confronting a different question than are Hufbauer, Schott, and Elliott. Hufbauer, Schott, and Elliott wish to know when sanctions, under a narrow definition of success, will lead to policy change by the target government. In terms of policy analysis, this is an important and interesting question. Baldwin, instead, examines the motivations of governments to impose sanctions even under conditions in which the probability of success is quite low so that policy change is only one of many goals. Both approaches have merit. In this work I use the term *success* in the narrow sense in which Hufbauer, Schott, and Elliott use it, in order to distinguish policy change in the target from other sender goals and in order to be consistent with the most common usage in the literature on sanctions.

## Explaining Coincidence

In general, the most straightforward explanation of cooperation is that states have a common interest in sanctions. As Kenneth Oye has pointed out: "When you observe cooperation, think Harmony—the absence of gains from defection—before puzzling over how states were able to transcend the temptations of defection."[23] The analyst, then, does not ask how cooperation was facilitated under difficult conditions, but why states have extensive common interests on a particular issue.

Answering the general question "When do states have common interests?" is an impossible task. When, however, we narrow our sample—to cases of post–World War II economic sanctions—we can begin to build hypotheses about the factors that tend to encourage cooperation. The following discussion assumes that states are rational actors in the sense that they are goal-driven and attempt to calculate costs and benefits associated with alternative courses of action. In addition, I assume that states respond to the pressures of the international system—in other words, that their interests are at least partly determined by the structure of the international system and their position in it. Some variables will account for systemic pressures, such as the need to balance other states' behavior or to act within institutional constraints. Other variables will account for unit-level factors, such as the costs of sanctions. What these variables have in common is their general applicability to the universe of postwar economic-sanctions cases.

Studies have shown that economic sanctions are most likely to be successful if they are targeted against a relatively weak, unstable country.[24] Sanctions are costly to the states that impose them, because they must forgo gains from trade. In fact, many authors have argued that one of the primary reasons sanctions fail is that they often are more costly to the senders than to the target.[25] Because sanctions are costly, states will be more willing to impose them if the expected benefits are high. Successful coercion of the target state constitutes one of the highest potential benefits. Thus, states considering sanctions must weigh the probability that their costly actions will have the intended effect on the target. A higher probability of success should create a greater willingness to impose sanctions.

One of the best indicators of potential success is the economic and political condition of the target state. Hufbauer, Schott, and Elliott find that "there seems to be a direct correlation between the political and economic health of the target country and its susceptibility to economic pressure."[26] Countries with extensive internal economic resources are unlikely to feel sufficiently pressured by external sanctions to make major policy changes, therein appearing to sacrifice their sovereign power over policy decisions. Likewise, economic pressure alone cannot topple governments that hold a strong, stable position vis-à-vis their own societies, nor can it force them to undertake major reforms.

Thus, sanctions are unlikely to succeed against economically and politically viable countries. Potential senders will be reluctant to engage in costly sanctioning activities directed against such countries. Poor, weak states, on the other hand, make attractive targets. States potentially could achieve policy change here with only modest application of economic pressure. For example, Uganda in the late years of Idi Amin's rule was experiencing great economic and political distress. Sanctions, led by the United Kingdom and the United States, are generally credited with playing a significant role in the 1979 toppling of his regime.[27] States that take into account the potential success of sanctions will be more willing to impose sanctions when the target country is poor and weak. We can hypothesize, therefore, that the political and economic health of the target has an impact on states' interest in undertaking sanctions and therefore has an impact on cooperation.

Another variable that can account for coincidence of interests among potential sanctioners involves structural factors such as those examined by neorealists in their reformulation of classical realism from 1945 to 1989, the international system was a bipolar one.[28] From a neorealist perspective, confrontation between the United States with its allies and the Soviet Union with its allies was the major source of conflict in this system. Thus, one would expect that states' interests in pursuing conflicts that crossed Cold War frontiers would be stronger than their interests in fighting against allies. When the United States was faced with responding to some activity it found disagreeable by a Western European state, for example, the complex and dense pattern of ties and interests it had with that state constrained its response. Responding to a similar action by the Soviet Union, however, was a simpler matter. Here, alliance interests tended to push the United States into a more-aggressive reaction. While the relevance of Cold War boundaries may have waxed and waned with the state of relations between the two major adversaries, it is difficult to identify any global political division of interests as significant as Cold War boundaries in the period of this study (1945–89).

In general, we should expect that states on one side of the East-West divide will have more-extensive common interests with their alliance partners than with states on the other side. Likewise, states should have a stronger interest in imposing sanctions in cases that cross Cold War boundaries than in cases that do not. Therefore, identification of a sanctions episode as a Cold War case should tend to increase common interests among allies in seeing sanctions imposed. This identification will tend to activate alliances and lead to definition of a particular sanctions case as part of a larger, ongoing struggle. I hypothesize, therefore, that we will find more cooperation in cases in which East-West conflict is central than in other cases.

Cold War alliances are only one example of what Kenneth Waltz calls "balancing behavior."[29] According to Waltz, states wishing to assure their survival will respond to the constraints of the international system by forming alliances and taking other actions to balance the alliances and activities of other states. Rather than bandwagoning, or tending to all join one side of an international conflict, states will make their choices in part with an eye to balancing the actions of others. They avoid bandwagoning because it would be disruptive to the stability of the system as a whole and thus to the survival of those who make up the system. Studies have found balancing behavior in the formation of alliances, for example.[30] Balances of power have always been the primary logic of international politics, according to realists.

We can apply the logic of balancing to economic sanctions. One frequently observed response to the imposition of sanctions is that some states will come to the aid of the target, for either political or economic reasons. Studies point to this form of balancing behavior as a reason for sanctions' failure. However, once the target country receives assistance, the logic of balancing should lead some countries to come to the aid of the major sender. They may do so for broad systemic reasons, if they consider this conflict important enough to be a test of the balance of power in the system as a whole. If balancing behavior directly applies, assistance to the target should increase cooperation among potential sanctioners. Below, I discuss the logic of bandwagoning as it applies among potential sanctioners. Balancing, if it occurs, involves a different group of countries—those who sympathize with the target. Potential sanctioners, while bandwagoning among themselves, may also balance against those who support the target.

In addition, assistance to the target will reduce the probability that unilateral sanctions will be effective. U.S. sanctions against Cuba in the 1960s, for example, should have had a good chance of working because of Cuba's dependence on the United States. Once the Soviet Union came to Cuba's aid, however, such sanctions were much less likely to be effective. If other countries—allies of the United States—had had an interest in seeing policy change in Cuba, they could have been induced by the Soviets' assistance to join the United States in sanctions. Such action would also have demonstrated their support for the United States in a confrontation with the Soviet Union. If balance-of-power theory applies to decisions to impose economic sanctions, assistance to the target country should have a positive effect on the level of cooperation observed.[31]

I have identified three overall factors that should contribute to congruence of interest among states in decisions on imposing economic sanctions; these factors should lead to a greater degree of observed cooperation when they occur in post–World War II cases of sanctions. One variable, the economic and political condition of the target state, relates to potential senders' expectations about the effectiveness of the sanctions. If the target is weak and vulnerable, sanctions are more likely to be effective, and states therefore should tend to be more willing to bear the cost. Thus, the stability and economic health of the target should be negatively related to the amount of cooperation observed.

Two other factors relate to systemic considerations. All else being equal, we should expect that states on the same side of the Cold War division will have common interests in sanctioning states on the other side of this divide rather than one another. Thus, cooperation should be greater on East-West issues. In addition, structural forces push states to engage in balancing behavior in situations of international conflict. If this sort of balancing takes place, we should expect that assistance to the target of economic sanctions will lead to a response by other states—that they will balance such assistance by imposing their own sanctions, in a process analogous to the formation of alliances. Thus, balance-of-power logic leads us to expect to see relatively more cooperation in cases where the target of economic sanctions receives assistance.

## Explaining Coercion

Another type of cooperation problem is actually a question of coercion and linkage. This condition results when one state has an unconditional strategy to impose sanctions and others are reluctant to join in. The major sender—the state that is going to impose sanctions regardless of the activities of others—has to persuade other potential sanctioners to cooperate. Such persuasion may take a number of forms and may be either explicit or tacit. In any case, the major sender must somehow link the sanctions issue to other issues in which it has power resources it can use to persuade others.[32] Ability to persuade, or coerce, rests on two factors: sufficient resources to change other potential sanctioners' incentives and willingness to use these resources. I postulate that two variables—declining U.S. hegemony and the costs of sanctions to the major sender—tap these two dimensions of coercion.

When would the major sender be motivated to put effort into persuasion? A key factor may be the costs of sanctions. The government of the major sender will be subject to domestic pressure to gain cooperation in a case of costly sanctions. As an example, consider a U.S. attempt to impose a grain embargo. A stringent embargo could be extremely costly for U.S. farmers. They would certainly complain about having to bear these costs, especially if their traditional markets were being taken over by farmers from other countries that were not imposing sanctions. U.S.

farmers would lobby the government to either end the sanctions entirely or at least assure the cooperation of other international grain suppliers. Costly sanctions will have similar effects in most sectors of a country's economy.

High costs for the major sender play a further role in coercion cases, one that appears frequently in the following case studies. As noted, the major sender (frequently the United States) will have to use threats or promises to change the incentive structure facing other potential sanctioners. One of the biggest dilemmas for the major sender is how to make these threats or promises credible. For example, if the United States threatened to cut off France's access to U.S. technology in order to persuade the French to impose sanctions against the Soviet Union, the French would evaluate the chances that Washington would carry through with this threat if they defied demands for sanctions. How could the United States demonstrate resolve and credibility? As Thomas Schelling and others have shown, self-imposed costs allow states to make credible commitments.[33] U.S. willingness to bear high costs could convince the French, in this example, that Washington cared enough about this sanctions episode to carry through with threats of countersanctions.

An extensive game-theoretic literature has developed on the topics of credibility, reputation, and signaling.[34] These factors can influence the outcomes of games under conditions of asymmetric information and iteration. Both of these conditions frequently obtain in cases of economic sanctions. In the hypothetical U.S.-France case, for example, it is reasonable to assume that the American administration has better information on its willingness and ability to carry through with threats or promises than the French government. In addition, bargaining over sanctions often goes on for weeks or months, constituting an iterated game. In this situation, the major sender can manipulate resources to send signals about its intentions. One important signal is self-imposed costs; they demonstrate the administration's ability to overcome domestic opposition. Use of only low-cost sanctions signals either that this case is not a high enough priority that the government is willing to overcome domestic opposition or that it is simply unable to do so. In this study, the 1982 pipeline episode provides the best opportunity to examine how self-imposed costs encourage other states to cooperate. Bringing sanctions under the purview of an international institution can also help establish credible commitments.[35] Thus, institutions can facilitate cooperation in coercion games, and we will see that they do so in coadjustment games as well.

The coercive abilities of the major sender depend on the resources it can link to the sanctions issue as well as on its credibility. In general, more-powerful states should have more resources for this purpose than weaker states. Studies of economic sanctions have begun to ask whether patterns can be found in the relation between U.S. power, for example, and the amount of cooperation it has achieved in various cases. Stephen Kobrin argues that as American power has waned relative to that of its allies, the United States has been less successful in convincing allies to cooperate in sanctions efforts.[36] Authors have pointed to U.S. failure to gain European cooperation in 1982 to impose pipeline sanctions on the Soviet Union as an example of the effect of declining U.S. power.[37]

That analysis is a specific application of more-general hegemonic-stability theories.[38] As the United States declines, such theories suggest, there will be a general breakdown of cooperation within the international system. Increasing autonomy of European countries combined with declining U.S. resources will lead to more-frequent situations where others ignore American calls for action. Indeed, according to the hegemonic-stability argument, in the early postwar period the United States frequently was able to gain the cooperation of other states without even asking. Dependence on the United States for security and economic reasons caused other states to follow its lead "automatically" on most issues, including economic sanctions. As American power declined, Washington more frequently had to make explicit threats and linkages in order to gain cooperation. Finally, perhaps only within the last decade, even explicit threats and arguments for cooperation may have ceased to be persuasive.

Anecdotal evidence has been offered on both sides of the declining-hegemony debate. On one side, Kobrin and Bruce Jentleson argue that there is clear evidence from the pipeline case that Washington now finds it extremely difficult to gain the active consent of European governments on sanctions issues. On the other side, Kenneth Rodman argues that the United States retains sufficient economic resources to manipulate others' perceptions of risk and thus to induce their cooperation. He examines the case of South Africa to find support for this argument. I will consider these hypotheses in the light of evidence from a broader range of cases. In general, if the hegemonic-stability argument is correct, we should expect, in cases where the United States is the major sender, a trend toward decreasing cooperation over time.

Overall, the logic of coercion games suggests that high self-imposed costs and the use of international institutions should enhance cooperation, while declining hegemony should undermine it.

## Explaining Coadjustment

The final type of cooperation problem is one of coadjustment. In this situation, epitomized by the Prisoners' Dilemma, no state has an incentive to cooperate unconditionally. States are in a situation of mutual discord, and their unilateral decisions against taking action make them all worse off than they would have been had they undertaken joint sanctions. Thus, the problem is to find a way to move away from this suboptimal equilibrium. Through coadjustment, states may be able to find ways to make themselves better off. Cooperation in such circumstances can be a rational, self-interested activity—provided, of course, that other states continue to cooperate as well.

Understanding the circumstances under which states will be able to use mutual policy adjustment to solve cooperation problems has engaged the attention of a number of international relations theorists. Building on works such as Robert Axelrod's *Evolution of Cooperation*, they have identified various factors as conducive to the emergence of cooperative strategies.[39] Here I focus on just one of these factors: the role of international institutions.

International institutions are a powerful tool for facilitating coadjustment. Institutions—defined as "persistent and connected sets of rules (formal or informal) that prescribe behavioral roles, constrain activity, and shape expectations"[40]—embody norms that offer states valuable standards by which to evaluate others' behavior. Institutions also help states monitor one another's activities. In addition, some organizations, such as the United Nations, have enforcement powers that can be used against defecting states. Although institutions rarely use such powers even if they have them, institutions are relevant. By providing an arena within which states can reach decisions, set standards, and exchange information, they reduce the transaction costs of coadjustment.[41] In this study, the role of institutions receives the most attention in the technology-embargo and Falkland Islands cases. In these cases, we see how institutional factors, such as the setting of standards and the provision of benefits in a range of linked issues, encourage cooperation.

Institutions can facilitate cooperation under conditions of coincidence or coercion as well. In coincidence cases that resemble an assurance game, where the fear of others' irrational or involuntary defection may make states reluctant to cooperate, institutions can provide the reassurance necessary to maintain multilateral sanctions. States should not have a difficult time cooperating in these conditions, particularly if they have good information about the preferences and actions of others. Institutions provide precisely this kind of information, so that states will not defect in an effort to protect themselves from the costs of unilateral sanctions. In coercion cases, institutions can facilitate the issue linkages that the leading sender will have to use in order to convince others to cooperate. Because international organizations encompass many individual fields of activity, dealing with a sanctions problem within such a forum emphasizes ties between the particular sanctions issue and broader institutional concerns. Thus, the leading sender can use these forums to convince other potential sanctioners to cooperate by raising the costs of defection, even though the others may not have much interest in acting on this particular issue. Institutions increase the credibility of these linkages by making them clear and public, at least among members.

This argument suggests that institutions have a role beyond that noted by neoliberal institutionalists, who focus on the role of institutions in facilitating attainment of mutual gains. In coercion games, one state might be able to manipulate institutional constraints, changing the incentives so that others are "forced" to cooperate. In this situation, only one state may benefit from the interaction, leaving the others worse off. On the other hand, the linking of issues and games may create possibilities for mutual benefit. The leading sender can make concessions on one issue in order to gain cooperation in the sanctions episode, leaving all members better off.[42] However, this perspective does stress the importance of asymmetrical interests and suggests that institutions can facilitate cooperation in the realist as well as neoliberal paradigm.

We should expect that international institutions will facilitate cooperation on economic sanctions. As the above discussion suggests, the role of institutions is complex, and it will thus have to be dealt with mostly in individual case studies. However, if institutions are to play any role at all, we should find at least one pattern across a large set of cases. If a formal international organization has called on its members to impose sanctions, we should see an increase in the level of cooperation.

## Bandwagoning

The hypotheses developed thus far from the model of strategic interaction have focused on the factors likely to influence the average level of cooperation in episodes of economic sanctions. However, for the statistical models and case studies that follow, this is not the only interesting aspect of the dependent variable of cooperation. We would also like to know about the process that leads to this average level of cooperation, about the pattern of decision making that gives rise to the observed outcome. In the statistical models, discovering such a pattern involves specifying a *variance function*. For the process of causal explanation, specifying a variance function is equivalent to determining whether states make decisions independently of one another or whether their decisions are somehow contingent on others' behavior. Different patterns of decision making are reflected in different variance functions for the statistical models, as discussed in chapter 4.

Clearly, the model of cooperation among potential sanctioners developed in this chapter implies that their decisions about sanctions are contingent, rather than being made independently. Only if a state has a dominant strategy will its behavior be independent of others' behavior.[43] In all other cases, the best policy choice depends on the behavior of others; so a state's decision on whether or not to impose sanctions will be based, in part, on what other potential sanctioners have decided. Consider an assurance game to see how this dynamic might work. In this case (an analysis restricted to only two states), both countries prefer bilateral sanctions. However, both also want to avoid the painful unilateral-sanctions outcome. Thus, they will decide to sanction only if they are quite sure that the other will behave the same way. If for some reason one of the two states refrains from imposing sanctions, the other will as well. The decisions in this case are clearly contingent, and contingent in a positive sense. One state's commitment to imposing sanctions greatly increases the probability that the other will behave the same way, while a refusal to sanction has the effect of greatly decreasing the probability that the other will sanction. In statistics, such a process is called *positive contagion*, in contrast to a situation of independence.

A similar pattern is likely to arise in coadjustment games, although the bilateral-sanctions outcome is not an equilibrium in a single-shot coadjustment game. As in assurance problems, states want above all to avoid the unilateral-sanctions outcome and so will not impose sanctions when others refuse to do so. Unlike in the assurance game, temptations to defect always exist; but the probability that a state will impose sanctions still increases when others establish a credible commitment to their own sanctions. This is the logic underlying the proposition that international institutions can help states overcome coadjustment problems. States can use institutions to bind themselves to act, with their actions contingent on similar behavior by others. Thus, institutions enhance the contingent nature of state decision making, by increasing the degree of positive contagion. We should find this dynamic in both assurance and coadjustment games, with states deciding to impose sanctions only after they have been assured that others are committed to behaving in the same way.

This description of the nature of decision making parallels in many ways the discussion about alliance formation in the field of international politics.[44] In this literature, the process of positive contagion is called *bandwagoning*; its opposite is *balancing*. In the context of economic sanctions, bandwagoning behavior is logically deduced from the structure of strategic interaction and state incentives among potential sanctioners. (As discussed above, we may see balancing behavior between states that sympathize with the target and states that are potential sanctioners.) Balancing behavior, if it is the opposite of bandwagoning, would imply a process of *negative* contagion, where the probability that a state will impose sanctions would *decrease* as others made a positive commitment to sanctions. Both positive contagion, or bandwagoning, and negative contagion, or balancing, should be distinguished from independent decision making, where no contagion exists and behavior is not contingent on how others behave.

In the literature on alliances, authors in the realist and neorealist traditions have argued that the nature of strategic interaction leads us to expect balancing, rather than bandwagoning, behavior. Their logic is that the pattern of state preferences in alliance decisions is quite different than that in sanctions decisions. Kenneth Waltz, for example, argues that states are playing an essentially zero-sum game because of the competitive nature of international politics.[45] Thus, when their survival is at stake, states will attempt above all to maintain their position in the system. Waltz concludes that this motivation leads to balancing behavior in alliances as well as other areas of interaction. Stephen Walt has subjected this proposition to empirical test and found some support for it.[46]

However, the discussion about balancing and bandwagoning in alliances is sometimes unfortunately confused. The confusion arises from the use of the words in at least two different ways. On the one hand, the terms are used to refer to the manner in which decision making is contingent—essentially the definition I have proposed here. Glenn Snyder, in a review article, offers a similar definition. He states that bandwagoning is a theory of "positive feedback or instability; a departure from equilibrium begets further departures. The opposite . . . is balancing, a process of negative feedback that maintains or restores equilibrium."[47] This description parallels closely my description of the processes of positive and negative contagion. On the other hand, the terms are sometimes used not to refer to characteristics of the decision-making process, but to identify a specific type of alignment. Walt explicitly uses this definition: "*Bandwagoning* refers to alignment with the source of danger."[48] In this case, balancing or bandwagoning refers to an outcome, rather than a process. States balance by forming alliances against threatening powers, and they bandwagon by forming alliances with them. Using these terms to refer to outcomes leads to conceptual difficulties. For example, in a multipolar system with multiple threats, a conciliatory action can amount to balancing vis-à-vis one threat, but bandwagoning vis-à-vis another. Glenn Snyder has addressed the ambiguity this creates when one attempts to understand Russian alliance behavior in the early twentieth century, for example.[49] I would argue that restricting *bandwagoning* and *balancing* to describe elements of the process rather than the outcome provides a logically consistent and conceptually superior understanding of these terms, and one that is consistent with much of the literature on alliances.

The logic of assurance or coadjustment games leads us to expect bandwagoning behavior, or positive contagion, among potential sanctioners. As Snyder's discussion suggests, this kind of behavior tends to be destabilizing, to lead away from equilibria. If a few states refuse to impose sanctions, others will respond in a similar way, and the result will be very low levels of cooperation. On the other hand, the contingent nature of decision making implies that this process could easily turn around and result in many states imposing sanctions. In cases of bandwagoning, compared to situations of independent decision making, we will find a high degree of variance in the number of states that impose sanctions. Thomas Christensen and Jack Snyder have called the former situation, where the ball never gets rolling, *buck-passing*. The latter, where the ball gets rolling and picks up speed, is *chain-ganging*. Both result from a process of positive contagion, in which states are constrained to copy others' decisions and in which incentives to avoid isolation or unilateral action are strong. Neither should occur under conditions of balancing, or negative contagion. Balancing would have the opposite effect from bandwagoning; the expected number of states imposing sanctions would be highly predictable and variances would be low. Thus, if bandwagoning occurs, we should find in the aggregate analysis a high variance in the number of sanctioners, and we should find in the case studies decisions that are positively correlated with the actions of other states.

## Conclusion

This chapter has developed the theoretical framework I will use to analyze problems of cooperation among states in cases of economic sanctions and a set of seven hypotheses about the conditions under which we can expect to see states cooperate. I began with a simple model of two states deciding about the level of sanctions they would impose against some third country, from no sanctions to a complete cutoff of economic ties with the target country. Imposing some reasonable restrictions on the utility functions of the two states, I found a set of games that describe the cooperation problems facing potential sanctioners.

Three types of equilibria characterize these games. In the first, both states choose to sanction at some level. I call this type of game a *coincidence game*, since it is the coincidence of interests between the states that explains their mutual decision to sanction. In these games, it is not difficult to understand why states cooperate; it would be irrational for either to defect, or refuse to impose sanctions. However, one class of coincidence games, assurance games, present more-complex cooperation problems. In this case, an irrational decision by one player to refrain from sanctions imposes high costs on the other. Even though both states have a strong interest in bilateral sanctions, they may hesitate to commit themselves fully, fearing irrational or involuntary defection by the other. Coincidence games fit within the liberal theory of international relations.

A second group of games has equilibria in which only one state imposes sanctions. I call these *coercion games*, since the leading sender has an incentive to convince others to impose sanctions as well. These efforts at coercion will involve threats or promises that create linkage between the sanctions issue and other issues on which the states interact. When we see cooperation in a coercion game, it means that one state has, through tactical issue linkage, successfully changed the incentives facing others. A realist approach to the study of international politics suggests that coercion underlies cooperation.

Finally, some games have equilibria in which neither state imposes sanctions, but both find this outcome inferior to the bilateral-sanctions outcome. I call these *coadjustment games*, since states can avoid the Pareto-inferior outcome only by mutual policy adjustment. In coadjustment games, states constantly face an incentive to defect, and maintenance of cooperation therefore requires outside mechanisms, such as international organizations. This type of cooperation problem, which includes Prisoners' Dilemmas, has received a great deal of attention in the international-relations literature in the last few years. It constitutes an explanation of cooperation consistent with neoliberal theorizing about international relations.

Consideration of these three types of cooperation problems led to seven specific hypotheses about conditions that could encourage or inhibit cooperation among states. Coincidence, coercion, and coadjustment should be considered ideal types, since real-world cases of economic sanctions typically involve elements of more than one game because of the involvement of more than two states. For this reason, it is not possible to split up the data set neatly into three different types of cases. Instead, the dynamics of more than one type of problem are typically seen in each case, justifying treating the data set as an aggregate. The following hypotheses form the basis for the aggregate data analysis and case studies in the rest of this book:

—States will be more likely to cooperate to impose sanctions against a weak, poor target country, because these sanctions have a higher probability of success than those imposed against strong, rich states.

—States will be more likely to cooperate to impose sanctions that cross East-West boundaries, since states on one side will have stronger common interests in these situations than in intrabloc disputes.

—States will tend to cooperate more when the target receives assistance from some other country, as potential sanctioners and the target's sympathizers balance against one another.

—We will find more cooperation when the major sender bears relatively high costs, since its incentives and ability to coerce others into sanctioning go up as self-imposed costs increase.

—In those cases where the United States is the leading sender, we will see, according to hegemonic-stability theory, declining cooperation over time due to the waning of U.S. power relative to that of other states.

—States will be more likely to cooperate in cases where an international institution has called for sanctions, as institutions help states avoid dilemmas of coadjustment and assurance and may give the major sender additional coercive tools.

—States' decisions to impose sanctions will exhibit a pattern of bandwagoning, or positive contagion.

The following chapter begins the empirical analyses of economic sanctions. It tests the hypotheses developed here against the patterns found in the history of sanctions since World War II. Later in the book, in-depth case studies probe beyond the aggregate patterns to trace the causal mechanisms specified in this chapter.

# 3

## Measuring Cooperation and Explanatory Variables

THE PRECEDING chapter outlined seven hypotheses regarding factors that, in general, should have an impact on the level of cooperation among states considering the imposition of economic sanctions against another country. In this chapter I discuss the operationalization of the independent variables specified in chapter 2 and develop three potential measures of cooperation, the dependent variable. Since each of the three measures of cooperation has some weaknesses, in the following aggregate analyses I work with statistical models appropriate for each proxy rather than relying on a single, inaccurate measure of a complex, unobservable variable.

This chapter also presents descriptive statistics for the independent and dependent variables involved in this study, using data from cases of economic sanctions between 1945 and 1989. Even before we address causal relationships in the next chapter, these descriptive figures provide some insight into the empirical side of economic sanctions. Analyses of a few major cases have dominated the literature and led to a sort of conventional wisdom about economic sanctions; the fact that most cases receive little analysis has skewed our understanding of the "typical" sanctions case. For example, critics of sanctions have argued that they are not an appropriate tool of foreign policy because they are too expensive, costing the sender more than the target. In fact, sanctions appear in this data set to be a relatively cheap means of taking action against another country, frequently leading to economic gains rather than losses for the sender. Simple descriptive statistics drawn from an unbiased set of sanctions cases thus contribute significantly to our understanding of this policy tool.

## Measurement and Description: The Dependent Variable

The extensive literature on international cooperation that has developed in the last decade lacks attempts to operationalize cooperation in such a way that we can measure it across a wide range of cases. While many authors clearly define cooperation or coadjustment, for example, their measurement of these quantities typically requires, in theory, estimation of concepts—such as the Pareto frontier—that are essentially unobservable.[1] Given this lack of an empirical foundation in the international-relations literature, the measures I develop in this section should be considered alternative estimates of an underlying unobserved quantity, cooperation. For this reason, I use a number of different measures and develop statistical models appropriate for each, rather than restricting attention to one plausible operationalization.

For the following analyses, I begin by using 101 cases of post–World War II economic sanctions as identified in Hufbauer, Schott, and Elliott's *Economic Sanctions Reconsidered* (second edition, 1990). In looking at the distributions of the variables, I argue that two cases—sanctions against South Africa and Rhodesia—should be eliminated from the rest of the analysis because they are outliers that unduly influence the results. More importantly, these two cases are unique because of the degree of consensus around the world about the immorality of apartheid and minority rule. Thus, for most of the analyses in this study the data set consists of the ninety-nine remaining cases.

Hufbauer, Schott, and Elliott have developed one measure of cooperation. They assign each sanctions episode a cooperation score, which can range from 1, indicating no cooperation, to 4, for significant international cooperation.[2] "No cooperation" means that only one country imposes sanctions. Many instances of U.S. sanctions against Latin American countries, such as those against Paraguay from 1977 to 1981, exemplify a cooperation score of 1. A value of 2 indicates "minor cooperation," typically meaning that the major sender is able to get some rhetorical support and, possibly, symbolic sanctions from other countries. U.S. sanctions against Poland and the Soviet Union in 1982, which I examine in more detail later in this study, receive a cooperation score of 2. Hufbauer, Schott, and Elliott give "modest cooperation" a value of 3, indicating that more than one state has imposed actual economic restraints but that they are limited in scope and duration. U.S. sanctions against Iran in 1979 over the taking of hostages are scored as a 3. Finally, a cooperation value of 4 indicates "significant cooperation," in which important trading partners of the target endeavor to restrict trade to a major degree—although enforcement of sanctions may not be perfect. The early years of CoCom, during which the United States and its allies were pursuing a form of economic warfare against the Soviet Union, illustrate a case with a cooperation score of 4. I call this variable COOP.

This categorical measure of cooperation has some advantages, as it estimates dimensions of the sanctions problem that are difficult to operationalize with more "objective" measures. For example, it takes into account whether sanctions involve control of significant goods or are merely symbolic, whether the target's major trading partners are included among the senders, and whether sanctions are actually enforced. Thus, COOP captures a dimension of cooperation related to the content of sanctions. However, this coding relies on a subjective assessment of the sincerity of those states claiming to be involved in the sanctions effort. We could increase confidence in the results if we could also develop a more-objective measure of cooperation and demonstrate that the relationships found in the data are consistent for both measures.

One plausible and simple measure of international cooperation might be the number of countries that impose sanctions. In the next chapter, I develop a model based on event counts that uses this measure, NUMBER, as a dependent variable. However, a moment's thought reveals weaknesses with NUMBER as a measure of cooperation. It reflects neither the significance of those countries imposing sanctions to the target nor the severity of the sanctions they impose. For example, Haiti's imposing sanctions against the Soviet Union would have the same effect on NUMBER as Germany's taking such a step, and an embargo of luxury items against some country would count as much as an oil embargo.

I correct for the first of these problems, the significance of the sanctioners, by weighting the number of sanctioning countries by the amount of their trade with the target. Thus, one might consider the percent of the target's trade accounted for by countries that impose sanctions as a potential measure of cooperation. This measure, however, has the drawback that if there is only one sender but that country accounts for a large percentage of the target's trade, the level of cooperation will appear high. In fact, all cases that involve only one sending country should have a 0 cooperation score. Thus, in weighting the number of countries by their trade with the target, I exclude trade between the target and the major sender. To prevent the trade data from being distorted by the effects of sanctions, I use the International Monetary Fund's *Direction of Trade* statistics for the year prior to that in which sanctions were imposed. The resulting variable, called NONMAJ, is therefore the percent of the target's trade accounted for by sanctioners after excluding trade with the major sender. Stating this mathematically, I use the formula

$$\text{NONMAJ} = \frac{\text{(value of target trade with sanctioners other than major sender)}}{\text{(total value of target trade excluding that with major sender)}}.$$

NONMAJ runs from 0, indicating that only one country imposed sanctions, to 100, indicating that all trading partners of the target imposed sanctions. An example might clarify the behavior of this variable. Consider a target state, 50 percent of whose trade is with one country (country A), with the rest evenly divided among five other countries (B, C, D, E, and F). If only one of these six states imposed sanctions, NONMAJ would be 0, indicating no cooperation. If A and B imposed sanctions and A were the major sender, the value of NONMAJ would be 20, indicating

**TABLE 3.1**
Descriptive Statistics for Dependent Variables (101 Cases)

| Variable | Mean | Standard Deviation |
|---|---|---|
| COOP | 1.82 | 0.974 |
| NUMBER | 5.67 | 11.88 |
| NONMAJ | 9.13 | 16.91 |

that 20 percent of the target's non-major-sender trade was with sanction-ing countries. If, on the other hand, country B were the major sender and A also imposed sanctions, the value of NONMAJ would be 55.5. This is appropriate because A's agreement to join B in imposing sanctions re-flects a higher degree of *cooperative* activity than would B's agreeing to join A. Because A is a more-important trading partner than B, B would probably have a harder time convincing A to cooperate than vice versa. If only countries B and C imposed sanctions, NONMAJ would be 11.1. In general, NONMAJ reflects the fact that obtaining sanctions from a num-ber of countries whose economic interdependence with the target is mini-mal signifies less cooperation than if sanctions are obtained from just a few major trading partners. Thus, the variable is sensitive to the costs for one country implicit in sanctioning another with which it has a significant trading relationship.

Descriptive statistics for the dependent variables COOP, NUMBER, and NONMAJ can be found in table 3.1; figures 3.1, 3.2, and 3.3 are histograms showing their distributions. In these figures, the horizontal

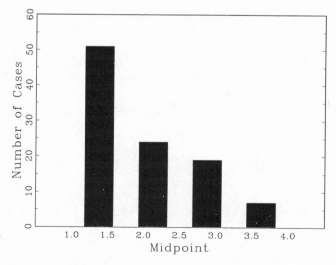

3.1. COOP Distribution (101 Cases)

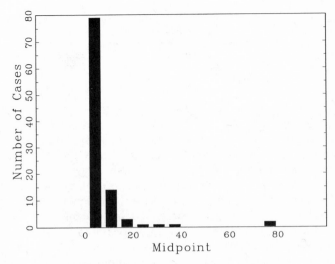

3.2.  NUMBER Distribution (101 Cases)

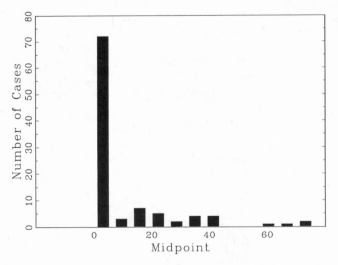

3.3.  NONMAJ Distribution (101 Cases)

axis indicates the value of COOP, NUMBER, or NONMAJ. The vertical axis, or height of each bar, indicates the number of cases with a particular value of the variable. For example, we see in figure 3.1 that just over fifty cases in our data set have a COOP value of 1. In this data set, the distribution of cooperation has a "long tail," particularly evident in the NUM-BER and NONMAJ histograms. For example, in the distribution of NUMBER we see two cases above 70, meaning that in each case over seventy countries imposed sanctions against the target. These two cases are those of sanctions against Rhodesia and South Africa. All the other cases are grouped under 40 on the NUMBER scale (the horizontal axis). A similar pattern appears in the distribution of NONMAJ. The two outliers, with a very high level of cooperation, cause large standard deviations in the measures. Because these two cases lie so far from the mean of the dependent variable, they will exert an unusually high degree of influence on the estimates of the effects of the independent variables.

However, we cannot exclude the South African and Rhodesian cases from the following analyses simply because they will have such an impact on the results. Excluding them is legitimate only if they are in fact unique in some way, having a common characteristic that separates them from the rest of the data set. I would argue that these two cases are sufficiently different from the others to justify their exclusion. Both deal with the same issue—ending white minority rule in black African states. The international consensus in support of this goal is unique, crossing East-West and North-South lines. While some states circumvented these sanctions for economic gains, the degree of international public support for government actions against Rhodesia and South Africa is unparalleled among the other cases in this study. The cases of anti-apartheid sanctions are important and interesting, but they are sufficiently different from the rest of the cases in this data set that including them would bias the findings significantly. Thus, I exclude these two cases from the rest of the analyses in this study.

Table 3.2 presents the statistics on the dependent variables once Rhodesia and South Africa are eliminated. COOP has a mean of 1.79 in these ninety-nine cases, showing that extensive cooperation occurs only rarely. The average case falls somewhere between "no cooperation" and primarily symbolic joint activity. The average value of COOP falls only slightly when the two outliers are removed. A mean of 4.22 for NUMBER shows that, on average, just over four nations participate in each sanctions episode. Because so many states participated in sanctions against Rhodesia

**TABLE 3.2**
Descriptive Statistics for Dependent Variables (99 Cases)

| Variable | Mean | Standard Deviation |
|----------|------|--------------------|
| COOP | 1.79 | 0.95 |
| NUMBER | 4.22 | 6.04 |
| NONMAJ | 7.95 | 14.81 |

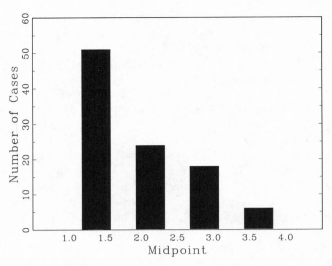

3.4. COOP Distribution (99 Cases)

and South Africa (although some of them did not enforce sanctions well), NUMBER changes substantially when we exclude these cases, falling from 5.67 to 4.22. The standard deviation of NUMBER also falls, from 11.88 to 6.04.

NONMAJ's average of 7.95 means that in the average case, just under 8 percent of the target's non-major-sender trade is accounted for by sanctioning countries.[3] Like NUMBER, NONMAJ is sensitive to the exclusion of the two outliers. Its mean falls from 9.13 to 7.95, while the standard deviation decreases from 16.91 to 14.81. In the next chapter, I run a regression including all 101 cases to allow comparison with the results obtained using only ninety-nine cases. As this model shows, excluding Rhodesia and South Africa does have some noticeable effects on the results. Figures 3.4, 3.5, and 3.6 show the distribution of the three dependent variables after excluding the Rhodesia and South Africa cases.

COOP, NUMBER, and NONMAJ all represent plausible, if rough, measures of cooperation. Thus, they should be positively correlated with one another. Examination of the correlation coefficients reveals that, while these variables do covary, they are not merely linear transformations of one another. The correlation between COOP and NUMBER is .709; between COOP and NONMAJ, .547; and between NUMBER and NONMAJ, .326. These figures, significantly below a perfect correlation of 1, reflect the fact that none of these measures is a perfect operationalization of cooperation and that the alternative measures pick up different dimensions of this concept. While NONMAJ and NUMBER may appear

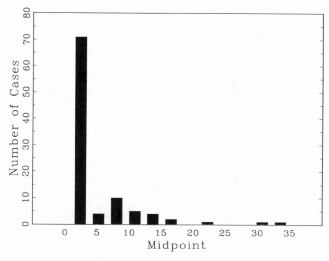

3.5. NUMBER Distribution (99 Cases)

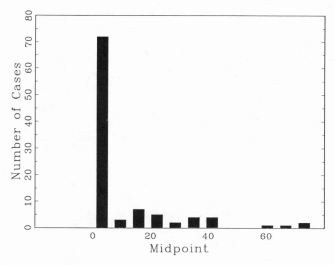

3.6. NONMAJ Distribution (99 Cases)

to be more precise than COOP, they miss aspects of cooperation such as the duration of sanctions and the significance of the embargoed goods. Thus, rather than using just one of these operationalizations of the dependent variable, I will estimate models appropriate for each and compare the results of the alternative models.

## Measurement and Description:
## Explanatory Variables

In the previous chapter, I identified five variables that could be expected to have an impact on the degree of cooperation observed in cases of economic sanctions. In addition, I hypothesized that in cases in which the United States is the leading sender, we should see a decline over time in the amount of cooperation observed, because of declining U.S. hegemony, and that we should see bandwagoning behavior. This section develops measures of the five explanatory factors. Since different dynamics may characterize different types of sanctions cases, I also control for the purposes of sanctions with the variable GOAL. Exploring the effect of U.S. hegemony and the existence of bandwagoning requires somewhat more complex models, whose development I leave until the next chapter.

The first factor expected to affect whether states have a common interest in sanctions, and thus whether they cooperate, is the condition of the target state. Hufbauer, Schott, and Elliott have constructed a three-point scale of the economic health and political stability of target countries; I call this scale TARGET. A value of 1 means that the target would have been distressed even in the absence of sanctions, suffering from severe economic problems and an unstable political atmosphere. Hufbauer, Schott, and Elliott code Uganda under Idi Amin as a 1 on this scale. They assign a value of 2 to countries with "significant problems" and a value of 3 to those targets in which the government was not seriously threatened and the economy was in relatively good shape. For example, they rate the Soviet Union in 1979, when it invaded Afghanistan, as a 3 on the TARGET scale.[4] Because many governments would believe it futile to sanction a strong, stable state, a higher TARGET value will tend to lower the level of common interest in sanctioning and therefore lower the level of cooperation. TARGET has a mean of 2.09 in this data set. This shows that states directed sanctions against countries that, on average, tended to have some economic or political problems but were not severely distressed.

A second factor expected to influence the level of common interest in sanctions and therefore the level of cooperation is whether sanctions crossed the Iron Curtain. I have coded a variable called COLDWAR to capture this factor; it takes a value of 0 if the sanctions were not imposed across East-West lines and a value of 1 if they were. In this data set, I coded 26 percent of the cases (twenty-six out of ninety-nine) as crossing Cold War boundaries. COLDWAR should have a positive effect on the level of cooperation states achieved, since these cases should tend to reflect greater coincidence of interests among potential sanctioners. Among the case studies we will look at in more detail following the aggregate analysis, two are East-West cases (with COLDWAR equal to 1) and two have more of a North-South character.

The final factor hypothesized to affect the coincidence of interests among states is whether the target receives assistance during a sanctions episode. Hufbauer, Schott, and Elliott have coded this dummy variable, which I call ASSIST. It has a value of 1 if the target received international assistance and 0 otherwise. If balance-of-power theory applies to decisions on imposing economic sanctions, ASSIST should have a positive effect on the level of cooperation observed.[5] In 23 percent of the cases included here (twenty-three out of ninety-nine), the target country received assistance from some other country or group of countries.

Turning to another ideal type, coercion games, we expect to find that high costs to the major sending country lead to greater cooperation. Hufbauer, Schott, and Elliott have calculated the costs of sanctions to the major sender in terms of welfare loss and have coded these costs on a four-point scale.[6] I call this variable COST. It takes a value of 1 if the sanctions resulted in a net gain to the sender (generally only in cases where sanctions took the form of withheld aid). A COST value of 2 means that sanctions had little effect on the sender; 3 means that they resulted in a modest loss to the sender; and 4 refers to a major loss, in which large trade dislocations occurred.[7]

Hufbauer, Schott, and Elliott have coded U.S. sanctions against Latin America during the 1970s for human-rights reasons as a 1 on the COST scale, a net gain. Because in these cases sanctions took the form of cutting economic and military aid to oppressive governments, the U.S. government actually bore negative costs by imposing them. An example of a case coded as a 2 (low cost to the sender) is U.S. sanctions against Iraq in 1980–82 to protest terrorism.[8] In this case, Washington prevented the sale of a few military aircraft and engine parts, costing U.S. firms about $22 million. The 1980 American grain embargo against the Soviet Union receives a value of 3 on the cost scale, since the U.S. government faced fairly high costs in reimbursing farmers for lost sales.[9] The data set contains only a few cases where COST equals 4, representing major trade dislocations. One such case is Arab League sanctions against Israel, dating from 1946.[10] These sanctions cut off nearly all economic ties between the members of the Arab League and Israel.

Table 3.3 shows the distribution of the ninety-nine cases across the four COST categories. Nearly 40 percent of the cases in this data set resulted in a net economic *gain* for the sender, while an additional 47 percent were only slightly costly. Only fourteen out of ninety-nine cases fall in the modest-cost or high-cost categories. The mean of COST in this data set is 1.78, reflecting the relatively low costs of most sanctions efforts

**TABLE 3.3**
COST Distribution

| COST | Number of Cases | Percentage of Cases |
|------|-----------------|---------------------|
| 1    | 39              | 39.4                |
| 2    | 46              | 46.5                |
| 3    | 11              | 11.1                |
| 4    | 3               | 3.0                 |

for the major sender. Thus, we need to reexamine the conventional wisdom that sending countries always incur high costs when they impose economic sanctions.

Many analysts have argued that sanctions often fail because they cost the sender more than the target.[11] This argument is fallacious, since the relevant calculation for the target is a contrast between the costs of sanctions and the costs of compliance for the *target* country. Unless credibility is an issue, there is no reason to take the sender's costs into consideration; if it is an issue, the direction of the relationship between costs and success is unclear. The argument is also based on the incorrect empirical assumption that the sender's costs are typically high. In fact, few cases of sanctions end up costing the sender very much. When we consider the range of foreign-policy actions available to states, economic sanctions may fall closer to the "cheap" end of the spectrum than analysts have typically assumed. One of the major findings of this study is that the low cost of most sanctions efforts is one factor inhibiting cooperation, since the credibility of the leading sender's commitment is also low in these cases. From this perspective, more-costly sanctions are actually preferable, at least for a state that cares much about gaining international cooperation. I would argue that the exclusive attention devoted to a few "big" cases of sanctions has skewed perceptions about the characteristics of sanctions in the more average case. This finding about costs to the sender provides support for the proposition that accurate inferences about the nature of economic sanctions require examination of a broad range of actual sanctions cases.

Hufbauer, Schott, and Elliott's coding of COST, however, raises some technical difficulties for the following quantitative analyses. First, this scale is unlikely to reflect interval-level measurements. We have no reason to believe that the difference between 1 and 2 on the cost scale reflects the same increase in expense for the sender as the difference between 3 and 4, for example. The models I use in the next chapter assume that the independent variables are measured on an interval-level scale. In addition, relatively few cases fall in the third or fourth categories. This means that the technique of using three dummy variables as a replacement for COST will probably not work, as the standard errors for categories three and four will be very large. Therefore, I have collapsed categories two, three, and four into a single group and renamed this variable COSTD.

COSTD takes a value of 1 if sanctions resulted in a net economic gain to the major sending country, while a value of 2 reflects cases where sanctions resulted in some economic cost to the sender, ranging from trivial dislocations to major welfare losses. In this set of cases, 39 percent of sanctions episodes resulted in a net economic gain for the sender, while 61 percent showed some level of welfare loss.

Considering coadjustment games, I hypothesized that the involvement of international institutions will be conducive to cooperation on economic sanctions. As the discussion in chapter 2 suggested, the role of institutions is complex and will thus be examined primarily through process tracing. However, if a formal international organization has called on its members to impose sanctions, we should at a minimum see an increase in the level of cooperation. I measure the concept of institutional involvement with the variable INST, which has a value of 1 if an institution has taken the step of calling for sanctions by its members and a value of 0 otherwise. Approximately one-third of the cases in this study (twenty-nine out of ninety-nine) had an institution involved in this manner, so INST has a mean of 0.29.

INST should be positively related to the level of cooperation observed, but this is a weak test of the multifaceted role of international institutions. In fact, it seems that by narrowing the operationalization of the effects of institutions to whether a formal organization has called for sanctions, we will miss most of the interesting consequences of institutionalization. For this reason, the question of institutions is one of the major focal points of the case studies in this book. However, if statistical analysis fails to show a relationship between INST and the level of cooperation, the validity of a transaction-cost approach to coadjustment should come under serious scrutiny. The statistical results should be seen as a weak test—a preliminary filter—for this approach; if a relationship holds up, we should study its nature with cases in which institutions did and did not play a role. In addition, we should ask whether institutions facilitated coadjustment, provided information in a harmony game, or allowed the leading sender to change the incentives facing other potential sanctioners in a coercion game. The case studies have been designed to address these questions.

The set of ninety-nine cases includes a wide range of different types of sanctions cases. Some deal with relatively modest demands for policy changes, while others involve attempts to compel major changes, such as a change in government. Thus, all three types of cooperation problems—coincidence, coadjustment, and coercion—are reflected in the data set. Ideally, we would prefer to be able to break up the data set by problem type to allow for more-accurate testing of hypotheses. Unfortunately, this is not possible. The major problem is that each sanctions case typically includes more than one type of cooperation game, since many countries are involved. The study of the control of high-technology exports to the Soviet bloc explores this multiplicity of games in greater detail. To simplify that story, it appears that the United States was playing a coercion game with its European and Japanese allies at many times, while the allies were playing a coadjustment game among themselves. Thus, classifying the high-technology case as either coercion or coadjustment would be misleading, since the dynamics giving rise to cooperation in each of these games should be reflected in this case. Similarly mixed patterns occur in most cases, making it impossible to sort the data set on the basis of problem type.

The inclusion of more than one type of cooperation problem could potentially create analytical difficulties. In essence, it introduces another variable that we should include in the analysis—one controlling for the kinds of cooperation problems faced in each case. One way to deal with this dilemma is to control for the purpose of sanctions. Such a control at least provides some leverage on the problem of assessing the "difficulty" of cooperation in each case. In addition, this control allows us to test an alternative model of cooperation on economic sanctions, which I call the goals model. It focuses on the incentives facing the leading sender and neglects the problems of strategic interaction I have focused on. Hufbauer, Schott, and Elliott use this model in analyzing the problem of international cooperation. They summarize it simply: "The pursuit of more ambitious objectives accompanied by much fanfare often goes hand in hand with efforts to enlist international cooperation."[12] They reason that a lack of international cooperation simply signals the leading sender's failure to put much effort into organizing cooperation. According to this model, the leading sender can generally gain cooperation if it tries, and it will try only when the stakes are high. Thus, the level of cooperation should be positively correlated with the ambition of the sanctions. Cases in which the goals are more ambitious should result in higher levels of cooperation among states, cooperation due to the efforts of the leading sender. This model differs significantly from the strategic model developed in this study, which recognizes that cooperation is always desirable but always difficult to achieve because of the incentives to free-ride on the leading sender's sanctions. Thus, even strenuous efforts to gain cooperation can fail, under certain specifiable conditions. The goals model is a partial-equilibrium model; I have attempted to build a more-general model, taking into account the strategic incentives facing all potential sanctioners.

To control for the purposes of sanctions, I include the variable GOAL in the following analyses. I have recoded this variable from Hufbauer, Schott, and Elliott's coding of the goals of each case. They put each case into one of five categories. The first category involves calling for "modest" changes in the target country's policies, such as resolution of expropriation disputes or limited improvements in respect for human rights. (While such improvements are not modest from the perspective of victims of human-rights abuses, limited improvements are well within the capacity of all governments). The second category involves destabilizing a government, and the third involves disrupting military adventures. A fourth category deals with impairing military potential, and the fifth is a residual category for other major policy changes.[13] From this categorization, I have created the dummy variable GOAL, which takes a value of 0 if the case falls into the first category (minor policy change) and a value of 1 if it falls into any of the other categories.

According to this distinction between minor and major policy goals, we find that in half (forty-nine) of the cases, the senders sought only minor changes in the target country's policies. In the other half (fifty cases), major changes were pursued. According to the logic of the nonstrategic goals model, this variable should be positively correlated with the level of cooperation achieved, once we have controlled for other factors. As a preliminary test of this model, we can look at the correlation between GOAL and the measures of cooperation. Here, we do find some positive correlation, although its significance is questionable. GOAL has a correlation of 0.162 with COOP, of 0.259 with NUMBER, and of 0.00908 with NONMAJ. However, the analyses in the next chapter show that even these small positive correlations disappear when we include other independent variables, suggesting that the goals model does not explain cooperation very well.

## Conclusion

The first problem in this chapter was finding an appropriate measurement for the dependent variable of cooperation. I introduced three potential measures. Hufbauer, Schott, and Elliott have coded a variable I call COOP that allows each sanctions case to be rated on a scale from 1 to 4, with 4 reflecting extensive international cooperation. While COOP captures some important elements of cooperation, it is a somewhat subjective measure. Therefore, I proposed two alternative measures. The first, called NUMBER, is simply a count of the number of countries imposing sanctions. While correcting for the subjectivity inherent in COOP, NUMBER does not take account of the significance of the countries imposing sanctions. The variable NONMAJ takes a step toward correcting this problem by adjusting NUMBER according to the amount of trade each sender carries on with the target (after excluding trade with the major sender). NONMAJ is thus a percentage, with 0 percent meaning that only one state has imposed sanctions and 100 percent meaning that all countries that trade with the target have imposed some sanctions. Because each of these variables has its own weaknesses and strengths, I use all of them as proxies for cooperation in the next chapter.

This chapter also developed measures for five of the hypotheses put forth in chapter 2. TARGET measures the economic health and political stability of the target country and should be negatively related to cooperation. COLDWAR is a dummy variable that specifies whether the sanctions case crossed East-West lines; it should have a positive impact on cooperation. ASSIST specifies whether the target received international assistance; if balancing behavior holds, ASSIST should also have a positive correlation with cooperation. COSTD measures the cost of sanctions to the major sender and should have a positive impact. INST is a dummy variable that takes a value of 1 if a formal international organization such as the United Nations called for economic sanctions. Clearly, this should have a positive effect on cooperation among states, although the role of institutions in coordinating sanctions is more complex than this simple measure suggests. Finally, GOAL controls for the purpose of sanctions. It differentiates between cases that aim at minor and at major policy changes in the target. The model developed in this book does not suggest any obvious relationship between GOAL and cooperation, but the implicit model used by other studies of sanctions suggests a positive relation.

At least one interesting finding has emerged from the purely descriptive analyses in this chapter. Contrary to the conventional wisdom on the costliness of sanctions for those countries imposing them, we find that the vast majority of sanctions are costless, or nearly so. Looking at an unbiased set of cases rather than the few "major" cases typically studied forces this kind of reconsideration of the characteristics of economic sanctions. The next chapter uses the variables discussed here in statistical analyses of the impact of various factors on cooperation.

# 4

## Estimating Models of Cooperation

TO THIS POINT, we have examined a model of cooperation on economic sanctions and some of the variables that might be used to explain when states cooperate. Chapter 3 discussed the operationalization of the independent and dependent variables in this study and presented some descriptive statistics. In this chapter, I begin testing the hypotheses developed in chapter 2.

The factors that should influence the observed level of cooperation fall along three dimensions: balance-of-power considerations, potential for success, and costs. With regard to the balance of power, this study looks for evidence of balancing or bandwagoning behavior among states. The variables COLDWAR and ASSIST attempt to help answer the question of how the logic of balancing affects cooperation in cases of economic sanctions. We should note, however, that ASSIST may also have an impact on the probability of success; sanctions are less likely to be effective against a target that receives assistance. Thus, balance-of-power and potential-success considerations may work against each other, mitigating the overall impact of the target's receiving international aid in response to sanctions.

States will also take into account the probability that sanctions will be effective; the primary variable measuring this dimension is TARGET, the economic health and political stability of the target state. Finally, states will consider the costs of sanctions. I explicitly consider two types of costs here: the economic cost of sanctions to the leading sender (as measured by welfare losses) and the transaction costs of coordinating sanctions efforts. I attempt to capture the effects of these two factors with the variables COSTD and INST. The variable GOAL controls for the purposes of sanctions.

This chapter subjects these hypotheses to a preliminary test with three alternative statistical models. Because I am dealing with an unobservable dependent variable—cooperation among states, and only roughly measured proxies for it—I present three different statistical models. The first uses NONMAJ as the dependent variable and relies on ordinary-least-squares regression. The second is ordered-probit analysis with COOP as the dependent variable. Finally, I test the same hypotheses with event-count analysis using NUMBER as the dependent variable. By comparing the results from these alternative models, we can have greater confidence in the impact of various factors on cooperation among states. This multi-model approach helps overcome some of the empirical difficulties introduced by the necessarily imprecise measurement of some of the variables in this study.

The results from this quantitative analysis will provide the framework for the focused case studies that follow. Although the methods of analysis used in this chapter perform well for discovering patterns that occur across large numbers of cases, they cannot answer questions about why these patterns occur. Those issues are best dealt with through microlevel examination of state decision making, as in the case studies in the following chapters.

## Regression Analysis

This section presents the results of a model that uses NONMAJ as the dependent variable. NONMAJ runs, in theory, from 0 to 100, with higher values reflecting higher levels of cooperation.[1] Since NONMAJ approximates a continuous variable, I use least-squares regression for this analysis. In the next section, using ordered-probit analysis, I set the variance of the underlying variable equal to the standard error of the regression. Thus, we can directly compare the estimated coefficients of the independent variables from this regression to those from the probit analysis. While NONMAJ is a more-objective measure than COOP, as it is based on readily available trade statistics, it may miss some of the more-subtle dimensions of cooperation captured by COOP. Alternatively, we could consider NONMAJ an attempt to measure directly the level of cooperation underlying the categorical COOP measurement. Thus, this model complements the following probit analysis.

The results of ordinary-least-squares estimation, which assumes a linear relationship between the independent and dependent variables, are shown in table 4.1. I have marked coefficients significant at the .05 level with an asterisk. In this regression, the variables TARGET and INST have statistically significant effects at the .05 level. As expected, the coefficient of TARGET is negative and that of INST is positive. Thus, cooperation as measured by NONMAJ decreases when states direct sanctions against relatively stable countries, while the involvement of international institutions appears to lead to more cooperation. According to the framework developed above, we could argue that states are less willing to cooperate on sanctions against stable countries, which are likely to fail; and that international institutions help states overcome barriers to cooperation. The coefficient of COSTD is not quite statistically significant according to conventional standards, with a $t$-statistic of 1.76. However, the coeffi-

**TABLE 4.1**
Regression Results; NONMAJ as Dependent Variable

| Independent Variable | Estimated Coefficient | Standard Error | t–statistic |
|---|---|---|---|
| Constant | 12.30 | 5.26 | 2.34 |
| COLDWAR | 0.503 | 3.33 | 0.151 |
| ASSIST | −0.887 | 3.50 | −0.253 |
| TARGET* | −7.14 | 2.11 | −3.39 |
| COSTD | 5.79 | 3.29 | 1.76 |
| INST* | 11.16 | 3.25 | 3.44 |
| GOAL | −3.81 | 2.98 | −1.28 |
| | | | |
| R-squared | | 0.210 | |
| Corrected R-squared | | 0.158 | |
| Standard Error of Regression | | 13.58 | |
| Number of Observations | | 99 | |

cient of COSTD is positive, as expected. The coefficient of COLDWAR is very small, as is that of ASSIST. Both of these variables appear to have negligible effects on cooperation as measured by NONMAJ. Thus, when these measures are used, balancing behavior does not appear to have much explanatory power for the level of cooperation achieved.

Finally, the coefficient of GOAL is negative but not statistically significant. This result suggests that the purpose of sanctions has no systematic relationship to the level of cooperation achieved, once we have controlled for other explanatory factors. If anything, the negative coefficient implies *less* cooperation when the goals of sanctions are more ambitious. This provides strong evidence against a model of cooperation that sees cooperation as the straightforward result of the sender's purposes. Such a goals model suggests, plausibly, that we should see more cooperation in cases with more-ambitious goals, since these are the cases where success requires international collaboration. Thus, in this nonstrategic, partial-equilibrium framework, the leading sender will bother to expend resources to gain cooperation only when the sanctions' purpose demands it. When ambitions are more modest, the leading sender will put little effort into organizing international cooperation.

The model I have adopted recognizes that some leading senders may put international cooperation low on their list of priorities. Strong leaders, in particular, may behave this way. However, the model of strategic interaction developed in this study diverges from the goals model in recognizing the difficulty of achieving cooperation even when it is a high priority. Because other potential senders have incentives to free-ride, the leading sender's efforts to organize international cooperation do not au-

**TABLE 4.2**
Regression Results; Dummies for TARGET

| Independent Variable | Estimated Coefficient | Standard Error | t–statistic |
|---|---|---|---|
| Constant | 6.49 | 5.08 | 1.28 |
| COLDWAR | −0.0167 | 3.39 | −0.0049 |
| ASSIST | −0.322 | 3.57 | −0.0900 |
| TAR1* | −9.66 | 3.67 | −2.63 |
| TAR2* | −14.48 | 4.23 | −3.42 |
| COSTD | 5.73 | 3.29 | 1.74 |
| INST* | 10.79 | 3.28 | 3.29 |
| GOAL | −3.66 | 2.99 | −1.22 |
| R-squared | | 0.216 | |
| Corrected R-squared | | 0.155 | |
| Standard Error of Regression | | 13.61 | |
| Number of Observations | | 99 | |

tomatically translate into results. Instead, achieving cooperation requires a credible commitment by the leading sender; and cooperation can be facilitated by tools such as international institutions. The regression results support this strategic analysis, showing clearly that more-ambitious policy goals do not result in more cooperation and drawing our attention to other explanatory variables.

Technically speaking, the TARGET variable has not been properly dealt with in this analysis. TARGET is a three-category variable, but there is no reason to assume that it is an interval-level measurement. Thus, it should be broken up into two separate dummy variables, TAR1 and TAR2. TAR1 is the dummy for TARGET = 2 and TAR2 the dummy for TARGET = 3. This procedure provides better estimates of the effect of the target's condition on cooperation, but it requires the estimation of an additional parameter from the data set, thus reducing the accuracy of the other coefficients.

Table 4.2 presents the regression results with TAR1 and TAR2 substituted for TARGET. This analysis shows that moving from TARGET = 1 (a poor, unstable country) to TARGET = 2 (a country with some problems) has a larger negative impact on cooperation than moving from TARGET = 2 to TARGET = 3. Moving from TARGET = 1 to TARGET = 2 decreases the expected level of cooperation by 9.66 percent, while moving to TARGET = 3 decreases it by an additional 4.82 percent. However, this difference in effect is within one standard error of the estimate of the coefficients. Thus, we cannot be confident that there is a significant difference between the coefficients of TAR1 and TAR2. In

**TABLE 4.3**
Regression Results; Outliers Included

| Independent Variable | Estimated Coefficient | Standard Error | t–statistic |
|---|---|---|---|
| Constant | 9.60 | 5.94 | 1.61 |
| COLDWAR | −2.52 | 3.73 | −0.676 |
| ASSIST | 0.667 | 3.90 | 0.171 |
| TARGET* | −6.70 | 2.37 | −2.82 |
| COSTD | 6.82 | 3.72 | 1.84 |
| INST* | 14.18 | 3.63 | 3.91 |
| GOAL | −2.50 | 3.37 | −3.91 |
| R-squared | | 0.217 | |
| Corrected R-squared | | 0.167 | |
| Standard Error of Regression | | 15.43 | |
| Number of Observations | | 101 | |

addition, including these dummies results in no significant changes in the values of the other estimated coefficients. For these reasons, and because including this additional variable puts more demands on a data set with a limited number of observations, I use TARGET for the remainder of the analyses in this chapter.

As discussed in the previous chapter, I have eliminated the cases of South Africa and Rhodesia from this analysis because they are unique outliers. For comparison, however, table 4.3 presents the results of the same regression when South Africa and Rhodesia are included. There are some significant and interesting influences on the results. First, the coefficient of COLDWAR changes from a small positive number, 0.503, to −2.52, although it is not statistically significant in either case. When we include the two white-minority-rule cases, which exhibit an extraordinarily high level of cooperation but were not mainly East-West issues, we find that the Cold War actually seems to have a negative impact on cooperation. Second, the coefficient of ASSIST changes from a small negative number, −0.887, to a positive number, 0.667, although neither is significant. Since Rhodesia did receive assistance from some states, ASSIST has a positive impact on cooperation when we include this case.

The coefficient of INST also changes when we include these two cases, increasing from 11.16 to 14.18. Because the United Nations played a central role in coordinating sanctions in these two instances, formal organizations appear to have a larger positive impact on cooperation. In order to avoid both exaggerating the importance of institutions and letting these two special cases dominate the interpretation of the aggregate results, I exclude them from the following analyses. However, it is interest-

**TABLE 4.4**
Fitted Values; Regression Model

| TARGET | COSTD | INST | Fitted NONMAJ |
|--------|-------|------|---------------|
| 3 | 1 | 0 | −3.33% |
| 3 | 1 | 1 | 7.83 |
| 3 | 2 | 0 | 2.46 |
| 3 | 2 | 1 | 13.62 |
| 1 | 1 | 0 | 10.95 |
| 1 | 1 | 1 | 22.11 |
| 1 | 2 | 0 | 16.74 |
| 1 | 2 | 1 | 27.90 |

ing to note that the literature on economic sanctions, in which the South Africa and Rhodesia cases have played a central role, has probably been skewed by the attention given to these outliers. Once again, working with an unbiased set of cases leads to a different understanding of the characteristics of economic sanctions.

Table 4.4 presents some fitted values for the original regression results, to facilitate their interpretation. These values assume that COLDWAR, ASSIST, and GOAL are fixed at 0, reflecting a case that did not cross East-West boundaries, in which the target did not receive assistance, and in which the policy-change goals were modest. Allowing these variables to take on different values would have no noticeable impact on the results, since their coefficients are small.

The first line of this table represents a case in which the target is strong, sanctions are a net benefit to the sender, and no institution has called for sanctions. U.S. sanctions against Paraguay for human-rights violations during 1977–81 have these values. This situation yields the lowest possible expected value of NONMAJ, which turns out to be negative. This result shows one weakness of the linear model: we can identify cases where the expected value of NONMAJ is less than 0, a value that is not meaningful. Cases in which the amount of cooperation is expected to be near 0 will sometimes be problematical. In fact, the realized value of NONMAJ for the Paraguay case is 0, as the United States failed to convince any other countries to impose sanctions.

On the second line of the table, we see what would be expected to happen if an international institution such as the Organization of American States (OAS) called for sanctions against Paraguay. The fitted value of NONMAJ increases by over eleven percentage points, to a value of 7.83 percent. Thus, we might expect in this case that countries accounting for about 8 percent of Paraguay's trade (excluding that with the United States) would impose sanctions. The impact of high-cost sanctions—for example, if the United States chose to cut exports to Paraguay, instead of merely cutting foreign aid—is shown in the third line. Here, we see some increase over the first case in the expected level of cooperation; but the level remains quite low, under 2.5 percent. When both an institution and high costs are involved, as shown in the fourth line, the level of cooperation rises to 13.62 percent.

The second half of table 4.4 presents results for sanctions against a poor, unstable country, such as Suriname in 1982. At that time, the United States and the Netherlands imposed sanctions in response to human-rights violations and suspicions of Cuban and Soviet influence. Here, we see a higher expected baseline of cooperation than in the hypothetical Paraguay case in the absence of high-cost sanctions or institutional involvement, with a fitted NONMAJ of 10.95 percent (line 5). In fact, many more states than predicted cooperated in this case, with a realized NONMAJ value of 39 percent. Again, increases in the major sender's costs and the approval of sanctions by an international institution raise the amount of cooperation expected, to a maximum expected value of 27.9 percent (last line of the table).

Overall, this regression model suggests that institutions and the target's condition have a significant impact on cooperation; that balancing behavior has no impact; and that self-imposed costs may have some impact, although the results are inconclusive. The model also demonstrates that the purposes of sanctions have no straightforward relationship to international cooperation.

## Ordered-Probit Analysis

This section turns to a different measure of cooperation, while using the same independent variables. The dependent variable COOP measures cooperation on a four-point scale. While we know that a value of 2 reflects more cooperation than a value of 1, we cannot say that the difference between 1 and 2 is the same as the difference between 3 and 4. In other words, COOP is an ordinal variable, reflecting an order but not an interval-level measurement.[2] One way to conceive of the process that generates such a variable is to consider an underlying unobservable scale of cooperation. Each case in the data set lies at a specific point along this scale, but we are unable to observe the actual cooperation value. However, we can break the underlying continuum up into four discrete pieces, labeled "none," "low," "medium," and "high." We can then say in which of these four categories any particular case falls and use this observation as the dependent variable. The appropriate method for analyzing a variable of this type, such as COOP, is ordered-probit analysis.[3]

**TABLE 4.5**
Ordered Probit Analysis; COOP as Dependent Variable

| Independent Variable | Estimated Coefficient | Standard Error | t–statistic |
|---|---|---|---|
| Constant | −8.69 | 6.54 | −1.33 |
| COLDWAR | 5.49 | 3.94 | 1.39 |
| ASSIST* | 12.85 | 4.12 | 3.12 |
| TARGET | −2.59 | 2.49 | −1.04 |
| COSTD* | 8.70 | 4.10 | 2.12 |
| INST* | 22.78 | 4.03 | 5.66 |
| GOAL | −5.97 | 3.68 | −1.62 |
| Thresh 1* | 21.21 | 2.38 | 8.91 |
| Thresh 2* | 40.45 | 4.15 | 9.75 |
| | | | |
| Log-likelihood | | −86.32 | |
| Percent Correctly Predicted | | 62.6 | |
| Number of Observations | | 99 | |

Ordered-probit analysis estimates threshold values for the points at which the underlying continuum of cooperation is divided into categories and produces estimates of the placement of each case on the unobserved cooperation scale. For this analysis, I assume that the underlying variable has a normal distribution with the same standard deviation as the standard error of the above regression, 13.58.[4] Setting the standard deviation equal to 13.58 affects only the scale of the estimated coefficients; it does not change the substantive interpretation of the results. However, choosing this value as opposed to an arbitrary number such as one (which ordered-probit models typically assume) allows direct comparison of the results from this probit model with those from the previous ordinary-least-squares analysis of NONMAJ.

Table 4.5 presents the results of the ordered-probit model, which uses the six independent variables described above. The most important finding here is that all coefficients go in the predicted direction; TARGET's coefficient is negative, and those of the other variables (except for GOAL) are positive. The coefficients of COLDWAR and TARGET, however, are not statistically significant at the .05 level. Thus, we cannot rule out the possibility that these variables actually have no impact on COOP and that the estimated coefficients are simply the result of chance. The coefficients of ASSIST, COSTD, and INST are all positive, as expected, and statistically significant at the .05 level. This indicates that cases in which the target receives assistance tend to have a higher cooperation score; that increases in the cost to the major sender lead to greater cooperation; and that the involvement of institutions increases the level of coop-

```
    1            2             3                 4        COOP Value
<--------|-----------|----------------|-------->
    6.97       21.21             40.45              Unobserved Cooperation
                                                    Variable
```

4.1. Estimated Thresholds (Probit Model)

eration. The findings on the impact of costs and institutions are consistent with those from the regression analysis, as is the lack of significance for East-West cases. Assistance to the target appears to have an impact only in the probit model, while the target's condition is significant only in the regression. Once again, more-ambitious sanctions are negatively related to cooperation, although this relationship is not statistically significant.

To interpret these coefficients, we need to look at the estimated thresholds, which are the points at which the underlying continuum of cooperation is divided to yield four segments. I have set the first threshold at 6.97, to make the underlying scale comparable to NONMAJ. By setting the first threshold at this level and by setting the standard error equal to the standard error of the regression, we fix the scale of the underlying cooperation measure to be the same as that for NONMAJ. Thus, the estimated coefficients from these two models can be directly compared. Setting these parameters changes only the scale, not the substantive interpretation, of the model's results. The second and third thresholds are estimated to be at 21.21 and 40.45 (Thresh 1 and Thresh 2, respectively). These thresholds are estimated using maximum-likelihood techniques to find the parameters that best fit the observed data. The underlying cooperation continuum that results is represented in figure 4.1.

In this analysis, the threshold estimates themselves contain information about the underlying cooperation variable, which is measured on the same scale as NONMAJ, a percentage. Because we assumed an underlying normal distribution, the lowest cooperation category is unbounded on the low end, while the highest is likewise unbounded on the upper end. The second category—COOP = 2—runs from 6.97 to 21.21 on the cooperation scale. The third category is approximately 40 percent wider, running from 21.21 to 40.45. With the actual COOP measure, 24 cases fall in the second category, while 18 fall in the third. We get a slightly different distribution of fitted COOP values, with just 16 cases predicted to fall in the second category and 22 in the third. The difference between these two distributions lies in the number of cases falling in the "no cooperation" category. Fifty-one cases actually have a COOP value of 1, while 60 are predicted to have this value. Thus, the probit model somewhat overpredicts the number of cases that will have no cooperation. In practice, factors not accounted for in this specification, or perhaps chance, result in a higher-than-expected incidence of low-level cooperation.

**TABLE 4.6**
Fitted Values; Probit Model

| COLDWAR | ASSIST | COSTD | INST | Fitted Value | COOP |
|:---:|:---:|:---:|:---:|:---:|:---:|
| 0 | 0 | 1 | 0 | −5.17 | 1 |
| 1 | 0 | 1 | 0 | 0.32 | 1 |
| 0 | 1 | 1 | 0 | 7.68 | 2 |
| 0 | 0 | 2 | 0 | 3.53 | 1 |
| 0 | 0 | 1 | 1 | 17.61 | 2 |
| 1 | 1 | 2 | 0 | 21.87 | 3 |
| 1 | 1 | 1 | 1 | 35.95 | 3 |
| 1 | 1 | 2 | 1 | 44.65 | 4 |

Using these results, we can also make some inferences about the universe of potential sanctions cases from which this sample of actual cases was drawn. The underlying cooperation variable has a mean of 7.95, the same as NONMAJ. This means that the COOP = 1 category, which runs from negative infinity to 6.97, contains 47 percent of the area of this normal distribution. The COOP = 2 category contains 36 percent of the distribution, COOP = 3 has 16 percent, and COOP = 4 has less than 1 percent. Thus, Hufbauer, Schott, and Elliott's categorization has broken up the cooperation continuum in such a way that, according to the thresholds estimated by the probit model, nearly half of the probability density, or potential universe of cases, falls into the lowest category of cooperation, while less than 1 percent falls into the high-level category.

Table 4.6 presents fitted values for various combinations of COLD-WAR, ASSIST, COSTD, and INST. For these calculations, I have held the value of TARGET at 2; the coefficient of TARGET is small enough that changes in the economic health and political stability of the target country appear to have a negligible impact on the amount of cooperation observed. GOAL is held at 0.

The first line of the table gives the expected results for a case in which there were no East-West issues, the target of sanctions received no assistance from other countries, the cost to the major sending country was negative, and no international institution called for sanctions. U.S. sanctions against Uruguay for human-rights violations, which were imposed during 1977–81, fit these parameters. Because these sanctions took the form of reduced military and economic aid, they actually resulted in a net economic benefit to the United States. In addition, Uruguay did not receive offsetting increases in aid from other countries, and the United States did not convince any international organization to call for sanctions against Uruguay. The predicted cooperation score in this case is −5.17, which would yield a COOP value of 1 (no cooperation). This result agrees with Hufbauer, Schott, and Elliott's coding of this particular case, as Washington could not convince other states to join in imposing sanctions against Uruguay.

According to this model, increases in the cost to the United States would increase the expected level of unobserved cooperation, but not sufficiently to move the case into a higher COOP category. Assistance from another state would just barely move the expected cooperation value into the next category (line 3). The approval of an international institution, however, would have a larger substantive effect. According to this model, if an international organization such as the OAS were to call for sanctions against Uruguay, we would expect an increase in the level of cooperation to 17.61 percent (line 5), which is large enough to move the case into the COOP = 2 category. Thus, the substantive importance of institutional approval appears to be greater than that of the other variables. Although assistance to the target and the cost of sanctions to the sender are large enough to be statistically distinguishable from 0, their impact on cooperation is smaller than that of institutions.

The last two lines of this table refer to cases in which the expected level of cooperation significantly exceeds that found in the U.S.-Uruguay case. For example, the second-to-last line presents the results for a case in which Cold War issues were involved an institution called for sanctions against the target, and the target received assistance in response to these sanctions. The major sanctioning country, however, bore negative sanctioning costs, perhaps by only cutting foreign aid. The model predicts a COOP score of 3 in this case.

Only one case in the data set fits all these criteria: Soviet sanctions against Yugoslavia in 1948–55. The Soviet Union imposed a range of sanctions, from a cutoff of tourist travel to Yugoslavia to delays in the signing of trade agreements. The Soviets imposed these sanctions in response to Prime Minister Marshal Tito's moves toward political independence, which included meetings with ambassadors from the United States and Britain. This model predicts a fairly large amount of cooperation in this case, with a fitted value of 35.95 percent and a COOP score of 3. In other words, countries accounting for nearly one-third of Yugoslavia's trade, excluding that with the Soviet Union, would impose sanctions. The model also suggests that if the Soviet Union were to impose sanctions more costly to itself, the fitted value would rise to 44.65 percent (last line), putting this case in the highest COOP category. In fact, in this specific case the Soviets were able to achieve a COOP score of 4 without imposing costly sanctions. The political situation between the Soviet Union and Eastern Europe during this period explains the unusually high level of cooperation—the Soviets did not have to bear high costs to demonstrate credibility.

**TABLE 4.7**
Probit and Regression Parameter Estimates

| Variable | Probit Estimate | Regression Estimate |
|----------|-----------------|---------------------|
| COLDWAR  | 5.49            | 0.503               |
| ASSIST   | 12.85           | -0.887              |
| TARGET   | -2.59           | -7.14               |
| COSTD    | 8.70            | 5.79                |
| INST     | 22.78           | 11.16               |
| GOAL     | -5.97           | -3.81               |

Overall, the ordered-probit model has given encouraging results. The variables ASSIST, COSTD, and INST had significant coefficients in the predicted positive direction. The results for TARGET and COLDWAR were not significant, although the coefficients for both were in the correct direction. We can directly compare the results of the probit and regression models; table 4.7 puts the estimated coefficients side by side.

One major difference between these two models lies in the effect of assistance to the target. While we found with the probit model that assistance led to an increase of 12.9 points on the underlying cooperation scale, in the regression model assistance actually had a small negative effect, although it was not significantly different from 0. This difference has implications for the sort of balancing behavior hypothesized to underlie the positive impact of ASSIST. The results suggest that potential sanctioners do balance against those who assist the target but that they do so in a way that is picked up by COOP and not by NONMAJ.

I would suggest two alternative explanations for this finding. First, balancing behavior may take the form of more-stringent sanctions rather than additional states' deciding to impose sanctions. This effect would show up in COOP but not in NONMAJ. For example, if the NATO allies responded to Soviet assistance to Cuba by extending the scope of their sanctions but did not include more countries in the effort, we would see an increase in COOP but not in NONMAJ. Second, balancing could occur through the imposition of sanctions by more states that have minimal economic relations with the target. This pattern would also result in increases in COOP but not necessarily in NONMAJ, since if additional sanctioners had little trade with the target they would have little impact on NONMAJ. The analysis of NUMBER later in this chapter supports the second of these two explanations, as ASSIST does have a significant positive impact on the number of countries imposing sanctions. Thus, we find some evidence of balancing behavior, but only among states that have minimal economic relations with the target. Comparison of the results from two admittedly imperfect measures of cooperation can, as this discussion suggests, lead to generalizations about the nature of the causal relationships between various factors and cooperation in cases of economic sanctions.

A second distinction between the probit and regression analyses lies in the estimated coefficients of TARGET. In the probit model, the economic health and political stability of the target country had no discernible impact on cooperation. In the regression, however, we find—as expected—a significant negative coefficient for TARGET, meaning less cooperation on sanctions directed against relatively rich, stable countries. This relationship between the target's condition and cooperation may be an artifact explained by the construction of NONMAJ. Small, poor countries tend to have their trade concentrated with a few major trading partners rather than spread among many. This means that sanctions imposed by only a few trading partners can result in an artificially large value for NONMAJ, one that reflects a higher level of cooperation than the "true" one. Therefore, the analysis of COOP may provide a better test of the impact of TARGET, leading to the conclusion that the target's condition has little effect on cooperation.

In both the probit and regression analyses, we find a negative but statistically insignificant coefficient for the goals of sanctions. The estimated coefficients for COLDWAR in the two models are within two standard errors of each other, as are those for COSTD. Thus, the regression results for these variables support the interpretation of the probit model. The estimate of INST's coefficient, however, is significantly larger in the probit than in the regression analysis. This may be due to error in Hufbauer, Schott, and Elliott's coding of COOP. Whereas COOP should measure cooperation among states as reflected in actual national policies, it is possible that Hufbauer, Schott, and Elliott's measurement was contaminated by the actions of international institutions. In other words, a call for sanctions by an institution should not have led to a higher value of COOP unless this action resulted in actual imposition of sanctions by more states. Some conflation of these two levels of analysis would lead to artificially high estimates of the impact of INST on COOP. Thus, the estimate of INST's coefficient from the regression analysis is probably more reliable than that from the probit analysis. What we find, using NONMAJ as the dependent variable, is that when an international organization calls for sanctions, states accounting for, on average, an additional 11 percent of the target's non-major-sender trade will join in the sanctions effort. The effect of institutions is slightly larger than that of the cost variable, COSTD.

In general, the results of the regression and probit analyses support one another and the hypotheses about cooperation developed in chapter 2. The models show strongest support for the influence of international institutions and the costs of sanctions; both factors have consistently positive effects on the level of cooperation observed. We found weaker support for the effects of the target country's stability, the Cold War, and assistance to the target; TARGET and ASSIST have significant effects in only one of the two models, and while the estimated coefficient of COLDWAR is positive in both models, it is not statistically significant in either. The variation across the two models suggests that while the hypotheses are supported, the variables COOP and NONMAJ measure somewhat different dimensions of cooperation. Neither variable should be considered a perfect measure of cooperation, as each contains some valuable information not found in the other. For example, comparing the results of these models allowed us to make some inferences about the nature of the balancing behavior that resulted from assistance to the target—namely, that only minor trading partners seemed to balance this way. Sorting out some of the puzzles these analyses present will have to be done through the focused case studies. First, however, I develop an additional statistical model of cooperation, one that corrects some of the inaccurate assumptions of the probit and ordinary-least-squares models.

## Event-Count Analysis

Earlier, I proposed a straightforward count of the number of countries imposing sanctions as a possible measure of cooperation, but rejected it because of its lack of sensitivity to the significance of the sanctioning countries. NUMBER does not appear to be an adequate direct measure of cooperation, if analyzed in isolation. However, it does seem plausible that it should be positively correlated with the level of cooperation. Thus, if we think about the process by which NUMBER is generated from unobservable factors, we can develop a model in which to use NUMBER to estimate the underlying level of cooperation. I adopt this approach here to develop an event-count analysis.[5]

As in the probit analysis, I begin by assuming that there is some unobservable underlying continuous level of cooperation. However, we could think of cooperation as the rate (represented by $\lambda$) at which countries decide to impose sanctions. While we cannot directly observe $\lambda$, we can count up the number of countries imposing sanctions and use this number as an estimate of the underlying variable. In this framework, the decision to impose sanctions is an event, and the only data we have are the number of events during each sanctions episode. In this context, the "rate" at which countries impose sanctions can be thought of as the probability that each country will decide to cooperate.

Researchers have typically estimated event counts using a Poisson distribution.[6] The Poisson distribution seems appropriate for event counts because it can take on only the values of non-negative integers and a count will also take on only these values. The Poisson distribution is

$$Y_t \sim f_P(y_t | \lambda_t) = \frac{[\exp(-\lambda_t)](\lambda_t)^{y_t}}{y_t!},$$

where $Y_t$ is the dependent variable (here, the number of countries imposing sanctions), $t$ refers to time (here, a particular sanctions episode), $y_t$ is a particular realization of $Y_t$, and $\lambda_t$ is the rate of event occurrence (here, the probability of cooperation). The distribution is unbounded on the upper end, so that theoretically we could count an infinite number of events in each episode. Clearly, there is an upper bound on the number of sanctioners; it is the number of countries in the international system. However, since the observed number of sanctioners never approaches this bound, the Poisson model is an adequate starting point.

The primary question asked in estimations of Poisson models has been whether the underlying process seems to approximate one that would give rise to a Poisson distribution. In other words, only the fit of the model as a whole has been estimated, not the effects of particular independent variables. However, using models that combine regression concepts and Poisson process models, we can estimate the effects of particular explanatory variables on the unobserved rate of cooperation.[7] The unobserved continuous process is specified as a function of these explanatory variables:

$$E(Y_t) = \lambda_t = \exp(x_t \beta),$$

where $x_t$ is a vector of explanatory variables and $\beta$ is a parameter vector, indicating the effect of each explanatory variable on the underlying rate of cooperation, $\lambda$. I estimate this model using the systematic and stochastic components just described, through maximum-likelihood techniques.

The regression and probit models estimated above suffer from a common weakness: they do not correct for selection bias present in the data. This bias results from the fact that there are no cases of zero sanctions in the data set—that is, I have not been able to include cases where no country has decided to impose sanctions. This kind of selection on the dependent variable tends to bias the resulting estimates of the effects of explanatory variables. In fact, the estimates are biased in a particular direction—*toward* zero. An intuitive feeling for why this is so comes from considering the impact of the variable INST. It is reasonable to assume that cases where no country imposed sanctions would be strongly corre-

**TABLE 4.8**
Truncated Poisson Results; NUMBER as Dependent Variable

| Independent Variable | Estimated Coefficient | Robust Standard Error | t–statistic |
|---|---|---|---|
| Constant | −0.746 | 0.574 | −1.30 |
| COLDWAR | 0.0515 | 0.264 | 0.195 |
| ASSIST | 0.228 | 0.283 | 0.806 |
| TARGET | −0.0217 | 0.0742 | −0.292 |
| COSTD* | 0.564 | 0.241 | 2.34 |
| INST* | 1.76 | 0.280 | 6.29 |
| GOAL | 0.264 | 0.304 | 0.868 |
| Log-likelihood | | 359.18 | |
| Number of Observations | | 99 | |

lated with INST. Theoretically, we should expect very few cases in which an international institution called for sanctions but no country imposed them, because getting sanctions on an institution's agenda requires that at least one country have a strong interest in them. Thus, when these "noncases" are excluded from the sample, we will tend to underestimate the effect of international institutions on cooperation. Including these cases where "the dog didn't bark" would presumably *increase* the absolute size of the estimated coefficients.

The Poisson distribution can be modified to take into account the fact that the data have been truncated at zero; with the modification, the event counts are always positive integers.[8] Table 4.8 contains the results of the truncated-at-zero Poisson model.[9] These results lend further support to our hypotheses about the effects of individual explanatory variables. Most impressively, these results, although derived from a model that uses a dependent variable measured completely independently of COOP, closely match the results of the probit model. As expected, the coefficient of INST is quite large, since we have now corrected for the downward-biasing effects of truncation. The variables COSTD and INST both have positive coefficients that are significant at the .05 level, indicating that when these factors (high cost or institutional approval) are present, the number of countries participating in sanctions increases. ASSIST also has a positive coefficient, as in the probit model, although it fails the test of statistical significance here. The coefficient of COLDWAR is positive, as predicted, and that of TARGET is negative; however, neither is statistically significant. GOAL has a positive coefficient—unlike in the two previous models, in which its estimated coefficient was negative. However, the coefficient of GOAL is not statistically different from zero.

**TABLE 4.9**
Fitted Values; Poisson Model

| ASSIST | COSTD | INST | Fitted NUMBER |
|--------|-------|------|---------------|
| 0 | 1 | 0 | 1.04 |
| 1 | 1 | 0 | 1.31 |
| 0 | 2 | 0 | 1.83 |
| 0 | 1 | 1 | 6.04 |
| 1 | 2 | 0 | 2.29 |
| 1 | 1 | 1 | 7.59 |
| 0 | 2 | 1 | 10.62 |
| 1 | 2 | 1 | 13.34 |

To help interpret these results, table 4.9 presents some fitted values, holding TARGET fixed at 2, COLDWAR at 0, and GOAL at 1. We can discuss these results using the same example employed in the analysis of the probit model—U.S. sanctions against Uruguay for human-rights violations. If, as was in fact the case, the United States imposed sanctions that were purely reductions in economic and military aid and that did not involve any international organization, and if Uruguay did not receive help from any other country, we would expect a total of only one country to impose sanctions. In other words, the United States could not expect any other state to join in the sanctions effort (line 1). With this low baseline of expected cooperation, assistance to Uruguay (line 2) or more-costly sanctions (line 3) would result in only small increases in the number of countries expected to sanction. A call for sanctions by an international institution, however, would have a much larger impact, increasing the expected number of sanctioners to six (line 4).

The last three lines of the table show that once an institution gets involved, assistance to the target and the costliness of sanctions have much larger expected impacts, because of the nonlinear nature of this model. With an institutional call for sanctions, assistance to Uruguay would increase the expected number of sanctioners to over 7.5 (line 6), while sanctions more costly to the United States would increase this number to nearly eleven (line 7). Finally, if institutions, assistance, and costly sanctions were all involved, we would expect thirteen countries to impose sanctions (line 8). These results have both statistical and substantive significance.

This analysis, while promising, rests on an untenable assumption. Specifically, the Poisson distribution results from an accumulation of a series of independent events. Formally, this means that the probability that an event will occur at time $t + 1$ is independent of what has happened up to time $t$. In this case, a Poisson distribution relies on the assumption that the probability that one country will impose sanctions is independent of the decisions of all other countries. The assumption of independence, which results in the specification of variance equal to $\lambda_t$ for all observations, is clearly incorrect in this case. In fact, the theoretical framework underlying the hypotheses being tested here assumes strategic interdependence—that states make their decisions based in part on what other states do.

We could think of strategic interdependence as "contagion" among states. Contagion can take two forms—negative and positive. Negative contagion appears as a type of balancing behavior. In this situation, a decision by one state to impose sanctions will *decrease* the probability that other states will impose sanctions; they will instead be more inclined to assist the target. We could infer negative contagion from these models if we saw a decrease in the variance of $Y_t$ from the variance of the Poisson distribution. Because states are balancing one another, repeated trials of the same hypothetical experiment will result in relatively few cases where an unusually large number of states impose or refuse to impose sanctions, compared to a situation where decisions are made independently. If states balance one another, the number of sanctioners, on average, will be closer to the expected number for any particular values of the independent variables. This effect would decrease the variance of $Y_t$ in repeated trials, so that $\mathrm{Var}(Y_t) < \lambda_t$.

Positive contagion, on the other hand, resembles a bandwagoning situation. Here, a decision by one state to impose sanctions will *increase* the probability that others will take a similar step. Likewise, a refusal to sanction will be followed by similar decisions from other states. In repeated trials, this process of positive contagion will lead to relatively many cases where an unusually large or small number of states impose sanctions; extreme results will occur more frequently than under conditions of independent decision making. In other words, the variance of $Y_t$ will increase, so that $\mathrm{Var}(Y_t) > \lambda_t$.

While balancing behavior leads to a process in which the results tend to stay close to the mean for each observation and so are relatively predictable, bandwagoning tends to lead to extreme results, so that the expected level of cooperation is relatively hard to predict. This proposition illustrates and puts into a testable form the common understanding that strategic interaction causes indeterminacy in results in international relations. However, we should note that only one type of strategic interaction—bandwagoning—has this effect. A second type of strategic interaction—balancing—will in fact lead to increased predictability about the level of cooperation.

The Poisson distribution can be modified to allow for contagion.

**TABLE 4.10**
Generalized Event Count Results; NUMBER as Dependent Variable

| Independent Variable | Estimated Coefficient | Robust Standard Error | t–statistic |
|---|---|---|---|
| Constant | 0.214 | 0.295 | 0.725 |
| COLDWAR | 0.0326 | 0.187 | 0.174 |
| ASSIST | 0.300 | 0.191 | 1.57 |
| TARGET | −0.0520 | 0.102 | −0.510 |
| COSTD* | 0.351 | 0.152 | 2.31 |
| INST* | 1.29 | 0.187 | 6.90 |
| GOAL | 0.0832 | 0.170 | 0.489 |
| Gamma* | 0.872 | 0.225 | 3.88 |
| Log-likelihood | | 371.03 | |
| Number of Observations | | 99 | |

Whereas $\mathrm{Var}(Y_t) = \lambda_t$ in the Poisson distribution, in the generalized event count (GEC) distribution we set

$$\mathrm{Var}(Y_t) = \lambda_t \exp(\gamma).^{10}$$

This distribution varies from the Poisson only in the inclusion of $\gamma$. A negative value of $\gamma$ (gamma) would decrease the variance of $Y$, while a positive value for gamma would increase the variance. If gamma is equal to 0, this equation simplifies to that for the Poisson distribution, so a negative value for gamma indicates that the assumption of independence is correct. Thus, negative contagion will result in negative estimated values of $\gamma$, independence in $\gamma = 0$, and positive contagion in positive values of $\gamma$. Table 4.10 shows the results of the GEC model. Gamma has an estimated value of 0.872, indicating that a significant amount of positive contagion may be present in the data. This finding is consistent with a hypothesis that sanctions episodes tend to show bandwagoning behavior, where states jointly decide either to impose or not to impose sanctions. We should expect this outcome, for example, if most sanctions episodes involve coadjustment problems, where unilateral sanctions are costly and ineffective but where cooperation can lead to the mutually beneficial outcome of multilateral sanctions.[11] One interesting implication of the positive value of gamma is that there is no evidence here of free-riding, in which one state's decision to sanction leads others to refuse to do so. Such a process would be reflected in a negative value of gamma. Thus, the results of this estimation differ from those of studies of alliance formation. In alliance formation, balancing behavior seems to predominate.[12]

With economic sanctions, we find stronger support for the existence of bandwagoning behavior among sanctioners. This finding deserves further exploration. I will examine the question of bandwagoning versus balancing more closely in the case studies.

The other parameter estimates of the GEC model are similar to those of the truncated Poisson, with COSTD and INST having significant positive effects. ASSIST, TARGET, COLDWAR, and GOAL again have effects that go in the predicted direction but that do not meet the criterion of statistical significance. The log-likelihood of the GEC model, 371.0, exceeds that of the truncated Poisson model, 359.2, indicating that the GEC model is more likely to have generated this particular data set than the Poisson model. Thus, the results indicate that allowing for contagion improves the model's performance.

An example may help to clarify the meaning of a positive value for gamma. In the case of independence, $\text{Var}(Y_t) = \lambda_t$. Thus, if $E(Y_t)$—the expected number of sanctioning countries for some particular set of circumstances—were four, the standard deviation of the distribution of $Y_t$ would be the square root of four, or two. However, the GEC model estimates gamma at 0.872, so that $\text{Var}(Y_t) = \lambda_t(e^\gamma) = 9.57$. The standard deviation of $Y_t$ thus would increase to 3.1, more than one and a half times greater than for the case of independent decision making. Substantively, this means that strategic interdependence has increased the variance in the expected number of countries participating in sanctions, making the outcome less predictable than it would if states made decisions independently.

We can contrast the two models by examining the probability distributions they produce. Figure 4.2 shows the probability distribution for the number of countries imposing sanctions, assuming independent decision making (no contagion). The chance that three or four countries will impose sanctions is highest, about 20 percent in each case. The chance that only one country will impose sanctions is quite low, less than 8 percent. There is almost no probability that more than ten countries will impose sanctions. Figure 4.3 illustrates what happens with positive contagion, where either buck-passing or chain-ganging behavior is likely to occur. The chance that only one country will act—that is, that buck-passing will occur—is now higher, about 14 percent. Likewise, there is a greater probability that many countries will impose sanctions as chain-ganging occurs, as seen in the thicker right-hand tail of the distribution.

We can make one further useful modification to the GEC model. The variance of $Y_t$ can itself be considered a variable, and we can attempt to specify how it will change with certain explanatory variables. In other words, we can try to identify factors that tend to increase the amount of bandwagoning observed. We might expect that international institutions,

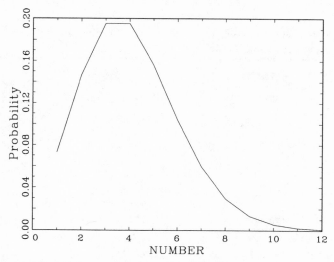

4.2. Probability Distribution under Independence

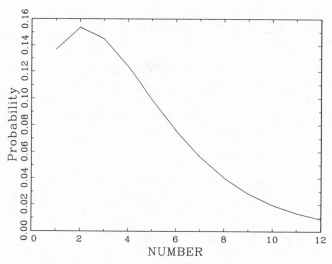

4.3. Probability Distribution with Positive Contagion

for example, will encourage bandwagoning among potential sanctioners—that is, that the involvement of institutions (besides increasing the
expected level of cooperation) might make state decisions more inter-
dependent. The neoliberal logic about the role of institutions, emphasiz-
ing issue linkage and reputation, suggests tighter coupling of decisions

**TABLE 4.11**
Truncated Negative Binomial Variance Function Results;
NUMBER as Dependent Variable

| Independent Variable | Estimated Coefficient | Robust Standard Error | t–statistic |
|---|---|---|---|
| Constant | −11.08 | 0.727 | −15.24 |
| ASSIST | 0.432 | 0.309 | 1.40 |
| COSTD | 1.01 | 0.708 | 1.43 |
| INST* | 11.28 | 1.86 | 6.06 |
| Gamma0* | 0.704 | 0.322 | 2.19 |
| INST | 0.930 | 0.513 | 1.81 |
| Log-likelihood | | 420.94 | |
| Number of Observations | | 99 | |

within institutions. This interdependence would be reflected in institutional involvement having a positive effect on gamma, reflecting more positive contagion. If in fact institutions do have this effect, it should increase our confidence that the positive value of gamma results from contagion, rather than from omitted variables or heterogeneity.

To estimate this model, I change the specification of the variance function somewhat. Because we now know that positive contagion exists, we can simplify the mathematics by using the negative binomial distribution, which is a special case of the GEC distribution in which the variance of $Y_t$ is always greater than $\lambda_t$. Rather than specifying gamma as a constant, I now use a vector of parameters, which quantifies the effect of the independent variables on the variance of $Y_t$. Thus, we can write

$$\text{Var}(Y_t) = \lambda_t[1 + \exp(z_t\gamma)],$$

where $z_t$ is a vector of explanatory variables. In this case, $z$ will include only one variable, INST. Table 4.11 presents the results of the truncated-at-zero negative binomial variance function (NBVF) model. I have eliminated the variables TARGET and COLDWAR, which we have found to have no significant effects on NUMBER.

Like the previous model, the negative binomial distribution allows for positive contagion. However, in this case contagion is measured by two variables: gamma and the second coefficient of INST. The major difference, which results from including INST in the variance function, is that contagion is now treated as a variable rather than a constant. The expected level of contagion for any observation is now gamma plus the value of INST for that observation. Thus, as further discussed later in this chapter, this model shows that positive contagion exists and that it increases when an institution becomes involved. Having an international

**TABLE 4.12**
Fitted Values; Negative Binomial Variance Function Model

| ASSIST | COSTD | INST | Fitted NUMBER |
|--------|-------|------|---------------|
| 0 | 1 | 0 | 0 |
| 1 | 1 | 0 | 0 |
| 0 | 2 | 0 | 0 |
| 0 | 1 | 1 | 3.35 |
| 1 | 2 | 0 | 0 |
| 1 | 1 | 1 | 5.17 |
| 0 | 2 | 1 | 9.21 |
| 1 | 2 | 1 | 14.18 |

institution involved in a sanctions case leads to chain-ganging or buck-passing, both forms of bandwagoning. This finding is important, since it implies that the measured effect of institutions on cooperation is actually a causal relationship, not just an epiphenomenal relationship or an artifact. If institutions merely ratified prior decisions to cooperate rather than having an independent effect on state decisions about sanctions, they would presumably have no impact on the degree of contagion.

The log-likelihood of 420.9 shows that this model performs better than the Poisson or GEC models. The standard errors of the estimated coefficients of COSTD and ASSIST have risen compared to the models presented above, so these coefficients are not significant by conventional standards. We see some fairly dramatic differences from the GEC or truncated Poisson. The large increase in the effect of INST on NUMBER is especially notable. When we separate the two effects of international institutions—the effects on the number of sanctioners and on the level of strategic interdependence—we find that the impact of INST on the expected value of NUMBER increases over eightfold. In the Poisson model, an organization's call for sanctions would increase the expected number of sanctioners from approximately 0.9 to 5.4. Now, the expected number of states never rises above 0 without action by an institution; with institutional involvement alone, we can expect that 3.4 states, on average, will impose sanctions (see table 4.12, line 4). In other words, the NBVF model predicts that no state will ever impose sanctions without institutional approval. We cannot fully accept this finding, as institutions acted in only one-third of the cases in our data set and at least one state imposed sanctions in each case. Nevertheless, this model does point to the importance of international institutions in facilitating cooperation. ASSIST and COSTD also appear to have somewhat larger effects than we found in the other event-count models, although the coefficients are imprecisely estimated.

Sanctions imposed by the European Community (EC) against Turkey during 1981–82, designed to encourage the restoration of democracy, provide a suggestive illustration of this model. Because the EC approved the delay of aid to Turkey, this case has been coded INST = 1 and COSTD = 1. Turkey did not receive international assistance in response to EC sanctions. The model predicts that between three and four nations should cooperate in this sanctions effort (line 4); in fact, eight did. Because the involvement of the international organization (the EC) makes the exact number of countries imposing sanctions less predictable, this difference between fitted and realized numbers is to be expected. If the EC imposed more-costly sanctions, such as agricultural-trade restrictions, the expected number of sanctioners would rise to nine (line 7), while if some country came to Turkey's assistance, the expected number would increase to just over five (line 6). While assistance and cost have no noticeable effect in the absence of institutional involvement in this model, they have considerable impact when an institution is involved, because of the nonlinear nature of the model.

Examination of the variance function (gamma and the second coefficient of INST) shows that in repeated trials we would find a great deal of variance in the size of the increase associated with institutions. In this NBVF model, the variance of $Y_t$ is given by

$$Var(Y_t) = \lambda_t[1 + \exp(\gamma_0 + \gamma_1 * INST)].$$

If an institution were to call for sanctions, while the target received no assistance but the sanctions were relatively costly, we would find that $E(Y_t) = 9.21$ and $Var(Y_t) = 9.21[1 + \exp(.704 + .930)] = 56.4$. Even when we take the square roots of these variances in order to find the standard deviation (symbolized by $s(Y_t)$), the approval of international institutions appears to cause a substantial increase in the variability of the number of sanctioning countries, in addition to a large increase in the average value of this number. If decisions were made independently but institutions had the same effect on $E(Y_t)$ as estimated by the NBVF model, the variance when $E(Y_t) = 9.21$ would be 9.21, much smaller than 56.4. Figures 4.4 and 4.5 illustrate these two probability distributions. (Of course, institutions do have an impact on the average level of cooperation, so figure 4.4 is purely hypothetical, presented just for purposes of comparison.)

To summarize the results of these event-count models, we have found that international institutions have a dual effect. On the one hand, they increase the amount of cooperation observed, as reflected in the number of countries imposing economic sanctions. On the other hand, they increase the amount of positive contagion, or strategic interdependence, among states. This means that although we should expect more cooperation if an institution is involved, we should also expect to find some

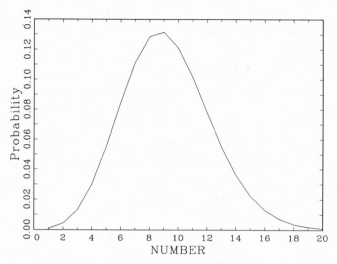

4.4. Probability Distribution with No Institution

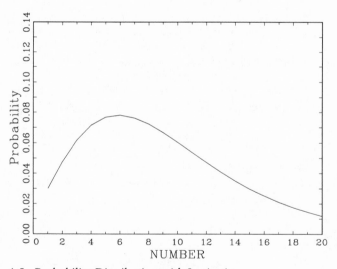

4.5. Probability Distribution with Institution

bandwagoning behavior. Bandwagoning makes it relatively hard for us to predict the exact number of countries that will participate when an institution calls for sanctions. These results also lend support to the hypotheses that assistance to the target and high costs for the major sender tend to increase cooperation. However, the effect of international institutions far exceeds that of assistance or costs.

## The Effect of Declining Hegemony

One hypothesis remains to be tested: that the United States has been decreasingly able to gain the cooperation of other states as its dominant position in the world order has eroded. As mentioned earlier, scholars have offered anecdotal evidence on both sides of this argument. In this section, I look for the effect of declining hegemony by examining changes, over time, in the level of cooperation when the United States is the leading sender.

I have coded the variable YEAR as the last two digits of the year in which sanctions were first imposed for each case. The variable US takes a value of 1 if the United States was the leading sender and 0 if some other state took the lead in imposing sanctions. I specify the model in the following way:

(1) $E(\text{NONMAJ}) = X\beta + \beta_1{}^*\text{US}$   ($X$ is a vector of explanatory variables)
(2) $\beta_1 = \delta_0 + \delta_1{}^*\text{YEAR}$

Equation 1 says that the expected value of NONMAJ is a linear function of some explanatory variables, such as those discussed above, and of whether or not the United States was the leading sender. $\beta_1$, the coefficient of US, is not constant throughout the period covered by the data set, since we expect the impact of having the United States take the lead to decline over time. Thus, $\beta_1$ is further specified as in equation 2. This formula says that $\beta_1$ is a linear function of the year in which sanctions were imposed. If the declining-hegemony hypothesis is correct, $\delta_1$ should be negative.

In order to estimate this model, I combine equations 1 and 2 to yield

$$E(\text{NONMAJ}) = X\beta + \delta_0{}^*\text{US} + \delta_1{}^*\text{US}{}^*\text{YEAR}.$$

Thus, we can test for the effect of declining hegemony by including a dummy variable, US, and an interaction term, US*YEAR, in the regression. If the United States is decreasingly able to gain the cooperation of other states, we should find that the coefficient of US*YEAR is negative. Table 4.13 presents the results of a regression and table 4.14 the results of a probit model including these terms.

The results disconfirm the hegemonic-stability thesis in two ways. First, the United States, which most scholars would agree was the most powerful state in the world during the period covered by this data set (1945 to 1989), tends to achieve *less* cooperation than other states when it takes the lead; the negative coefficient of US, which is statistically significant at the .05 level in the regression model, shows this. Second, the coefficient of the interaction term, US*YEAR, is *positive* and significant. Thus, although the United States does not get much cooperation from

**TABLE 4.13**
Regression Results; Interaction Term for US and YEAR

| Independent Variable | Estimated Coefficient | Standard Error | t–statistic |
|---|---|---|---|
| Constant | 16.37 | 6.28 | 2.60 |
| COLDWAR | 2.39 | 3.40 | 0.710 |
| ASSIST | −0.657 | 3.48 | −0.189 |
| TARGET* | −6.62 | 2.09 | −3.18 |
| COSTD | 3.41 | 3.25 | 1.05 |
| INST* | 10.70 | 3.12 | 3.43 |
| US* | −28.03 | 11.87 | −2.36 |
| US*YEAR* | 0.309 | 0.157 | 1.97 |
| | | | |
| R-squared | | 0.254 | |
| Corrected R-squared | | 0.196 | |
| Standard Error of Regression | | 13.27 | |
| Number of Observations | | 99 | |

**TABLE 4.14**
Probit Results; Interaction Term for US and YEAR

| Independent Variable | Estimated Coefficient | Standard Error | t–statistic |
|---|---|---|---|
| Constant | −5.76 | 7.55 | −0.763 |
| COLDWAR | 6.76 | 4.01 | 1.69 |
| ASSIST* | 11.98 | 4.10 | 2.92 |
| TARGET | −2.19 | 2.48 | −0.883 |
| COSTD | 6.71 | 4.01 | 1.67 |
| INST* | 21.30 | 3.84 | 5.55 |
| US | −21.18 | 14.56 | −1.45 |
| US*YEAR | 0.222 | 0.190 | 1.17 |
| Thresh 1* | 21.12 | 2.36 | 8.95 |
| Thresh 2* | 39.85 | 4.02 | 9.91 |
| | | | |
| Log-likelihood | | −86.12 | |
| Percent correctly predicted | | 61.6 | |
| Number of Observations | | 99 | |

other states, it has done better recently than in the early postwar period. If the hegemonic-stability thesis applied here, we should expect that the United States would gain more cooperation than others, but that cooperation would decline over time. The probit results also show a tendency for the United States to receive less cooperation than other senders, on average, although the upward trend over time is somewhat smaller here.

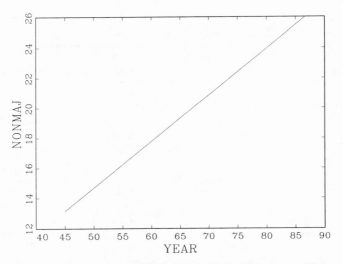

4.6. Changes in Cooperation with the United States over Time
(Regression Model)

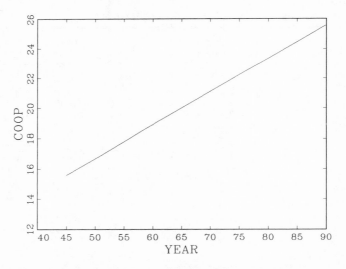

4.7. Changes in Cooperation with the United States over Time
(Probit Model)

Figures 4.6 and 4.7 show plots of cooperation on U.S.-led sanctions over
time. All variables except the interaction term have been held constant in
these graphs.

The literature on cooperation in international relations suggests a
number of possible explanations for the above findings. One is that de-

clining hegemony is a myth. Susan Strange, Bruce Russett, and others have argued that the U.S. decline has been greatly exaggerated.[13] This hypothesis, however, cannot explain the fact that the United States receives less cooperation than other countries. If American power had not declined, remaining greater than that of other states, we should see a relatively flat level of cooperation over time, with the United States typically gaining *more* cooperation than other states, not less.

A second way to approach this puzzle is to claim that the United States never actually received much cooperation. This explanation fits Michael Mastanduno's description of the behavior of Western Europe in CoCom. According to Mastanduno, the Europeans always made decisions about trade with the Soviet Union based on their own preferences, not the coercion or encouragement of the United States.[14] The Mastanduno thesis, however, cannot explain why the United States has been doing somewhat better in recent years. Again, this explanation would predict a fairly flat level of cooperation, not an upward-sloping one.

A third explanation has been offered by Kenneth Rodman. Rodman argues that, although overall U.S. power has declined, the United States maintains sufficient control over economic and political resources to be able to manipulate others' perceptions of risk, thus encouraging them to support sanctions efforts.[15] This hypothesis, however, suffers from the same weakness as the first: it overpredicts the amount of cooperation the United States has been able to achieve.

Robert Keohane's work suggests a fourth explanation: cooperation may be facilitated in the face of declining hegemony by international institutions and regimes.[16] While this explanation conforms to this chapter's findings on the importance of international institutions, it may also overpredict the level of cooperation Washington achieves. Focusing on institutions provides an explanation for why the level of cooperation does not decline, but not for the finding that the United States tends to achieve less cooperation than other states.

Finally, we could base a fifth explanation on a game-theoretic view of the situation, such as that offered by Duncan Snidal.[17] In this framework, smaller states had strong incentives to free-ride during the period in which the United States had overwhelming power; they knew that the United States would provide public goods unilaterally. For example, in the case of high-technology trade with the Soviet Union, other states had little reason to refrain from cheating at the margin when the United States was the major source of such trade. However, with relative U.S. decline, cheating at the margin comes to mean a substantial loss of control over the flow of goods to the Soviet bloc. Thus, according to Snidal's reasoning, it may be rational for a few medium-size powers to cooperate more extensively than a single large power and numerous small ones. In addition, as American dominance waned, Washington's incentives to gain the cooperation of others increased. In the area of high-technology trade, once other countries had become significant potential suppliers, the United States had a stronger interest in gaining their cooperation and might have even refused to continue with unilateral sanctions. Chapter 7 examines the technology-control case in greater detail.

This sort of explanation, especially if combined with an understanding of the facilitating role of international institutions, fits the findings both about the relative lack of cooperation with the United States and about the increase in cooperation over time. While the United States is the most powerful nation, others will free-ride and avoid paying the costs of economic sanctions. However, as relative U.S. power declines, others will face increasing incentives to stop free-riding and impose sanctions themselves. To put this in the framework developed in chapter 2, the early postwar period may have been dominated by coercion games, while coadjustment games are more common in recent years. Thus, as long as institutions are available to facilitate mutual adjustment of policies, we see increasing cooperation over time.[18]

The question of declining hegemony, and more-careful analysis of why this hypothesis appears to fail in cases of economic sanctions, are central to the Siberian-pipeline case study in chapter 8.

## Conclusion

This chapter took a first cut at explaining cooperation on economic sanctions by using quantitative analysis of ninety-nine cases of sanctions to test the hypotheses developed earlier. By comparing the results of the three types of analysis—linear regression, probit, and event counts—undertaken in this chapter, I come to several conclusions about the factors that might influence cooperation. I find strong support for the hypotheses that international institutions, high costs to the major sender, and assistance to the target tend to increase the level of cooperation. When an institution calls for sanctions, the level of cooperation increases dramatically in all three specifications. High costs for the major sender have a similar effect, though not quite as large. Assistance to the target tends to increase cooperation in the probit and event-count models, but not in the regression. This finding suggests that balancing behavior takes the form of imposition of sanctions by small states—those with little trade with the target—when the target receives assistance. Since the assistance effect is questionable, I focus on costs and institutions in the following case studies.

The role institutions play, however, is most likely more complex than simply increasing the number of sanctioning countries. For example, the involvement of institutions encourages bandwagoning among potential sanctioners. In the following case studies, I will focus on deepening our understanding of the impact of institutions. In these studies, we should also find evidence that the major sender gains more cooperation when it bears relatively high costs. Microlevel evidence will allow us to assess the role of credibility in generating this relationship between costs and cooperation. One additional result arose in the analyses in this chapter: the event-count models showed a high degree of bandwagoning behavior among potential sanctioners. Considering the characteristics of economic sanctions, this result makes sense, since states typically derive little symbolic benefit and achieve few policy changes through imposition of unilateral sanctions. The following case studies will look for evidence of actual bandwagoning behavior—an increasing probability that a state will impose sanctions as the number of sanctioners goes up.

I find somewhat weaker support for the effects of the Cold War and the stability of the target. Although Cold War cases do tend to show more cooperation, this effect is not always statistically significant. Likewise, a strong target tends to discourage cooperation, although this effect is also weaker than we might expect. Case studies may shed some light on whether these factors do in fact have a noticeable effect. In addition, I find no support for the hypothesis that cooperation is positively related to how ambitious the goals of sanctions are, as would be suggested by a partial-equilibrium model focusing on the leading sender's incentives rather than considering the strategic nature of interaction among senders—as in the model I have developed. Table 4.15 summarizes in verbal form the results of the three primary models we have considered in this chapter.

Finally, I find no support for the declining-hegemony thesis. In fact, the United States tends to receive less cooperation than other states, but this effect may have decreased over time. While we can suggest numerous possible explanations for this finding, one based on an understanding both of different types of collective-action dilemmas and of the facilita-

**TABLE 4.15**
Summary of Support for Effects of Independent Variables

|  | *Regression* | *Probit* | *Event Count* |
|---|---|---|---|
| INST | strong | strong | strong |
| COSTD | some | strong | strong |
| ASSIST | none | strong | some |
| COLDWAR | none | none | none |
| TARGET | strong | none | none |
| GOAL | none | none | none |

tive role of international institutions appears the most promising. Sorting out the various explanations will require careful process tracing in the following case studies. The two East-West cases prove especially useful for examining the impact, if any, of declining American power.

Beyond testing specific hypotheses, the analyses in this chapter and the previous one demonstrate the value of quantitative studies of cooperation. Certainly, this approach leaves many questions unanswered—some of these form the basis of the rest of this book. However, careful examination of descriptive statistics helped clear up common misconceptions about economic sanctions, such as their cost to the major sender. This chapter has allowed us to narrow the range of hypotheses deserving more-detailed analysis by suggesting that some hypotheses, such as that regarding the relation between purposes and cooperation, have little empirical support. For those variables that showed statistically significant effects, the analyses complement the case studies by improving our confidence in the generalizability of our results. Both the quantitative and case-study approaches have much to offer, and the benefits of quantitative analysis for the study of international cooperation should be further exploited by students in this field.

# Part Two

## CASE STUDIES

THIS STUDY now turns from general models and aggregate results to detailed case studies. The previous three chapters have looked for general patterns in post-1945 cases of economic sanctions. The following four chapters focus on particular cases in order to examine the explanations underlying these results and to show how the concepts and hypotheses developed above can improve our understanding of actual instances of economic sanctions. Some of the following cases have already received extensive attention from political scientists. I argue that the variables identified above provide an improved and more-generalizable understanding of the dynamics leading to cooperation.

Before turning to these case studies, let me summarize the hypotheses and their status following the statistical analysis. This analysis has decisively refuted one hypothesis—that declining U.S. hegemony should make cooperation more difficult in recent years. Chapter 8 looks at U.S. attempts to coordinate natural-gas-pipeline sanctions against the Soviet Union in 1982, which authors have presented as a classic example of the effects of declining hegemony. I argue that the lack of involvement by international institutions and the lack of self-imposed costs provide a better explanation of the American failure.

Two other hypotheses did not receive much support in the aggregate analysis—that East-West cases tend to result in more cooperation than cases that do not cross this divide, and that states tend to cooperate more fully when sanctions are directed against a poor, unstable target. The results for both of these hypotheses showed coefficients in the expected direction but were not statistically significant. This leads us to expect that North-South cases will not differ much from East-West cases in the level of cooperation achieved, and that the condition of the target has only a minimal impact on cooperation. However, since many scholars would argue that East-West cases differ in important ways from North-South ones even if the aggregate results do not reveal these differences, I have controlled for this dimension in the following cases.

Three independent variables received fairly strong support: assistance to the target, the costs borne by the leading sender, and international institutions. We found more cooperation when the target received international assistance and when the leading sender bore significant economic costs. In addition, international institutions had a large impact on cooperation, as the number of countries imposing sanctions and other measures of cooperation rose significantly when an institution called for sanctions. These results fit the hypotheses developed in chapter 2.

One additional result appeared in the statistical analysis. The data support the hypothesis of a significant degree of bandwagoning behavior among potential sanctioners, as the analysis of strategic problems led us to expect. The following cases examine whether this overdispersion is in fact due to bandwagoning—when imposition of sanctions by one state increases the probability that others will impose them as well—or whether it is an artifact. Do states seem to make their decisions independently of one another, or on a contingent basis?

Of the following four case studies, two look at sanctions directed by the West against the Soviet Union and two involve North-South issues. I have sought to control for another dimension as well—whether a formal international institution called for economic sanctions. In U.S. human-rights sanctions against Latin America, the first case study, no organization became involved in coordinating sanctions (except in the case of Chile), although U.S. officials did make some halfhearted attempts to get this issue on the agendas of organizations such as the World Bank. On the other hand, in British sanctions against Argentina during the Falklands War—the second case study—the European Community played a central role in organizing the sanctions effort. In one of the East-West cases, the United States used CoCom to gain agreement on restricting sales of high-technology goods to the Soviet Union in 1980, after the latter's invasion of Afghanistan. In 1982, however, when using sanctions to respond to events in Poland, the U.S. government could not use the CoCom mechanism since the goods it wished to embargo, pipeline materials, were not on the CoCom list.

Skeptics could argue that the strong relationship between institutions and cooperation found in the data shows nothing. They could make a case that states make their decisions on sanctions without regard to any organizational constraints and then turn to institutions to ratify or justify these decisions. In the cases, I show that institutional calls for sanctions actually had an impact on state behavior. While support for this hypothesis shows up throughout the studies, the clearest evidence comes in the Falklands case, where even states that did not support British actions or claims in the Falklands followed the EC lead and imposed sanctions on Argentina.

In the following cases, besides looking for evidence that institutions constrained behavior and that actual bandwagoning occurred, I ask about the processes underlying the fact that high costs to the leading sender lead to more cooperation. At least two processes could explain the relationship: increased domestic pressure on the sending government to gain cooperation and the signals that high costs send to other potential sanctioners. Thus, I look for evidence to support either of these two mechanisms. The role of costs receives especially close attention in the pipeline case.

Unfortunately, because the target did not receive significant international assistance in any of these four cases, they cannot add much to the aggregate results on this final hypothesis. Exploring the relationship between assistance and cooperation among potential sanctioners could provide puzzles for additional case studies focusing on the effects of international aid to the target.

Although I have chosen the cases to allow testing the hypotheses discussed above, other factors inevitably appear that seem to have had a significant influence on cooperation in particular cases. Because few authors have focused on the question of cooperation in cases of economic sanctions, I devote some attention to these factors when they arise, rather than keeping my analysis within the bounds of the hypotheses outlined in chapter 2. For example, in the Falklands case the relationship between military action and economic sanctions seems to play an important role. Rather than censoring this finding, I go back to the data set to see whether it can be generalized. The case studies thus suggest additional hypotheses that could form the basis for future research on issues of economic sanctions and international cooperation.

I hope that the following cases, beyond testing hypotheses, will show the utility of the model used in this book for understanding the emergence of cooperation. In particular, I argue that the distinction among coincidence, coercion, and coadjustment helps clarify the discussion of why states succeeded or failed in their efforts at cooperation. Thus, we should evaluate these case studies not just on their significance for the specific hypotheses of this study, but also on what this model contributes to previous discussions of these instances of economic sanctions.

# 5

## Human Rights in Latin America: Explaining Unilateral U.S. Sanctions

TO UNDERSTAND the causal relationships underlying cooperation on economic sanctions, we need to study an unbiased set of cases. This means looking at cases where cooperation failed to occur as well as those where it succeeded. Selection of cases should be based on the values of the independent variables, particularly costs and institutions, as described in the previous chapters. Too frequently, cases are chosen for study because of the value of the dependent variable; instead, we should maximize variation on the independent variables, particularly costs and institutions. The first case we will study is widely understood as one where costs were low and international institutions not a factor, for the most part. Conventional wisdom sees economic sanctions imposed by the United States against various Latin American countries for their human-rights records as an unmitigated failure. Analysts claim that U.S. human-rights policy failed both in terms of the impact of sanctions on the target countries and in terms of the extent to which Washington was able to gain the cooperation of other countries in undertaking joint action. Hufbauer, Schott, and Elliott, for example, code the level of cooperation as a 1, equivalent to "no cooperation," in all cases of U.S. sanctions against Latin American countries for human-rights reasons.

In this chapter, I make two major arguments. One major conclusion is that some sanctions efforts resulted in a slightly higher level of cooperation than commonly reported in the academic literature. Specifically, in the case of Chile under Pinochet there were widespread reductions in bilateral and multilateral foreign aid. However, in spite of this qualification, analysts correctly conclude that cooperation on human-rights sanctions was, in general, minimal and largely symbolic. A second dimension explored is the factors underlying the general lack of cooperation on human-rights sanctions. At first glance, little explanation appears necessary, as these cases closely fit the model presented earlier. The leading sender, the United States, bore only very low or negative economic costs. These cases were not considered part of the East-West conflict, and sometimes human-rights activism worked at cross-purposes to the demands of Cold War politics. Typically, no state came to the active assistance of the sanctions' target, and no international organization called for economic sanctions. Thus, we would expect little or no cooperation, on average. The human-rights cases provide a baseline for an understanding of the emergence of cooperation by providing support for expectations about when cooperation will fail to emerge.

However, this kind of analysis raises questions on a different level. We are led to ask why the United States, especially during the Carter administration, refused to impose sanctions that would have proven at all costly to itself. In addition, we ask why the United States failed to gain the approval of any international institution for sanctions. Process tracing can reveal how these factors entered into the decision-making processes of other states that may have been considering the imposition of sanctions. In view of the strong rhetorical commitment of President Jimmy Carter to an aggressive human-rights policy, along with support for such a policy in a Democratic Congress, these puzzles deserve an explanation, one that must be grounded in the demands of U.S. domestic politics.

In this chapter, I first summarize the course of U.S. economic sanctions against Latin American countries for human-rights reasons in the 1970s. In the first two sections of the chapter, I attempt to unravel the strands of U.S. policy. Next, I examine more closely the area in which we might expect to have seen the most active attempts to gain cooperation—U.S. policy in international institutions such as the multilateral development banks. Following this, I discuss in greater detail the case of Chile, the major exception to the generalization that only the United States imposed sanctions for human-rights reasons. I find that the conventional view of the Chilean case as one where the United States did not convince other states to cooperate is in essence correct, since Washington followed, rather than led, international action against Pinochet. I conclude that the human-rights cases have implications for a more-general understanding of when cooperation fails. They point to the need for future research to build on the systemic model by adding a systematic understanding of the role of domestic politics in decisions on imposing sanctions.

To give a brief preview of the argument of this chapter, these human-rights cases differ from the other cases of sanctions examined in this book in that the sanctions were not imposed in response to a specific provocation by the target. Although the level of human-rights abuse in Latin America may have intensified in the 1970s, this problem has a disturbingly long history. Instead, the motivation for sanctions came from forces within the United States. Thus, analysis of the rationale for economic sanctions must focus more intensely on domestic politics than in many of the other cases examined here. In addition, the complexity of human-rights politics in the United States led to a policy in which U.S. actions were much weaker than the rhetoric that accompanied them. While this divergence between rhetoric and policy actions frequently occurs, it is especially pronounced in the area of human rights. This ambivalence led other potential sanctioners to believe, correctly, that the price they would have to pay for refusing to cooperate would be negligible in comparison to the potential political and economic risks of a vigorous international human-rights policy in Latin America. In addition, they questioned the commitment of the U.S. government to a consistent, long-term human-rights policy. Thus, the ambivalence of U.S. policy was responsible for the half-hearted efforts to gain the cooperation of other states and for the predictably dismal level of international cooperation, even though many U.S. politicians recognized the potential benefits of internationalizing the policy. In this respect, this case most closely resembles the 1978 attempt to impose technology sanctions on the Soviet Union, discussed in chapter 7.

## Congress versus the President: U.S. Human-Rights Policy, 1973–76

The impetus for the imposition of economic sanctions against countries perceived as consistent violators of human rights came, in the early 1970s, from Congress rather than the executive branch. Although President Carter commonly receives credit (or blame) for putting human rights on the U.S. foreign-policy agenda, Congress in fact took the initiative in this area long before Carter arrived on the national political scene.[1] During the Nixon and Ford administrations, congressional activism on human-rights issues clashed sharply with the executive's foreign-policy stance, leading to a story of repeated confrontations and frustration on the part of many in Congress.

In the backlash against foreign and domestic policies widely perceived as amoral or immoral, a backlash that was part of the fallout of Vietnam and Watergate, the U.S. Congress assumed an increasingly activist role in foreign affairs. Congress asserted itself especially in the area of international human rights. The permissive conditions for this activism arose in part from institutional changes within Congress that allowed junior representatives and senators, including those swept in with the post-Watergate "class of 1974," to play an unusually large role in the formation of foreign policy. Junior members of Congress with an interest in Latin America had an opportunity to influence policy toward this region, about which most of their colleagues expressed little interest and put little effort into educating themselves. With the immediate heritage of Vietnam and the recent experience of the domestic civil-rights movement, international human rights became a cause with significant public and congressional support. Junior members could make significant political gains by adopting an aggressive stance on this issue.

Legislation influencing U.S. human-rights policy took two paths:

general and country-specific. Country-specific legislation began with restrictions on aid to Chile in the aftermath of General Augusto Pinochet's overthrow of President Salvador Allende in 1973. I will discuss these restrictions in more depth later in this chapter. The Chilean coup was also a proximate cause of general legislation tying human rights to economic and military assistance.

## General Legislation

The issue of human rights gained the congressional spotlight through an unprecedented series of hearings held in 1973 by the International Organizations and Movements Subcommittee—chaired by Donald Fraser, Democratic representative from Minnesota—of the House Foreign Affairs Committee. Previously, Congress had not given sustained attention to the role of human rights in U.S. foreign policy. Representative Fraser's subcommittee held fifteen hearings on human-rights issues between August and December 1973; in the Ninety-fourth Congress (1975–76), the subcommittee held forty hearings on this topic.[2] These hearings brought in witnesses from nongovernmental organizations and other people familiar with human-rights conditions in a wide range of countries, in order to gain information on the status of human rights that was not easily accessible through the bureaucracy. In addition to nongovernmental witnesses, officials from other arms of government, particularly the State Department, testified about the role of human-rights considerations in U.S. foreign policy.

The subcommittee's hearings had the immediate effect of putting human-rights concerns on the agenda when the Foreign Affairs Committee undertook markup of foreign economic-assistance authorization bills. Beyond this, the hearings generated unwelcome publicity for the regimes whose treatment of citizens was called into question. The most tangible output of the hearings was a report entitled *Human Rights in the World Community: A Call for U.S. Leadership*, which contained twenty-nine specific policy recommendations.[3] These included integrating human-rights considerations into U.S. bilateral and multilateral relations, upgrading the competence of the United Nations and other international organizations, and reorganizing some of the bureaucracy within the executive branch. The process started by these hearings led to legislation tying human rights to foreign aid.

General legislation on human rights affected the executive branch in two ways. First, Congress called for increasing amounts of information on the status of human rights in other countries and on the impact of human rights on executive-branch decision making. Second, the legislation imposed ever-tighter restrictions on the provision of economic and military assistance to countries that consistently violated internationally accepted human-rights norms.

In 1973, Congress amended Section 32 of the Foreign Assistance Act of 1961 (P.L. 93–189) to call on the president to deny aid to countries that violated human rights. This amendment, which was introduced by Senator Edward Kennedy and which did not receive much attention in Senate or House debate, stated that "it is the sense of Congress that the President should deny any economic or military assistance to the government of any foreign country which practices the internment or imprisonment of that country's citizens for political purposes."[4] Because this declaration merely expressed the "sense of the Congress," it did not bind the executive. The legislation, although prompted in part by the September coup in Chile, was not directed at any particular country or set of countries. It apparently had no impact on the administration's policies, although the State Department did cable its embassies the text of the amendment and ask them to begin preparing reports on the state of human rights in aid-recipient countries.[5] In June 1974, Assistant Secretary of State for East Asian and Pacific Affairs Robert Ingersoll testified that the Nixon administration had not in any manner implemented Section 32.[6]

In 1974, Congress passed legislation that it hoped would have a more-noticeable impact on U.S. policy than Section 32. Section 502B of the Foreign Assistance Act declared the sense of the Congress that the president should reduce or terminate all security assistance to governments engaging in "a consistent pattern of gross violations of internationally recognized human rights," except in "extraordinary circumstances."[7] Although this legislative provision countered one executive argument— about the definition of human rights—by explicitly giving examples of "gross abuses of human rights," such as torture or inhuman punishment, it left the president a great deal of leeway by not defining "extraordinary circumstances." The "sense of the Congress" language kept this legislation from directly changing the course of executive-branch decision making.

Soon after, Congress added Section 116 to the International Development and Food Assistance Act of 1975, to tie economic as well as military aid to human-rights concerns. This legislation was quite similar to Section 502B, with one important exception: the legislature removed the non-coercive "sense of the Congress" language.[8] Thus, Section 116, which became the first of many "Harkin amendments," specifically prohibited development aid to a particular class of governments. Congress tightened the legislative language because of its frustration with the refusal of the administration—specifically, the State Department under Henry Kissinger—to comply with earlier provisions. However, State's legal office and the Treasury Department quickly set out "to develop guidelines that would enable the Executive Branch to take greatest advantage possible of the needy people loophole," according to a July 1976 State Department memorandum.[9] This loophole allowed the continuation of aid addressed to "basic human needs" in spite of a government's human-rights record.

The State Department did instruct some embassies to prepare reports on human-rights conditions in response to reporting requirements in the 1974 Foreign Assistance Act. While the embassies apparently prepared such reports, Secretary Kissinger vetoed their submission to Congress at the last minute. He submitted, instead, a one-page report that claimed that all countries violated human rights and that he therefore could not discriminate among aid recipients on this basis.[10]

Other actions by Kissinger further contributed to congressional anger. For example, the *New York Times* reported on 27 September 1974 that he had rebuked the U.S. ambassador in Santiago, David Popper, for bringing up issues of torture and other human-rights problems in a meeting on military aid with Chilean officials.[11] Kissinger added this marginal comment on a memorandum about Popper's discussions: "Tell Popper to cut out the political science lectures." While human-rights activists in Congress found some sympathetic responses within the State Department, the secretary of state vigorously opposed complicating traditional foreign-policy issues with such a sensitive subject as government torture of citizens. As one State Department official explained, "We can't have an Ambassador going into a meeting with the Defense Minister for one issue and discussing something else."[12] In addition, Kissinger argued that Congress and others were judging Chile too harshly, given the state of near civil war there.[13] Ambassador Popper responded to Kissinger's rebuke by drastically cutting back his correspondence with Washington on human-rights issues, which had been the subject of approximately one cable per week up until this time.

Another condition that favored passage of restrictions on economic and security assistance was an unusual coalition—some have called it an "unholy alliance"—between conservatives and liberals in Congress.[14] On the one hand, some conservative members were willing to vote for restrictions based on human-rights criteria for the simple reason that they would vote for anything likely to cut the aggregate level of U.S. foreign economic assistance. On the other hand, liberal members who typically voted to increase levels of assistance also voted in favor of these restrictions because of their commitment to the human-rights agenda.

Even more stringent controls on security assistance were soon imposed, in the form of a revised Section 502B in the International Security Assistance and Arms Export Control Act of 1976. This bill differed from the 1974 amendment to the Foreign Assistance Act in that the "sense of the Congress" language was replaced with a more straightforward statement of "the policy of the United States." On 7 May 1976, President Gerald Ford vetoed this bill.[15] One of his arguments against it was that the bill allowed Congress to veto foreign aid by concurrent resolution, which would not require the signature of the president.[16] Congressional action then changed the language to allow an aid cutoff through a joint resolution; such action would require presidential signature. Thus, the joint-resolution provision gave the executive more control over aid flows, and President Ford signed the bill on 30 June 1976.

We can summarize the pursuit of economic sanctions during 1973–76 against Latin American countries considered to violate human rights as a classic struggle for power between the legislative and executive branches of the U.S. government. A number of factors converged to create strong pressure for attention to human rights as a dimension of U.S. foreign policy within Congress, but the executive was opposed in principle to this pursuit. Thus, Congress passed increasingly stringent legislation in an attempt to bind the executive and gain access to information on the relationship between the status of human rights and U.S. policy actions. However, this general legislation was not legally binding on the Nixon or Ford administrations, as it contained numerous loopholes large enough to continue funding even after the United States found that a government consistently abused the rights of its citizens.

What impact did general legislation have on Ford-Kissinger foreign policy? Nearly all analysts agree that the impact in terms of redirecting aid flows was negligible.[17] Apparently, however, Kissinger did respond to congressional pressure in one way—by increasing the attention he gave to the general issue of human rights in public appearances.[18] Analysis of his public rhetoric shows a dramatic increase in the number of references to human rights from 1971 to 1976.[19] Kissinger's speech to the General Assembly of the OAS on 8 June 1976 in Santiago, Chile, stressed human-rights issues in a newly blunt manner and called for support from the Inter-American Commission on Human Rights (IACHR). Thus, while general legislation through 1976 failed to change directly U.S. policy, it did succeed in getting human rights on the policy agenda, setting the stage for more-cooperative policy-making under the Carter administration.

### Country-Specific Legislation

In the meantime, Congress used another tactic to push for executive compliance, passing country-specific legislation in addition to general restrictions on assistance. Chile was the first target of specific legislation. In 1973, Section 35 of the Foreign Assistance Act called on the president to request that Chile protect human rights and called on the IACHR to investigate events following the September coup.[20] The following year,

Section 25 of the same act prohibited all military assistance to Chile and limited economic aid in fiscal year 1975 to $25 million. President Ford opposed these provisions, but he did sign the bill. However, as I discuss below, the administration and the Agency for International Development (AID) found ways to circumvent these restrictions. Congress limited economic aid to $90 million in 1975 and reduced it to $27.5 million in 1976. With evidence of the administration's maneuvering to evade these restrictions, the legislature put stricter conditions on the disbursement of this $27.5 million in an attempt to gain executive compliance.[21] Congress terminated all military aid in 1976.

Uruguay was the only other Latin American country subject to country-specific legislation prior to the Carter administration. Representative Ed Koch, in the Foreign Operations Subcommittee of the House Committee on Appropriations, initiated a move to go beyond the provisions of Section 502B and to cut off all military aid to Uruguay in 1976. Since the projected level of military assistance to Uruguay was only $3 million, this did not appear to be a major step. However, it provoked angry responses from the administration and in Latin America.[22] The move to use country-specific legislation was a response to strong resistance from the Ford administration and to the extremely cumbersome methods that Congress would have had to use in order to invoke the joint-resolution provisions of Section 502B. In fact, Congress never used the powers it spelled out for itself in the general legislation. Prior to the Carter administration, only country-specific legislation changed the level of foreign aid for human-rights reasons.

## The Carter Administration

Conventional wisdom holds that President Carter zealously pursued the cause of human rights, frequently to the neglect of other foreign-policy goals. He is criticized from the right for having been too tough on authoritarian regimes and perhaps contributing to the overthrow of conservative governments in Nicaragua and Iran.[23] Simultaneously, however, the left attacks Carter for having focused too heavily on the Soviet Union, subjugating the cause of human rights to East-West politics.[24] Clearly, there remains some confusion about the real nature and intensity of Carter's human-rights policy. In this section I argue that, while President Carter did have a fundamental commitment to international human rights, the elevation of this issue to a dominant place in U.S. foreign policy was in part the result of astute political calculations. Tensions between the executive and legislative branches of government, while moderated, did not disappear under Carter. Most importantly from the viewpoint of international cooperation, the domestic motivations of Carter's human-rights policy meant that attempts to gain the cooperation of other countries were relegated to a low priority and pursued halfheartedly. Other countries thus perceived a lack of commitment and ignored Carter's occasional requests for cooperation.

## The Politics of Carter's Human-Rights Policy

Candidate Carter faced a difficult problem in gaining the Democratic party's nomination. Put simply, a candidate for the party's nomination in 1976 had to appeal to both the "Jackson Democrats"—such as Patrick Moynihan, Ben Wattenberg, and Jeane Kirkpatrick—and the "McGovern Democrats." These two groups had split over Vietnam and had widely diverging ideas about the proper contours of U.S. foreign policy. A human-rights strategy, broadly defined, was one of the few issues capable of generating support from both wings of the Democratic party.[25]

Human rights could generate broadly based support because both factions could believe that the policy would be focused on a particular group of countries. The Jackson Democrats could see Carter's emphasis on human rights as an extension of the Jackson-Vanik amendment strategy, which tied most-favored-nation (MFN) status for the Soviet Union to its policies on emigration. Those who placed somewhat less emphasis on the dominance of East-West conflict could anticipate that U.S. actions to support human rights would be directed as they had been in Congress for the last few years—against authoritarian regimes. Thus, emphasis on this issue united, at least superficially, a divided party, while simultaneously providing a distinction the Democratic party could use to emphasize its isolation from an era when "the American presidency was in the hands of harsh and amoral conservatives."[26]

This perspective on the role of human rights in the campaign should not be interpreted as a statement that Carter's commitment to the issue was a cynical political move. However, electoral considerations contributed to the centrality of human-rights issues in the campaign. Carter's national security adviser, Zbigniew Brzezinski, later explained that "the commitment to human rights reflected Carter's own religious beliefs, as well as his political acumen. He deeply believed in human rights. . . . At the same time, he sensed . . . that the issue was an appealing one, for it drew a sharp contrast between himself and the policies of Nixon and Kissinger."[27] In Carter's campaign appearances, we find no references to the human-rights issue prior to the adoption of the party's platform on 13 June 1976. Beginning with Carter's talk to the Foreign Policy Association on 23 June, and especially in his B'nai B'rith speech in early September, we find frequent references to this topic.[28]

After the election, human rights and other "global" issues became important symbols of the new administration, as reflected in Carter's inaugural statement that "our commitment to human rights must be absolute."[29] Indeed, human rights was one of the few issues on which Carter, Brzezinski, and Secretary of State Cyrus Vance were in total agreement on principles, although they did differ on tactics.[30] However, the combination of moral commitment and domestic political goals left little room to coordinate U.S. human-rights strategy with that of other states. The administration took actions with almost no attention to their impact on international cooperation.[31]

### Legislative Action

Congress, willing to give Carter a chance to set his own priorities in the human-rights area, waited for several months after his inauguration before passing any legislation on this subject. For example, Senator Edward Kennedy agreed to push back the deadline on arms-sales cutoffs to Argentina from October 1977 to October 1978, in order to give the State Department some time to explore other avenues of diplomacy.[32] However, perhaps motivated by a belief that Carter was not being sufficiently aggressive or by a desire to protect human-rights policies against the whims of the executive, by late 1977 Representative Fraser and others once again began introducing both general and country-specific legislation.

The general legislation encompassed three tactics: further tightening of legislative provisions on bilateral aid, bureaucratic changes designed to give higher priority to human rights, and attempts to link human-rights considerations to loans from international financial institutions (IFIs). (Since the IFI story provides a chance to emphasize U.S. interaction with other potential sanctioners and international institutions, I deal separately with it later in this chapter.) In 1978 Congress attempted to make Section 502B more binding on the executive by deleting the "policy of the United States" language, so that the amendment now stated bluntly that "no security assistance may be provided to any country, the government of which engages in a consistent pattern of gross violations of internationally recognized human rights."[33] However, President Carter never officially certified that any government consistently and grossly violated human rights, although he did take actions to cut aid to countries privately considered violators.[34]

In addition to actions on security assistance, Section 116 of the International Development and Food Assistance Act, dealing with economic aid, was tightened. Congress also added human-rights language to P.L. 480, which provides credits for agricultural sales.[35] Congress considered putting restrictions into legislation that affected U.S. trade, restrictions that would have made sanctions more costly for both the United States and the target countries. For example, in 1977 Congress amended the Export-Import Bank Act of 1945 to require that decisions about export credits "take into account" human rights. However, reluctance to interfere with trade resulted in an overwhelming House vote (286–103) against further strengthening the human-rights language of this act.[36] Concern about unemployment and the U.S. trade balance meant that Congress limited its efforts to the area of economic and military aid. As Senator Hubert Humphrey explained, "There is always the question that comes up, 'If we do not do it, the French will, or the British will, or somebody else will, and you want us to lose the business? We need exports, we need jobs.' "[37]

A proposed Argentine purchase of turbine generators from Allis-Chalmers illustrated the uproar that business could create when human-rights policy threatened to interfere with sales. In the summer of 1978, the Carter administration denied a request for a $270 million Export-Import Bank loan for the purchase of this nonmilitary equipment.[38] Spokesmen for the industry reacted with outrage, claiming that this denial had cost the industry $813.5 million, the U.S. economy numerous jobs, and the U.S. government influence over the behavior of the Argentine government. Commerce secretary Juanita Kreps was against the decision, arguing that concerns with balance-of-payments difficulties should come first. Under pressure, the administration reversed its decision in September, having received a promise from Argentine president Jorge Videla to allow the IACHR to visit Argentine prisons.[39] According to the logic of cooperation, this unwillingness to bear the costs of sanctions had anticipated negative consequences on international cooperation, as other states took it as a sign of ambivalence and refused to join in sanctions efforts.

In the area of bureaucratic arrangements, the Nixon and Ford administrations had undertaken some reorganization in the State Department in order to appease congressional demands for action. Soon after the completion of Fraser's initial set of hearings in 1973, a human-rights officer was designated in each regional bureau. These officers, however, continued to have other functions and did not exert much pressure on policy. Donald Renard, a former foreign-service officer, has admitted that the creation of this bureaucracy was merely a "sop to public opinion."[40]

Anticipating further legislative action, State appointed a coordinator for humanitarian affairs in April 1975. The International Security Assistance and Arms Export Control Act of 1976 upgraded this position to create a coordinator for human rights and humanitarian affairs in the State Department, so that the executive could not destroy this position without congressional approval.[41] However, it became clear in congressional hearings that regional bureaus, rather than the coordinator, controlled the framework of U.S. policy. Representatives from the Inter-

American bureau sounded especially defensive in these hearings.[42] In 1977, Congress upgraded the office of the coordinator, creating the Bureau of Human Rights and Humanitarian Affairs, called HA, for Humanitarian Affairs, to be led by an assistant secretary.[43] President Carter appointed Patricia Derian, a civil-rights activist, to this position in August 1977. In contrast to some officials charged with human rights, Derian took her responsibilities seriously, expanding her activism into the realm of international human rights.[44]

Another bureaucratic development came at the initiative of the president rather than Congress. The Interagency Committee on Human Rights and Foreign Assistance was formed by a National Security Council directive in April 1977 and was chaired by Deputy Secretary of State Warren Christopher. This committee, known as the Christopher Committee, focused on bilateral and multilateral loan decisions, while also considering arms-export control issues at times. All bureaus whose work touched on human-rights issues, including the Treasury Department and the Agency for International Development, were represented on this committee.[45] It considered loan decisions on a case-by-case basis, instructing representatives in the IFIs, for example, on which loans to oppose on human-rights grounds.

Congress continued to pass country-specific legislation during the Carter administration, both to bolster the administration's own efforts and to push it further than it sometimes wished to go. In 1977 and 1978, Congress denied Uruguay any funds for military assistance, international military education and training, or military credit sales. It also eliminated proposed military aid to Argentina, Brazil, El Salvador, Guatemala, Nicaragua, and Paraguay in 1977.[46] On 30 September 1978, Congress prohibited any U.S. military assistance to Argentina and established a human-rights certification procedure for future aid to that country. Military sales to Brazil, El Salvador, and Guatemala were prohibited in 1978. Also in 1978, the Senate attempted to prevent Nicaragua and Paraguay from receiving military education and training funds. However, a conference committee cut this provision in favor of a strategy that would generalize denial of such funds to repressive regimes. It cut the overall account for international military education and training by the amount that would have been sent to Nicaragua and Paraguay.[47]

While working within the framework set by Congress, the Carter administration retained a great deal of discretion as to the application of legislation. Thus, some of the sanctions imposed during 1977–80 came as the result of executive rather than congressional action. On 24 February 1977, Secretary of State Vance informed the Senate Appropriations Committee's Subcommittee on Foreign Operations that the administration had decided to cut aid to Argentina, Uruguay, and Ethiopia because of concern with human-rights violations.[48] This represented a clear break with past executive-branch practice, as it was the first time any administration had publicly made such an announcement.[49] Specifically, the Carter administration cut military credits to Argentina from the $32 million allocated by the Ford administration to $15 million for fiscal year 1978; $48 million in credits for 1977 was denied. Uruguay's allocation of $3 million in military credits was eliminated, and its economic aid was reduced from $220,000 to $25,000. Some commentators saw the Uruguay cut as something of a "throwaway," as Congress had already signaled its intention to terminate aid to this country.[50]

Administration and congressional aid reductions, combined with the release in March 1977 of negative and specific State Department reports on the status of human rights in various countries, brought strong negative reactions in Latin America. El Salvador, Argentina, Brazil, Guatemala, and Uruguay protested by rejecting all remaining U.S. military aid.[51] These actions relieved the administration of considering whether to renew assistance the next year. In fact, the Carter administration's enthusiasm for applying human-rights sanctions appeared to be dampened after this initial burst of activism. While quiet diplomacy in bilateral relations and some activity in international organizations continued, these actions were not backed by a credible threat of administrative sanctions.

## Economic Sanctions and the Multilateral Development Banks

The "Harkin amendment," originally referring to Representative Thomas Harkin's 1975 amendment to the International Development and Food Assistance Act tying economic aid to human-rights considerations, soon became a generic term in Congress. Legislators added a Harkin amendment to various forms of aid authorization; it directed the president to deny aid to governments that consistently engaged in gross abuses of internationally recognized human rights.[52] At first, these amendments were added only to bills authorizing various forms of bilateral aid. The impact of these restrictions on overall aid flows shrank as U.S. assistance was increasingly directed through multilateral organizations. Thus, Representative Harkin pushed for inclusion of Harkin amendments in authorizations for U.S. contributions to IFIs, especially the multilateral development banks (MDBs). President Carter and other members of the administration strongly disagreed with this strategy. Because the MDBs are an area in which we might expect to find explicit efforts to gain the cooperation of other donors, these maneuverings deserve closer attention.

## Legislative Action

Congress first added human-rights language to legislation authorizing funds for the African Development Fund and the Inter-American Development Bank (IDB) in 1975.[53] Although the Ford administration expressed opposition to this provision, it passed with little comment in both the House and the Senate, and President Ford signed the bill into law in May 1976. This version of the Harkin amendment required that U.S. representatives in these institutions vote against any loans to repressive governments, unless such loans would directly benefit needy people. Congress added this loophole in an attempt to reconcile the restrictions with the argument that depriving poor populations of multilateral economic aid could only hurt them and would have little effect on their governments' actions.

This legislation had a negligible impact, for at least two reasons. First, the United States did not have veto power over loans in either of these organizations, except for the soft-loan window (Fund for Special Operations) of the IDB, which lends only small amounts of money. Thus, unilateral U.S. abstention or opposition would have practically no impact on the flow of multilateral funds to recipient countries.[54] Second, the Ford administration proved adept at using the "needy-people" loophole to evade the intent of Congress. The executive enforced the Harkin amendment only once, in an attempt to block an IDB loan to Chile in 1976.[55] However, the administration continued to give its support to other multilateral loans to Chile, in the face of disapproval from both Congress and other donor countries, particularly in Western Europe. As in the case of bilateral assistance, resistance from the administration led to legislation imposing tighter restrictions on multilateral aid. However, because the next bill authorizing MDB funds did not come before Congress until 1977, the showdown was with Carter rather than Ford.

Somewhat surprisingly, given his campaign rhetoric and actions in office, President Carter strenuously objected to an amendment that would require U.S. representatives to oppose loans in the World Bank and other MDBs. In 1977, Congress was considering authorization for five MDBs. Carter worked with Representative Henry Reuss, the influential chair of the House Committee on Banking, Finance, and Urban Affairs, to develop a human-rights provision that would leave the executive with a great deal of flexibility. They settled on a provision that required U.S. representatives to use their "voice and vote" to "advance the cause" of human rights.[56]

In various subcommittee hearings, administration witnesses, including Assistant Secretary Derian and representatives from Treasury, argued against the mandatory language of the 1976 MDB authorization bill. They contended that this legislative restriction reduced their bargaining power vis-à-vis other donors and recipient governments and that it could lead to "politicization" of these institutions that would undermine their effectiveness on purely economic issues. Deputy Secretary Christopher argued, in congressional hearings, that further MDB restrictions required careful consideration, and he pointed to the potential "downside" of restrictive legislation: "If you begin to politicize those international lending organizations, we may have some effects that are more harmful than helpful."[57] While in general, institutional linkages created among members can support cooperation, in this case institutional parameters created significant barriers to forging particular tactical linkages—those between multilateral aid and human rights. If a linkage had been created between multilateral aid and political issues such as human rights, it could later be turned against U.S. interests, by introducing political concerns where the United States would prefer to exclude them. In addition, the MDBs' voting rules made it impossible for the United States to create this linkage unilaterally, unlike in the CoCom case discussed in chapter 7.

Representative Harkin introduced an amendment that was much stronger than the administration's proposal, requiring a "no" vote on loans to repressive regimes. Congress, given its experience with the previous administration, greeted the Carter-Reuss argument for "flexibility" with great distrust. Previously, executive flexibility had translated into total disregard for congressional mandates. Although the bill was reported to the floor with the weaker Reuss language, it was easily defeated and replaced by the Harkin amendment. The Senate, however, was more sympathetic to President Carter's arguments. This may have been due in part to an aggressive lobbying effort, including a news conference and a letter from Carter to the Foreign Assistance Subcommittee chair Hubert Humphrey, both of which explained Carter's argument for flexibility.[58] The letter stated, "There may well be times when we can bargain with prospective borrowers to release prisoners or stop other offensive practices if we have our vote as leverage. We need this flexibility if we expect to influence borrower countries or the overall programs of the banks."[59] The Senate passed the bill containing the weaker "voice and vote" language.

The bill went to conference committee for reconciliation of the Senate and House versions. The conference committee returned a sort of compromise, but one that came much closer to the "voice and vote" language than to the provision for a mandatory "no" vote. The House overwhelmingly rejected the compromise version, and the Senate finally gave in and accepted the stronger Harkin amendment. Admitting defeat, Carter signed this bill into law in October 1977.[60]

Congressional proponents of strong human-rights provisions were not as successful at inserting this type of language into the 1977 authorization for the International Monetary Fund (IMF). Specifically, debates arose over including human-rights language in authorization for the Witteveen Facility, which the IMF was creating to aid countries with balance-of-payments difficulties due to rising oil prices.[61] In this case, administration representatives and many members of Congress made the argument that the IMF served an essential economic purpose, that its charter forbade consideration of non-economic criteria in making loan decisions, and that introducing such concerns would jeopardize an institution that the United States found valuable for helping maintain world economic stability.[62]

In the face of mobilized administration opposition and an attitude of some ambivalence from traditional supporters of human rights, such as Representative Reuss, Harkin's pleas to extend the limitations placed on funds for the regional banks and World Bank were insufficient to persuade his colleagues.[63] He was unable to gain the passage of a bill that introduced human-rights considerations into the IMF, although he tried again in 1978. Thus, the Carter administration succeeded with the IMF where it had failed with the regional banks, largely because it persuaded important members of Congress that the institution itself was extremely valuable and that extending its functions to include protection of international human rights would undermine its ability to perform purely economic functions. As in the case of bilateral aid, the United States found itself unwilling to take potentially costly steps in pursuit of human rights in Latin America; the costs outweighed the benefits of such sanctions, in the eyes of key officials.

### Application of the Legislative Provisions

Most decisions about application of the legislative provisions were made by the Christopher Committee. The committee sometimes decided to support particular multilateral loans to countries with repressive governments on the basis that the loans would serve basic human needs. For example, in 1977 the United States voted in favor of an $81 million IDB loan to Argentina that was designed to improve the water-supply system, as well as IDB loans to Nicaragua and Paraguay for similar projects.[64] Because the basic-human-needs emphasis of U.S. foreign-aid policy frequently conflicted with human-rights policy, the Christopher Committee engaged in a careful balancing act, supporting selected projects and sending finely calibrated signals by differentiating between "no" votes and abstentions.[65] In addition, the United States sometimes informed a country applying for loans that the U.S. representative would have to oppose any proposal. Administration representatives claimed that this action led to the withdrawal of many loan applications before they could be voted on, to avoid the negative publicity of a U.S. "no" vote on human-rights grounds.[66]

The complexity of the process leading up to decisions on U.S. votes left little room for attempting to coordinate strategy with that of other donor governments with an interest in pursuing international human-rights concerns. The decision-making process consisted of a balancing of domestic economic and political concerns. Once a decision was made on this basis, it was nearly impossible to make it contingent on other states' actions. The United States behaved, in these instances, more as a shortsighted utility maximizer than as a strategic actor, and U.S. representatives to the MDBs made no real efforts to persuade other members or to act contingently.[67] This factor, combined with the resistance of European and Latin American countries to introducing non-economic concerns into the MDBs, led to a lack of cooperation on human-rights sanctions.

An early sign of trouble came with a June 1976 vote on a $21 million IDB loan to Chile. Because of congressional pressure, the United States voted against this loan.[68] However, all Latin American members of the IDB voted in favor of the loan, including Mexico and Venezuela, who had previously led efforts to isolate the Pinochet regime. Venezuelan representative Juan P. Perez Castillo explained that "the bank is not a forum for considering political questions." Deputy Assistant Secretary of State Joseph Grunwald, who had helped coordinate the U.S. "no" vote, worried that many actions like this could put the bank out of business, since so many Latin American countries violated human rights.[69] Some members of the U.S. team were sensitive to the same concerns of politicization that motivated some Latin American members.

Congressional staff members, accustomed by now to State Department maneuvering to evade human-rights legislation, claimed that the United States had voted against the loan only after counting up the votes of other IDB members to assure that the loan would be approved regardless of the U.S. action.[70] While Assistant Secretary Grunwald denied that the delegation had done this, Jonathan Sanford of the Congressional Research Service reported that "executive branch sources indicate . . . that the Administration never made much effort at persuading other governments to emulate the U.S. vote on these issues or to dissuade bank management from bringing forth proposals of these sorts in the future."[71]

This evidence raises an interesting possibility for the general model of cooperation developed in this study. One of the model's basic assumptions has been that governments will always prefer multilateral sanctions to unilateral ones, since multilateral action will increase the effectiveness of sanctions. However, in the case of Chile the U.S. government applied sanctions at the insistence of Congress, and the administration had little concern for their impact on Chile. In fact, Kissinger and Ford preferred that relations with Pinochet remain as calm as possible, given congressional interference. Thus, the executive may have actually preferred unilateral to multilateral action. In the language of the model developed in chapter 2, the payoff for unilateral sanctions was greater than for mutual sanctions; contrary to the assumptions used there, $u > m$. In this way, Washington could signal its domestic constituencies that it was playing an active role in human-rights issues in Latin America, while maintaining amicable relations with the target country. In effect, the intended audience for some sanctions is domestic rather than international. In such a situation, the benefits of international cooperation are marginal and certainly not worth the expenditure of resources necessary to establish credibility. Some authors have suggested that the Carter administration had similar preferences, actually valuing a unilateral human-rights campaign over a multilateral one: "The international effects of the campaign are incidental, and in certain instances may even be unwanted."[72] Whether the government actually opposed international cooperation or merely relegated it to a low priority, the halfhearted attempts to gain cooperation and the resulting lack of success are explicable in this framework.

Under the Carter administration, the rhetorical commitment to multilateral action increased. State Department publications noted the need to work with many other governments through the UN, the OAS, and other institutions. In December 1978 one such publication reported, "We consult regularly with our West European allies and others on promoting broader international cooperation on human rights. We have found strong support for giving human rights a higher priority in international affairs."[73]

Deputy Secretary Christopher, testifying before Congress in 1977, emphasized the need for international cooperation. The United States, he argued, could not create the right climate for a human-rights policy on its own: "In order to get the help of our allies and of the other nations around the world, we are going to have to work with them very carefully to try to get them to appreciate the deep concern that we have in the values of human rights."[74] Derian, human rights coordinator-designate in 1977, also stressed the need to work with other states and international organizations: "We don't want to stand on the street corners of the world, shaking our tamborine [sic] alone, as though we were the moral arbiters of the world. . . . we must take the lead; but we must not hope to stand alone. We are trying to get other governments to work with us."[75] The main problems, she said, were convincing others that the U.S. commitment to human rights wasn't a "gimmick," that U.S. actions were for the common good, and that "we are in this together."[76] Clearly, other states, having experienced the previous administration's refusal to commit to a human-rights policy, were somewhat skeptical about the real purposes of the new administration's efforts. The credible-commitment problem inhibited efforts at coordination of policies.

Congress wished to formalize this rhetorical commitment to multilateral action; the legislation tying human rights to IFIs included requirements for the administration to push for cooperation. An October 1977 act, P.L. 95–118, called on the executive branch in Section 703 to "initiate a wide consultation" to the end of channeling multilateral loans toward governments that respected human rights.[77] Administration officials later testified that the government was living up to this obligation, although in very general terms. Derian explained that the United States was consulting widely with other governments, seeking "support for the position that the multilateral development banks are appropriate and effective instruments for the enhancement of human rights."[78] She claimed that the administration used many different forums for these discussions, including bilateral contacts, multilateral conferences, and discussions with bank management. However, she admitted that achieving consensus remained an elusive goal.

One common problem facing U.S. representatives to the MDBs had to do with these organizations' charters. Most of them included a provision stating that loan decisions must be based solely on economic grounds. Other countries frequently cited these provisions as a justification for their opposition to U.S. policy.[79] In response to such arguments—which U.S. Treasury officials, who dealt most frequently with the banks, also made—Representative Bill Young proposed in 1978 that the United States seek the adoption of an amendment to the MDBs' charters explicitly setting human-rights standards for loans.[80] Assistant Secretary Derian explained that the United States had raised this possibility informally with other donor governments but had met with a universally negative response. In view of requirements that between 75 and 85 percent of the members of an MDB must approve changes to its charter, she argued against pressing forward with this proposal. She concluded, "Increasingly, other bank members share our views. But the process of developing an international consensus on these issues takes time."[81] In this instance, institutional constraints inhibited rather than encouraged cooperation, as the introduction of human-rights concerns would have undermined members' convergent expectations about MDB standards.

In congressional testimony in 1978, Deputy Assistant Secretary of State Mark Schneider stressed that the administration's goal was effectiveness in combating human-rights abuse, not posturing.[82] He conceded that there was not universal support for U.S. actions in the banks but insisted that the administration recognized the need for cooperation with other bank members. He mentioned a State-Treasury team that consulted with officials in Canada, Britain, West Germany, Sweden, Denmark, France, Belgium, and the European Community in fulfillment of Section 703's provisions.[83] While Schneider noted that "the response was sympathetic and generally positive," he provided no details on the content of these discussions or the specific responses of any country.

Schneider also stated that the government was attempting to increase the level of communication among donor countries. He noted that many European countries and Venezuela did in fact occasionally oppose loans to human-rights violators. Again, Schneider provided no specifics, but he was probably referring to votes on loans to Chile. However, other analysts have found that the United States nearly always stood alone in its "no" votes and abstentions. According to Sidney Weintraub, "the United States has been supported in its voting opposition on human-rights grounds by virtually no other country, with the rare exception of the United Kingdom and even the rarer [sic] exception of some Scandinavian countries, and occasionally Venezuela in the IDB."[84] The signs of progress that Schneider noted in early 1978 did not develop into fuller or more-consistent cooperation over the next few years. Overall, the United States never succeeded in blocking any MDB loan on human-rights grounds, except for a few in the Fund for Special Operations of the IDB, where the United States had veto power.

Thus, administration representatives strove to convince Congress that they were indeed fulfilling their mandate to "initiate wide consultations" with other bank members on the human-rights issue. There is little doubt that they did discuss the issue with other governments at some time, although it was probably in quite general terms. Closer examination of the evidence, however, suggests that efforts to gain cooperation were not a high priority for the administration and that the Christopher Committee made decisions to oppose loans without considering the likelihood that other donors would agree with its assessment of any particular case. For example, when Schneider explained to Congress the criteria according to which the Christopher Committee made its decisions about which loans to oppose and which to support, he did not mention consultations with other donors.[85] In addition, the government made no effort to link cooperation on human-rights sanctions to other dimensions of bilateral or multilateral relations—and indeed shied away from this kind of linkage policy, as its policy toward the IFIs shows. According to one participant in these processes, Patrick Flood, the State Department was restrained in its efforts to gain cooperation, in order to maintain good relations with the target: "We did not lobby our allies for support for our position in the banks. . . . A more active lobbying effort could have been more effective."[86]

Descriptions of the process used to express opposition to particular loans leave a clear impression of a policy poorly designed to bring about multilateral action. The Christopher Committee's sessions were bureaucratic battles rather than opportunities to discuss the multilateral dimensions of policy. The first few executive-board meetings of the MDBs after the Carter administration began opposing loans were reportedly stormy, as the United States had given the banks little warning of the switch in policy. Eventually, the administration developed a more-orderly procedure. Countries with loan applications the United States was likely to oppose were warned in advance, so they had a chance to withdraw their application. Weintraub describes what would happen if they did not withdraw the application and it came before the board: "The U.S. director is normally silent and at the very end of the procedure merely states that he is abstaining on or opposing the loan under instructions, and that generally is that. The U.S. action is usually quietly received as a political statement."[87] The new, orderly procedure left little room to persuade other donors to cooperate, as the United States did not discuss specific loans with them and did not announce its intentions until other countries had already voted.

In other words, the United States' decisions were made in isolation from considerations of the likely actions of other states and were in no way contingent on its ability to gain cooperation. Although other donors did not fully agree with the U.S. position, there was some variation in their willingness to cut aid, as discussed below. Other potential sanctioners could safely assume that the United States would make its point regardless of their own actions. If their preferences were to see some state take action but to remain out of the fray themselves, there was little reason for other donors to join the U.S. action. If the United States had adopted a more-strategic position and made its decisions after consultation with allies, the chances of gaining cooperation would have been greater. The next section addresses this argument by discussing the preferences of other potential sanctioners.

## Attitudes and Responses to U.S. Human-Rights Sanctions

While there was general support for an emphasis on human rights, other states were not pleased with the manner in which the United States attempted to use certain institutions such as the MDBs. U.S. policy toward international institutions perplexed many European governments, who took the constraints imposed by these institutions more seriously. In addition, they were puzzled by the U.S. refusal to ratify the standard multilateral human-rights treaties and thus suspected that the government was motivated more by political considerations than genuine concern with promoting international human rights. With respect to their own human-rights policies, Europeans were generally unwilling to engage in unilateral sanctions, with the exception of sanctions against Chile immediately after the 1973 coup. However, there was a basis of support on which the United States could likely have built a more-cooperative approach to human-rights problems, if its policy decisions had been more consistent and if it had put the issue of cooperation closer to the top of its agenda.

Where did the Western European public stand on Carter's human-rights policy? While European journalists typically expressed a great deal of skepticism, a study of public opinion in four countries in the late 1970s showed a high degree of acceptance of the idea that countries should criticize others on human-rights grounds. Of those who were aware of the U.S. stand, 79 percent in West Germany, 64 percent in Italy, 56 percent in France, and 64 percent in Britain thought that governments should criticize human-rights abuses by other countries.[88] Thus, European publics seemed generally open to the idea of an active human-rights policy, although we cannot estimate from these data the degree to which they might have been willing to bear the costs or risks of economic sanctions.

European analysts have pointed out the importance of public opinion in determining governments' human-rights policies. For example, Evan Luard argues that how far a state goes in criticizing another's human-rights abuses depends more on public opinion than on "the absolute scale of its atrocities" or on relations with other states.[89] Because publics now have greater knowledge of human-rights abuses, constituencies demand government action.[90] Luard uses this argument to explain why the British government spoke out on Chile. Its silence on other Latin American cases was due to a lack of attention to these situations from the British public and nongovernmental organizations. Luard also argues, however, that it did not make much sense for Britain to pursue a vigorous human-rights campaign unilaterally: "However committed its government and however active in this field, Britain can do little, acting bilaterally, to secure more effective promotion of rights elsewhere. One of our aims, if we are concerned to make progress in this field, must, therefore, be to secure better *international* action to bring this about" (emphasis in the original).[91] He concludes that Britain should strive for more joint action. If this analysis is correct, Britain should have been receptive to U.S. calls for cooperation. David Owen, a former foreign minister, also emphasizes British receptivity to multilateral human-rights campaigns.[92]

One of the instances in which international disagreement on human-rights issues first arose was President Carter's first seven-power economic summit, in London in May 1977. Carter attempted to introduce initiatives on nuclear energy and human rights into the conversation, challenging the prevailing view that the summits should be restricted to economic issues. The "irritant" of human rights "was dispensed with fairly briefly, as Carter expounded his forthright policy, and [Chancellor Helmut] Schmidt [of West Germany] defended the quieter approach of his government."[93] In a decision similar to that on the IMF, Carter came around to the viewpoint that the summits were valuable economic institutions that could be destroyed by the introduction of foreign-policy issues. Europeans typically held this viewpoint more strongly than U.S. officials, which explains their emphasis on using the "proper" international institutions, such as the UN and the Council of Europe. This institutional focus resonates with European reluctance to go along with U.S. opposition to loans in the MDBs on human-rights grounds.

The differences between U.S. and European thinking on the role of publicity and international institutions also surfaced at a private meeting of governmental officials held in England in November 1978. While participants from the United States emphasized the benefits of their public diplomacy, the British explained that while they had a rating system for evaluating the status of human rights in various countries, these assessments were not made public. They were, however, used in governmental decisions on aid distribution, and they led to a suspension of aid to Bolivia in 1977.[94] The British minister for overseas development, Judith Hart, also noted that the British public's interest in human rights in developing countries had "exploded" in the last few years.[95]

British participants also stressed that international institutions could not be bent to serve the purposes of U.S. foreign policy. As Douglas Williams, deputy secretary in the Ministry of Overseas Development, explained, the United Kingdom "is more concerned about complying with the constitutions of the multilateral aid organizations and would not agree that a resolution of Parliament could override them. . . . international aid organizations *must* operate within their constitutions."[96] Because these organizations served valuable developmental goals, the European officials would not consider a change in their constitutions to allow consideration of human-rights issues. In addition, British participants referred to specific UN provisions to justify their occasional cuts in aid or public criticism.

To generalize, human rights could be described as basic to most Europeans' worldviews but not central to their governments' foreign policies. Thus, "the states of Western Europe have sheltered behind the argument that sanctions are an ineffective or counter-productive form of leverage."[97] While the European Community passed more than seventy resolutions condemning various countries, the European Commission did not take action on any of these resolutions. The foreign ministers of the EC rejected the notion of producing an annual report on the status of human rights in specific countries similar to that produced by the U.S. State Department. The EC could have included human-rights concerns in agreements on dealings with other countries, such as the Lomé Convention. The Lomé Convention, while discussing economic rights and development assistance,[98] has no provision for the imposition of sanctions on human-rights grounds.[99] International institutions do seem to matter for multilateral human-rights sanctions, but in a negative sense. Since human-rights issues were outside the recognized scope of international economic institutions, the United States was inhibited in efforts to use these mechanisms to gain cooperation. The lack of U.S. veto power further inhibited such efforts.

Western Europe, however, has a much better record on accepting international human-rights documents than does the United States. The European system for safeguarding human rights is the most highly developed such regional system in the world, with extensive procedures for individual appeals. The European Convention on Human Rights is quite effective, having been incorporated into national law in eleven countries.[100] Most European states have ratified the four major universal human-rights treaties negotiated in the UN.

The United States, on the other hand, has ratified none of these treaties, despite playing a major role in their negotiation just after World War II. While President Carter signed these four treaties in October 1977, as a signal of his commitment to a multilateral approach to human rights, the Senate never scheduled them for debate. Old battles over human-rights treaties were replayed in Senate debates over the Genocide Convention.[101] The United States apparent unwillingness to accept universal human-rights standards for its own behavior only increased European skepticism about the fundamental motivations of U.S. human-rights policy and thus exacerbated the credibility problem.

The smaller European states adopted a slightly different approach to human rights than Britain. They placed more emphasis on economic and social rights, generally arguing in favor of positive measures designed to promote basic rights rather than negative sanctions intended to improve governmental behavior. In addition, they argued that because of their small size, their most effective contribution to international human rights could be made through multilateral mechanisms, particularly the UN.

The Netherlands, for example, undertook an extensive policy-review exercise in 1979 on the subject of human rights. The resulting document pointed to major advances in the development of universal norms of "classic" (political and civil) and "social" (economic, social, and cultural) rights. The Dutch government recognized human rights as an essential part of its foreign policy, but it stressed the need to avoid "arrogance" and to respect the sovereignty of other states.[102] Thus, it focused on improving the international legal order in a way that would promote human development.

The Dutch government pointed out in this review that criticism from the Netherlands alone would be unlikely to have much impact on the target country: "As far as drastic measures such as sanctions are concerned, it will only be acceptable to take such measures if there is participation by a sufficient number of countries for achieving the desired effect, preferably on the basis of a decision by the UN Security Council."[103] This statement strongly supports this study's proposals about the logic of bandwagoning and the effect that institutions can have in increasing the level of positive contagion. In bilateral aid programs, the Dutch government might consider positive measures to reward governments for good behavior, but not aid cutoffs as punishment for human-rights violations.[104] Thus, U.S. efforts to gain the cooperation of the Netherlands on sanctions would likely have succeeded only if the U.S. government had focused its efforts on the UN and created broader international consensus. However, many European countries, including the Netherlands, did impose sanctions against Chile in 1973, demonstrating that there were special circumstances in which they considered the international consensus broad enough to engage in punitive behavior.

Canadian human-rights policy was quite similar to that of the smaller European states.[105] Margaret Doxey's analysis of the role of human rights in Canadian foreign policy notes the importance of UN norms and decisions. In addition, she reports that Canadians found the U.S. policy frustrating for its apparent inconsistencies; the task, she says, was to "design and promote constructive cooperative international action in the field of human rights which will combine consistency of principle with efficacy in application."[106] Parliament had much less impact on Canadian human-rights policy than did Congress on U.S. policy.[107] Canada, like Europe, was suspicious of aggressive U.S. policies, especially given U.S. reluctance to work within established frameworks.

Overall, U.S. allies may have been sympathetic to the basic goals of human-rights policy, but they disagreed with the tactics the United States used to pursue these ends. Although President Carter did sign the international human-rights instruments and recommend improving the capabilities of the OAS human-rights system through the Inter-American Commission on Human Rights, major U.S. efforts went outside of these traditional human-rights forums. This led to a rather lukewarm response in Europe and Canada, which, combined with the lack of strenuous bilateral efforts to gain cooperation on sanctions, resulted in the United States pursuing its policies in isolation. Without the use of more-consistent signals about the intent and nature of its human-rights policy and without the use of relevant institutions, Washington had little chance of gaining the cooperation of other potential sanctioners.

## Pinochet's Chile: U.S. Leadership or Resistance?

According to Hufbauer, Schott, and Elliott, the United States took the lead in condemning the Pinochet regime for its abuse of human rights and received no cooperation from other states in imposing sanctions, although the UN consistently voted to criticize the human-rights situation in Chile after 1973.[108] As I show in this section, this interpretation of the international reaction to Pinochet's abuses misses many of the most important dynamics of this case. In fact, a large number of states, including nearly all of Western and Eastern Europe, imposed sanctions in the form of aid reductions against Chile soon after the September 1973 coup.[109] Against this background, the U.S. decision to cut military and economic aid in December 1974 seemed both belated and inadequate, especially since the Ford administration found ways to circumvent the aid cutoff. This case illustrates U.S. difficulties in coordinating its domestic policies sufficiently to establish credibility.

From 1970 to 1973, Chile was governed by democratically elected President Salvador Allende, who introduced numerous reforms that had the cumulative effect of destroying the Chilean economy. A combination of the economic situation, expropriations, and U.S. pressure brought multilateral lending to Chile nearly to a halt by 1973.[110] Allende's rule had the effect of polarizing Chilean society, creating a fertile ground for the military coup of 11 September 1973. The Ford administration welcomed Allende's overthrow, as it had spent significant sums of money supporting his political opposition.[111] The United States quickly recognized the new regime and found that its economic policies, which encouraged new foreign investment, were far more congenial than Allende's.

The military junta, however, immediately engaged in a campaign of repression that included massive detention and murder. By December 1973, Congress called upon the president to discuss human-rights issues with Chile, although it did not impose restrictions on foreign aid until 1975. In May 1974, the UN Economic and Social Council passed a resolution condemning human-rights abuses in Chile, which was followed by a similar General Assembly resolution in November.[112]

The imposition of military rule in a country that had a strong tradition of democracy shocked Europe and brought swift action from many European countries.[113] The Finnish government froze all credit agreements with Chile immediately after the coup and canceled them in January 1974.[114] Actions against Swedish citizens and embassy staff led the Swedish government to cut financial aid in November 1973.[115] The Netherlands suspended development cooperation and credit guarantees. Norway also suspended all bilateral aid. West Germany suspended development aid, discontinued supplies of weapons and military equipment, and insisted on harsher terms in debt-rescheduling negotiations.[116] Many Western European countries voted against loans to Chile in the World Bank and IDB, while most socialist countries cut all ties to the military government.[117]

The reaction of the British government was somewhat more complex, because of the change in government after the Labour party won the elections in March 1974. Immediately after the coup, Britain recognized the new government. Labour criticized the Tory government's "indecent haste" and made the reduction of aid to and trade with Chile one of the issues of the election campaign.[118] In November, Labour argued that the government should follow Sweden's lead and refuse to supply arms to the new regime.[119] However, Minister of State, Foreign, and Commonwealth Affairs Julian Amery insisted that Britain would fulfill its contracts, which were important for British employment. He argued that the naval contracts were worth 61 million pounds and that there was no need to suspend military contracts because there was no civil war in Chile. Judith Hart, an opposition member of Parliament at this time, took a strong stand in favor of terminating arms sales, withholding future aid and credits, and using British influence to withhold World Bank and IMF assistance.[120]

Hart became the new minister for overseas development after the Labour party's victory. On 27 March 1974, she announced that the government was ending all British aid to Chile, because "the present Chilean so-called government indulges in murder of opponents on a scale unknown by any government since Stalin."[121] She also revealed that the government had discussed Chile with other members in the IMF and the World Bank. In response to this action, Chile threatened to suspend shipments of copper to Britain. This would have entailed substantial transition costs as Britain searched for new sources, since Chile accounted for 18.8 percent of all British imports of copper. However, it was generally believed that Chile was unwilling to implement this threat; Britain accounted for 15 percent of Chilean copper exports, making the domestic costs of an embargo high for a government striving for international economic respectability.[122] Chile never did embargo copper exports.

At this time, Britain was in the process of building four warships for Chile and was actively testing one in spite of the threatened arms embargo.[123] On 9 April, Foreign Secretary James Callaghan announced that the government would not prevent the delivery of these ships to Chile. This decision outraged many members of the Labour party, who were unsatisfied with the decision to fulfill existing contracts in spite of selling no new arms. It led to a crisis within the party, and many saw it as a test of the "socialist intentions" of the new government. On 5 May, there was a demonstration in London in which thousands marched to protest the sales. In the end, however, the government held firm—arguing that it had to honor its contracts—and delivered the ships.[124]

At the same time, the government decided to suspend a Rolls Royce contract for overhaul of aircraft engines and supply of spare parts, although this decision would not take effect for three months.[125] This story suggests that, as in the United States, domestic politics in this case influenced sanctions decisions at least as much as international considerations. However, the British government relied on the decisions of international institutions to a greater extent than the United States—for example, justifying its decision to continue shipments by reference to UN decisions to condemn Chile but not call for mandatory sanctions.

Against this background of action by European countries, the United States seemed to have exceptionally warm relations with the Chilean junta. U.S. aid, which had come to a halt under Allende, quickly rose. Bilateral aid peaked in 1975 despite congressional attempts to reduce economic and military assistance. Chile ordered large amounts of military goods from the United States until Congress put an end to this in December 1974.[126] Congress had allowed aid to Chile to continue in fiscal year 1974, requesting that the president press human-rights issues with the junta. When it became clear that the administration had instead refused to discuss this topic with the junta, Congress imposed a $25 million ceiling on economic aid and prohibited all military aid and sales for fiscal year 1975.[127]

The administration managed to evade the economic-aid restriction through a legal finding that the limits did not apply to Public Law 480 food aid or to housing guarantees.[128] Although Chile had not received any P.L. 480 assistance prior to 1975, as its per capita income exceeded that of most other countries in Latin America, in 1975 it received $57.8 million under this program while the rest of Latin America received only $9 million.[129] Although Congress attempted to close some of these loopholes, in fiscal year 1976 Chile again received significant bilateral U.S. assistance. For example, the administration reclassified certain dual-use equipment that had been formerly considered military, so that it now was classified as commercial equipment and could thus be sold to Chile.[130] In October 1976, Chile renounced all U.S. aid, claiming that congressional human-rights provisions constituted interference in Chile's internal affairs.[131] However, funds continued to flow through P.L. 480 and housing guarantees.

After the 1973 coup, multilateral lending to Chile, which had dried up under Allende, suddenly resumed—largely because of U.S. support for new loans. Multilateral lending peaked at 52.7 percent of all external aid to Chile in 1975; it fell sharply thereafter as many countries voted against or abstained on loans because of human-rights considerations.[132] However, the drop in official lending was more than compensated by a dramatic increase in private lending, as private banks came to see Chile as an excellent outlet for excess liquidity.[133]

Under the Carter administration, restrictions on aid to Chile were more strictly enforced, although U.S. representatives sometimes voted in favor of multilateral loans and the Carter administration refused to put restrictions on private lending to Chile. A slight intensification of sanctions came in November 1979, in response to Chile's failure to investigate the August 1978 assassination—on Pinochet's orders—of Orlando Letelier and Ronni Moffitt, representatives of the Chilean opposition, in Washington.[134] However, actual sanctions at this time did not cover trade with Chile and were much less substantial than Carter had threatened. They were a unilateral move on the part of the United States. Meanwhile, Israel and France picked up sales of military equipment cut by Carter.[135]

How should we interpret the course of economic sanctions against Chile? In the early years of the Pinochet regime, we find a surprisingly high degree of cooperation among states, although the United States was reluctant to join in the international effort. Sanctions actually imposed by European states included reductions in aid and arms sales to the Pinochet regime. Once the United States began genuinely enforcing its own sanctions, in 1977, other governments had no interest in intensifying their own efforts in response to U.S. actions. In this case, dismay at the loss of democratic government in Chile and the junta's brutality initially led to international political isolation of the new government and willingness to impose mild, symbolic sanctions. When the Carter administration decided to impose sanctions against Chile—three years later—it found some support within the MDBs, making this the case with the highest degree of cooperation within the set of Latin American human-rights cases. U.S. policy does not explain this level of cooperation, which occurred in spite of inconsistencies in U.S. actions and rhetoric. It was the result of coincidence of interests among most European states, fitting the pattern of a coincidence game rather than one of coadjustment or coercion.

## Conclusion

The case of Chile is anomalous within the set of cases of sanctions against Latin American regimes in that countries other than the United States got involved. It is also unique in that sanctions were initially imposed by Europeans without the participation of the United States. Europeans felt compelled to respond to the military overthrow of a democratically elected government in a country with a relatively strong tradition of democratic rule. Thus, the Chilean case is unusual because the initial motivation for sanctions developed not from U.S. domestic politics but from dramatic events in the target country. This led to a different pattern of European interests than in other human-rights cases.

Because other cases of sanctions against Latin American countries had their roots in domestic U.S. political battles rather than specific events in target countries, much of the story of failed cooperation lies in the battles between Congress and the president. Between 1973 and 1976, Congress attempted to force the Nixon and Ford administrations to cut aid to various countries for human-rights reasons. When the executive refused to comply with general legislation, Congress reacted by tightening the general laws and passing country-specific legislation. Even these restrictions, however, had only minimal impact on State Department actions during Kissinger's reign.

President Carter brought a new commitment to human rights to the executive branch. Especially in the first few months of his administration, we see sudden compliance with congressional demands, along with initiatives from Carter to cut aid to some egregious violators. However, the administration remained reluctant to press vigorously for sanctions in international financial institutions or other international forums. The decisions to act depended solely on domestic factors, not anticipation of other states' reactions. No attempts were made to threaten countersanctions or provide inducements for cooperation. Overall, attempts to gain the cooperation of other countries appeared as an afterthought rather than a central part of the administration's human-rights strategy.

In addition, the administration refused to take actions that might have proven costly to the United States, such as denying export credits. In the area of trade—the only one in which sanctions could have been costly and U.S. firms demanded that the government seek other countries' cooperation—the administration backed down, as in the case of the Allis-Chalmers sales to Argentina. Thus, other countries concluded that it was not worthwhile to get involved in the complex situation of human rights in Latin America. As in the 1982 pipeline episode discussed in chapter 8, unwillingness to bear self-imposed costs reflected underlying divisions regarding the wisdom of sanctions and undermined U.S. credibility. The credibility problem was exacerbated by U.S. failure to ratify human-rights treaties. Although European countries were sympathetic to the goals of Carter's policy, they were suspicious of his motivations and disapproved of the manner in which the United States threatened to use "inappropriate" international institutional mechanisms to multilateralize its policies.

The U.S. government never succeeded in gaining institutional approval for sanctions. Again, this failure seems due in large part to a lack of effort. U.S. representatives to the MDBs admit that the United States never tried very hard to gain the support of others within these institutions. Thus, other potential sanctioners never had to calculate the risks of defying institutional decisions to impose sanctions. Instead, the costs of changing fundamental institutional standards determined their actions. The administration's reluctance to push this issue reflected its recognition of the value of the economic functions these institutions performed, functions that would be threatened if the institutions were linked to political issues. In addition, the institutional rules gave U.S. representatives little leverage, since the United States did not have veto power. This contrasts with the situation in CoCom discussed in chapter 7, where the United States had and used veto power—and got cooperation.

What does this case suggest for a more general understanding of when cooperation fails? First, it supports the general findings of the model used in this study, where the costs borne by the major sender and the role of international institutions provide a great deal of explanatory leverage. Without high self-imposed costs and without the involvement of international institutions, Washington was unable to establish a credible commitment to human-rights sanctions and thus failed to generate international cooperation. However, this case also allows us to go one level deeper, to ask why the government adopted policies that decreased the probability of getting cooperation from other states. What led to the government's neglect of steps that could increase cooperation?

Except in the case of Chile, the human-rights sanctions were imposed not in response to specific events in the target countries but as a result of a complex political process within the United States. This process led to decisions to impose sanctions in which the likelihood that other states would also take this step was, essentially, irrelevant. Although U.S. officials generally preferred cooperation to unilateral action (with the possible exception of some members of the Nixon and Ford administrations), the United States adopted a noncontingent strategy of sanctions and engaged in only feeble attempts to multilateralize them. I would speculate that, in general, economic sanctions that result from domestic political motivations are less likely to become multilateral than those that are a reaction to specific outside events. The pattern of interests in such cases will typically constitute a coercion game, but one in which the incentives for the leading sender to use linkage to gain cooperation are low.

The next chapter presents another North-South case, British sanctions against Argentina during the 1982 Falklands War. In contrast to the United States with its human-rights sanctions, Britain achieved a high level of international cooperation. Comparison of these two cases allows exploration of the factors that facilitate cooperation among Northern countries to impose sanctions against Southern countries.

# 6

## The Falkland Islands Conflict

AT THE BEGINNING of April 1982, a long-festering dispute between Great Britain and Argentina over sovereignty in the Falkland Islands (called the Malvinas in Latin America) turned into open conflict when Argentine military forces invaded the islands. During the next two months, numerous states imposed economic sanctions against Argentina at Britain's urging; sanctions both preceded and accompanied British military action. In this chapter, I examine Britain's success in gaining the cooperation of other states, particularly the members of the European Community and the United States. (Technically, it was the European Economic Community [EEC] that undertook the actions discussed in this chapter; since the distinction between the EEC and the EC is of no significance for my argument, I refer only to the EC here.) Some authors have described British success as surprising. However, according to the model used in this study, we should expect a high level of cooperation in this case, because of the involvement of the EC and the high costs borne by Britain. The discussion in this chapter focuses primarily on the institutional rather than the cost argument.

This chapter begins with a brief chronology of the Falklands War and of the economic sanctions imposed during this episode. While Britain took the lead in imposing sanctions, gaining the cooperation of other states and the approval of international institutions was a matter of high priority for the British government.

After this overview, I discuss in more depth the involvement of the EC and the decisions that led to its imposition of sanctions. Intra-EC politics show that in a situation of coercion, linkage across issues is vital to the leading sender's success in gaining the cooperation of other states. I argue that a link between ongoing EC budget discussions and the Falklands issue became central to the renewal of sanctions in mid-May. The central argument of this chapter is that the cooperation of reluctant sanctioners resulted from institutional involvement. In addition, the actions of other organizations, particularly the United Nations, influenced EC decisions. Thus, we find bandwagoning on a grand scale, with a sort of snowball effect in which institutional decisions led to decisions by individual states to impose sanctions on Argentina. This situation had a mirror image in Latin America, where the failure of the OAS to agree on action to support

Argentina meant that the Argentines were isolated in their sanctions against Britain. While chain-ganging occurred in Europe, buck-passing resulted in Latin America.

Within the EC, Ireland found itself in a unique position as a neutral country. The third section of this chapter focuses on Ireland's decisions first to impose sanctions and then to back off once the shooting war started. This episode gives us some insight into the larger question of the relationship between military activity and economic sanctions. The aggregate data show that there is no significant positive correlation between military action and the level of cooperation observed in the imposition of economic sanctions, as we might expect from a consideration of the costs involved. The Irish case suggests that because many states understand sanctions as an alternative, rather than a complement, to actual fighting, they are less willing to impose sanctions when they accompany military actions.

Finally, I examine the decisions of non-EC states on imposing sanctions. The United States provides an interesting case, as the U.S. government found itself in the acutely embarrassing position of having to take sides when two of its allies began fighting with one another. The decisions of other states, such as members of the Commonwealth, Japan, and Latin American states, show a typical pattern of bandwagoning and reliance on the guidance of international organizations. Overall, the Falklands case shows that although different institutional mechanisms are used, the dynamics of North-South cases resemble closely those of East-West ones, such as the following two cases. In this case, the high level of cooperation cannot be explained as the coincidence of individual state interests, but only through the incentives to cooperate generated by the EC. Thus, the Falklands case allows us to examine the dynamics underlying the aggregate positive relationship between institutions and cooperation. This case also presents a nice analogy to sanctions against Iraq in 1990–91. In both cases, issue linkages were the key to maintaining cooperation, and the relationship between sanctions and military action was of central concern.

## The Falklands Crisis, 1982

Argentina and Britain have contested the sovereignty of the Falkland Islands for the last two centuries. The Falklands are located in the South Atlantic Ocean, 480 miles northeast of Cape Horn. Their discovery is variously claimed by representatives of Spain and England at different dates in the sixteenth century. Spain forced out a small British colony on the islands in the 1770s; the Spanish settlers then withdrew in 1811 because of the high costs of maintaining a colony in such cold, barren surroundings. In 1820, Argentina declared sovereignty over the Falklands, sending settlers to stake its claim. In 1831, the United States became briefly involved in this drama, deporting the Argentine settlers and declaring the islands free of any government. The Argentines, however, returned to establish a penal colony. In 1833, British warships landed on the islands to reclaim them. The Argentine settlers left peacefully, but under protest. Britain has exercised sovereignty over the islands since then, although Argentina has continued to argue that the Falklands were illegally taken by force.[1]

In 1965, Argentina took the Falklands case to the United Nations, which sporadically sponsored negotiations between the two claimants until 1982. These negotiations made little progress, as neither side was willing to concede on the central issue of eventual sovereignty. In March 1982, negotiations broke down once again, with Argentine representatives warning that they would have to seek more-effective measures to advance their cause.[2] Apparently, this warning was not taken seriously in London, and there is no evidence that the Argentine government had a definite plan for invasion in early March.

As of 1982, the Falklands were inhabited by about eighteen hundred "kelpers" of British origin. The Falklanders are fiercely loyal to Britain, and just as fiercely disdainful of the Argentines. Most refuse to learn to speak Spanish and maintain a willful ignorance of anything about Argentina.[3] Thus, the Falklanders want their islands to remain a British dependency, and the British argument for sovereignty rests on claims about islanders' right of self-determination. Yet, because Argentina refuses to maintain regular communications and other services with the islands, the British government has found the cost of maintaining the Falklanders quite high.[4] The "Falklands lobby" in Parliament is disproportionately powerful and has frustrated occasional attempts by the Foreign and Commonwealth Office to consider seriously mechanisms that eventually would transfer sovereignty to Argentina.[5] One such option was "leaseback," a proposed arrangement similar to that used for Hong Kong.[6]

The 1982 Falklands crisis began somewhat haphazardly on 19 March when an Argentine scrap-metal merchant landed on the island of South Georgia, another British dependency about six hundred miles east of the Falklands, and raised the Argentine flag. The captain apparently had the implicit backing of the Argentine navy, which expected little or no British response. Instead, Prime Minister Margaret Thatcher sent the HMS *Endurance* from the Falklands to South Georgia.[7] The Argentine government, headed by President Leopoldo Galtieri, was under intense domestic pressure due to rapidly deteriorating economic and political conditions. It felt it had to respond, and it did so by landing Argentine commandos on

South Georgia on 25 March. The junta also decided to go ahead with an invasion plan for the Falklands, apparently believing that the South Georgia incident provided a window of opportunity and that the invasion would direct domestic attention away from new austerity measures.[8]

By 30 March, British foreign secretary Lord Carrington warned Parliament that Argentina had created a "potentially dangerous" situation in the South Atlantic. At Britain's request, the United Nations Security Council took up the Falklands issue on 1 April, and the president of the council called on both sides to exercise restraint and avoid the use of force.[9] Carrington's fears were confirmed when Argentina invaded the Falklands, South Georgia, and the South Sandwich Islands that night. About three hundred marines landed in Port Stanley, the capital of the Falklands. The British forces defending the islands killed four Argentines and wounded two before surrendering; the Argentine forces were under orders not to harm the British forces and did not return fire.

Sir Anthony Parsons, the British permanent representative to the UN, immediately called an emergency session of the Security Council, on the morning of 2 April. He demanded a vote within twenty-four hours on a resolution drawn up by Britain that called for an immediate cease-fire and Argentine withdrawal. On 3 April, the Security Council approved the British document, Resolution 502, by a vote of ten in favor (including the United States), only one against (Panama), and four abstaining (including the Soviet Union, which declined to use its veto power to kill the resolution).[10] Later, UN diplomats called the rapid passage of Resolution 502 "miraculous."[11] Delighted by this unexpected level of international support, Britain based its future actions on Resolution 502, refusing to ask for further Security Council or General Assembly action. British officials believed that attempts to enforce 502 by forcing Argentina to withdraw would meet with a Soviet veto. Thus, the UN's role in the unfolding conflict became more limited after 3 April.

On 3 April, the British government also broke diplomatic relations with Argentina and imposed economic sanctions. These sanctions, which were clarified over the next few days, included a freeze on Argentine assets (valued at about $1.5 billion) in British banks, embargo of arms sales to Argentina, suspension of export-credit insurance, and a ban on Argentine imports. However, the sanctions did not cover goods already in transit, nor Argentine assets in overseas branches of British banks. The freeze on assets was potentially the most damaging of these economic measures, as the already-acute financial problems in Argentina meant that the government would need to borrow more than $7 billion on the international market in the remaining months of 1982. The leading role of the City of London in syndicated loans meant that international financing for Argentina might dry up.[12] Thatcher told the House of Commons, recalled on a Saturday for the first time in more than thirty years, that she saw the freeze of assets as "an appropriate precautionary and, I hope, temporary measure."[13]

London banks worried that the financial measures could harm their reputation as reliable sources of funds, and they pressed the Bank of England for an "enlightened interpretation" of the sanctions regulations that would minimize damage to their long-term interests.[14] When the Bank of England came out with its clarified guidelines on 13 April, they covered a wide range of transactions; British banks were not allowed to make any new loans to Argentina or to disburse funds from existing lines of credit. However, these restrictions did not apply to overseas branches of British banks and so were acceptable to the City.[15] Argentina responded to these measures by freezing British assets in Argentina, banning British imports (worth about $411 million annually),[16] and suspending payments to British banks. However, both British and Argentine financial interests were strongly against declaring Argentina formally in default on its British loans. One such declaration could trigger a spider's web of cross-default clauses, with drastic effects on the international financial system. Thus, Argentina claimed that it was continuing to make payments on British debt to an escrow account set up in New York, and London banks were spared the necessity of finding Argentina in default.

Coincidently with its own imposition of sanctions, the British government asked other states to take economic measures against Argentina. On Tuesday, 6 April, at a meeting in Brussels, Britain formally asked the EC to impose economic sanctions. The attempt to organize EC sanctions had actually begun over the weekend, and British officials described intensive discussions with EC states as the centerpiece of diplomatic efforts to isolate Argentina.[17] These efforts focused on West Germany, Argentina's largest trade partner in the Community and a significant source of military goods.[18] The initial response of the EC ambassadors to requests to ban imports and export credits was described as "positive and sympathetic but non-committal," although they did agree to an embargo on arms sales.[19] Thus, British officials were somewhat surprised by the unanimous EC decision of 10 April to ban imports from Argentina, effective 17 April.

Prime Minister Thatcher also communicated personally with the leaders of Commonwealth states, Western European nations, Japan, and the United States, asking for expressions of support. Many nations responded immediately by embargoing arms sales to Argentina, including France, West Germany, Belgium, Austria, the Netherlands, and Switzerland.

Australia, New Zealand, and Canada withdrew their ambassadors from Buenos Aires, and New Zealand banned all trade with Argentina.[20] The United States and Japan were more reticent.

The U.S. government found itself in the difficult position of being asked to choose between two allies. Faced with this dilemma, the government decided the best course was to remain neutral for the time being and to take all possible measures to prevent the conflict from escalating to open warfare. Thus, Washington refused to impose sanctions and sent Secretary of State Alexander Haig on a mission to attempt to negotiate a settlement to the dispute. However, evidence that has come out since 1982 shows that, at least in the lower levels of government and within the military, the United States was never neutral. The Defense Department, in particular, provided important assistance to the British task force from the beginning.[21]

For most of the month of April, the course of the crisis was dominated by Haig's shuttle diplomacy and the approach of the British task force to the Falklands. The task force of more than one hundred ships and twenty-eight thousand men provided a de facto time limit to negotiations, although the Argentines and many others remained unconvinced that the British were actually willing to risk lives over a few barren rocks eight thousand miles from Britain. However, domestic political pressures and Thatcher's own preferences meant a low probability that Britain could back down from its stand on the Falklanders' right of self-determination at this time. At home, the conflict led to a surge of support for Thatcher's Conservative party, which otherwise was in electoral trouble.[22] In the House of Commons, support for a strong response to the actions of the "tinpot fascist junta" was almost universal.[23] Any outcome that looked like a British surrender would almost certainly have led to demands that Thatcher resign.

On 8 April, Britain announced a two-hundred-mile blockade around the Falklands, effective 12 April, and threatened to sink any Argentine vessel within this area. Haig continued his negotiations, but Argentina repeatedly rejected any deal that did not guarantee eventual Argentine sovereignty over the islands. The OAS formally began to discuss the conflict on 21 April, and the majority of votes predictably went in Argentina's favor. However, the OAS never called for sanctions against Britain.

Until 25 April, the Falklands dispute remained a matter of diplomacy rather than military confrontation. On that date, the task force reached South Georgia Island and recaptured it in a two-hour battle. By 30 April, Britain would have sufficient forces in the area to attempt to enforce the two-hundred-mile blockade, and warned it would do so. However, even this threat was insufficient to convince the Argentines to back down. At this time, many observers had doubts about Britain's ability to win a military confrontation. Argentina had a logistic advantage, with British forces having to operate eight thousand miles from home. Argentine military forces were equipped with advanced armaments, some of them purchased from Britain. In addition, the Argentine forces had the advantage of defending, rather than trying to invade, the islands.

When it became obvious on 30 April that neither Argentina nor Britain would back down, the United States announced its unqualified support for Britain. The U.S. government imposed some limited sanctions against Argentina, including an arms embargo, and offered support to the British task force. The next day, fighting began in the Falklands with British bombers attacking airfields on the islands. On the night of 2–3 May, a British submarine sank the Argentine cruiser *General Belgrano*, which was outside the declared exclusion zone. More than three hundred Argentine sailors were killed in the attack. This action shocked most of the world, as it realized the potential for widespread casualties in the Falklands. The sinking had a negative impact on sympathy for the British in Europe, where many felt that Britain had acted too aggressively. Ireland called for an end to EC sanctions.[24] On 4 May, Argentina retaliated for the attack by sinking the HMS *Sheffield*, killing thirty.

After the failure of Haig's negotiating efforts, UN Secretary-General Javier Pérez de Cuéllar attempted to find a solution to the conflict. However, despite personal appeals to Prime Minister Thatcher and President Galtieri, his efforts were fruitless. Peru, which had sided with Argentina from the beginning of the conflict, also attempted to play the role of mediator, without success. Fighting continued, with Britain gaining a foothold on the islands on 21 May despite stiff Argentine resistance. British forces continued to gain ground, and Argentina finally surrendered to the British at Port Stanley on 14 June. Over the next week, arrangements were made for the exchange of prisoners, and the British governor of the Falklands returned on 26 June. The defeat led to the fall of the Argentine military junta within a matter of months.[25]

While military defeat dealt the final blow to the junta, analysts have credited sanctions with having put severe strain on the Argentine economy. In early July, the government was forced to devalue the peso and place strict controls on interest rates, imports, and currency. M. S. Daoudi and M. S. Dajani conclude that "collectively, the sanctions imposed by the EEC quickly made Argentina's already desperate economic situation worse."[26] The EC accounted for approximately a third of Argentine trade in the 1975–80 period, and Argentina's loss of export income exacerbated the difficulties of repayment of its huge foreign debt. While the emphasis of this study is on politics within Europe rather than sanctions' impact on Argentina, the evidence suggests that the sanctions had significant effects on the target country.

## The Falklands and the European Community

After its initial success in the UN, Britain's efforts to gain international support centered on the EC. In this section, I examine the series of EC decisions on economic sanctions. I argue that Britain had to persuade other EC members, who would not have imposed sanctions—especially after the start of hostilities—without sustained British efforts. In such a situation, issue linkages provide one of the few levers for gaining the co-operation of recalcitrant states. In this case, the linkage was provided by an ongoing dispute over the EC budget and the Common Agricultural Policy (CAP); British concessions on the budget issue were linked to renewal of EC sanctions in mid-May. Examination of EC involvement provides persuasive evidence of the importance of international organizations in facilitating cooperation. Many of the smaller member states did not impose sanctions until the EC formally called for them, as the larger problems of Community solidarity and political cooperation became intertwined with the somewhat-obscure issue of sovereignty in the Falklands.

For analytical clarity, I have divided EC sanctions into three phases. During the first, many EC states were willing to support Britain with multilateral sanctions, seeing them as an alternative to military conflict. In this phase, the EC as an organization provided member states with assurance that they would not be acting unilaterally; the EC functioned as a neoliberal perspective would predict it would. The second phase began as military action broke out, and this stage presented Britain with a more-difficult cooperation problem. Now, some members became quite averse to continuing with sanctions and maintained them only because the EC as a whole would not agree to their withdrawal. Finally, the third phase of sanctions involved crucial negotiations over their renewal in mid-May. At this time, most EC members were unwilling to continue cooperating unless they received a side payment from Britain, which took the form of concessions on a budget rebate.

### Initial EC Sanctions: An Assurance Game

Most EC members were basically willing to support Britain with sanctions prior to the military engagement, as long as they were assured that the rest of the Community would act in the same manner. Because European states believed that a broad ban on Argentine imports would provide sufficient leverage to force the junta to back down, they saw multilateral sanctions as an effective alternative to military conflict. In addition, because EC members did not expect sanctions to last longer than a few weeks, governments anticipated low costs. Although some members were more reluctant than others to impose sanctions, either because of higher direct costs to themselves or because of a greater unwillingness to support Britain, all eventually acquiesced in the European Commission's initial decision to take action.

One of the most striking features of EC involvement in the Falklands is the speed with which the normally slow-moving Community acted. One EC official said, "We have done in a day what it usually takes a year to do."[27] British diplomacy deserves the credit for this rapid response, as gaining the cooperation of others in imposing sanctions received sustained attention at the highest levels of government. The prime minister, foreign secretary, and various ambassadors immediately called on other nations to support the British cause, framing the issue as a response to unlawful international aggression. On Monday, 5 April, just four days after the Argentine invasion, the secretary of state for trade informed Parliament that "any helpful economic response in this dispute can best proceed if we are supported fully by our nearest allies in the European Community."[28] The British government quickly realized that its economic pressure on Argentina would be minimal unless other states also cut imports, export credits, and arms exports. Since the EC accounted for approximately 20 percent of Argentina's exports, a Community-wide ban on imports could, politicians believed, put intense economic pressure on Buenos Aires.[29]

West Germany was Argentina's largest trading partner in the European Community in 1982, with Argentine exports to Germany worth almost $565 million and German exports to Argentina worth $1 billion. Thus, British efforts first centered on the West German government. Foreign Minister Hans-Dietrich Genscher had extensive discussions with Lord Carrington on Thursday and Friday, 1 and 2 April. On 5 April, the British ambassador to West Germany, Sir Jock Taylor, met with Foreign Ministry State Secretary Bernd von Staden. At this time, German representatives felt that it was too early to discuss economic sanctions. However, they reached an informal agreement with the British to stop the shipment of German-built frigates if the conflict escalated. One German diplomat said, "We would do our utmost to comply with Britain's wishes."[30] Belgian foreign minister Leo Tindemans, then serving as the president of the EC Council of Ministers, also became the target of British lobbying efforts. His initial response was generally supportive.

Although the EC quickly condemned Argentina's use of force and called for its withdrawal from the islands, the question of imposing economic sanctions that could be costly for the Community if they stayed in place for any significant time remained undecided. EC trade with Argentina in 1980 totaled about $4 billion, with a $460 million trade surplus.[31] Banning Argentine imports would not cost much for the Community as a whole, since most Argentine imports, such as meat and other agricultural products, were already overproduced by member states. However, Italy and Ireland could suffer from termination of leather imports for their shoe industries. In addition, the EC fully expected that Argentina would retaliate by banning Community imports, as it had banned British imports when Britain announced sanctions on Argentine imports.[32] Thus, the cost of sanctions lay not only in lost imports, but in the near certainty of losing the Argentine market as well. In fact, on 9 April Argentina formally protested EC discussions of sanctions and threatened to adopt "pertinent measures responding to those liable to affect its foreign trade and international economic relations."[33]

By 6 April, initial soundings from Community members were encouraging enough for Britain to call formally for EC sanctions against Argentina. Britain wisely asked only for measures that did not exceed steps it had taken unilaterally. It requested an embargo on arms sales, to which the Netherlands, West Germany, Belgium, and France, had already agreed. The French were highly supportive of the British position, probably because Argentine success in the Falklands would set an unwelcome precedent for various disputed French possessions. Most importantly, Britain asked for a ban on some Argentine imports (including beef, steel, textiles, and leather goods), an end to preferential treatment of other Argentine imports, and termination of export credits.

Over the next few days, EC ambassadors consulted with their governments on the issue of sanctions. While Germany and France seemed willing to go along with the British request, some of the other EC members were more reluctant. Ireland, in particular, questioned the wisdom of sanctions. Prime Minister Charles Haughey was cool to the British request and believed that sanctions would be "counter-productive."[34] During four hours of talks on 8 April, the political directors from EC foreign ministries decided to defer a decision on sanctions, awaiting further instructions from their governments.[35] They did, however, agree to terminate all supplies of arms and military equipment. In spite of general support for Britain, as of 9 April reports from EC sources suggested that Community action would fall short of British requests for an import ban.[36] Denmark stated that it would not accept any sanctions that were not administered on the national, as opposed to supranational, level. Italy, in addition to benefiting from leather imports, had a large emigrant population in Argentina and so was reluctant to break off relations. Germany was worried about proposed limitations on export credits.[37]

On Saturday, 10 April, the EC overcame its reservations and imposed a total ban on Argentine imports, along with an embargo on arms exports.[38] Press reports called this action the "toughest sanctions ever imposed" by the Community, expressly comparing them to the "almost laughable" sanctions imposed against the Soviet Union and Poland in the previous two years.[39] The date on which sanctions would come into effect and their duration remained unclear.

Thatcher, speaking to Parliament, noted the government's "heartening degree of success" in convincing the EC to take action, calling it a "very important step, unprecedented in its scope and the rapidity of the decision." The prime minister also observed that short-term self-interest could not explain the EC action: "The decision cannot have been easy for our partners, given the commercial interests at stake."[40] Other governments agreed with this assessment. A spokesman for Tindemans corroborated Thatcher's point, noting that both Ireland and Italy had required a great deal of persuasion to join in the sanctions effort.[41] A German official said, speaking of the negotiations on the import ban, "Here was a case where we were doing something for the Community with no national profit to be gained, in fact quite the opposite."[42]

Given the economic and political interests at stake, European states were willing to participate in multilateral sanctions as an alternative to war, but they were not willing to bear the costs of unilateral sanctions, which they saw as ineffective. This led to an assurance game within the EC, in which the institution provided information to its members about the policies and preferences of other members. Such information was necessary to prevent suspicions that any members were taking advantage of the others' actions to benefit from the redirection of Argentine trade. In addition, involvement of this formal multilateral organization meant that states agreed on the precise obligations of each in the sanctions effort; such agreement established standards about what constituted cooperation or defection. Through the provision of information and setting of standards, the EC allowed members to overcome doubts about the utility of their own sanctions, facilitating cooperation in this assurance game.

EC members viewed sanctions not as an adjunct to military activity, but as an alternative to it. British officials recognized that the EC ministers were willing to impose sanctions quickly because they hoped that this action might prevent escalation of the conflict into a military confrontation. This hope seemed justified because of the poor state of Argentina's economy; British foreign secretary Francis Pym, who replaced Lord Carrington in the first week of April, claimed that the sanctions caught Argentina by surprise and were "a body blow to its already rather shaky economy."[43] The "European plan" was to use economic and diplomatic pressure to force Argentina to compromise.[44] In Parliament, one member noted, "We are fortunate in having the EEC's backing, but I suspect that it wants not only to provide us with support but to act as a restraining force on any over-adventurousness on our part."[45] As events were to prove, this member's assessment was correct. The Community's under-standing of the purpose of sanctions had been articulated earlier by the founders of the United Nations and by scholars thinking about alterna-tives to military settlement of disputes.[46] These authors argued that col-lective economic sanctions could force aggressors to back down without resort to military action. Although twentieth-century experience with sanctions had called this assumption into question, EC members hoped that joint sanctions, with cooperation from Commonwealth members and potentially the United States and Japan, could have a significant im-pact on Argentina because it was highly dependent on the international economy.

However, as in the Argentines' assessment of British motives, the Euro-peans underestimated the importance of domestic political pressures on the junta. Like Thatcher, Galtieri could not afford to back down once he had taken his stand on the Falklands.[47] Argentina hoped to counter sanc-tions with assistance from Latin American countries and the Soviet Union. It also calculated correctly that international financial markets could not afford to force the country into default. Thus, even the impres-sive level of cooperation exhibited by the EC and other countries was not sufficient to prevent the Argentines from fighting over the Falklands.

The EC did not immediately implement its 10 April decision to ban imports. Over the next week, representatives struggled with a number of legal and technical difficulties. Reports suggested that the import ban would likely be limited to two weeks.[48] However, by 14 April, offi-cials had sorted out these difficulties. Sanctions went into effect on 17 April and were initially approved for a period of four weeks. After four weeks, the Community would lift the sanctions if progress toward a dip-lomatic solution was evident. Approval of the one-month import ban was considered a victory for the British, since the European Commission had proposed a two-week limit.[49] The economic interests of member states received one crucial concession in the final negotiations: contracts con-cluded prior to 16 April were exempted from the import ban.[50] Given the time it takes for goods to travel from Argentina to Europe, as well as expectations that the conflict would be settled within a few weeks, this provision meant that the ban could have only a minor economic impact. In spite of this concession, Italy continued to express reservations about the proposed sanctions and refused to approve the official documents until the last minute, on Friday, 16 April.

Ireland and Belgium also showed a notable reluctance to impose sanc-tions without getting something in return from Britain. Other EC mem-bers expressed more wholehearted support for Britain. In France, Presi-dent François Mitterrand and the rest of the government fully supported the British effort, although the French press continued to portray the conflict as a farce. One analysis suggested that the French "government's reason for rallying early to the British cause has been to provide a precedent for joint EEC action in the event of a threat to France's overseas territorial possessions."[51] In West Germany, public, government, and press support appeared strong. Analogies were drawn to the situation in Berlin. Economics Minister Otto Lambsdorff sounded one discordant note, declaring that EC sanctions against Argentina did not change his belief that economic sanctions were not very useful as a political lever.[52] He hoped that the dispute would be settled quickly so that the Community could lift its sanctions.

Thus, there was a range of opinion in Europe about the utility of supporting Britain with sanctions at this stage. However, in spite of their misgivings, European states were willing to take economic measures because they were an alternative to military conflict and because they were not expected to cost much, as long as they worked. British requests had been designed to keep costs relatively low—avoiding, for example, a Community-wide freeze on Argentine assets that German representatives had opposed.[53] States' willingness to cooperate had one strong condition: that other EC members also impose sanctions. Measures taken by just a few countries would have had little impact on Argentina, so governments were willing to participate only in a multilateral effort. The EC machinery provided assurance that all states were taking the same measures and thus provided a solution to this collective-action dilemma. In other words, the EC, by deciding on specific measures, clearly defined what constituted "sanctions" against Argentina. Members' reputations were now tied to national enforcement of particular measures. As a result, EC action helped reduce fears of cheating among all members.

### Sanctions after the General Belgrano Sinking: Institutional Coercion

EC solidarity began to waver as soon as the first shot was fired in the Falklands War. As mentioned above, EC members hoped that economic pressure would be sufficient to prevent Argentina from going to war with Britain. Some, especially Ireland, were strongly opposed to imposing sanctions that could be seen as an adjunct to military activity. In addition, the economic costs of sanctions would now increase, as it became obvious that the conflict would not be resolved overnight. As early as 20 April, Tindemans, the EC president, refused to agree that EC support for Britain would continue if force was used.[54] Newspapers reported that if Britain began firing, strong public and governmental backing for Thatcher would likely evaporate.[55] During this second phase of sanctions, preferences became more asymmetric, with Britain needing continued strong support while other states grew less willing to keep sanctions in place. The game moved away from assurance preferences to one where Britain had to exert significant pressure on some members to gain their continued cooperation, as the payoff for multilateral sanctions decreased. The EC framework provided this leverage.

After the British recapture of South Georgia on 25 April, EC foreign ministers met in Luxembourg on 27 April to discuss the status of sanctions. Although some reports suggested that officials urged Thatcher to continue negotiating with Galtieri and warned that they would have to reevaluate their support for sanctions if force was used, the public stance of solid EC support remained firm.[56] Tindemans announced continued backing of Britain. On the other hand, Irish diplomats argued that with the start of military action, the EC was involved in "a whole new ballgame."[57]

West Germany, however, remained committed to sanctions. Foreign Minister Genscher argued that solidarity was in the interest of NATO as well as the EC; since only Ireland was not a member of NATO, this inter-institutional tie could have persuaded some representatives. Genscher contended that the value of EC backing would be diluted if internal EC differences were made public; thus, Tindemans's public statements downplayed any dissent. At the Luxembourg meeting, Britain did not request any further sanctions, and there was apparently no formal discussion of what actions the EC might take if fighting became serious.[58] Tindemans did, however, link continued EC support to continued negotiations between Britain and Argentina, and particularly to Haig's ongoing shuttle diplomacy. Other officials, including Italian foreign minister Emilio Colombo, expressed similar views. One official said, "The aim of Common Market sanctions was to put diplomatic pressure on Argentina, and the whole ball game will be completely different if the British attack the Falklands."[59] Newspapers in Europe echoed this sentiment.[60]

In spite of these warnings, on 2 May British forces sank the Argentine cruiser *General Belgrano*, outside of the declared two-hundred-mile exclusion zone around the Falklands. Immediately, Tindemans reiterated EC support for Britain and for a negotiated settlement to the dispute, saying that no government had yet formally changed its stance on sanctions.[61] However, in Ireland, Denmark, and West Germany, officials quickly began to question their position. The Irish minister for defense, Patrick Power, said on 3 May that Britain was now the aggressor in the Falklands, and he compared the British to a hit-and-run driver. Reports in Irish newspapers suggested that renewal of sanctions when they expired on 17 May was now "extremely unlikely."[62] In addition to the sinking of the *Belgrano*, air attacks on Port Stanley, which had begun on 30 April, and U.S. support for Britain were cited as factors that had changed the situation considerably. Leaders of most European countries, including France and Germany, called for an immediate cease-fire.[63]

When the news of the *Belgrano* sinking reached Dublin, Irish cabinet ministers were relieved about a decision they had made earlier in the day—to ask the EC to agree to a lifting of sanctions and to call for an emergency UN Security Council meeting in light of the likelihood of military conflict. There was now little ambiguity about the Irish position. The new policy, calling Britain an aggressor and calling for an end to sanctions, was adopted in a cabinet meeting on Tuesday, 4 May. The government's statement said it was "appalled by the outbreak of what amounts to open war . . . and at reports that hundreds of lives have already been lost. They see the present situation as a serious threat to world peace. . . . The Irish Government regard the application of economic sanctions as no longer appropriate and will, therefore, be seeking the withdrawal of these sanctions by the Community."[64]

Prime Minister Haughey declared, however, that Ireland would not lift sanctions unilaterally. A Dublin paper explained this reasoning: "There is no compulsion on Ireland or any other country to fall into an EC line, but the desirability of such solidarity itself becomes a factor in deciding policy."[65] Afraid of threatening its Community benefits, particularly farm subsidies and access to the British market at favorable tariff rates, the government was worried about unilateral withdrawal from sanctions to which it had previously agreed.

Haughey explained that Irish neutrality was the major obstacle to continuing sanctions, now that they were a complement to British military action. Neutrality meant that Irish options were "more limited" than those of other EC members (an interesting interpretation of neutrality). Haughey stated, "We were never very enthusiastic about the imposition of sanctions but the argument was persuasive that they could be instrumental in applying pressure to achieve the implementation of Resolution 502 and so lead to a diplomatic solution."[66] He justified the timing of his decision to oppose sanctions by saying that prior to the attack on the *Belgrano*, the British task force had appeared to be on a mission of blockade rather than invasion. Now, he reiterated that he wanted to maintain EC solidarity but stated that he would try to convince others to lift sanctions. He continued to be "very averse" to unilateral action.[67]

West Germany and Italy continued to favor an arms embargo but questioned the continued utility of trade sanctions. If their purpose was to prevent fighting, there seemed to be little reason to continue the ban on imports now that the shooting had started. Germany also expressed fears that escalation of violence in the Falklands would provide an opportunity for the Soviet Union to increase its influence in Latin America.[68] Germany in particular was disappointed and surprised by the failure of U.S. efforts at mediation. Officials noted that U.S. negotiations had been an important factor in convincing the EC to impose sanctions. However, the failure of negotiations made sanctions look like a blank check for British military action, which was not what the Community had intended.

Germany said that a "grave question mark" hung over the future of EC sanctions and noted that its initial support had been given only with "serious misgivings," considering significant German economic interests in Argentina and the fact that sanctions were unlikely to work.[69] German businesses began to worry more about the economic impact of sanctions, especially since Argentina was threatening that extension of the sanctions past 17 May could result in long-term damage to relations.[70] While the credibility of this threat remains open to question, the prospect of losing a market worth over half a billion dollars annually because of a colonial dispute between Britain and Argentina was unsettling.

By 4 May, support for continued sanctions seemed to be in serious trouble. Prime Minister Haughey publicly called for the EC to lift its sanctions immediately; but he said that if the EC would not agree to lift sanctions, Ireland would not do so unilaterally. Given the outrage in Ireland over the *Belgrano* sinking and the general antipathy toward the British, this condition was a strong statement of the power of institutional decisions on national policies. The rest of the EC, however, was unprepared for the Irish request and was unlikely to agree quickly. This cautious attitude was reinforced on 4 May, when Argentina retaliated for the sinking of the *Belgrano* by sinking the HMS *Sheffield*. After this event, it was more difficult for governments to consider the initial British action unjustifiable.

The escalation of the Falklands conflict to the military level had profound implications for states' preferences. Some, like Germany, found themselves questioning the level of support they had given Britain. Others, particularly Ireland, now faced strong domestic pressure to pull out of the sanctions. However, the EC decided to put off a decision until the original sanctions expired, on 17 May. In this situation, Ireland anticipated that its EC benefits, such as farm subsidies and access to EC markets, would be threatened by a unilateral withdrawal from the Community's policy. Thus, institutional considerations forced Dublin to stick with the sanctions in spite of domestic demands to pull out. Only the pressure of institutional commitments can explain continued Irish cooperation. Although the conflict between institutional and domestic pressures became most public in Ireland, other EC members faced a similar conflict, to varying degrees. The EC's decision to maintain the original agreement helped push governments toward continued sanctions.

*Renewing Sanctions: Issue Linkages*

In this final phase of sanctions, most EC members were reconsidering their costs and benefits, while Britain continued to look for cooperation. It was becoming obvious that the conflict was likely to drag on, leading to much higher costs of imposing sanctions than states had originally anticipated. In addition, many Europeans felt that since sanctions had failed to avert hostilities, they should now be dropped. In light of these higher costs, EC members demanded a side payment from Britain in the form of a concession on a persistent budget problem. In the face of now highly asymmetrical interests, the organization fostered continued cooperation by allowing its members to link these two issues. The nature of strategic interaction and coercive bargaining that led to the continuation of sanctions conforms more closely to realist than neoliberal expectations, but the institutional dimension remained essential to the cooperative outcome.

Over the weekend of 8–9 May, European foreign ministers met in Belgium in what was described as an "extremely acrimonious" meeting to discuss renewal of sanctions, which were due to expire on 17 May.[71] Other issues were on the agenda as well, including the British contribution to the EC budget. British sources began to suggest that refusal to renew sanctions, or linkage of sanctions to other issues, might lead Britain to pull out of the EC. They also emphasized that British ships were being lost and that the government was now cooperating in UN efforts at negotiation, under the secretary-general. These efforts would, diplomats hoped, convince their EC partners that Britain was genuinely interested in a negotiated solution to the conflict and so increase the chances of renewal of sanctions.[72]

Throughout the crisis, some EC members had quietly suggested that Britain should be willing to make concessions in a long-running intra-Community budget dispute in exchange for EC solidarity on the Falklands issue. Britain had been demanding a reduced contribution to the budget, arguing that it was one of the poorest countries in the Community and therefore its budget assessment was out of line. In an attempt to force other members to concede on the budget issue, Britain had been holding up an increase in farm-price supports under the Common Agricultural Policy.

Suggestions of linkage first arose in Ireland and Belgium. As early as 12 April, the *Irish Times* had suggested, "In return for this show of solidarity Britain may now be expected by her partners to take a more conciliatory approach to the review of farm prices, already a week overdue."[73] On 16

April, the *Financial Times* noted the sentiment in favor of linkage in Belgium: "Belgium, at any rate, has not forgotten that the intra-EC disputes of budget payments and farm prices that tend to separate Britain from the rest of the EC had to be hurriedly shelved on the outbreak of the crisis."[74] One Belgian farmers' weekly carried a headline suggesting that European farmers were being held hostage to eighteen hundred Britons in the Falklands. The *Financial Times* reported that questions of linkage were "floating eerily on the diplomatic breeze" and that Foreign Secretary Pym was working hard to keep the Falklands issue separate from all others.[75] In West Germany, hints of linkage emerged as expressions of hope that the quick EC response would improve the Community's image in Britain.

Irish sources, in the early phases of sanctions, were the most open about potential linkage. One paper reported in late April, "To maintain EC solidarity with Britain in the Falklands crisis, the Irish Government would like to see Britain show solidarity inside the EC by approving this week the 1982–83 farm price increases."[76] A few days later, the Irish minister for foreign affairs Gerard Collins claimed that there had been no direct trade-off between EC sanctions and the farm-price deal, but he noted that he did not expect continued British obstruction of price increases. He went on to say that "there had been an expectation that Britain would soften its line on the farm price issue following the EC's solidarity over the Falklands."[77] Other reports claimed that Pym had been given an ultimatum on this issue. By early May, West German farm minister Josef Ertl had joined the Irish, Belgians, and French in suggesting that Britain would now have to make concessions on the budget–farm price dilemma in order to gain continued support for sanctions.[78]

Irish and French sources, on the weekend of 8–9 May, continued to suggest that Britain would have to concede on the budget issue in order to get their cooperation on sanctions.[79] While EC officials still avoided making an explicit link between the two issues, they did suggest that Britain could not expect backing in the Falklands if it continued to antagonize its partners on other issues. A West German official went so far as to say that "solidarity is not a one-way street."[80] Thus, linkage between the two issues could have transformed two games of deadlock into a single game where both sides—Britain and the rest of Europe—could benefit.

However, Pym adamantly rejected any such linkage at the weekend meeting. Britain opposed all suggested deals on the budget, precipitating a crisis in the organization. The Community also failed to come to a decision on the sanctions issue. Although Ireland agreed to continue its sanctions until 17 May, the ministers did not agree to British requests to extend them past this date.[81] Tindemans reported continued EC solidarity behind Britain and said that a decision on the renewal of sanctions would be made the next Sunday, 16 May—just one day before sanctions were due to expire. The *Financial Times* noted the implicit link between the budget and sanctions: "In taking the final decision [on sanctions], governments such as Ireland, Italy and Denmark may well be influenced by the fact that the UK has refused to soften its 'no farm price increase without a budget deal' stand, while still expecting supporting action over the Falklands."[82]

Over the next week, individual countries clarified their positions on the renewal of sanctions. Italy began to emerge as a major problem for Britain, as the Italian Socialist party, a member of Italy's ruling coalition, came out strongly against any renewal while military action continued. Bettino Craxi, leader of the Socialist party, said that he could see no reason to approve extension of the sanctions. Europeans saw this as a major embarrassment for Italian prime minister Giovanni Spadolini, who was known for his pro-European attitudes and had supported continuing EC solidarity.[83] The British press, however, guessed that Spadolini would win this domestic debate and that Italy would be unwilling to drop sanctions if West Germany and France called for their renewal.[84] In other words, some analysts expected that institutional incentives would overcome domestic opposition to sanctions in Italy, as they had in the Irish case. Although the German public expressed opposition to continued sanctions if this might draw Germany more deeply into the conflict, the government was expected to continue supporting sanctions unless Britain took the rash step of attacking the Argentine mainland.

Ireland continued to oppose renewal of sanctions, arguing that its position of neutrality made it especially difficult for it to support sanctions if fighting continued. In addition, Ireland had much to gain from the proposed farm-price increases Thatcher was blocking. Anti-Anglo sentiment was running high in Ireland for this reason, and also because of a mishap in which a British submarine caught an Irish trawler's nets, sinking it. In spite of these factors working against Irish approval of new sanctions, the government delayed a formal decision until the last minute, hoping to avoid isolation within the EC.[85] As in Italy, systemic pressures working against isolation were competing with domestic pressures to pull out of sanctions. By Friday, 14 May, the Irish government was reportedly ready to veto sanctions.[86] Other EC members were unlikely to grant it an exemption from the requirement to impose sanctions; by vetoing sanctions, Ireland would avoid some of the stigma attached to refusing to go along with an institutional decision approved by majority vote.

During this week, the French position, which had been strongly pro-British, underwent an interesting revision. French officials seem to have realized that they could use the sanctions issue to get concessions from Britain on the budget and farm prices, problems that had been plaguing the Community for years. Foreign Minister Claude Cheysson went to

London on 14 May for talks with Pym and other officials. In an extended interview with the BBC he explicitly recognized the linkage between the budget and sanctions. He accused Britain of not appreciating EC solidarity and of being interested only in financial gains, and he said that the impressive solidarity shown in the Falklands crisis had much to do with other issues of Britain's presence in the Community.[87]

The foreign ministers' meeting took place as scheduled in Brussels on Saturday, 15 May. However, the ministers failed to reach any agreement then and so moved to Luxembourg, where a NATO meeting was due to begin on Monday. By Sunday night, they had not yet struck a deal on either sanctions or the British budget contribution. The ministers used an ambiguity in the language of the sanctions order to determine that sanctions would not expire until midnight on 17 May, thus giving themselves one more day in which to reach agreement.[88] The most vociferous opposition to sanctions came, unexpectedly, from Italy rather than Ireland. The Italian foreign minister argued that he could not approve continued sanctions because of domestic opposition, despite a personal visit from U.S. Secretary of State Haig urging him to support a renewal. The Irish representative said nothing during the debates.

On the budget issue, the ministers renewed an earlier offer to reduce Britain's contribution by $810 million, and Pym again rejected it. While British officials continued to insist that the budget and sanctions were separate issues, representatives of the other nine EC members privately said that they would find approval of sanctions easier if the British showed some willingness to concede on the budget. On Monday, a series of bilateral meetings took place throughout the day. Representatives could not agree on the budget, farm prices, or sanctions. Finally, the ministers, led by the French and German representatives, decided to renew sanctions for just seven days, rather than the minimum of four weeks that Britain had requested.

Irish aversion to isolation continued during this series of negotiations, and the Irish government delayed making its own decision in the hope that the EC as a whole would refuse to extend sanctions. However, when Britain refused to accept the budget-rebate offers, Ireland would not go along with a continued trade embargo. It was saved from the embarrassment of complete isolation by the fact that the Italian representative was forced to argue and vote against a renewal. Italy and Ireland invoked the Luxembourg Compromise to declare sanctions a matter of vital national interest, thus allowing their abstention.[89] Both countries agreed to continue the arms embargo against Argentina, while the Irish government informally agreed to avoid circumventing the EC import ban by trans-shipping Argentine goods.[90]

Spadolini found his government's decision difficult to accept, but his coalition partners had vowed to bring down the government if he went ahead with sanctions, even for seven days.[91] Craxi stated that he believed sanctions were "a mistake from the beginning," and he supported the government's decision not to go along with the rest of the EC.[92] Foreign Minister Colombo, however, revealed the division between the Socialist and Republican parties by stating that Italy still considered Argentina the aggressor and by stressing that the arms embargo remained in force.[93] Thus, Britain lost the cooperation of two states, while achieving a temporary commitment to continued cooperation from the other EC members.

On Tuesday, 18 May, a crisis arose over the question of farm-price supports. Britain continued to refuse to allow increases to go through. Traditionally, the EC had allowed member states to exercise veto power over such decisions on the grounds of "vital national interest," under the terms of the Luxembourg Compromise. However, on 18 May the ministers of the Council of Agriculture decided to go ahead with the price increases against Britain's wishes, precipitating a constitutional crisis.[94] This decision also created a political crisis for Thatcher, as calls arose for Britain to change its status in the EC or withdraw completely from the organization.[95] Although she protested the Community's action loudly, calling it a dangerous move toward majority rule, she took no concrete actions to retaliate. Considering that sanctions were due to be renewed again in just six days, she could not afford to continue to press on the budget issue. Reports suggested that the farm-price decision had been politicized by the Falklands issue.[96]

On 21 May, British forces landed on the Falkland Islands. EC members largely refrained from commenting, particularly on the impact of this move on the renewal of sanctions. Tindemans said the Community would look for ways to continue pressuring Argentina, but he did not mention sanctions.[97] Diplomats in Brussels suggested that sanctions might not be renewed, although France and West Germany still favored them.

A foreign ministers' meeting beginning Monday, 24 May, lasted until three o'clock the next morning; but the ministers finally reached a deal. Britain accepted a budget rebate of $875 million, very close to what had been offered a week earlier, while EC members—except Ireland and Italy—agreed to an indefinite renewal of sanctions.[98] As of Monday morning, the British delegation had still been looking for a rebate of $1.1 billion, but negotiations during the day forced Pym to "compromise to an extent unacceptable two months ago."[99] The members also agreed during these negotiations to a proposal from the French foreign minister Cheysson for an indefinite extension of sanctions.[100] Ireland and Italy remained "neutral" on the sanctions decision and agreed not to circumvent the embargo. By conceding on the budget and CAP issues, Britain achieved a firm commitment to continued sanctions from the other EC members.

EC observers declared the settlement of the farm-price, budget, and sanctions issues a victory for the institution. The *EC Bulletin* said that a crisis had been overcome but denied that linkage among the issues had contributed to the settlement.[101] Given the series of events, however, this assertion seems implausible. Analysts described the decisions on the Falklands as a success for the process of European political cooperation, the gradual movement toward coordination of foreign policies among EC members.[102] Even taking into account the withdrawal of Italy and Ireland, the level of cooperation achieved within the EC is impressive.

In this final phase, states used the renewal of sanctions to gain British concessions on a long-standing institutional dilemma. Thatcher, although livid at the Community's override of the farm-price veto, could not pull back from the institution because she needed the others' support on sanctions. The linkage between these issues, a linkage created and sustained by the Community's organizational framework, accounts for the high level of cooperation expressed by the indefinite renewal of economic measures against Argentina.

## Summary

In each of the three phases of sanctions, the EC as an institution contributed to the high level of cooperation Britain achieved. At first, other EC members found themselves playing an assurance game, where each was willing to impose sanctions as long as others would as well. Low expected costs of sanctions created these assurance preferences. The EC framework provided the necessary assurance that others would not defect from this agreement, by specifying the nature of sanctions and publicizing government commitments to the joint policy. Although the importance of the institution became more pronounced in the two later phases, its role was not negligible in this first phase.

Once the EC had approved sanctions, individual countries found it difficult to back down, even when domestic opinion turned against these measures during the second phase. This is most evident in the case of Ireland, where the government was ready to call for an end to sanctions after the *Belgrano* sinking. However, when other members refused to go along, Ireland continued to impose trade sanctions for two weeks, until the expiration of the original four-week period. Even after Ireland and Italy backed out of the trade sanctions, they continued to enforce the arms embargo and agreed to avoid diverting trade to circumvent the EC embargo. Fear of being isolated within the Community and of losing EC benefits influenced government decisions on sanctions during this phase. This study of decision making during the Falklands crisis contributes to our understanding of the pattern of bandwagoning found in cases throughout this book and of the role of institutions in increasing the level of bandwagoning. Clearly, the probability of states imposing sanctions increased as they became assured that others were going to behave the same way. Institutions increased the bandwagoning effect by contributing to this assurance and providing diffuse benefits that would be threatened if a state backed out of sanctions.

During the third phase, an important factor in the renewal of sanctions—a factor overlooked by many analysts—was the linkage between the EC-budget issue and the Falklands. Although Britain worked hard to avoid such a linkage, the existence of the budget dispute was fortunate for cooperation on the Falklands. Because the Falklands case was a game in which Britain had to engage in "high-level arm twisting" to gain the cooperation of others, issue linkage created conditions for cooperation.[103] British budget concessions allowed the Community to agree to an indefinite extension of sanctions on 25 May. One group studying the Falklands crisis concluded, "The fact that the EEC cooperated with Britain at all was a result of intra-community politics. The effective quid pro quo was the abandonment of the Luxembourg Compromise which had allowed Britain to veto EEC farm pricing policies."[104] Therefore, the British should have been thankful for the existence of an intra-institutional issue easily linked to the Falklands crisis. As the strategic incentives would suggest, Britain had to rely on this type of linkage in order to achieve cooperation, and the EC structure lowered Britain's transaction costs.

## Sanctions and War: The Case of Ireland

As the preceding study of EC sanctions showed, calculations about imposing economic measures changed considerably when military actions began. This finding suggests a possible answer to a puzzle about multilateral sanctions: why the level cooperation does not appear to be higher when sanctions accompany military activity. In this section I discuss this puzzle, focusing on Irish decisions about sanctions. Because Ireland is not a member of NATO and because of its traditional reluctance to support any British military activity, the significance of sanctions for Ireland changed dramatically when fighting began at the end of April 1982. This case, besides showing how institutions constrained national actions, provides insight into states' and analysts' various understandings of the purposes of sanctions and the impact of these understandings on states' decisions.

The willingness of the leading sender to bear significant costs, we have seen, greatly increases the level of cooperation achieved from other states. A state unwilling to bear significant costs will have a difficult time convincing others of its credibility and intentions in a particular sanctions episode, thus making it unlikely that others will be willing to join in the sanctions effort. In addition, if the costs to the leading sender are low, domestic pressures to gain the cooperation of others may not be very strong, so that the government will not find it worthwhile to engage in difficult international negotiations or resort to threats or promises to gain the cooperation of other governments.

Given these facts, we might expect to find a high level of cooperation in cases where sanctions accompanied military activity. If anything would demonstrate the credibility of the leading sender, it would be willingness to incur the risks and costs of actual fighting. Thus, we should find that military action is positively related to the level of cooperation observed in sanctions cases. However, as the following regression and probit analyses show, there is no statistically significant positive relationship between military involvement and cooperation. In tables 6.1 and 6.2, MILITARY is a dummy variable, coded 1 if the sanctions episode involved military action and 0 otherwise. Other independent variables are included as in the earlier analyses.

Military activity accompanied sanctions in 14 percent of these cases (fourteen out of ninety-nine). In both the probit and regression analyses, MILITARY has a slight positive effect on the level of cooperation observed, but this effect is not significantly different from zero, because of the large standard errors of the coefficients. Thus, military action appears to have a negligible effect on cooperation. Apparently, some factor is working against the increase in credibility generated when the leading sender engages in military action. I argue that the countervailing factor is a perspective that sees sanctions as an alternative to military action. According to this viewpoint, collective sanctions should put sufficient pressure on a state that disputes can be resolved without resort to military force. This viewpoint is especially influential in neutral countries such as Ireland, which wish to remain distant from any military undertakings.

In Ireland, the issue of neutrality has been closely associated with the problem of Northern Ireland. Membership in the European Community has threatened Ireland's neutral stance in some ways, leading the Irish to distinguish between political and military neutrality. They argue that they can be militarily but not politically neutral. A desire to maintain EC solidarity convinced the Irish government to go along with sanctions as long as they appeared to be a support for British attempts to negotiate with Argentina. However, neutrality, combined with traditional antipathy toward Britain, prevented Ireland from supporting sanctions once the con-

**TABLE 6.1**
Regression Analysis; NONMAJ as Dependent Variable

| Independent Variable | Estimated Coefficient | Standard Error | t–statistic |
|---|---|---|---|
| Constant | 12.58 | 5.33 | 2.36 |
| MILITARY | 1.74 | 4.43 | 0.394 |
| TARGET* | −7.06 | 2.13 | −3.32 |
| COLDWAR | 0.664 | 3.37 | 0.197 |
| ASSIST | −1.24 | 3.63 | −0.342 |
| COSTD | 5.47 | 3.40 | 1.61 |
| INST* | 11.29 | 3.28 | 3.45 |
| GOAL | −4.17 | 3.13 | −1.33 |
| | | | |
| R-squared | | 0.211 | |
| Corrected R-squared | | 0.150 | |
| Standard Error of Regression | | 13.65 | |
| Number of Observations | | 99 | |

**TABLE 6.2**
Probit Analysis; COOP as Dependent Variable

| Independent Variable | Estimated Coefficient | Standard Error | t–statistic |
|---|---|---|---|
| Constant | −1.10 | 0.487 | −2.25 |
| MILITARY | 0.308 | 0.380 | 0.811 |
| TARGET | −0.178 | 0.184 | −0.969 |
| COLDWAR | 0.433 | 0.292 | 1.45 |
| ASSIST* | 0.892 | 0.311 | 2.87 |
| COSTD | 0.582 | 0.310 | 1.88 |
| INST* | 1.71 | 0.300 | 5.70 |
| GOAL | −0.512 | 0.286 | −1.79 |
| Thresh 1* | 1.06 | 0.176 | 6.00 |
| Thresh 2* | 2.47 | 0.305 | 8.10 |
| | | | |
| Log-likelihood | | −85.99 | |
| Percent correctly predicted | | 61.6 | |
| Number of Observations | | 99 | |

flict escalated. Ireland did not, however, back out of its institutional commitment until the original EC sanctions expired on 17 May.

Ireland remained neutral in World War II and refused to join NATO after the war; it is the only member of the EC that is not a member of NATO. The refusal to join NATO was linked to British membership in the alliance; Ireland expressed some interest in pursuing a bilateral alliance with the United States, although the U.S. government did not. In a statement rejecting NATO membership, the Irish government said, "Any military alliance with the state that is responsible for the unnatural division of Ireland would be entirely repugnant to the Irish people."[105] The partition became the justification for neutrality, and Ireland's stance as a neutral country subsequently became an issue beyond the realm of political debate in the country, a sort of sacred cow.[106]

Involvement in the EC, as well as in the UN, has been a major factor in Irish foreign policy, as these are arenas in which Ireland can demonstrate its independence from Britain. As the Community moved closer to political cooperation in the 1980s, Ireland found it increasingly difficult to maintain its stance of neutrality. Nevertheless, it would be politically difficult for any Irish leader to drop the formal pretense of neutrality. This was demonstrated in 1980–81, when Prime Minister Haughey caused an uproar by appearing to consider an exchange with Britain—trading neutrality for a deal on Northern Ireland.

The EC plays a central role in Ireland's foreign policy, especially because of the economic benefits its farmers derive from membership. The UN also played a role in 1982, when Ireland had a temporary seat on the Security Council. From a legal perspective, Ireland sided in the UN with the Argentines' position in the Falklands matter; the Irish drew parallels between the Falklands, where inhabitants vetoed a change in sovereignty, and Northern Ireland.[107] Irish UN votes on the Falklands issue had tended to favor the Argentine position over the British until December 1976, when human-rights abuses in Argentina and Irish EC membership led Ireland to change its perspective.[108] In April 1982, the Irish representative to the UN decided to condemn Argentina's invasion of the islands, while remaining neutral on the underlying territorial dispute. Even if the Irish sympathized with Argentina's claim, they could not agree with the means used to achieve this goal. Thus, the Irish representative, Noel Dorr, voted on 3 April in favor of Resolution 502.[109]

Some of Prime Minister Haughey's supporters later suggested that Dorr had acted without Haughey's approval. However, Dorr has been described as a "meticulously precise diplomat," and he was in contact with Haughey on the day of the vote.[110] The attempt to dissociate the government from the vote came only after Haughey had changed his mind about the resolution, after Britain attempted to use it to justify its military action in the islands. The Irish government wanted deep UN involvement in the dispute, feeling that this forum was more appropriate than the EC. The government may have preferred the UN because it was unlikely to call for mandatory actions against Argentina. Haughey was cool to EC sanctions from the beginning, in part because the EC was in disfavor with the Irish government in 1982; British obstinacy was costing Irish farmers, the basis of Haughey's electoral support.[111]

Haughey's then-current government had been in office only three weeks when the Falklands crisis broke. Haughey was known for putting the issue of Northern Ireland high on his political agenda, making for difficult relations with Britain. He also had some differences with the Irish Foreign Office (Iveagh House), feeling that diplomats did not put enough emphasis on the Northern Ireland issue. The Falklands crisis brought these tensions to a head.[112]

When Britain sent notes to the nine other EC members asking them to impose sanctions, Haughey's response was restrained. He stated that sanctions might be counterproductive, a rationalization for opposition to helping Britain in this forum. However, observers judged that "should the other nine members of the EC agree to the imposition of trade sanctions against Argentina at a meeting of ambassadors in Brussels today, it would be highly unlikely that the Government would then stand aloof, despite its expressed reservations on the issue."[113] From the beginning of the crisis, the diffuse benefits of institutional membership appeared to outweigh the short-term costs of imposing sanctions. Before 10 April, the Irish cabinet took no position on the issue of trade sanctions, waiting to decide on the best way to prevent hostilities until after the "EEC decides its collective attitude."[114]

Public discussion before 10 April on the possibility of sanctions showed that there were divisions on the issue. On the one hand, the Irish Export Board pointed out that Irish trade with Argentina was quite small, so that the economic impact of the sanctions would be minimal. On the other hand, the Irish Sovereignty Movement argued that participation in EC sanctions would be a clear breach of neutrality and would erode confidence in Ireland's commitment to remain neutral in future conflicts.[115]

During EC debates, Irish representatives tended to stick to the line that the Community should not take sides on the underlying question of ownership of the islands, but could act to condemn Argentina's use of force and support Resolution 502. Ireland quickly agreed to the arms embargo—a nominal gesture, since Ireland exported no arms to Argentina. Ireland joined other EC members in being less than enthusiastic about sanctions, especially in the face of British intransigence on the budget and farm-price questions, but Britain was "pulling out all the stops in the search for support and was demanding solidarity."[116] Ireland found itself in a dilemma: refusal to go along with the EC could seriously harm the progress of political cooperation and could threaten Ireland's Community benefits, but supporting sanctions could eventually lead to Ireland's appearing to support British military action.

The Irish Foreign Office recommended that the government vote for sanctions, arguing that good relations with Britain could prove useful with respect to the Northern Ireland question. By 9 April, the balance in the EC appeared to have shifted in favor of sanctions as a measure to prevent hostilities, and Ireland joined this consensus under heavy pressure from the British. When the vote came, Ireland voted in favor of sanctions, while some more-reticent members required further British persuasion before it became unanimous.[117] Ireland's change of heart was described as being "in the interests of EEC solidarity."[118] Irish spokesmen emphasized that this decision had no implications for Irish neutrality and was made only to support Resolution 502, not to support British military action.[119]

Ireland's actions throughout the remainder of the crisis have been discussed above. As noted, the *Belgrano* sinking drastically shifted the balance of opinion in Ireland, as sanctions now seemed to support British military action. However, despite domestic pressure to pull out, Ireland reluctantly agreed to continue sanctions through the original deadline, for fear of jeopardizing other benefits it derived from EC participation. After it did pull out, Dublin agreed not to take actions to undermine other members' sanctions. Ireland gained significant benefits from the EC, particularly in agricultural subsidies, and the government paid a domestic political price to guarantee the continuation of these benefits.

This discussion of Ireland emphasizes two points—the influence of international organizations on national decision making, and the distinction between sanctions with and without war. Ireland would never have imposed sanctions if the rest of the EC had not called for them. Both bandwagoning (fear of isolation) and institutional incentives (fear of losing the benefits of EC membership) contributed to its decision. Even when Irish opinion turned strongly against sanctions at the beginning of May, the government refused to lift sanctions unilaterally.

The Irish change of position after the start of hostilities offers an answer to the puzzle presented earlier—why military action does not increase the level of cooperation observed. Some countries—especially small, neutral ones such as Ireland—hope that sanctions can act as a substitute for military conflict. It was with this understanding that Ireland initially approved sanctions. However, when Britain began firing shots, its support decreased—not just in Ireland, but around the world. What Inis Claude has described as "quasi-pacifism" took over.[120] Countries, including Ireland, backed off from sanctions to avoid the appearance of condoning military action. Thus, the outbreak of war actually decreased the level of cooperation observed in this particular case. In general, this effect offsets the increased credibility generated by commitment to military action, making such conflict a poor predictor of international cooperation.

## Responses of the United States,
## Latin America, and Others

The United States found itself in a dilemma, torn between two countries with which it wished to maintain good relations. Like the EC, the United States much preferred a negotiated solution to the conflict. Unlike the EC, however, it was not concerned about the implications of imposing sanctions after hostilities began. Most Latin American countries sympathized with Argentina's claim to the Falklands and wanted to maintain an appearance of solidarity. However, they were reluctant to condone the methods Argentina used, given other outstanding territorial disputes in the region. A few other countries also imposed sanctions after some delay, specifically some Commonwealth nations and Japan. These decisions were all contingent on the actions of the EC and/or the United States.

### The United States

The Reagan administration found itself in a difficult position when Argentina invaded the Falklands. It had been cultivating General Galtieri's government as part of its security policy in South and Central America, and it strongly wished to maintain good relations there.[121] At the same time, the United States could hardly approve of Argentina's act of aggression and would have found it difficult to turn against its strongest NATO ally in a military conflict. Secretary of State Haig was driven to search for a negotiated solution to the conflict. Most Europeans supported his mission, although there was some grumbling in the EC about the U.S. refusal, during April, to impose sanctions. Thatcher also supported Haig's efforts—although, as the task force approached the islands, demands grew for the United States to "come off the fence" and openly support Britain.[122]

Haig realized that he had little room in which to find a solution acceptable to both parties. As one of the members of his team has noted, "It was also clear that any political solution that would permit the survival of one of the two governments would likely bring down the other."[123] Despite the difficulties, Haig believed that only the United States had sufficient influence with both sides to have any hope of success. One of Haig's major problems was to convince the Argentine government that Britain actually was willing to fight for these islands, contrary to the evidence of the past few years. However, even had he convinced the Argentines that Britain would fight—and that the United States would side with Britain in case of hostilities—it was unlikely that the Galtieri government could agree to any settlement that did not give Argentina eventual sovereignty over the islands, something Britain was not prepared to concede.

Until 30 April, the United States continued to play the role of neutral broker, although members of Parliament were calling for Washington to show greater support for the British cause.[124] During Haig's peace efforts, the United States refused to make any statements on possible sanctions, believing that such statements would compromise its role as an impartial mediator. These signals convinced some European observers that the United States might actually side with Argentina, or at least refuse to impose sanctions, if negotiations failed.[125]

However, despite public affirmations of neutrality, the U.S. government sent Britain numerous signals that it would side with the British. Haig privately told Sir Nicholas Henderson, the British ambassador in Washington, that the administration was not impartial and could not be evenhanded.[126] The administration quietly stopped arms deliveries to Argentina on 6 April.[127] From the beginning of the crisis, military contacts between the British and American forces led to extensive cooperation, with the approval of Secretary of Defense Caspar Weinberger.[128] Within the United States, public and elite opinion favored Britain. One prominent exception was Jeane Kirkpatrick, the U.S. representative to the United Nations. Kirkpatrick, concerned about American relations with Latin America, preferred that Washington steer a neutral course between its two allies. However, public and congressional demands that the government side with Britain increased as the negotiations' chances of success appeared slimmer. Senators Daniel Patrick Moynihan and Henry Jackson, for example, called on the United States to join the EC sanctions against Argentina.[129]

When the task force reached the Falklands and Haig concluded that his mediation had no chance of success, the United States announced that it was imposing military and financial sanctions against Argentina and providing "materiel support" to Britain.[130] The United States made this declaration on 30 April, after U.S. ambassador Harry Schlaudeman talked with President Galtieri for fifteen minutes. Sales of arms to Argentina had been prohibited since 30 September 1978 because of human-rights abuses. However, deliveries covered under contracts signed before this date had continued; the sanctions eliminated these deliveries.[131] Commodity Credit Corporation export-credit guarantees, used to finance U.S. agricultural exports, were denied, and a previously announced $2 million credit was halted. In addition, the government stopped disbursement of some Export-Import Bank loans.[132] Six preliminary commitments worth $230 million in loans were affected by this order.[133]

The Argentine economy minister Roberto Alemann called the U.S. sanctions "innocuous."[134] Certainly, they were much weaker than the EC's measures, not touching most trade between the two countries. U.S. desires to maintain good long-term relations with Argentina, as well as U.S. economic interests, led the government to take a cautious approach.[135] Although the British may have been disappointed with the level of U.S. sanctions, publicly they thanked Washington for its support and did not press for more-stringent measures. It would not have been in London's interest to demand that the United States freeze financial assets, as New York banks had been serving as escrow agents for prohibited transactions between London and Buenos Aires. Britain satisfied itself with the sanctions the United States did impose, along with the logistical help the task force received.

### The Third World, the Commonwealth, Spain, and Japan

Judging by previous UN votes, Argentina expected a high level of support for its action from many less-developed countries (LDCs) and members of the nonaligned movement. It was therefore disappointed when these states lined up, for the most part, on the British side of the dispute. While having some sympathy for the Argentine claims, most LDCs saw a threat in the precedent that Argentine success would set.[136] For example, the Kenyan delegate to the UN argued that the Argentine action ignored the wishes of the inhabitants of the Falklands. He pointed out that the Argentine claim was a purely historical and territorial one, which he could not support because its implications would introduce chaos in Africa.[137] Thus, the nonaligned nations did not rush to Argentina's defense.

Members of the Commonwealth, including Canada and New Zealand, "followed the EEC" and imposed sanctions early in April.[138] At Britain's request, Canada and New Zealand withdrew their ambassadors from Buenos Aires.[139] Canada also banned imports and export credits, while New Zealand banned all trade with Argentina. Australia imposed a ban on imports. Hong Kong also banned imports, except for those heading for China. In these cases, EC actions encouraged others to satisfy Britain's demands for sanctions, as these countries were more willing to participate in collective sanctions than in those imposed by only a few of Argentina's minor trading partners.

Spain found itself in a particularly difficult position. Like the United States, Spain had ties to both sides of the conflict and hoped to avoid antagonizing either side too severely. Spain had a historical commitment to Argentina, and over one million Spanish were living there. Spanish trade with Argentina did not reflect this historical commitment, however; it ran at only about $250 million a year.[140] Spain's foreign policy in 1982 was centered strongly on Europe—its NATO and EC memberships were both pending. Considering these applications, Spain could not afford to side aggressively with Argentina. On the other hand, the echoes of the situation in Gibraltar kept the Spanish from siding with Britain. Thus, the Spanish representative on the Security Council abstained on Resolution 502.[141] After Spain quietly joined NATO on 30 May, it reiterated that it did not support Britain in the Falklands conflict.[142]

Japan, as in the other cases in this study, took its cues from the United States and the EC. Prime Minister Zenko Suzuki began by speaking cautiously about the conflict in response to Thatcher's letter of 7 April requesting support. Thatcher apparently asked that Japan show restraint in extending credits to Argentina. Suzuki said he preferred to see what moves other countries took before deciding the Japanese response—clear evidence of a bandwagoning strategy.[143] He pointed out that Japan sold no arms to Argentina and made few loans to the country. On 13 April, Foreign Minister Yoshio Sakurauchi said Japan was watching U.S. mediation efforts before deciding whether to take any actions. On the same day, Suzuki announced that the government had decided not to impose sanctions, saying that it wanted to maintain friendly relations with both sides.[144] Some British politicians later suggested that the United States should convince Japan to impose economic measures against Argentina.[145]

Two days later, Japan reiterated its opposition to sanctions, citing international obligations in GATT (the General Agreement on Tariffs and Trade) and bilateral treaties with Argentina as factors preventing Japan from taking action. However, trade ministry officials said they would impose sanctions if the UN Security Council called for them.[146] Nevertheless, after the United States imposed sanctions on Argentina on 30 April, Japan did take similar measures. Initial reports out of Tokyo were somewhat confused. First, the Japanese foreign ministry announced that it was not going to follow the U.S. lead.[147] However, on the same day, the Japanese government informed Britain that it was going to impose sanctions in response to official British requests.[148] Apparently Suzuki had told Thatcher in a letter on 26 April that he was ready to take action, but he had waited for the U.S. decision before announcing the measures. Japan suspended Argentine imports and halted official export credits. The government described these actions as "strengthening the economic sanctions imposed against Argentina by the United States and the European Economic Community."[149]

The foreign ministry continued to insist, however, that these actions were not economic sanctions, but merely measures designed to support the EC sanctions. The official statement said only that the government would advise its traders not to undermine the Community's sanctions and that the government "cannot expect applications for new export credits from the governmental Export-Import Bank of Japan to Argentina for the time being under the present tense situation."[150] Thus, the ministry maintained that it would not impose formal economic sanctions without a mandate from the UN Security Council. Japan appears to have been concerned with the legal aspects of sanctions, and it looked for institutional approval from the one relevant organization to which it belonged—the UN. Japan, like the Commonwealth countries, followed a bandwagoning strategy. These decisions contrast with U.S. decisions, which appear to have been made as part of a unilateral strategy directed at Argentina, without much concern for others' actions.

### Latin America and the Soviet Union: Argentina's Supporters?

Argentina looked for support from two sources: Latin America and the Soviet Union. Both gave verbal support, but they refused to impose sanctions against Britain to complement Argentina's.

In Latin America, most countries supported the Argentine claim to the Falklands and saw British resistance as a form of imperialism. However, many also had outstanding territorial disputes with Argentina or other neighbors. Chile, for example, had a long-running dispute with Argentina over islands in the Beagle Channel. The use of force to assert a territorial claim made most countries in the region nervous. Therefore, while Latin America supported Argentina vocally in the UN, it took no more-concrete measures.

The forum in which Argentina hoped to organize a Latin American response to Britain was the Organization of American States. One obvious problem was that the United States and the Caribbean nations sympathetic to Britain were also members of the OAS. However, approval of two-thirds of the members would make economic sanctions mandatory. Latin American countries began by expressing their support for Argentina in the UN. Panama, the only Latin American member of the Security Council, was also the only member to vote against Resolution 502. Throughout UN debates over the next two months, Jorge Illueca, the foreign minister of Panama, was the most aggressive speaker attacking Britain.[151] At times his rhetoric approached the absurd—for example, blaming Thatcher's intransigence on "female hormonal cycles" and refusing to use Sir Anthony Parsons's title.

On 16 April, Venezuela was reportedly considering imposing economic sanctions against Britain. Specifically, a British Petroleum oil-technology contract was threatened.[152] However, these sanctions never materialized. No other countries in the region volunteered to join Argentina in imposing sanctions.

On 26 April, an OAS meeting convened in Washington to discuss the organization's response to the Falklands crisis. Argentina had called this special meeting of foreign ministers under the terms of the 1947 Inter-American Treaty of Reciprocal Assistance (the Rio Treaty). Observers expected Argentina to ask for a vote on economic sanctions and thought that there was some chance it would gain the necessary two-thirds majority for approval.[153] However, the Argentine foreign minister, Nicanor Costa Méndez, merely asked the organization to demand that Britain withdraw its fleet and end sanctions against Argentina.[154] Some reports suggested that U.S. opposition to sanctions explained Argentina's decision.[155] However, information later came out suggesting that the opposition to sanctions was much more widespread and had been communicated to Costa Méndez before the meeting.[156]

The final product of this OAS meeting was a statement that supported Argentina's claims to the islands and that called for a truce, a troop withdrawal, and an end to sanctions against Argentina. The United States, still officially neutral, did not vote against this resolution. It passed 17–0, with the United States, Chile, Colombia, and Trinidad and Tobago abstaining. The United States explained its abstention as opposition to the statement on Argentine sovereignty. Territorial concerns probably explained Chile's and Colombia's decisions. Colombia even called the Argentine invasion a "military occupation" and described the British response as "not entirely an act of outside aggression."[157] Another emergency OAS meeting called on 29 May again refused to call for sanctions, although a resolution approved 17–0 did call on the United States to stop aiding Britain.[158]

The United States gave up negotiations and imposed sanctions against Argentina just after the April meeting. Latin American countries reacted angrily. Peru, for example, called this decision a "grave mistake."[159] Other diplomats criticized the timing of the U.S. decision, coming just after the OAS meeting. One said, "For Latin America, this is a bad day. This is the first time that the United States has come to the aid of an outside force." The Peruvian foreign minister added that the United States, "which has been propounding the thesis of the Americas for the Americans, now appears to be propounding the thesis of the Americas for Great Britain."[160]

After its defeat in the OAS, Argentina turned to the Latin American

Economic System (SELA) for support. A ministerial meeting was not scheduled until July, too late for sanctions to be of much use.[161] However, on 3 June SELA did adopt a resolution condemning European sanctions and offering to help Argentina overcome their effects.[162] Following up this resolution, a major Venezuelan trade delegation visited Argentina on 7 June, although no significant deals were forthcoming.[163] One final attempt to organize assistance for Argentina took place at a meeting of the Association for Latin American Integration (ALADI) on 29–30 June. By this time, the EC had dropped its sanctions against Argentina, although the United States and Britain still had some in place. ALADI agreed to increase its imports of Argentine goods to offset the effects of European sanctions.[164] Overall, Argentina did not receive much more than rhetorical support from other Latin American countries. Even those countries that clearly sided with Argentina, such as Venezuela and Panama, refused to impose sanctions if only a few states were going to participate. In this case, failure to gain institutional approval meant that Argentina was isolated in its economic measures against Britain, as buck-passing behavior dominated.

One other potential source of assistance for Argentina was the Soviet Union and other Communist countries. The Soviet Union traditionally had supported Argentina's sovereignty claims in the UN. Thus, the Soviet decision to abstain on, rather than veto, Resolution 502 came as a blow to Argentina, as well as a pleasant surprise to Britain. The Soviets were probably influenced, as were Chile and Colombia, by concern about the precedent a successful Argentine use of force would set, since the Soviet Union had more than a few outstanding territorial disputes with other countries.[165]

Since 1980, Argentina had developed a strong trading relationship with the Soviet Union. In the aftermath of the U.S. grain embargo, Argentina began exporting large amounts of grain and meat to the Soviets and had become their its largest supplier of these goods. The friendly relations that had developed were ironic because the Argentine government had been staunchly anti-Communist since the early 1970s. Argentina assumed it could take advantage of this friendship to offset European sanctions. However, while rumors circulated about possible Soviet military aid to Argentina, no good evidence of military or economic aid surfaced. Soviet diplomatic support for Argentina continued, but Moscow kept a low profile throughout the crisis.[166] One other socialist country, Czechoslovakia, made some preliminary moves to take this opportunity to increase trade with Argentina.[167] However, these moves did not come until mid-June, and they did not amount to much. Overall, Communist support for Argentina was even weaker than that received from its regional allies. The bandwagoning dynamic meant that states were unwilling to get involved in costly sanctions supported by only a few states, and this meant that the Argentines received no cooperation in this case.

## Conclusion

Sanctions imposed during the Falklands crisis highlight some of the major points raised by the theoretical and quantitative analyses of earlier chapters. Most striking are the roles of institutions, issue linkage, and bandwagoning.

The EC quickly called for sanctions against Argentina, despite reluctance from some of its members. This decision had a direct impact on the foreign policies of member states, as they followed the EC decision and banned imports from Argentina. Institutional influence was particularly strong in the case of Ireland, which maintained sanctions until the original deadline of 17 May despite a drastic change in the Irish attitude toward sanctions after hostilities began. However, the potential drawbacks of pulling out of the original sanctions convinced Ireland to maintain them for two more weeks. Similar considerations, while less explicit, account for the sanctions imposed by other reluctant EC members. The EC actions offer a clear contrast to those of the OAS. Argentina failed to organize a call for sanctions in this regional organization, and no OAS member imposed sanctions against Britain.

Britain was involved in a coercion game vis-à-vis other potential sanctioners, including EC members. Although these potential sanctioners opposed the Argentine use of force, they were not eager to get involved in a potentially costly British adventure with colonial overtones. Thus, we are led to expect that Britain would use issue linkage to gain the cooperation of other states. The EC provided a good forum for such linkage, although Britain resisted a tie between other issues and the Falklands. However, without the existence of the budget and farm-price issues, on which EC members were looking for British concessions, it is unlikely that sanctions would have been approved quickly and unanimously by the EC, or renewed in mid-May. This chapter thus provides important microlevel evidence on the role of institutions and linkage in international cooperation. The EC provided diffuse benefits that would have been threatened for individual states that failed to cooperate. In addition, this forum for negotiation and standard-setting body made possible the specific linkage between sanctions and the budget. We will see similar institutional dynamics in the following chapter.

Finally, we find bandwagoning dynamics in the Falklands crisis, as in the other cases in this study. Bandwagoning took place within regional institutions, as countries took pains to avoid the appearance of isolation even in the face of domestic resistance. Bandwagoning also took place outside institutions. Japan, Canada, and others found their foreign policies influenced by the decisions of the EC and the United States. These medium-size powers were unwilling to impose potentially costly sanctions unless a number of other states did so, and they stated this policy publicly. Assured that sanctions would indeed be a collective effort, they took some measures against Argentina. On the other side, Argentina was unable to provide similar assurance to its potential allies and so gained no cooperation. Both the chain-ganging and buck-passing sides of bandwagoning appear in this case.

This case also suggests an approach to understanding the relationship between economic sanctions and military actions. We might expect, given the central role of credibility in explaining cooperation, that military actions by the leading sender would increase the observed level of cooperation. This effect does not appear, however, in the aggregate. The change in the Irish stand on sanctions provides a tentative answer to the question of why cooperation does not increase with military activity. Because many small states see collective economic sanctions as a plausible alternative to military activity, they are reluctant to cooperate in sanctions efforts that accompany such action. This effect offsets the credibility gains generated by hostilities, leaving no significant correlation between war and cooperation.

A final note: the Falklands case provides a number of interesting analogies to recent sanctions against Iraq. Both Argentina and Iraq used military action to claim territory forcibly from another sovereign state. Neither apparently expected reactions from the rest of the world that would go much beyond rhetoric. Like Britain, the United States turned to multilateral organizations, particularly the UN, to coordinate support for sanctions. Although the Iraqi case requires further research, the Falklands episode leads us to expect that UN approval significantly enhanced the level of cooperation and bandwagoning.

However, we also see in both cases that some states were concerned about the use of military force by the leading sender and that they became less enthusiastic about sanctions over time. Like Britain, the United States turned to issue linkages to sustain cooperation when it began to use force in January 1991. In the early months of 1991, these linkages took the form of promises of debt relief (e.g., for Egypt) and other measures. Although future research will have to examine the extent and credibility of U.S. threats and promises, the parallels between these two cases are striking in spite of the vastly different values at stake—barren rocks versus oil wealth. Once again, the goals of sanctions appear to be a poorer predictor of success than strategic variables such as institutions and credibility.

The next two case studies examine East-West conflicts to see whether the patterns found in this chapter and the previous one hold in East-West sanctions as well. The next chapter emphasizes institutional considerations in an examination of controls on high-technology sales; the final case study will focus on the role of costs in the 1982 pipeline dispute.

# 7

## Western Technology-Export Controls

SINCE 1949, the United States and its allies have controlled the flow of their technology to the Soviet Union and its allies. For much of this period, export control was a matter of controversy within the Western alliance, with the United States pressing for more-stringent controls than the Europeans or Japanese preferred to impose. In early 1991, these controls remained a matter of controversy in spite of major changes in the Soviet Union. Despite this persistent political controversy, Western control of technology with potential military applications presents an instance of a relatively high degree of cooperation among states. This chapter examines the factors underlying this success, which contrasts to the failures of U.S. human-rights sanctions and the 1982 pipeline embargo.

Cooperation is especially evident in the West's response to the Soviet invasion of Afghanistan in December 1979. While most studies of the 1980 sanctions have focused on the U.S.-inspired grain embargo, the United States and its allies also tightened the flow of technology to the Soviet Union.[1] In fact, the United States managed to overcome significant resistance to gain approval of a more-stringent policy within CoCom, the Coordinating Committee for Export Controls.

In this chapter, I examine the history of controls on exports to the Soviet bloc, focusing on the post-Afghanistan embargo on high technology and the 1978 sanctions responding to Soviet trials of dissidents. The technology case fits this study's general model quite well. We expect a high degree of cooperation in 1980—when an international organization (CoCom) was involved and the United States bore relatively high economic costs—but not in 1978, when these factors were absent. Therefore, the technology-transfer cases allow us to examine the processes underlying the aggregate effects of institutions and costliness. In this chapter, I argue that CoCom, as an institution, exerted a strong influence on the nature of sanctions imposed by various states in 1980. In addition, I find that the willingness of the United States to bear a fair share of the costs of sanctions increased the degree of cooperation it was able to achieve. These two factors allowed the United States to demonstrate a credible commitment to multilateral sanctions and to credibly threaten to punish defections. These factors were absent in 1978, and the Carter administration gained no cooperation at that time.

The export-control case as a whole does not fall neatly into any of the three categories of cooperation problems described earlier. While control of exports in some periods, such as the Korean War, may have approached a situation of coincidence, more-recent sanctions episodes, including the 1980 case, are more complex. I argue that while the United States found itself in a coercion game vis-à-vis each of its allies, the Europeans and Japanese were playing a coadjustment game among themselves in 1980. This structure of interests led to an interesting pattern of cooperation, with European and Japanese decisions dependent on both assurances of cooperation from other allies and American threats of retaliation through CoCom.

Both theory and the statistical evidence presented in earlier chapters lead us to look for bandwagoning—either chain-ganging or buck-passing—among European states and Japan in this case. Because it would be costly and ineffective for these states to impose sanctions without allied support, we should find them making their decisions contingent on others' decisions. Specifically, we should find Europeans and Japanese arguing that they will not impose sanctions unless they can be assured that other potential suppliers will. Organizations such as CoCom can be especially useful in such a situation, providing guidelines for sanctions and information on others' actions.

If the United States' dominant strategy is to deny technology to the Soviet Union regardless of the degree of cooperation it receives, as in the 1980 case, we should find it using linkage among issues to convince other states to join in the sanctions effort. If the United States cannot credibly threaten to keep from imposing sanctions, it must find some other form of persuasion. In this case, by linking the response to Afghanistan to broader national-security controls within CoCom, the American government succeeded in persuading its allies to cooperate in the technology sanctions. Admittedly, European and Japanese cooperation fell short of the U.S. ideal. However, it exceeded the level of sanctions we could expect from an examination of national preferences without consideration of strategic interaction. The 1980 sanctions were not simply a case of coincidence of interests.

The first section of this chapter examines U.S. and allied views on East-West technology transfer. While the allies recognized they had a common interest in slowing the flow of militarily significant technologies to the East, numerous factors converged to guarantee there would be a substantial degree of conflict over the stringency and nature of controls. I next examine the history of CoCom and multilateral export controls since World War II to provide a background for study of the Afghanistan sanctions. I describe the 1980 technology embargo, then evaluate the success of cooperation in this case and the contribution of different variables to this result. Specifically, I attempt to sort out the contribution of American linkage efforts to cooperative behavior, the role of U.S. willingness to bear the costs of sanctions, and the importance of CoCom's existence and involvement. Finally, I contrast this success to the failure to impose multilateral technology sanctions in 1978.

## American, European, and Japanese Views on East-West Technology Transfer

Conflicting views and debate between the United States and its European and Japanese allies on the costs and benefits of East-West trade result from many sources. Factors such as geographical position, economic incentives, political coalitions, domestic institutional process, roles in the alliance, and ideology all lead to conflicts of interest. The United States values the benefits of trade with the East less highly than do European countries, and it is more willing to sacrifice these benefits for potential political gains. In this section, I examine the views of the United States, Britain, France, West Germany, and Japan on export controls. This description of the configuration of interests and national export-control policies will provide a basis for analyzing multilateral controls and specific responses to the invasion of Afghanistan. All countries feel the need to balance the pulls of national-security concerns and economic gains, but the ways in which they perform this balancing act vary widely.

In order to sort out complex Western views on East-West technology transfer, we need to differentiate two dimensions: the *goods* being controlled and the *purpose* of the controls. Goods can be arrayed along a continuum of "military relevance." For simplicity, I break this continuum into three parts. First, one category of goods, such as munitions, has direct and obvious military applications. Second, there is a large gray area of "dual-use" goods, such as computers—products with both military and civilian applications. The third group consists of goods whose military relevance comes only in that they release resources that society can shift to military applications; agricultural products, for example, fall into this category. I refer to the first group of goods as munitions, the second as dual-use goods, and the last as nonstrategic goods.[2]

States find it difficult to specify with precision the boundaries between these categories. Debate over where the boundaries lie has led to significant conflict within the NATO alliance.[3] In this chapter, I argue that the European preference ordering on munitions approximates that found in a harmony game. For a small category of goods with direct military applications, each state would refuse to sell to the Soviet bloc regardless of others' actions. On the other end of the spectrum, European states have never had an interest in controlling nonstrategic goods, so the United States always faced a coercion game when it tried to pursue controls in this area.

The category of dual-use goods can be further subdivided, based on the configuration of state preferences. Among dual-use goods, there is a shifting boundary between goods that have substantial military relevance and those closer to the nonstrategic end of the spectrum. With respect to the first subcategory, states face an assurance game; all are willing to maintain controls as long as others do as well. In this variation of a coincidence game, states prefer multilateral controls but are afraid of the costs if others cheat. However, with respect to the second, growing subcategory of dual-use goods, Europeans face a coadjustment dilemma, where each state has strong incentives to defect from multilateral controls. For these goods, the strategic importance of a few sales to the Soviets cannot outweigh the economic benefits of exports for each state individually; however, governments recognize the potential contribution to Soviet military strength of unrestricted sales by all CoCom members. I call those dual-use goods with the most direct military relevance "type I" goods and those closer to the nonstrategic endpoint "type II" goods. Figure 7.1 represents these distinctions.

The second and third boundaries—between type I and type II goods and between dual-use and nonstrategic goods—have shifted over time. Changing international political and economic conditions and domestic pressures have led to these shifts. States have not succeeded in developing objective measures to differentiate strategic from nonstrategic goods, but they continue to use this distinction. In general, both boundaries have moved to the left since 1945, with the nonstrategic sector growing as Europeans become less willing to give up economic gains for what they see as questionable security benefits. U.S. policy preferences, in contrast to those of the Europeans, vacillate, but with a trend toward looser controls. In general, however, the United States shows a greater willingness to impose unilateral controls than the Europeans, especially on type II goods. In an exception to this rule, U.S. preferences during the 1970s seemed to approach those of the Europeans, as Washington became unwilling to impose strict controls on type II goods. This created a credibility problem for the Carter administration in 1980.

In practice, decision makers frequently relate the question of which goods to control to a second dimension—the purpose of controls. We find two distinct purposes cited in arguments about export controls: national security and foreign policy. The U.S. Congress recognizes these two pur-

```
Game:  Coincidence   Assurance   Coadjustment
<----------------|----------|-------------|---------->
Goods:  Munitions     Type I      Type II     Nonstrategic
                   {          Dual-Use          }
```

7.1. European Preferences on Export Controls

poses in legislation such as the 1979 Export Administration Act.[4] States use national-security controls as a long-term strategy, to prevent potential adversaries from gaining an advantage through trade. Thus, controls imposed for national-security reasons are contingent not on specific actions of the target country but on underlying strategic factors. Unlike for most economic sanctions, states do not specify conditions for lifting national-security controls. In the East-West context, governments have usually justified controls on strategic goods with arguments about national security, so that some controls would remain in place even with "good behavior" on the part of the Soviet Union.[5]

Foreign-policy controls, on the other hand, tend to be short-term in nature, as their goal is some change in behavior from the target. Thus, states will, in theory, lift such controls once an acceptable change in behavior has occurred. The United States, and at times its European allies, has imposed controls on nonstrategic goods for foreign-policy reasons. In practice, the distinction between the two purposes of controls is sometimes lost. For example, in response to the Afghanistan invasion the U.S. government justified its actions both as a reevaluation of national-security problems and as a desire to put pressure on the Soviet Union to withdraw from Afghanistan.[6] However, U.S. allies find the distinction valuable for the degree of predictability it would add to export-control policy, and they prefer that the United States not confuse its motives in this manner.[7] In general, the United States has been more willing to embargo all sorts of goods for political ends than have Europe or Japan.

Albert Hirschman, in his classic work *National Power and the Structure of Foreign Trade*, notes two effects of foreign trade, which help clarify the two purposes of controls just discussed.[8] First, trade has a *supply effect*, meaning that imports will allow a state to use its resources more efficiently and thus potentially increase its military capabilities. National-security controls relate to this supply effect; these controls do not have specific foreign-policy goals but are intended to prevent their target from increasing its military potential. Second, states can use the threat of trade denial coercively, leading to an *influence effect*. Foreign-policy sanctions are an example of attempts to use the influence effect of trade, relying on economic denial to pressure the target into changing its policies.

Theoretically, the distinction between supply and influence effects does not necessarily coincide with a distinction between any particular denied goods. However, in practice, most CoCom members have argued that only denial of goods with some military significance is justified by national-security concerns. This argument relies on an underlying belief, which some American analysts question, that the Soviet economy is inefficient in translating the benefits of trade in most sectors of its economy to the military. Foreign-policy sanctions tend to address a broader range of goods than national-security controls. Europeans generally resist imposition of foreign-policy controls more strongly than national-security controls, for two reasons. European states are skeptical that foreign-policy controls will work—an observation that, like the earlier statistical evidence, calls into question the assertion of a simple positive relationship between cooperation and the ambitiousness of the goals of sanctions. Second, since these controls tend to cover a broader range of goods, they demand greater economic sacrifices.

The following sections discuss state export-control policies in some detail to clarify and support the general classification of goods and preferences just described. This background of state interests then provides the framework for analysis of the 1980 sanctions.


### The United States

Soon after the end of hostilities in World War II, the United States adopted a strategy of economic warfare vis-à-vis the Soviet bloc.[9] This strategy initially took the form of stringent unilateral U.S. licensing criteria, administered by the Commerce Department, on most exports to the Soviet Union and Eastern Europe.[10] From the beginning, the United States adopted a policy that was not dependent on the response of Western Europe; U.S. controls have consistently exceeded those applied by other countries. In 1948, this approach seemed reasonable, as Europe was in no condition to export much of significance to the East. As Representative Thomas Ashley later explained, Washington "believed, comparing our industrial might with both Eastern and Western Europe at the time, that goods withheld from the Soviets by means of controls on American commodities could not elsewhere be obtained."[11]

In 1949, Congress passed the Export Control Act (ECA), giving the president broad authority over peacetime control of exports to Communist nations.[12] This act remained the basis of U.S. export-control policy until 1969, when it was replaced by the Export Administration Act (EAA); however, the EAA did not change the complex U.S. licensing process. The control mechanism established in 1949 uses a system of general and validated licenses to control trade, requiring licenses for all exports.

The Commerce Department administers the system of validated licenses for exports to the East.

In the late 1940s, some of President Harry Truman's advisers, such as Under Secretary of State Robert Lovett, argued in favor of a control policy that focused on fewer, more-significant goods, rather than a near-total embargo.[13] However, the concept of a "strategic embargo" that expanded into genuine economic warfare won out. In 1949, Congress passed the Mutual Defense Assistance Control Act, more commonly known as the Battle Act (named after Senator Laurie Battle). This legislation tied economic and military assistance to other states to their cooperation in controlling exports to the Soviet bloc.

By 1969, the preferences of legislators had changed significantly, resulting in the passage of the Export Administration Act of 1969 (P.L. 91–184). The change in name from "control" to "administration" signified a deeper shift in the American strategy of economic relations with the East. The U.S. government had now moved from economic warfare to a strategic embargo, increasing exports of agricultural goods and slightly liberalizing controls on industrial items. The 1969 act also made "foreign availability" one of the criteria to be taken into account in licensing decisions, suggesting a move to a contingent strategy with regard to items such as type II goods, whose potential contribution to military capabilities was questionable.[14] Pressure from American business, which claimed that European companies were gaining a competitive advantage because of stringent U.S. export controls, pushed Congress toward this strategy.[15]

The Nixon administration had a more pro-trade attitude than its predecessors, but for political rather than economic reasons. The administration held that trade could contribute to more-stable relations between the United States and the Soviet Union. National Security Adviser Henry Kissinger's linkage strategy called for an increase in the level of U.S.-Soviet trade, an increase that would be conditional on improved political conditions.[16] The administration objected to the growing, unconditionally pro-trade attitude of Congress, which favored increasing trade regardless of political developments in the East. In response to executive lobbying, Congress, in passing the 1969 EAA, left the president with a great deal of flexibility to control exports, through "national-security" loopholes.[17] The early and mid-1970s saw a more-lenient U.S. export-control policy, based on this legislation and administration strategy. It resulted in an increase in U.S. exports to the Soviet Union, which rose from $144 million in 1971 to nearly $3.8 billion in 1979.[18] However, the United States continued to account for only 10 percent of Soviet imports of machinery and equipment, with grain sales accounting for most of the increase in trade.[19]

The political motivations of détente provided the major impetus for U.S. policy in the 1970s. Thus, when détente seemed to fail, U.S. policy turned back toward a more-cautious attitude on trade with the East. Some authors would date the demise of Kissinger's linkage strategy from the passage of the Jackson-Vanik amendment to the Export Administration Act of 1974; the amendment explicitly tied most-favored-nation (MFN) status for the Soviet Union to its emigration policies.[20] By 1979, debate in Congress focused on a report from the Defense Science Board (the Bucy Report) that called for tighter national-security controls on technology.[21] This attitude signaled a further move away from détente.

The Carter administration returned to a linkage strategy, although it favored more explicit and public linkages than did its predecessor. In August 1977, Presidential Directive No. 18 called for a strategy of economic diplomacy that would use both carrots and sticks to gain political concessions on human rights and foreign policy from the Soviet Union.[22] President Carter took advantage of the executive discretion written into the EAA to impose controls for foreign-policy reasons, such as protesting the trials of dissidents Aleksandr Ginzburg and Anatoly Shcharansky in 1978.[23] During the Carter administration, the use of sticks, or negative sanctions, appeared to predominate over the use of carrots, or positive inducements. Except for the 1980 grain embargo, these negative sanctions involved type II goods.

The domestic legacy of stringent export-control policies is a labyrinthine system for their administration, which has become increasingly complex even while underlying attitudes about the wisdom of stringent controls have wavered.[24] The U.S. system is considerably more complex and politicized than that of any of its allies.[25] It involves input from the departments of Commerce, State, and Defense, in addition to other participants; and it has resulted in lengthy delays for businesses seeking export licenses.[26]

Within the executive branch, the Department of Defense tends to be the most reluctant to approve licenses; the State Department tends to focus on the multilateral aspects of policy and so usually favors making decisions contingent on support from other states; and the Commerce Department seems to follow no consistent strategy, being torn between its functions of promoting trade and controlling it through the Office of Export Administration. The complex U.S. licensing system directly affects Europeans too, as it requires firms outside the United States to obtain re-export licenses before exporting any goods containing American components. These re-export controls frequently lead to conflict between Washington and other governments, as well as frustrating American business.

Throughout shifts in philosophy and strategy, the United States has maintained a unilateral control list (the Commodity Control List) that is considerably longer than the multilateral list agreed to in CoCom. As of 1979, the United States controlled 38 categories of items not on the multilateral lists.[27] However, the "U.S. differential" had declined significantly during the 1970s; in 1972, the United States formally controlled 461 items in addition to the 495 on the CoCom list.[28]

In general, American policy on East-West trade has tended to be dominated by political rather than economic considerations. As both a cause and an effect, U.S. trade with the Soviet Union never reached a level where American business as a whole had economic stakes comparable to those of European firms. For example, in 1981 total U.S. trade with the Soviet Union was $2.8 billion, only 5.6 percent of total Soviet trade with the West.[29] Considered in the aggregate, the economic benefits to the United States of trade with the Soviet Union are not large, although individual firms have considerable stakes in the completion of particular deals. In addition, the United States' role as leader of the Western alliance pushes the executive branch to give greater weight to national-security and foreign-policy concerns than do its allies.

Given the increasing ability of other suppliers to overwhelm the impact of unilateral export controls, we might expect to see U.S. preferences shift from coercion to coadjustment, and strategy from unconditional control to more-contingent measures. In practice, preferences and policies have fluctuated with the shifting balance of power between liberals and conservatives in Congress and in the presidency, in addition to responding to changing economic and political incentives. In general, the U.S. government continues to favor tighter controls than the Europeans; but a substantial faction has developed that recognizes the drawbacks of unconditional control—higher costs for domestic producers and incentives for allies to free-ride. As with the other case studies in this book that involve the United States, divisions such as this within the government raise serious questions of credibility and intentions when Washington undertakes coercive actions or promises benefits to gain cooperation. Other potential sanctioners need to guess at the likely outcome of American factional struggles, and the United States is forced to prove its credibility in order to gain cooperation. Self-imposed costs and international institutions are essential in this process.

The situation in the United States contrasts with those in the other CoCom members who are major technology exporters—Britain, France, Germany, and Japan. Attitudes, economic interests, and political structures vary across these countries, leading to characteristic policy positions on export controls.

## Britain

Among the European countries, Britain's attitude toward export control comes closest to that of the United States, although a large gap remains.[30] Britain typically follows a policy of separating economic from political issues when not under pressure from the United States. It is more dependent on international trade in general than is the United States, and it has a long tradition of free trade. Thus, there is a broad consensus that trade with the East is in the national interest.[31] Unless Britain is pressed by the Americans to adopt a specific restrictive policy, this consensus tends to dominate British export controls, pushing the recognized boundary between dual-use and nonstrategic goods to the left.

Britain has reached a series of agreements with the Soviet Union on economic relations, which contributed to Britain's attainment of a significant share of Western trade with the East before the country's position began to slip in the 1970s.[32] By 1977, Britain accounted for only 2.2 percent of Soviet high-technology imports from the West, and 6 percent of manufactures.[33] London appears to control carefully the export of goods of direct military significance but is skeptical of stringent controls on dual-use technology.[34] This dichotomy is evident in Britain's occasional denial of licenses that CoCom has approved, on national-security grounds, while it was Winston Churchill who took the lead in the 1950s in pushing for the end of the Western alliance's economic warfare against the Soviet Union.[35]

Britain often gives in to U.S. pressure to control type II goods, because of its strong commitment to the overall security relationship and because the economic stakes are low. However, it resists when it feels significant principles are at stake, such as extraterritoriality. For example, in 1970 the British threatened to veto all U.S. license requests in CoCom unless the United States removed a block on certain British computer exports to the Soviet Union. The United States backed down in CoCom but attempted to use re-export controls to prevent the sales, as the computers contained some American components. This effort failed.[36] The British suspected U.S. motives; it appeared that the American government might be attempting to buy time for its own computer firms, especially IBM, to build up their own marketing position.[37] This episode foreshadowed the pipeline case discussed in the next chapter, but such cases of serious conflict between the United States and Britain on national-security controls are relatively rare.

Britain does not have a political imperative to trade, as West Germany did (until 1990); and British firms prefer to focus on the English-speaking world rather than the less-familiar East European market. In addition, they are more reluctant to use methods such as countertrade (a form of barter) to overcome constraints imposed by shortages of hard currency. Thus, while there is no anti-trade lobby in Britain, as there is in the United States, there is no vigorous pro-trade lobby either. Instead, we find a consensus on normalization and consistency of economic relations with the East. These economic interests, as well as a low overall level of British trade with the East, make Britain more susceptible to U.S. pressure than France, for example. Export-control authority is contained in the Export of Goods (Control) Order under the Import, Export, and Customs Powers (Defence) Act of 1939. As in the United States, responsibility for export-control policy is spread among many agencies, and the defense ministry plays a significant role.

Overall, Britain appears to occupy a middle ground between the United States and continental Europe in terms of export-control policy. This has made British policy somewhat unpredictable, as the United States cannot always be sure which direction the government will lean in any particular conflict. In general, however, the British government will tend to support the United States on issues of national security; on foreign-policy questions, it tends to side with the other Europeans. These preferences lead to an assurance game with the United States on type I goods controlled for national-security reasons, but to coadjustment or coercion games on foreign-policy controls. Thus, American efforts to control type II or nonstrategic goods for foreign-policy reasons meet with some British resistance—although significantly less than in the case of France.

## France

If Britain is the European country most willing to control dual-use goods, France is the country most likely to refuse to impose such controls. A French scholar has summed up the underlying attitudes determining France's policy on East-West trade in this way: "France considers itself a power which seeks, with all available means, to preserve or expand its freedom to act."[38] France has felt that its foreign-policy and national-security interests are best served by a strong commitment to good relations with the Soviets, keeping economics and politics in separate spheres, and maintaining a position of relative independence from the United States. These attitudes lead to stiff resistance to controls for foreign-policy purposes.

Until approximately 1980, France ran a trade surplus with the Soviet

Union, but in the 1980s it ran a deficit as French imports of Soviet fuel rose. Overall trade with the East is not a large proportion of total French trade (only 4 percent in 1979), but some sectors depend quite heavily on the Council for Mutual Economic Assistance (CMEA) market.[39] For example, in 1980, 50.4 percent of French steel-pipe exports went to the East; the figures are 41.3 percent for compressors, 30 percent for steel strips, and 75.6 percent for metallurgical-testing machines.[40] Thus, some large firms have a significant stake in East-West trade, and they exert greater pressure on the government than do their counterparts in the United States. No clearly identified anti-trade lobbies have organized.

Until the late 1960s, French economic interests leaned heavily toward compliance with U.S. initiatives, in spite of underlying political incentives. French industry relied on U.S. technology and trade with the East was minimal, a situation that allowed Washington to exert coercive pressure. By the late 1970s, France had adopted a strongly pro-trade policy, trying to push the recognized boundary between dual-use and nonstrategic goods to the left in allied negotiations. It became the member of the alliance most skeptical of the benefits of CoCom, and the United States accused France of excessive laxity in its export-control system. France's policy led it to become the third-largest supplier of Western technology to the Soviet Union by the end of the 1970s, behind only West Germany and Japan—in spite of the fact that technology does not weigh heavily in French exports to the rest of the world.[41] Despite countervailing pressures, French officials claim to recognize the imperative for some strategic export controls; they have assurance preferences on at least a few goods.

No single export-control law covers all categories of goods in France. Instead, strategic goods are controlled under a 1944 decree, while munitions exports are covered by a 1939 law. A special commission made up of representatives from the ministries of finance, foreign affairs, and defense reviews applications for munitions sales.[42] French firms appear to work quite closely with government throughout the licensing process. In contrast to the American situation, the French government periodically publishes lists of controlled items, so that firms can quite easily predict the results of the licensing process.[43] As of 1980, customs officials made nearly all licensing decisions.

From this brief overview of underlying economic and political pressures, we might expect that France would offer the greatest resistance to American calls for sanctions in 1980. Concentrated economic interests, political pressures, dominant theories about the relationship between trade and security, and the structure of the domestic export-control process all tended to favor the continuation of normal trading relationships with the Soviet Union. These factors had to be weighed against the value of maintaining solidarity with the United States and retaining access to American technology, as well as against the severity of the security threat represented by the Soviet action in Afghanistan in December 1979.

### West Germany

If France's attitude toward export control is determined by its desire to maintain independence from the United States, West Germany's attitude was determined by the necessity of maintaining strong links to East Germany. (This discussion covers the period through 1989, and references to "Germany" mean West Germany.) One fact symbolizes this situation: trade with East Germany was considered, under West German law, as domestic rather than international trade.[44] Unlike the British, French, or Japanese, the Germans could not easily argue that they disdained the linkage of economics and politics, since they frequently made trade concessions in exchange for humanitarian actions in the East. Instead, they emphasized the benefits for both East and West of using positive inducements instead of negative sanctions.[45]

Since 1950, economic and political relations with the East have been bound up with each other in West German policy.[46] While close ties to East Germany pulled West Germany strongly to the East, for much of the postwar period military dependence on the United States exerted an equally strong pull to the West. At the same time that the West German government played an active role in negotiating trade agreements with CMEA countries, it avoided any open conflict with the United States, unlike France or Britain.[47] The traditionally high levels of trade between Germany and the East and a general perception that such trade is normal and desirable introduced a further complication.[48] The openness of West Germany's economy, in which foreign trade accounts for 30 percent of GNP, bolstered this consensus.[49] Thus, there were relatively few goods about whose control Germans had assurance preferences, but Germany seems more susceptible to U.S. pressure in coercion situations than France.

Since the 1970s, positive linkage policies and economic considerations made West Germany the East's major Western trading partner. In 1978, West German trade with Communist countries (including East Germany) totaled 38 billion deutsche marks, or 7.2 percent of total West German trade. West Germany also accounted for 21 percent of OECD (Organization for Economic Cooperation and Development) exports to Communist nations. In 1977, 34 percent of Soviet imports of high-technology goods came from West Germany.[50] Not surprisingly, some sectors of the West German economy relied heavily on exports to the East. The post-1969

German policy of creating "webs of interdependence" appears to have succeeded.

In contrast to the situation in the United States, under German law exporting was a right that can be interrupted by the government only for national-security purposes. The foreign economic law and decree of 1961 regulate trade with Eastern countries other than East Germany. The government created lists of controlled goods, which were nearly identical to the CoCom lists. The German government had no legal provision for applying controls for reasons other than national security, and the legislature had veto power over any export regulations. In 1978, when President Carter announced limited sanctions on the Soviet Union for human-rights reasons, the German foreign ministry announced that it would never link exports to domestic developments in the Soviet Union.[51] This argument, however, fits somewhat uncomfortably with the frequent use of positive sanctions to influence East German emigration policy. A more-accurate assessment would be that politically, it was difficult for the German government to cut exports to the East for reasons other than national security.

However, West Germany cooperated closely with CoCom on exports of goods with potential military applications. In spite of a desire to increase trade, it did not push other members to reduce the number of goods controlled for national-security reasons. Although the question of leakage through Berlin or East Germany frequently arose, the West German government applied CoCom regulations to trade with East Germany, and there was no evidence of large-scale evasion.[52]

The preferences that result from these conflicting pressures on West Germany's export-control policy mean that trade was valued more highly than in Britain but that West Germany was more open to U.S. pressure than France. West Germany offered little resistance to long-term national-security controls, but it opposed the imposition of negative sanctions intended to achieve foreign-policy goals. However, for much of the postwar period West Germany was highly susceptible to U.S. pressure, so these preferences did not lead to refusals to join in American-inspired sanctions. The Germans complied because issue linkages—through NATO, for example—made resisting the United States a costly proposition.

## Japan

On the surface, Japanese export-control policy resembles the German policy quite closely: economic demands pull strongly in one direction while security incentives pull strongly in the other. One important difference lies in the fact that Japan does not use positive incentives to gain political concessions to the same extent as West Germany. Nevertheless, business pressures and a desire to avoid antagonizing the United States mean that Japan's East-West trade strategy resembles the German one in many respects. Industry and trading consortiums play a larger role in determining Japan's control policy than they do in other CoCom nations. However, the Japanese government is highly responsive to American policy—although it will not institute economic sanctions on its own initiative. According to Gordon Smith, "While the government of Japan does not simply mimic U.S. policies, American policies and pressures are keenly felt and present Japanese leaders with real constraints in formulating their trade policies toward the USSR and Eastern Europe."[53]

Japan does not have a history of significant trade with the Soviet Union prior to the 1960s. However, for a country that imports over 99 percent of its oil, Soviet oil and gas reserves were bound to prove tempting. Beginning in the mid-1960s, Japanese businessmen quietly set about negotiating deals with the Soviet Union, including three major joint projects to provide Japan with energy imports.[54] Following the American lead, the Japanese government more openly encouraged trade in the 1970s. While a major deal to develop the Tyumen oil field fell through in 1974, bilateral trade grew rapidly in this decade.[55]

Japan also imports significant amounts of raw materials other than energy from the Soviet Union.[56] In return Japan exports technology; in 1977 it accounted for 18 percent of the technological goods and 87 percent of the oil-refining equipment the Soviet Union imported from the West.[57] Although Japan runs a slight trade surplus with the Soviet Union, a study by the U.S. Office of Technology Assessment (OTA) concluded that it was probably more dependent on Soviet imports than vice versa. Thus, adoption of a policy of interrupting trade for foreign-policy reasons would be quite costly.[58]

The legal framework for export controls derives from the Foreign Exchange and Foreign Trade Control Act of 1949. Drafted while Japan was under U.S. occupation, this act emulates the old U.S. Export Control Act.[59] The law now specifies that exporters should be allowed to operate with a "minimum of restrictions," although the Ministry of International Trade and Industry (MITI) may impose embargoes for up to one month and punish companies that violate these regulations. The Japanese control lists closely resemble the CoCom lists, although they also include chemicals that could be used for chemical warfare. The government, prior to the Toshiba Corporation's evasion of controls that was revealed in 1987, put little effort into following up its licensing decisions with monitoring or enforcement.[60]

If Japan did not rely on the United States in matters of national security and did not value access to American technology, we might expect the government to control only those items with the most direct military applications. However, the United States has used its bargaining power to gain Japanese cooperation in CoCom, and the Japanese have not mounted a sustained resistance to this pressure. As is evident in the other cases in this study, Japan follows a bandwagoning strategy, acting in concert with Europe and the United States. Taking these factors into consideration, we might expect that in 1980 the United States would quietly receive some minimal acceptable level of cooperation from Japan, but we should not expect to see the Japanese taking the initiative in imposing sanctions, especially on technology.

## Summary

This overview of the national export-control policies of the major CoCom members provides the framework for a study of multilateral coordination of export-control policies. While we find differences among the attitudes and interests of the Europeans and Japanese and numerous crosscutting pressures, it is possible to distinguish a "Euro-Japanese" viewpoint from that of the United States. With greater dependence on international trade, more-significant economic ties to the East, and domestic political pressures (in the French and German cases), these states have strong incentives to free-ride on the foreign-policy sanctions of the United States. For national-security reasons, the Europeans and Japanese control munitions and type I goods. However, U.S. foreign-policy sanctions ask them to extend controls to type II goods or even some nonstrategic items. Here, the United States faces a coercion game.

Regarding national-security controls, each country would impose export controls on munitions regardless of the policies of the others, but the extent of these controls might be minimal. Governments are willing to control dual-use goods with obvious military relevance (type I goods) as long as they are sure that others are not free-riding. Type II goods present a more-difficult cooperation problem that offers greater incentives to defect. The United States, because of its role as alliance leader and its low level of economic ties to the East, tends to put more weight on the political benefits of sanctions and so adopts them more frequently than the Europeans and Japanese would. This balance also means that the United States would prefer more-expansive controls for national-security reasons than would the Europeans and Japanese, although the preferred extent of these controls has varied over time. Internal divisions have their greatest impact on policy in the United States, where the legislature and the Department of Defense play an unusually significant role in export-control policy.

## Institutional Coordination of
## Export Controls: CoCom

In 1980, the United States used an existing institution, CoCom, to gain agreement on tightening controls on technology sales to the Soviet Union in response to the invasion of Afghanistan. The NATO allies established CoCom on 22 November 1949 for the purpose of coordinating their export-control policies. Today, CoCom's membership consists of all members of NATO (except Iceland), Japan, and Australia.[61] CoCom is an informal organization not covered by any treaty; it is sometimes described as a gentlemen's agreement. Because public debate about CoCom would cause problems in some European states, its workings are not made public. Only the United States publishes any information on the organization. Its formal purpose is to establish three lists of controlled goods—munitions, atomic-energy products, and industrial goods—and to decide on requests for exceptions to allow specific exports of goods on these lists. In addition, CoCom informally provides information on members' national export-control policies and allows some coordination of enforcement efforts.

In this section, I look at the history of multilateral export controls since 1947. The major point of this examination is to determine to what extent the CoCom regime allows the West to overcome a collective-action problem, provides a forum for the United States to pressure the Europeans and Japanese into cooperation, or is simply irrelevant. The distinctions used in the previous section—types of goods and purposes of controls—will help us understand the changing nature of multilateral export-control policy and the attitudes of various states toward CoCom. With this background, I will go on to ask more directly about the role of CoCom in determining responses to the invasion of Afghanistan and to dissident trials.

### Economic Warfare: The Early Years of Export Controls

There is a debate in the sanctions literature about the nature of cooperation between 1947 and 1954, when CoCom pursued an extremely stringent export-control policy. On the one hand, many authors have argued that extensive cooperation during this period was the result of U.S. coercion, possible because of the United States' overwhelming power vis-à-vis Europe.[62] On the other hand, recent research calls this finding into question, arguing that common interests among the allies accounted for cooperation during this period. Michael Mastanduno, for example, finds that the Korean War convinced the Europeans of a genuine national-security threat from the East and made them more than willing to impose extensive export controls.[63] Framing the question in the terms used in this study, we need to ask whether the cooperation problem during 1947–54 is coercion or coincidence. Both sides in the debate offer persuasive evidence.

The United States unilaterally began to control exports to the Soviet Union in 1948. The control policies of the Western European states, given the condition of their economies in that year, were not of vital importance. However, the United States intended, through the Marshall Plan, to help rebuild their industrial capacity as quickly as possible. Thus, in 1948 the American government initiated a series of bilateral talks with Marshall Plan aid recipients on the topic of East-West trade. In the same year, Britain and France established their own joint list of embargoed goods, although it was much more restricted in scope than the U.S. list.[64]

To coordinate these bilateral efforts, the United States set up the multilateral Consultative Group on Export Control (CG) in 1949; its formation was coincident with the passage of the Export Control Act. While the CG was a high-level group that set overall export-control policy, a committee that met more frequently had to be established to carry on day-to-day business. This committee became known as the Coordinating Committee, or CoCom.

The multilateral discussions within CoCom began with the items on the Anglo-French list and added goods to this list until CoCom covered approximately four hundred categories of goods by April 1952.[65] Meanwhile, the American unilateral list covered an additional one hundred categories. Clearly, even from the beginning the United States was not able to impose absolutely its preferences on the Europeans and chose to follow more-stringent unilateral guidelines. U.S. representatives were quite pleased with their accomplishments in CoCom, however, explaining that "coordinated and simultaneous action was essential to effective regulation to dispel the feeling that Country A was doing more than Country B was willing to do."[66] This assessment suggests that the regular multilateral meetings did help overcome some type of collective-action problem such as an assurance game.

However, U.S. officials felt that since CoCom had no enforcement procedures, some threat of punishment was needed to back up the multilateral agreements. Accepting the role of enforcer, the United States began to link export controls to American military and economic assistance. Congress passed legislation tying such aid to recipients' observance of export controls. The first moves came with the Cannon amendment of 1950 and the Kem amendment of 1951, both of which allowed the government to cut off aid to any countries that exported goods to the Soviet bloc that were embargoed by the United States.[67] It is interesting that these amendments referred to the American rather than the multilateral lists. This suggests that the legislation was not only a backup to CoCom, but also an effort to coerce the allies into accepting a more-expansive embargo than they preferred—to engage in economic warfare. While the Europeans may have been engaged in a coadjustment game among themselves on goods of less-than-direct military significance, the U.S. government perceived itself as playing a coercion game vis-à-vis each of its allies on these goods and thus needing to forge a link between technology transfer and aid.

In the Cannon and Kem amendments, there were limits to the types of aid that the United States could cut and the situations under which the amendments applied. In late 1951, both were superseded by the Battle Act. This act allowed the president to cut military, financial, and economic aid; Congress saw cutoffs of Marshall Plan assistance as a potent threat. The Battle Act applied in peacetime as well as during hostilities. It called for a cutoff of all American aid if a country was found to ship any "category A" items—munitions and atomic-energy materials. Sales of "category B" items—those with strategic value—would result in aid termination unless the president determined that this step would be detrimental to the security of the United States.

In practice, the hostilities in Korea, combined with general strategic uncertainty, created a high degree of common interest in not shipping category A goods even without U.S. threats. The U.S. government had uncovered no instances of shipment of such goods by the end of 1956.[68] Mastanduno's assessment that cooperation in imposing controls on this category of items was a case of "congruent interests," or coincidence— rather than U.S. coercion—seems amply supported.[69] In other words, during the Korean War Europeans had harmony or assurance preferences on a large range of items, although never as large a range as the United States.

The situation was more complex in the area of category B, or dual-use, goods—those that were not munitions but had strategic value. As of the end of 1956, the United States had uncovered twenty-nine separate incidents of shipment of such goods by seven different countries.[70] However, the president determined in every case that cutting assistance would be detrimental to national security, and took no action. This failure to cut aid suggests that the credibility of the U.S. threat was quite low and that Europeans were willing to cheat and sell some type II goods in spite of this threat. The next chapter examines a similar lack of credibility in the 1982 pipeline case. However, the fact that Washington backed down in the 1950s undercuts arguments that the 1982 failure was due to declining U.S. hegemony, since hegemony was not the cause of extensive cooperation earlier. The Europeans in the 1950s were sufficiently dependent on the United States that they avoided openly threatening the institutional framework, but they realized they could get away with occasional free-riding.

In Congress, Senator Laurie Battle (of the Battle Act) continued to insist that U.S. negotiators relied on threats of aid cutoffs and that these threats persuaded the Europeans to cooperate.[71] In fact, there is little evidence to back up this assertion, and interpretations that see multilateral agreements on strategic goods as the solution to a collective-action dilemma rather than as a coercion game conform better to the facts. The United States preferred more-stringent controls than the Europeans, and the government could not credibly threaten to sell its own technology if the Europeans did not control theirs—domestic outcry in the United States would have prevented such sales. In addition, threats to cut aid were not credible, since the United States valued highly the recovery of friendly nations. Thus, while the American government found itself in a situation of coercion on nonstrategic goods, it was unable to find a linkage that allowed it to impose all of its preferences on the Europeans.

U.S. pressure probably did extend the embargo to a slightly larger range of goods than the Europeans would have controlled on their own, into the type II area; and it backed up agreements reached in CoCom. It helped the Europeans to overcome the coadjustment dilemma they faced on type II goods and the assurance problem on type I goods. European states claimed to be willing to control many goods as long as the others did as well.[72] While they had "congruent interests" on controlling goods with clearest military significance—type I goods—Europeans needed reassurance that other Europeans would recognize these common interests and prevent their firms from exporting. Thus, common interests alone were not sufficient to insure cooperation on type I goods; the CoCom forum, backed up by American pressure, helped alleviate suspicion that other states were cheating and thus increased willingness to cooperate.

To summarize, Europeans' perceptions of Soviet aggressiveness during the Korean War meant that they faced an assurance game on many goods, and CoCom allowed them to cooperate. After 1954, the range of goods recognized as type I—the area of congruent interests—shrank considerably. In addition, consistent U.S. pressure led to agreements to control some type II goods; but states did sometimes defect from these agreements, not believing American threats to cut aid.

In 1951, the members of CoCom established an "exceptions" procedure that allowed a country, with the unanimous consent of the other members, to sell particular goods that were formally subject to the CoCom embargo. As Mastanduno and others have argued, the United States agreed to this exceptions procedure to allow other members to make sales without the United States' having to invoke the provisions of the Battle Act.[73] In other words, this procedure allowed European members to defect "legally" from agreements on type II goods. In the 1970s, in an ironic twist, the United States frequently availed itself of this loophole. Deciding on exceptions came to constitute one of the major functions of the weekly CoCom meetings. The exceptions procedure also provided, in 1980, a mechanism that the United States could use to pressure other CoCom members into cutting high-technology sales to the Soviet Union. Because each exception requires approval by all CoCom members, the United States could veto requests, thus forcing members to evade CoCom if they wished to make such sales. I will discuss U.S. utilization of the exceptions procedure later in this chapter.

### Gradual Relaxation of the Strategic Embargo: 1954–79

As the situation in Korea cooled off, the European allies became disenchanted with the broad scope of the strategic embargo. Defection began with a speech by Winston Churchill on 25 February 1954 that called for relaxing the embargo on nonmilitary goods.[74] Churchill wanted, that is, to push the cutoff point for controlled goods closer to the militarily-significant end of the spectrum, validating the occasional evasion already occurring. Secretary of State John Foster Dulles responded by stating that the United States desired tighter control but could not impose its own views on others.[75] Given the waning of the Marshall Plan aid lever, this argument convinced Congress as well as the executive branch. In the first of many such moves, the United States agreed in August 1954 to reduce the scope of the CoCom lists in exchange for European promises to improve enforcement of the new, shorter lists. The move toward controlling only goods closer to the direct-military-significance end of the spectrum continued with further reduction of the lists in 1958.[76] The United States relaxed its efforts to coerce others into control of nonstrategic and many type II goods, restricting CoCom to those issues on which members had a coincidence of interests and played a harmony or assurance game.

During the 1960s, the scope of the CoCom lists did not change drastically. In this period, U.S. officials came to value CoCom more highly, because unilateral American controls on technology appeared less likely to have any impact on the Soviet Union as other CoCom members gained the capacity to export significant amounts of comparable technology to the Soviet bloc. In 1962, Secretary of State Dean Rusk argued against unilateral action, pointing both to the political friction it created with allies and to the fact that "the economic effect of a unilateral embargo would be trivial because of the small amount of trade we have with the Sino-Soviet bloc."[77] Echoing this statement, George Ball, then the U.S.

ambassador to the UN, argued that "we can no longer, merely by our own unilateral action, limit the economic strength of the Communist countries in any significant way."[78]

This process continued into the 1970s, with the United States backing down from its traditional leadership position within CoCom. Instead of pushing for more-stringent controls, the United States became the CoCom member requesting the largest number of exceptions. Prior to 1969, the number of exceptions granted in CoCom remained quite low; for example, the organization approved only $19 million of exceptions requests in 1969. However, by 1977 CoCom approved $214 million in exceptions.[79] The explanation for this change lies almost entirely in changing American behavior. In the years 1974 to 1977, CoCom considered a total of 5,322 exceptions requests, approving all but 101. Of these 5,322 requests, the United States accounted for 2,241, or 42 percent. Only one of the disapproved cases originated in the United States, suggesting that the U.S. representatives were essentially the only ones to use their veto power.[80] Thus, the United States attempted to enforce rules on some type II goods in the late 1970s, but not against itself.

Given this behavior from the country that was supposed to be providing unwavering commitment to export control, it is not surprising that CoCom experienced institutional decay during the 1970s. As former U.S. representative to CoCom William Root explained, U.S. allies "want the United States to continue to discipline the system."[81] They could not overcome coadjustment problems with Washington acting this way. Some officials later described CoCom during the 1970s as a "sleepy backwater," operating with a hand-cranked mimeograph machine until 1981 and on an annual operating budget of only $500,000.[82] As in the other cases in this study, uncertainty about the intentions of the United States undermined cooperation efforts.

During that decade, American interests came to resemble those of the European countries more closely, with greater weight given to economic interests and less willingness to impose unilateral controls. The Europeans and Japanese began to suspect that the United States was cheating, using CoCom to gain commercial advantages by vetoing others' sales while approving sales from its own firms.[83] Therefore, the institution lost some of its value, and it exerted few constraints on sales of type II goods. Suspicions of U.S. defection even threatened cooperation on type I goods, where members had assurance preferences. While U.S. behavior was more likely the result of uncoordinated actions by various agencies than a well-planned strategy to achieve a competitive edge, this period demonstrates the need for states to avoid creating the perception of cheating in order to maintain cooperation in an assurance game under conditions of uncertainty.

CoCom members continued to value the organization for its role in regulating type I goods. However, CoCom exerted little influence on sales of type II technologies in the 1970s. During this period, CoCom's principal function was to provide information on others' preferences, to show where the game shifted from assurance to one where states had incentives to defect from multilateral controls. CoCom was not strong enough to maintain cooperation in the latter situation, and some members worried about its competence in the former. Thus, when the Soviets invaded Afghanistan, President Carter found himself faced with a weak institution within which to pursue new controls on technology exports.

## Responding to the Soviet Invasion of Afghanistan, 1980

Beginning on the night of 25 December 1979, the Soviet Union sent its troops into Afghanistan, replacing Prime Minister Hafizullah Amin with Babrak Kamal, considered a pro-Moscow Marxist.[84] The invasion followed two years of internal upheaval in Afghanistan. The American government had seen signs of a possible Soviet move as early as September but had engaged in only preliminary talks with its allies to formulate possible responses.

### American Reaction to the Invasion

The Carter administration saw the Soviet move as profoundly disturbing for two reasons. First, as Secretary of State Cyrus Vance explained, this was the first military occupation of a non–Communist bloc country since World War II.[85] As Carter notes in his memoirs, the Soviets had used proxy troops for such actions before. "However, this was the first time they had used their troops to expand their sphere of influence since they had overthrown the government of Czechoslovakia in February 1948."[86] In addition, Secretary Vance saw the invasion as threatening because it moved the Soviets closer to the West's oil supplies.

The United States responded with actions in three areas: efforts to build a regional security framework, reexamination of the U.S. strategic doctrine and defense budget, and economic sanctions. While the U.S. government called for the Soviet Union to withdraw immediately from Afghanistan, National Security Adviser Zbigniew Brzezinski admits that he had no illusions that sanctions could make the Soviet Union withdraw, although they were necessary so that the Soviets would at least have to "pay a price" for their actions.[87]

Beginning on 30 December 1979, the administration undertook a series of meetings in which officials decided on a number of unilateral and multilateral sanctions. Deputy Secretary of State Warren Christopher traveled to Europe to consult with the allies. Sanctions implemented included restrictions on sales of grain and on high-technology exports, as well as restrictions on exports of phosphates to supplement the grain embargo. Exports for a Kama River truck plant were terminated, on evidence that trucks from this plant had been used in the invasion. Later, the United States also banned exports of goods and services connected to the 1980 Moscow Summer Olympics and boycotted the games. In addition, Washington cut back Soviet fishing and landing rights and scientific and cultural exchanges.[88]

According to Brzezinski, a decision on 4 January to link the grain and technology embargoes was important. The administration realized that the grain embargo would meet stiff resistance in Congress and from farmers but felt that the technology ban would not stick without it. Brzezinski, "feared that without such an embargo the business community would be more effective in lobbying against the more stringent controls on technology transfer that I strongly favored."[89] This statement points to the domestic impact of the costs of sanctions. If the administration was not willing to bear the economic and political heat of a grain embargo, it would have a hard time facing down its own exporters of high technology. As the next chapter shows, the willingness to impose a grain embargo was also essential on the international level, to persuade other states to cooperate.

While the administration mistakenly believed that the Soviet Union would have a difficult time quickly finding new sources of grain—the Agriculture Department reported that Argentina was not a significant supplier—it immediately recognized the need for cooperation on technology controls and took a multilateral approach. However, it also was clear that the United States would not be able to convince its allies to bear heavier costs than it did itself. The administration had to confront the problem of taking the lead in imposing sanctions, but without appearing to bully other nations into cooperating. Carter noted in his diary on 4 January that CoCom should become a forum for multilateral sanctions against the Soviet Union.[90]

President Carter announced the imposition of economic sanctions on 4 January. Actions taken immediately included an embargo on seventeen million tons of grain (although eight million tons previously contracted for would be delivered), termination of Soviet fishing rights, and delay of diplomatic and cultural exchanges. Carter announced that all high-technology sales would be discontinued until further notice, pending a review of export-control policy.[91] This delay would give the United States time to coordinate high-technology sanctions with its allies, who expressed strong political support for the U.S. actions but were more reticent about imposing their own sanctions. Britain, Canada, and Japan expressed approval of U.S. sanctions and claimed to be studying possible responses of their own, although these would more likely be diplomatic than economic.[92] Some governments threatened to ignore potential formal U.S. vetoes of high-technology sales, signaling resistance to economic steps.[93] The allies, seeing the United States take strong steps and aware of the high domestic costs they would have to pay to impose foreign-policy sanctions, preferred to let the United States act alone, as in a typical coercion game. Washington would have to turn to other mechanisms to gain their assistance.

The French government was initially more restrained in its support of the United States than the British. President Valéry Giscard d'Estaing, however, assured Carter that French firms would not provide supplies cut off by the United States—a relatively strong expression of cooperation, given previous French behavior (such as that in the 1978 case, discussed below). Chancellor Helmut Schmidt of West Germany warned the United States that his country could not engage in "reprisals" or follow the American lead on denying grain or credits; he did not specifically mention technology.[94] Schmidt pointed out the need for solidarity in the West, however, and also agreed not to replace sales lost because of U.S. sanctions.[95]

On 9 January, the U.S. government clarified its position on high-technology sales, freezing all current shipments and suspending all existing licenses. The administration predicted that the freeze would last for four to six weeks while U.S. policy was reviewed. Administration spokesmen stressed the importance of persuading others to cooperate in the technology embargo, noting that consultations had begun but that the reaction of other states was still uncertain. The six-week limit allowed the United States to "take the lead," while putting the allies on notice that they might not be able to free-ride on these controls indefinitely.

Officials attributed the mildly positive response they had received so far partly to the American grain embargo, arguing that it had given the United States "credibility."[96] These statements are especially interesting, as they support the finding that high costs for the leading sender tend, in the aggregate, to increase the level of cooperation on sanctions. They suggest that because the United States was willing to bear the costs of the grain embargo, it gained bargaining power on the high-technology issue. The costs of the grain embargo helped convince the Europeans that the U.S. government was serious about imposing sanctions, would not cheat on multilateral sanctions agreements, and would attempt to make the Europeans pay if they refused to impose high-technology sanctions. In this coercion game, the United States had to make credible threats and promises in order to gain its allies' cooperation; bearing high costs helped make these threats credible. The next chapter further explores the link between costs and credibility, showing what happened when Washington rejected a grain embargo in 1982.

On 11 January, the administration took more steps to bolster its credibility. Secretary of Commerce Philip M. Klutznick announced that eight applications for licenses to sell technology to the Soviet Union had been denied. However, questioning from journalists revealed that these licenses would have been denied for national-security reasons even before the invasion of Afghanistan and that the Department of Commerce had been instructed by the White House to find and publicize some cases of denial; the administration was apparently attempting to take actions to enhance its credibility.[97] The Department of Commerce also released figures to quantify the direct costs to the United States of the technology embargo. It predicted that the sanctions would reduce U.S. technology exports to the Soviet Union from a previously expected value of $200 million to just $50 million.[98]


### European Responses

In studying European countries' decisions on economic sanctions, we find strong evidence of bandwagoning behavior. Above all, no European state nor Japan wanted to be isolated, and their statements about sanctions always stressed the importance of unity.[99] For example, when Britain announced diplomatic sanctions on 24 January but stopped short of cutting trade, London said that decisions on economic sanctions depended on the results of consultations among the Western allies.[100] When British attempts to "spearhead" European sanctions failed, Foreign Secretary Lord Carrington announced that the government would continue to apply the principle of mutual advantage to British-Soviet trade, suggesting that London would not impose sanctions without European support.[101] The U.S. government expected some kind of contingent behavior, as Under Secretary of State for Economic Affairs Richard Cooper stated: "Very few countries on their own can have the kind of impact through their own actions on the Soviet Union that the United States can, so it is quite natural that they follow the U.S. lead in this regard."[102]

West Germany appeared to be close to the British position—mildly pro-sanctions—thus threatening to leave France alone in resisting U.S. pressure, a position France wanted to avoid in this highly public case.[103]

Regarding other European states, "the smaller allies [were] somewhere in the middle, hoping for a cue from their larger partners."[104] On 5 February, the French and West German foreign ministries announced that their opposition to sanctions was fading as support for action against the Soviet Union increased throughout the world.[105] As the Congressional Research Service later concluded, while the Europeans eventually pledged not to take advantage of U.S. restrictions on technology, "in most cases such willingness was predicated on like responses by the other CoCom countries."[106] As in the Falklands case, European responses were dominated by positive contagion, or bandwagoning. Overall, the Europeans seem to have found themselves in a coadjustment game with one another, while responding to serious pressure from the American government to impose sanctions. This configuration of interests led to chain-ganging behavior, as U.S. actions supported the precarious multilateral sanctions outcome within Europe. Each country's incentive to defect was reduced by the strong possibility of U.S. retaliation.

In February, with the content of European sanctions still undefined, the administration sent Secretary of State Vance to Europe to coordinate a meeting of foreign ministers, tentatively scheduled for 20 February.[107] However, France continued to resist U.S. pressure, preferring to stick to a policy of avoiding confrontation with the Soviet Union, and so pulled out of the meeting.[108] Instead, Vance met with Foreign Minister Hans-Dietrich Genscher of West Germany and then moved on to France for bilateral talks.[109] As the Europeans were meeting to coordinate their own policies at this time, Vance's visit was intended to persuade them to lean toward imposing sanctions.[110] However, Vance found that the allies thought they should have been consulted much earlier. As he explains in his memoirs, "upset at what they viewed as inadequate consultations on a common Western approach before we announced far-reaching punitive steps, some felt we had adopted a confrontational strategy without taking European interests into account."[111] This trip achieved some agreement on the general need for sanctions, but Vance was unable to persuade the French government to move closer to the U.S. position.[112]

By this time, the United States was nearing the deadline on its "policy review" and needed to determine whether to impose longer-term sanctions on technology, bringing the question of European actions to a head. The key player was Bonn. If the German government decided to impose sanctions, the French would go along to avoid being isolated, and "Japan [was] expected to go along basically with whatever economic sanctions against the Soviet Union may be agreed to by the U.S. and its NATO allies."[113] By this time, Carter had identified CoCom—specifically, the use of the exceptions procedure and increasing the scope of the lists—as potential multilateral foci.

### CoCom's Role in the Afghanistan Sanctions

With hindsight, we can see that the exceptions procedure provided an especially promising venue for cooperation. Because the United States requested more exceptions than any other country, it would bear a large share of the costs of implementing a no-exceptions policy; such a demonstration of commitment could lead to cooperation in the Europeans' coadjustment game. In addition, institutional considerations made the exceptions procedure an attractive tool. Because approval of exceptions requests required a unanimous vote in CoCom, the United States could simply announce that it would veto all exceptions requests. Other states could evade this action only by avoiding the CoCom forum entirely, using national-discretion clauses to approve licenses without the agreement of other CoCom members. However, large-scale use of this escape clause would have threatened CoCom's viability. Because CoCom played a valuable role in assurance games, members were reluctant to destroy it by massive defiance of restrictions in a coadjustment game. Such action would undermine CoCom's information-providing function on type I goods.

The United States thus managed to force other CoCom members to agree to a "no-exceptions" policy on sales to the Soviet Union in retaliation for the invasion.[114] The Carter administration announced on 18 March that it would request no exceptions for sales to the Soviet Union.[115] Although a few instances of states—particularly France—evading this policy have been revealed, there is no evidence that Europeans routinely ignored CoCom restrictions.[116] William Root, the U.S. representative to CoCom from 1976 to 1983, has said that "the only multilaterally supported sanction in response to the Soviet invasion of Afghanistan . . . was the no-exceptions policy on exports of security items to Moscow."[117] Because states had come to recognize the value of CoCom over the last thirty years, they were unwilling to put the entire institution at risk by defying the policy.

As we would expect from the statistical analysis presented earlier in this study, involving CoCom increased the level of bandwagoning. Some states, such as Japan, made their sanctions policies directly dependent on the agreements reached within CoCom.[118] Japan adopted this policy because it "did not want to sacrifice trade with the Communist countries through measures sought unilaterally," according to Prime Minister Masayoshi Ohira.[119] Chancellor Schmidt made a similar argument, saying that "West Germany would go along with additional tightening of the rules governing export of strategic goods—providing all Western Bloc allies do the same."[120] He singled out the European Community and CoCom as institutions whose decisions would affect the decisions of the West German government.[121] Even some officials in the United States argued for making continued restrictions on high-technology exports dependent on CoCom's decisions. One argued that "if we act alone and our CoCom partners pick up the business, the Soviets aren't hurt but we are."[122] Again, CoCom provided essential information about the extent to which others imposed sanctions, helping to maintain the fragile coadjustment outcome.

While some officials in Washington argued against unilateral controls on technology, the administration never decided that the United States would impose such controls only if it gained the support of other CoCom members. Thus, the American government found itself in a situation of coercion—of linking other issues to high-technology sanctions in order to gain others' cooperation. The no-exceptions policy constituted a case of foreign-policy sanctions, since it led to increased denial of high-technology exports. CoCom provided a linkage between these sanctions and national-security controls. Not surprisingly, given this logic, we find Washington defining the question of technology controls as one of national security rather than simply a foreign-policy matter.[123] William Root credits this strategy with helping the United States gain British support for technology controls.[124] President Carter made this linkage more explicit by stating that "some countries had failed to live up to their obligations to the United States while expecting its protection."[125] U.S. statements attempted to tighten the linkage between national-security controls on militarily significant goods and foreign-policy sanctions. In addition, negotiators appear to have used quiet suggestions that European access to American technology could be restricted if the U.S. government could not trust the Europeans to refrain from re-exporting American components to the Soviet Union.

### Summary

In 1982, the European Parliament undertook a study of economic sanctions, based in part on an examination of the 1980 sanctions that were a response to the invasion of Afghanistan. Two of the recommendations of this report point to the factors I have focused on here—bandwagoning and costs. The parliament recommended that "the unconditional support and full cooperation of all the EEC member states and other countries involved in the imposition of sanctions must be established before any such measures are taken."[126] In addition, the parliament urged that efforts be made to spread the costs of sanctions as evenly as possible across national economies. Although Washington never achieved the "unconditional support" called for in this report, it was able to achieve enough *contingent* support to maintain cooperation.

Overall, the United States was able to achieve a modest amount of cooperation from Europe and Japan on imposing high-technology sanctions on the Soviet Union in 1980, in spite of substantial resistance. Unlike cooperation in 1950, with the outbreak of war in Korea, this was not a simple case of common interests naturally leading to independent decisions to impose sanctions. Instead, states expressly made their own willingness to sanction dependent on the decisions of other states and of an international institution. Thus, we see a great deal of bandwagoning behavior in the pattern of government decisions to impose or not impose sanctions. In addition, in this case we find that relatively high costs borne by the United States, both from the grain embargo and the high-technology sanctions, had a positive impact on its ability to persuade others to cooperate. These costs increased Washington's credibility, putting substance behind the American commitment to multilateral sanctions. CoCom facilitated cooperation by covering both type I and type II goods—thus linking assurance and coadjustment games—and through its exceptions mechanism, which the United States could manipulate to raise the costs of defection.

## Responding to Dissident Trials, 1978

In 1980, the Carter administration successfully used CoCom to overcome resistance from its European allies to imposing sanctions on high-technology exports to the Soviet Union. This outcome contrasts sharply with that of a similar case—attempts to restrict high-technology exports in 1978. I discuss this case briefly in this section, because it supports the claim that self-imposed costs and the CoCom institution were central to success in 1980. Two years earlier, while imposing similar sanctions on the Soviets, the Carter administration failed to use these two means to establish a credible commitment to the sanctions. As we would expect, no cooperation resulted. In fact, other countries, particularly France, refused even to go so far as to avoid taking advantage of the U.S. actions. This case emphasizes the causal roles of institutions and, particularly, self-imposed costs.

During 1977 and 1978, the Soviet government arrested a number of dissidents, charging them with treason. These actions came on top of others that had bothered Washington, including the arrest of an American businessman and the harassment of two U.S. journalists who were charged with libel.[127] Two of the arrested dissidents were well known in the West—Aleksandr Ginzburg and Anatoly Shcharansky. In July 1978, a week after they were tried, found guilty, and sentenced to prison, labor camps, and exile (for Ginzburg), President Carter responded by canceling the sale of a Sperry-Univac computer to the Soviet news agency Tass and by announcing that all exports of oil technology to the Soviet Union would now require validated licenses.[128] The Sperry computer was intended largely for use during the 1980 Moscow Olympics, although it would continue to be used by Tass after this event. Sperry had "lobotomized" the computer—modifying it to reduce its capabilities in order to prevent military applications—prior to this cancellation.[129]

The validated-license procedure for oil-technology exports reversed a 1972 decision by the Nixon administration to allow export of these goods, except those with military applications. Now, the Commerce Department had to review every potential sale and had veto power over each. This move was seen as an attempt to gain leverage over the Soviets and was enforced over the strong objections of representatives from State and Commerce; it had the support of National Security Adviser Brzezinski and Secretary of Energy James R. Schlesinger. The largest pending deal at stake was the export of a $144 million high-technology drill bit by Dresser Industries. While parts of this sale had been approved in May, the package as a whole still required a validated license. The sale of this package had been controversial, since there were fears that the technology could be modified to allow production of armor-piercing projectiles. Fred Bucy had undertaken a Defense Science Board study of the proposed export and concluded that no foreign source could provide equipment of equal quality on the data-package and tungsten-carbide elements of this sale.[130] Nevertheless, Dresser had anticipated that the sale would go through, and it threatened a suit against President Carter if it was now denied.[131]

Reaction in Congress to the administration's moves was mixed. Senator Henry Jackson applauded the restrictions, while his fellow Democrat, Senator Frank Church, chair of the Foreign Relations Committee, said he was doubtful that they would have any impact on the Soviets.[132] Reaction from other countries was muted. On 20 July, the leader of the British Tory party discussed the possibility of ending aid to Moscow with the Soviet ambassador in London, but there was apparently no follow-up on this discussion.[133] The Netherlands froze contacts with Moscow.[134] The European Community publicly criticized the trials but took no steps to sanction the Soviets.[135]

The Carter administration took few steps to organize cooperation from its allies, and it seemed to waver in its determination to stick with

sanctions when firms and some members of Congress responded negatively to these sanctions. On 21 July, Carter announced that he would
take no further retaliatory actions and that he hoped the steps he had
taken would not lead to an Olympics boycott.[136] In addition, the administration made no efforts to get these issues on the agenda of CoCom or
any other multilateral organization. Secretary of Commerce Juanita
Kreps, who opposed the sanctions, testified before Congress to this effect
in 1979: "I don't know of any efforts that have been made, say, by the
State Department to have [the allies] join us."[137] Under Secretary of State
for Economic Affairs Cooper concurred, stating that the administration
had not asked any other states to restrain exports.[138] In addition, the
U.S. commitment to the oil-technology sanctions was quickly called into
question, as the validated-license procedure resulted in no refusal of
contracts, including the Dresser deal. As Cooper testified, "We put them
under license, but we have granted all of the licenses that have been
requested."[139]

Not surprisingly, given the lack of commitment or even threats of linkage from the administration, the level of cooperation achieved was very
low. Japan, Britain, and West Germany did exhibit a minimal level of
cooperation, as they did not allow their own firms, such as ICL or
Siemens, to pick up the canceled Sperry contract.[140] However, they did
not go beyond this to impose their own sanctions. The French government refused to show even this minimal level of cooperation, allowing
CII-Honeywell Bull SA and other firms to provide an Iris 80 computer,
ancillary equipment, programming, and software to Tass.[141] Paris
guessed that Washington was not committed enough to the sanctions to
respond vigorously to this sale.

This guess was absolutely correct. The administration made no objections to this export, contending that it was technically different from
the original Sperry computer, had no national-security implications,
and therefore did not need to be brought to CoCom for a formal exceptions request.[142] In using this reasoning, the administration openly
shifted its justification for the Sperry denial from the initial foreign-policy
argument—that it was retaliation for the dissident trials—to a national-
security argument. Once the French had decided to allow the Honey-
well Bull sale, the administration quietly reversed its decision on the
Sperry case, approving export of a slightly modified system in April
1979.[143] However, since the French deal was already sealed, Sperry lost
the sale.

U.S. officials charged with negotiating with the allies on East-West
trade issues were dismayed by this series of actions, as it showed European assessments of the lack of U.S. commitment to be correct. Lawrence
J. Brady, deputy director of the Office of Export Administration in the

Commerce Department until January 1980, explained, "The French did not take us seriously, and when we suddenly granted Sperry Univac a license a few months later, their reasoning was proven to be essentially correct. The Japanese, who had passed up a contract in order to heed our request, felt betrayed." He concluded that this wavering was a consistent pattern in U.S. behavior: "Because these suspensions were often so short-lived, however, it became difficult to take them seriously, or to transmit our seriousness to our CoCom partners."[144]

Brady and others also argued that the United States' behavior in CoCom, particularly the large number of exceptions requests, undermined its credibility. As Brady put it, "the United States seeks the largest share of exceptions to the embargo, and in so doing persuades other countries that they have nothing to lose by submitting requests for exceptions as well."[145] Clearly, U.S. officials shared the perception that the unwillingness to bear costs severely undermined attempts to gain cooperation from the allies. Senator Jackson brought up this argument in congressional hearings: "The U.S. leadership in seeking CoCom exceptions and its readiness to race to Moscow to beat the competition in selling security-sensitive items indicates to our allies that we are more interested in advancing our national commercial interests than the security of free world nations."[146] One does not have to accept Jackson's assumptions about the dangers of dual-use exports to share in his assessment of the signals U.S. actions sent to other potential sanctioners. As one analyst concluded, "It is hard to see how the U.S. can expect to gain the cooperation of its allies in denying strategic technology to the Soviet Union if we ourselves continue to supply it in abundance. In fact, the relaxation of U.S. controls over the last decade is a major reason for the diminishing effectiveness of CoCom."[147]

As argued above, the major problem the United States had to overcome in gaining the cooperation of its allies on sales of high technology to the Soviet Union was establishing a credible commitment to the controls. British, West German, and Japanese actions in 1978 showed at least some willingness to consider sanctions, but U.S. actions gave the allies no confidence that the coadjustment dilemma would be overcome in this case. Correctly reading the signals sent by the American unwillingness to bear high costs and by the lack of efforts to use multilateral organizations to organize sanctions, the French decided to pick up sales denied to U.S. firms. In 1980, when the administration put a higher value on multilateral sanctions, it took steps to overcome these perceptions by imposing a grain embargo and instituting a no-exceptions policy in CoCom. The contrast between the outcomes of the two cases is clear-cut, with essentially no cooperation in 1978 but grudging acceptance of the no-exceptions policy in 1980.

## Conclusion

The Soviet invasion of Afghanistan presented the Carter administration with a dilemma. The American response had to be strong and immediate; at the same time, the U.S. government strongly preferred multilateral to unilateral sanctions, especially in the proposed embargo of high-technology items. Across the Atlantic and Pacific, reactions to the U.S. measures were mixed. On the one hand, allies were pleased to see the United States taking a strong stance and showing willingness to bear a large portion of the costs of economic sanctions. On the other hand, many were reluctant to give up the gains of détente and resented *post facto* demands from the American government to impose sanctions. Above all, these governments did not want to be isolated in their response; unilateral sanctions could entail unacceptable costs with few benefits.

The United States managed to use the institutional mechanism of CoCom to gain European cooperation on restricting exports of high-technology items to the Soviet Union. Two factors appear to have been essential to this agreement. First, the United States itself would bear a large share of the costs of the embargo. Combined with the costs of the grain embargo, this willingness demonstrated commitment to the sanctions effort and strengthened U.S. ability to persuade its allies to cooperate. Europeans felt that the United States and other CoCom members would not disregard outright evasion of the no-exceptions policy. Chapter 2 suggested two possible ways in which high costs to the leading sender could increase cooperation: through greater domestic pressure to gain international cooperation, and through enhanced credibility on the international level. In this case, we find substantial support for the latter suggestion; allies believed the administration was committed to the CoCom restrictions. Willingness to bear the costs of the grain embargo also increased the administration's credibility vis-à-vis domestic interest groups, supporting the former argument as well.

Second, CoCom itself increased the leverage of the United States. Approving exceptions requests required a unanimous vote by the body; therefore, refusal to cooperate with the United States would have forced potential exporters to evade the CoCom mechanism entirely, bringing the viability of a valued institution into question. CoCom allowed states to cooperate in an area where they had strong common interests—on goods with direct military significance—but where suspicion that others were taking advantage of them could undermine cooperation. Governments resisted the temptation to defect from foreign-policy sanctions because this step would involve defying the entire institutional arrangement and thus threatening national security.

Initial European and Japanese responses to U.S. suggestions that they impose sanctions were what we could have predicted from the examination of national export-control policies. All were more reluctant than the United States to impose sanctions for foreign-policy reasons. The British showed the most willingness to support the American position, even making a short-lived attempt to organize a European response. The French were the most resistant to pressure to follow the U.S. lead. West German policy represented something of a "swing vote"; initial resistance to using negative sanctions gradually moved, under U.S. pressure, toward a position more like the British one. The Japanese wanted above all to avoid conflict with the Americans or Europeans, and they tended to sit on the sidelines until official decisions had been made on multilateral sanctions. In the end, however, the bandwagoning dynamic prevailed; each country decided it was willing to impose some sanctions as long as it was sure others would as well.

The Afghanistan case also sheds light on the larger question of long-term national-security export controls. In 1980, the United States used CoCom to impose multilateral sanctions on the Soviet Union. It was able to do this partly by defining the issue as a more fundamental national-security problem, the sort of issue CoCom was designed to handle. However, since 1980 other CoCom members have complained that this was simply another example of American "light-switch diplomacy," the "on-off" use of export controls for short-term foreign-policy goals. Given the importance many Europeans attach to the distinction between the two purposes of export controls, and given the fact that CoCom is valued principally for the consistency it should impart to export-control policy, the institution may not survive repeated instances of U.S. manipulation. The following case study examines the difficulties the United States experienced in gaining cooperation when it was prevented from using the CoCom mechanism.

The Afghanistan case stands in contrast to the attempt to impose high-technology sanctions in 1978 in response to dissident trials. In this case, the administration took no steps to overcome the perception that it was not committed to multilateral sanctions. It backed down quickly in the face of domestic complaints, imposing only limited sanctions. This unwillingness to bear costs, along with the lack of attempts to use CoCom or any other multilateral institution to organize sanctions, convinced the Europeans that they had little to lose and much to gain from picking up lost U.S. sales. The French were the first to do this, and the United States responded merely by reversing its initial sanctions decisions. The contrast between 1978 and 1980 emphasizes the role of credible commitment in gaining international cooperation—and the role of self-imposed costs and international institutions in sending signals about such commitment.

# 8

## The Polish Crisis and Gas-Pipeline Sanctions

IN DECEMBER 1981, the Polish government declared martial law. The U.S. government responded with a set of economic sanctions directed at both Poland and the Soviet Union. Its European allies participated in some sanctions but balked at an embargo of gas and oil equipment. In the succeeding months, U.S. policy conflated the goal of responding to the Polish crisis with a long-standing objective of reducing European dependence on natural gas imported from Siberia. The Reagan administration demanded that European firms abrogate their contracts to supply pipeline equipment to the Soviet Union. Many analysts have pointed to U.S. failure to gain European cooperation in pipeline sanctions as a prime example of the difficulty of coordinating multilateral sanctions; as an illustration of the potential negative impacts of sanctions on sending countries; and as evidence of U.S. decline.

While it is difficult to dispute the conventional wisdom regarding the extent of American policy failure in the pipeline episode, the dominant causal explanations lack empirical support. Two explanations are prominent. The first relies on declining U.S. hegemony to explain successful European resistance to American demands. According to this argument, the decline of American power relative to that of other countries meant that the United States could no longer impose its will on them, as it had earlier in the postwar era. Thus, the pipeline crisis revealed an underlying shift in power across the Atlantic.

A second argument focuses on economic conditions rather than power shifts as the source of failure. According to this view, Europeans simply had no alternative to Soviet natural gas as an energy source. France, West Germany, and Italy could not afford to forego building the Siberian pipeline, and so U.S. efforts were doomed to failure. While this argument has more empirical support than the previous one, I contend that the economic benefits of the pipeline contracts were not sufficient to explain the tenacity of European resistance.

In contrast to the proponents of these two arguments, both of which emphasize the inevitability of American failure, I find that the United States potentially could have achieved a significantly higher level of cooperation. While American pressure could not have prevented construction of the pipeline, most European governments could have been persuaded to impose more-stringent sanctions against the Soviet Union and Poland—*if* the United States had been willing to bear higher costs itself. By refusing to bear the costs of a grain embargo, Washington lost its bargaining power on the pipeline issue. Thus, the pipeline case is not an example of unavoidable failure; it was a failure by the Reagan administration to carry out a coordinated policy designed to achieve European and Japanese cooperation.

In the aggregate data presented earlier in this study, the costs borne by the leading sender had a significant positive effect on the level of cooperation observed. While I have touched on the role of these costs in the other case studies, this incident allows a fuller exploration of why and how they influence the process of cooperation. During the pipeline crisis, the unwillingness of the United States to bear significant costs was epitomized by the government's refusal to impose a grain embargo. This refusal, the result partly of divisions within the government on the value of sanctions, sent a double signal to the Europeans. It told them that American threats of countersanctions were not credible and it raised questions about the real objectives of U.S. policy. Others have pointed to the importance of self-imposed costs in signaling credibility and intentionality. From this perspective, U.S. policy was ultimately self-defeating.

Other dynamics found in the aggregate results are also apparent in the pipeline case. Specifically, this incident shows the negative side of bandwagoning—that is, buck-passing, where each European country's refusal to impose sanctions encouraged others to do the same. The United States was unable to "divide and conquer," as European decisions were highly contingent on one another. In addition, international institutions, particularly NATO and CoCom, constrained decision making. However, the pipeline case is interesting primarily for the insight it provides into the mechanism underlying the aggregate result that costs are positively correlated with cooperation.

In this chapter, I begin by presenting a brief chronology of the crisis in Poland and the U.S. response. The chronology details the Reagan administration's decision to attempt to prevent sales of pipeline equipment to the Soviet Union and the allies' responses. The second section explores the declining-hegemony explanation for U.S. failure to gain cooperation and finds this explanation inadequate. The third section considers Western European economic interests and finds that these do not fully explain European resistance. The final section shows how assessments of U.S. credibility influenced European calculations and how the refusal to impose a grain embargo undermined U.S. threats.

## Martial Law in Poland and the Siberian Gas Pipeline

Because of the dramatic nature of the U.S. policy failure in the pipeline crisis, there is an extensive literature on it. Entire books and numerous articles have been devoted to chronicling the crisis and drawing lessons from it.[1] In this section, I summarize the events leading up to and constituting the pipeline crisis, to provide a background for analysis of the dynamics behind American and European actions.

### Responding to Martial Law in Poland

During 1980, the Polish labor union Solidarity began demonstrating and demanding reforms in the Polish system. This situation raised fears among NATO members of a Soviet invasion of Poland to suppress dissent.[2] In response to these fears, President Carter—having learned from the problems caused by a lack of prior planning in the Afghanistan crisis—began a series of consultations with NATO members to draw up a contingency plan for a Soviet invasion of Poland. While the details of this plan have not been made public, it reportedly included strong, coordinated economic sanctions, including halts to exports of grain, CoCom technology, and oil and gas equipment. The West German government appeared reluctant to endorse these sanctions but said that it would back out of ongoing natural-gas deals in case of an invasion.[3] The coordinated Western response—while not clearly specified, in order to complicate the Soviet Union's decision-making process—was expected to exceed the response to the Afghanistan invasion. More-intense European interest in Poland explains the broader extent of the proposed sanctions and makes the eventual failure of sanctions surprising.[4] The Western response in case of Soviet intervention that fell short of invasion, or in case of internal Polish repression, remained undecided.

While Western European governments were planning to restrict economic relations with the Soviet Union under specified conditions, they were pursuing increased trade involving natural gas on the assumption that political conditions would not interfere. As discussed below, the oil crisis of 1978–79 had convinced many Europeans that natural gas was the best energy alternative for the 1980s and 1990s; and the Soviet Union was an obvious, and cheap, source of gas. Thus, a number of European firms entered into contracts to sell the Soviet Union wide-diameter pipe, compressors, and other equipment to build a major natural-gas pipeline from Siberia to Western Europe. Sales of these goods were financed on favorable terms, to be paid off by exports of Soviet gas to Europe once the pipeline was completed. Contracts obligated European firms to buy specified amounts of gas over the next decade. One aspect of these contracts assumed vital importance later. Most of the technology sold to the Soviet Union, especially turbines and compressors, was produced under license from American firms such as General Electric (GE), or by subsidiaries of American firms.

The original plans to transport gas from Siberia to Western Europe envisaged two parallel pipelines running from the huge Urengoy gas field to Western Europe, a distance of about three thousand miles. Five additional pipelines would supply parts of the Soviet Union and Eastern Europe. Initial plans called for Western Europe—particularly France, West Germany, and Italy—to import as much as forty bcm (billion cubic meters) of gas per year by 1990. Eventually, in part because of decreased demand, the project was scaled back to one pipeline with a maximum capacity of thirty bcm/year.[5] Nevertheless, even this reduced volume of imports would increase importers' dependence on Soviet gas from about 15 percent of their total gas supplies in 1980 to approximately 30 percent by 1990, while gas would become a more-important part of total energy consumption in Western Europe.[6] Soviet gas would then supply between 5 and 6 percent of total energy consumed.

Conservatives in the United States became alarmed at the degree of energy dependence these imports could create in Europe. Members of Congress and the Reagan administration expressed concern and looked for ways to convince the Europeans to back out of the deal. Their arguments focused on two potential problems that could be created by imports of Soviet gas. First, there was the possibility that the Soviets could threaten to withhold gas in order to extract political concessions. Second, the administration was concerned about the amount of hard currency the Soviets would earn from these exports, arguing that they would use this hard currency to purchase Western technology and so increase the military strength of the Soviet Union.

Senator Jake Garn expressed one of these concerns in a letter to President Ronald Reagan in June 1981: "Such dependence upon Soviet sources of energy would clearly provide the USSR with tremendous economic and political leverage over NATO, leading to a potential Finlandisation of Western Europe."[7] Richard Perle, assistant secretary of defense for international security policy, told a congressional subcommittee that he believed that "the increasing dependence of our European allies on Soviet energy, and especially natural gas, will weaken the alliance politically and militarily, shifting an already adverse military balance still further in the direction of Soviet advantage and threatening the unity of purpose on which our collective security ultimately depends."[8]

The Reagan administration pursued a number of private and public initiatives to convince the Europeans to pull out of the Urengoy project. Administration representatives visited Norway to explore the possibility of rapidly increasing gas exports from giant, newly discovered fields in the North Sea and Far North.[9] The most visible of the administration's early efforts came at the Ottawa economic summit meeting in July 1981, as companies from France, West Germany, Italy, and Britain were about to sign contracts worth approximately $15 billion for equipment to build the pipeline. President Reagan made no progress in convincing the Europeans that the pipeline was a bad idea, although he did achieve agreement to hold a high-level CoCom meeting in 1982.[10] Apparently, Reagan did not offer Europe any alternatives to Soviet gas or threaten reprisals if the project went through. Bruce Jentleson calls the effort at the Ottawa summit a "consciousness-raising" exercise relying on American prestige, rather than an effort to make a deal linked to other issues.[11] By the end of September 1981, European firms had completed negotiations with the Soviets and begun to sign contracts.

From the beginning, the Europeans and Japanese had doubts about the true motivations of the Reagan administration for opposing the pipeline project. U.S. handling of negotiations during the Ottawa summit did little to allay these concerns. For example, President Reagan reportedly asked Prime Minister Suzuki of Japan to prevent Komatsu, a Japanese firm, from completing a contract to sell pipelayers to the Soviet Union. Suzuki complied, asking Komatsu to delay supplying the pipelayers. However, within ten days the Commerce Department gave Caterpillar, an American firm directly competing with Komatsu, an export license for equivalent pipelayers.[12] While this action probably resulted from lack of coordination among agencies rather than intentional misleading of the Japanese, it fed the notion that U.S. concerns were more commercial than security-oriented. This kind of suspicion about the real goals of the United States flows through the history of the pipeline crisis as it did in the technology-export case, complicating efforts to achieve cooperation. Confusion over American motives undermined Reagan's credibility.

Escalation of the Polish crisis came on the night of 12 December 1981, when the Polish government declared martial law and imprisoned many of Solidarity's leaders. In spite of NATO's contingency plans, this action appears to have caught the West off guard. The Soviet Union, perhaps deterred by threats of sanctions in case of direct intervention, tried to keep a low profile, although U.S. officials insisted they had evidence of direct Soviet involvement in the Polish government's actions. On 14 December, the NATO foreign ministers met in Brussels, while EC officials met in London. All issued communiqués condemning the Polish action, but they did not agree on further joint steps other than future meetings.[13]

European leaders, feeling that the threat of sanctions had worked to prevent a Soviet invasion, saw no need for further action against the Soviet Union at this stage. They argued that they needed time to evaluate the situation in Poland and determine appropriate responses.

In the United States, debate began about the appropriate American response. While everyone agreed that the U.S. government needed to "lead the alliance" in some way, a split developed between those who favored stringent sanctions, even if unilateral, and those who stressed the overriding need for cooperation with the allies. Within the administration, this split was personified by Secretary of State Alexander Haig, who insisted that "only through unified action could we achieve results within the range of actions rationally available to us," and Secretary of Defense Caspar Weinberger, who saw the crisis as an opportunity to cut drastically economic ties with the Soviet Union.[14] The division was between a faction with coercion preferences, which was willing to undertake unilateral sanctions, and a coadjustment faction, which wanted to impose sanctions only if they were supported by U.S. allies. The interplay between these two groups characterized American domestic politics on the pipeline issue during the next year, with the outcome of the struggle always in doubt. Would the United States really be willing to bear the costs of unilateral sanctions for more than a few months, or the even-higher costs of countersanctions?

One piece of evidence suggested, from the beginning, that the answer was no. Although the two factions within the administration had deep differences, they did agree on one point—the infeasibility of imposing another grain embargo. President Reagan had campaigned on the issue of lifting Carter's grain embargo, and he did so soon after taking office. In addition, Congress passed legislation prohibiting sanctions that would hurt American farmers disproportionately. Haig noted that this legislation made a grain embargo an expensive proposition: "Reimposition of the American grain embargo would cost the treasury at least $3 billion in payments to farmers in compensation for taking 30 million tons of wheat off the market."[15] Thus, although hard-liners might have wished for a total Western embargo on trade with and credits for the Soviet Union, they never pressed hard for an end to sales of U.S. grain. As discussed below, the administration's inability or unwillingness to impose a grain embargo both infuriated the Europeans and convinced them that American threats to take costly actions were empty.

In looking at sanctions imposed during this crisis, it is important to distinguish between those directed at Poland and those directed at the Soviet Union. Although later events obscured the fact, the United States and the EC did manage to impose some sanctions on Poland, and even on the Soviet Union in luxury goods. Both the United States and Europe found themselves searching for ways to redirect foreign aid away from the Polish government and directly to the country's people. Even with respect to the Soviet Union, Europeans were willing to go along with demands to take some action, although they would not have done so without U.S. prodding.

The United States began by suspending economic aid to Poland on Monday, 14 December.[16] The ten EC foreign ministers met for two days, and their final statement warned against further Soviet intervention. The U.S. Senate likewise warned against further Soviet actions, while threatening a complete trade embargo in case of direct intervention. However, the question of how to respond to internal repression remained unresolved. While demonstrations against martial law took place and demands for a Western response were heard in Ottawa, London, and other capitals, governments other than that of the United States deferred decisions on future economic aid to Poland.[17]

Meanwhile, the U.S. administration sent a delegation to Western Europe in an attempt to develop a joint response. Assistant Secretary of State for European Affairs Lawrence S. Eagleburger and Assistant Secretary of State for Economic and Business Affairs Robert Hormats made the rounds of European capitals and met with support for some cautious moves, along with promises of more-severe actions in case of further Soviet intervention.[18] The ambassadors of Japan, New Zealand, and Australia were invited to the State Department to discuss possible sanctions.[19] In view of these contacts, later complaints that the United States had not consulted with its allies do not appear justified. Nevertheless, it is true that the administration went ahead with unilateral actions in spite of the cool allied response, perhaps assuming that American leadership would persuade others to join in. In other words, the administration was hoping to find itself in an assurance rather than coercion game, so that American sanctions would increase the willingness of others to go along. This assumption may have been correct with regard to sanctions short of those on pipeline equipment; but the American position was undercut by the refusal to include grain in the list of embargoed goods.

In Washington, President Reagan met a number of times with the National Security Council to plan the American response. Even in this relatively hard-line group, some members felt that actions against the Soviet Union were not justified until there was evidence of more-direct involvement in Poland.[20] However, the NSC did agree on a series of sanctions directed against Poland, which the President announced in his Christmas address on 23 December.[21] Food aid to Poland would continue, but only through private channels; government-sponsored shipment of agricultural and dairy products to the Polish government was halted. In addition, the United States cut the Export-Import Bank's line of export-credit insurance to the Polish government; suspended Polish civil-aviation privileges in the United States; suspended Polish fishing rights in American waters; and suggested that CoCom consider further restrictions on technology sales to Poland.[22]

Less than a week later, the administration announced that it was going ahead with unilateral sanctions against the Soviet Union. According to Alexander Haig, U.S. allies were given less than five hours' notice of this extension of sanctions, which took them by surprise.[23] Declaring that the Soviet leaders bore a "heavy and direct responsibility for the repression in Poland," Reagan announced a series of sanctions. These included suspension of Aeroflot flights to the United States; closure of the Soviet Purchasing Commission; suspension of licenses for all high-technology exports; suspension of negotiations on a new long-term grain agreement; suspension of negotiations on a new U.S.-Soviet Maritime Agreement; expansion of the list of oil and gas equipment requiring export licenses and suspension of all such licenses; and review of U.S.-Soviet exchange agreements.[24]

Two elements of this list are notable, one for its exclusion and one for its inclusion. Although the administration suspended negotiations on a new grain agreement, it did not cut off continuing sales under the terms of the old agreement. Most of the other steps announced would have minimal economic impact on the United States, since the sale of high-technology goods was already severely constrained by the Afghanistan sanctions. Gas- and oil-equipment sanctions, however, had the potential for a serious impact, depending on how the government interpreted and enforced them. Secretary Haig and members of the Department of Commerce were concerned about these regulations. If they were interpreted to apply retroactively, it would imply that European contracts involving U.S.-licensed technology should be broken. This "coadjustment" group convinced the president to hold off on applying the sanctions retroactively or extraterritorially until they had had a chance to discuss the issue further with the Europeans, and they sent off a delegation to Europe. The Commerce Department did enforce the oil- and gas-equipment regulations in the United States, however, meaning that Caterpillar lost its bid to sell pipelayers for the Siberian pipeline project.

After the United States' surprise decision to impose sanctions against the Soviet Union, its allies felt increased pressure to join in with their own measures. In spite of strong economic incentives against sanctioning the Soviets, the bandwagoning dynamic combined with public opinion to push the Europeans toward taking some steps.[25] Various meetings were scheduled to discuss European steps within NATO and the EC. In addition, Chancellor Helmut Schmidt of West Germany met with President Reagan in Washington. This meeting did not resolve the differences between Reagan and Schmidt on sanctions against the Soviets, but Schmidt was careful to characterize their disagreement as a "routine" one, not a crisis.[26]

Schmidt also met with Haig, who agreed not to push for sanctions against the Soviet Union at an upcoming NATO meeting but to settle for a strong joint condemnation of the Soviet role in Poland.[27] Schmidt and Haig's agreement held up at the NATO meeting in Brussels on 11 January 1982. A joint statement condemned the Soviet Union for its support of "systematic suppression" in Poland, meeting the U.S. government's wishes for recognition of a direct Soviet role in the crisis. While NATO announced no sanctions against the Soviet Union, European members threatened possible measures, including restrictions on Soviet imports and on export credits, if repression continued. The statement noted that "Soviet actions toward Poland make it necessary for the allies to examine the cost of future economic and commercial relations with the Soviet Union."[28]

Secretary Haig gained allied agreement to refrain from undercutting American sanctions and called the meeting a "solid success." In addition, the allies took some minor steps to reduce economic relations with Poland, holding back export credits for goods other than food and suspending debt-rescheduling negotiations.[29] These measures, however, were motivated more by economic conditions than political pressures, as Poland had suspended payments on its international debt. A former deputy assistant commerce secretary from the Carter administration praised Haig's efforts to reach agreement with the allies, saying that "the initial impression that Europe would do nothing was unduly pessimistic."[30]

The meaning of "not undermining U.S. sanctions" remained purposely vague. Immediately after the NATO meeting, West German economics minister Otto Lambsdorff clarified his government's interpretation by declaring that the pledge applied only to new contracts.[31] In other words, the West Germans (and others) intended to go ahead with the pipeline contracts that had already been signed, even if they involved American-licensed technology. Since Haig had never expected the Europeans to back down on the pipeline issue, this understanding was most likely implicit in the agreement reached at the NATO meeting.

In addition to these developments within NATO, another institution served as a focal point for joint European action on Poland—the European Community. On 4 January, the EC issued a statement declaring its "utter disapproval" of the declaration of martial law in Poland. It also issued a "solemn warning" against any further Soviet intervention and undertook to avoid compromising the actions taken by the United States. The ministers planned future meetings to consider commercial relations with the Soviet Union and economic and financial relations with Poland.[32]

Like the United States, the EC discontinued its food aid to the government of Poland, redirecting it through nongovernmental channels.[33] As it did in NATO, Greece refused to endorse any of the Community's actions.

By February 1982, the Community appeared poised to move on its pledge to impose sanctions against the Soviet Union if repression continued. On 24 February, the European Commission called for a 50 percent reduction of some Community imports from the Soviet Union. The proposed measures would affect approximately 8 percent of all EC imports from the Soviet Union, mostly manufactured goods and luxury products such as diamonds, vodka, and caviar.[34] One source calculated that these moves might reduce imports of Soviet goods by about $425 million and emphasized that this level of import reduction would impose about the same costs on Moscow as had U.S. sanctions.[35]

However, when the Community actually adopted a regulation carrying out this call for sanctions, the level of trade affected was only about half what the Commission had called for. A meeting of EC ambassadors in Brussels adopted this regulation on 15 March; it covered about sixty products, reducing imports by 25 percent for some goods and 50 percent for others.[36] Overall, imports were reduced by about $150 million, or just 1.4 percent of Community trade with the Soviet Union.[37] The ambassadors gave no explanation for the reduction in sanctions from those proposed by the Commission.

### Focusing on the Pipeline

The U.S. government did not react strongly, either positively or negatively, to the EC's action. The administration had turned its attention to other issues, especially the possibility of a link between U.S. concessions on the pipeline and a European agreement to tighten up credit extended to Poland and the Soviet Union. Over the next three months, the American credit initiative was directed at both the EC as a whole and individual countries.

Meanwhile, individual U.S. allies responded to American pressure by taking minor additional steps. Britain, as in other East-West crises, appeared the most willing to join the United States in imposing sanctions. Secretary Haig met with Prime Minister Margaret Thatcher near the end of January. Thatcher's statements captured European frustration with American unwillingness to bear significant costs while expecting its allies to do so, frustration we would expect in an assurance game: "Britain, and the other members of the alliance, wanted desperately to follow the American lead on Poland in a policy that would protect the Polish people and discomfit the Soviets and the regime in Warsaw. But it was too much to ask that they punish their own economies and their own interests in support of policies that would inflict no noticeable wound on Moscow's interests."[38]

With respect to Poland, Britain and other creditors agreed to put off negotiations on rescheduling Polish debt, although they refused to go along with Defense Department demands to find Poland in default. While Secretary Weinberger pushed for a declaration of Polish default, other groups within the U.S. government agreed with the Europeans that this step would have unpredictable and perhaps dangerous consequences on world financial markets.[39] Britain also halted any new credits to Poland. With respect to the Soviet Union, the British took steps to restrict travel, exchanges, and fishing rights. These measures were announced on 3 February at one of a series of NATO meetings.[40]

West Germany and Japan announced similar measures in February, suspending negotiations on trade agreements and imposing travel restrictions. Both West Germany's and Japan's statements emphasized that their national actions were dependent on the decisions made by other states and the decisions of international organizations—evidence of bandwagoning behavior. West German officials pledged "FRG participation in future EC and OECD agreed measures," while Japan committed itself to "follow the European lead."[41] In addition, both states agreed not to undermine U.S. sanctions. These steps, however, did not involve any direct reductions in trade with the Soviet Union, so that the joint EC measures represented the only immediate economic impact on the Soviet Union.

Between March and June 1982, attempts to coordinate American and European policies focused on the possibility of restricting commercial credits to the Soviet Union. In mid-March, the U.S. government sent a delegation led by Under Secretary of State James Buckley—with representatives from Defense, Commerce, Treasury, and the NSC—to European capitals. In Bonn, Paris, London, Rome, and Brussels, this delegation asked for a "financial embargo" of the Soviet bloc, but it met stiff resistance. Since trade between Western and Eastern Europe is highly dependent on credit from the West, the extreme measures Buckley proposed would have practically stopped Western exports to the East.[42] During these talks, Buckley appears to have adopted the position favored by Haig, in which the United States would back down on its opposition to the pipeline if the Europeans would make some concessions on the credits issue. This linkage had the potential to cement cooperation, if the administration would live up to it.

Near the end of March, some agreement appeared near on credits to the Soviet Union. An OECD meeting was scheduled for 6 May to discuss export-credit policies. The OECD at that time considered the Soviet Union a "Category II," or "intermediate-income" borrower, which allowed lenders to extend low interest rates. These interest rates, which according to OECD criteria should have been set at about 10.5 to 11 percent, were important elements of the various pipeline contracts.[43] Soviet negotiators had skillfully played off potential suppliers against one another; firms competed to offer concessionary export credits. While good data on the actual rates offered are not available, it appears that the Soviet Union managed to get rates substantially below the agreed 10.5 to 11 percent range through Western governments' financing of the difference between market rates and those offered to the Soviets.[44]

While European governments refused to go along with Buckley's suggestions to suspend all trade credits for ninety days and end government guarantees against Soviet defaults, they did agree to reconsider the Soviet Union's classification within the OECD Consensus.[45] U.S. officials claimed to have achieved agreement that at the May meeting, the Soviet Union would be reclassified as a "Category I," or "relatively rich," borrower.[46] This step would raise agreed interest rates for the Soviet Union to between 11 and 11.25 percent. By mid-March, Buckley had reportedly achieved agreement from EC countries to raise rates to this level before the arrangement was formalized in the May OECD meeting.[47]

At this meeting, which took place in Paris, the United States managed to reclassify the Soviet Union and achieve other concessions to strengthen cooperation on credit policies. The interest rates for Category I countries were raised to 12.15–12.49 percent and maturities reduced to a maximum of five years; and OECD members agreed not to cheat on these guidelines.[48] However, these agreements were clearly in the economic interests of all participants, since financing concessionary rates was expensive for governments. While the Polish crisis may have contributed to Europeans' desire to overcome a long-standing collective-action problem, they were careful to avoid portraying the credit arrangements as a form of economic sanction against the Soviet Union.[49]

The administration was not satisfied with the OECD credit restrictions; it sent Secretary of State George Shultz to Europe in May to ask for further concessions, showing that it was not willing to make the necessary concessions on this issue to gain substantial cooperation. Shultz wanted to reach an agreement that could be ratified by the heads of government at the Versailles economic summit in June. As the summit neared, the State Department used the threat of retroactive sanctions on oil and gas equipment in an attempt to gain European concessions on credit. Retroactive sanctions would restrict European firms from selling U.S.-licensed goods to the Soviet Union, and the administration claimed that it could take this step through a simple reinterpretation of existing controls. With the Europeans under pressure, the outlines of a deal began to emerge near the end of May.

French president François Mitterand was central to this deal. French firms had a large stake in the Siberian pipeline, France had traditionally been the Western European state most reluctant to apply foreign-policy sanctions in response to U.S. demands, and the French government led the competition to offer concessionary rates to the Soviets. Thus, if the United States and France could make a deal, other European states would probably go along. France demanded concessions on exchange-rate management. Paris found itself confronted with domestic economic problems caused by a weak franc and wanted the United States to intervene on international markets to bolster the currency's value. The Reagan administration, an outspoken advocate of the free market, was reluctant to undertake this kind of intervention. However, State negotiated a deal with Mitterand in which Washington would intervene in international markets if France would take the lead in limiting credits to the Soviet Union.[50] Implicitly, the administration agreed to back down on the pipeline dispute.

However, as the summit approached, divisions within the administration threatened this delicate linkage. Defense and the NSC remained adamantly opposed to the pipeline and refused to endorse any deal. Haig's stature within the administration had been undercut by his failure to negotiate a settlement in the Falklands dispute, and Secretary Weinberger and National Security Adviser William Clark were able to override the deals made by the State Department. As the summit began, Reagan refused to endorse the linkage forged by Haig, stating that any decision on the pipeline would have to wait until an NSC meeting scheduled for mid-June. While Reagan did not endorse Haig's deal in internal discussions, his own position remained unknown. The possibility remained open that Reagan would make concessions on the pipeline and monetary policy if this was the only way to gain European cooperation on trade credits. As later events were to show, Reagan's refusal to take a clear stance reflected the failure by top administration officials to agree upon a strategy and fallback position.

In spite of American ambivalence, some European representatives hoped that the deal would stick. Prime Minister Thatcher seemed to endorse the proposal; and Gaston Thorn, the president of the European Council, explicitly called for a trade-off: "All Europeans are ready to recognize the principle that we ought to harmonize our approaches to East-West trade. . . . There must first be a gesture to say, 'We're also going to make a contribution to Western economic solidarity in the form of an effort to correct the malfunctioning of the monetary system.' "[51]

The subject of East-West trade proved to be the most-contentious issue on the allies' agenda in Versailles. Afraid that Mitterand would avoid the entire question until the last minute, Reagan brought it up at a dinner early in the summit. Chancellor Schmidt defended West Germany's policies, pointing out that American and Japanese exports to the Soviet Union had increased during the last couple of years, while West German and French exports had decreased. The matter remained unresolved until the next day's meeting.[52]

In those discussions, Reagan threatened to withhold his approval of a text on North-South relations if Mitterand would not endorse the trade credits–monetary policy link. Finally, Mitterand and Schmidt gave in, and all parties seemed satisfied that they had reached agreement on both East-West trade and exchange-rate issues. Although the heads of government had not publicly discussed the Siberian pipeline, they appeared to reach an understanding that the United States would not extend its regulations extraterritorially or retroactively, allowing the Europeans to go ahead with their contracts.

The summit's final statement on East-West trade fell short of what Washington had hoped to achieve, as it did not explicitly call for an end to government-subsidized credits. Instead, it referred to "caution" and "commercial prudence" in economic relations with the East. Once again, the Europeans were reluctant publicly to attach political motivations to their concessions on trade finance. Treasury Secretary Donald Regan, however, said he was "more than satisfied" with the final agreement on credits, as it harmonized the West's financial policies with its diplomatic and military policies.[53] The allies had apparently settled the transatlantic dispute over the Siberian pipeline, after intensive U.S. efforts to construct the appropriate linkages.

However, the agreement quickly collapsed. Immediately after the summit Regan, who either did not know about the linkage between the East-West credit deal and monetary policy or refused to ratify it, said that the summit communiqué in no way committed the United States to exchange-rate intervention. Infuriated at what he perceived as American treachery, President Mitterand held a press conference and announced that since France had already increased its interest rates on credits to the Soviet Union, it was not bound by the Versailles agreement to take any steps. Mitterand said that while he would cooperate in defensive measures, he was not interested in pursuing economic warfare or participating in an "economic CoCom."[54] National Security Adviser Clark, who had never been satisfied with the credit arrangement, responded to Mitterand's announcement by taking steps to extend U.S. oil- and gas-equipment controls. While authors have offered numerous explanations for this "failed" summit, the simple answer appears to be that influential players in the administration were not satisfied with the outline of the deal reached in Versailles and believed that tougher U.S. action could force the Europeans to make a better deal.

## The Pipeline Crisis Erupts

When the summit deal fell apart, administration officials developed a new strategy for blocking completion of the pipeline, maintaining a belief that U.S. technology was essential. A number of studies had explored the degree to which denial of American technology could complicate building the Siberian pipeline. The Soviets insisted that they could get along without any Western technology, although without GE-licensed turbines major design changes would be required. Some administration officials argued that if oil- and gas-equipment restrictions were extended to U.S. subsidiaries in Europe, construction of the pipeline could be delayed by up to two years.[55]

Even if Europe resisted complying with U.S. regulations, complications introduced by extension of American sanctions could potentially raise the price of Siberian gas to the point where it would not be greatly preferable to other energy sources. If the United States could raise the cost of gas sufficiently, the Europeans might find it worthwhile to pay for American coal or increase gas imports from the Netherlands and Norway, according to this logic.[56] As Perle told Congress, "we can take action that will make the costs of Soviet energy higher and the costs of non-Soviet alternatives lower."[57] At an 18 June NSC meeting, Clark took steps designed to implement the first part of this strategy. He scheduled this meeting for a day when Haig, the main proponent of conciliation, would be in New York.

Although Haig was out of town, some representatives at the meeting favored dropping all opposition to the pipeline and allowing American firms to compete for contracts. The secretaries of Commerce, Agriculture, and Treasury; the U.S. Trade Representative; and Assistant Secretary of State Eagleburger all opposed extraterritorial extension of gas-equipment regulations. However, Secretary of Defense Weinberger, White House Counsel Edwin Meese, and Clark argued in favor of the "toughest option"—full extension of U.S. regulations to all subsidiaries and licensees, effective retroactively. After little discussion, President Reagan approved the position put forward by Clark.[58]

In a terse statement that same day, Reagan announced that sanctions were being extended "to include equipment produced by subsidiaries of U.S. companies abroad, as well as equipment produced abroad under licenses issued by U.S. companies."[59] Europeans reacted with shock, anger, and a bit of incredulity. Haig had convinced them that the administration would not go ahead with the pipeline sanctions, and the costs to the United States of enforcing the sanctions could be high. The administration threatened to blacklist European firms that fulfilled their contracts with the Soviets, preventing such firms from obtaining any technologies or intermediate goods from U.S. exporters. This came perilously close to threatening a full-scale trade war with huge costs for both sides. Secretary of Commerce Malcolm Baldrige warned that enforcing the blacklist rules would bring high direct costs, even if the dispute did not escalate.[60]

The language that accompanied the extension of sanctions did nothing to alleviate the hostility these controls were bound to generate in Europe. Under Secretary of Commerce for International Trade Lionel Olmer talked about exploiting European dependencies on the United States to gain compliance: "If they're going to thumb their nose at these kinds of controls, maybe they'll find that they require goods and services from the United States in other areas and they would be fair game for the application of sanctions."[61] Such talk exemplifies a purely coercive strategy. Because the United States could not persuade the Europeans to impose pipeline sanctions, it threatened to link the pipeline issue to one where it felt it had an advantage, thus forcing Western Europe to give in on the sanctions issue. In order for such a coercive strategy to work, the linkage threat must be credible. If European governments believed the administration was bluffing, they could simply ride out the storm of rhetoric and go ahead with their contractual commitments.

For a while, Europe responded to the U.S. action mainly with rhetoric. In Bonn, a government spokesman called the move a "direct contravention of agreements reached by the western allies."[62] *The Economist* complained that American grain sales would continue while these European firms were suffering.[63] A West German newspaper called the U.S. moves "sheer imperialism."[64] When the ten EC heads of government met in Brussels on 28 June, they listed a series of grievances with the United States, including the pipeline. The EC officials stated that the U.S. administration showed no concern for consulting with its allies or cooperating with them and that it made decisions on the basis of its own narrowly defined national interest.[65] However, the EC did not take any action to defy the U.S. sanctions directly.

It appeared that European firms would comply with the sanctions unless their governments prohibited them from doing so. Faced with the choice of the Soviet market or U.S. technology, they would give in to American demands in spite of the sales and jobs they would lose. Four firms figured most prominently in this dispute: AEG-Kanis of West Germany, John Brown of Britain, Nuovo Pignone of Italy, and Alsthom-Atlantique of France. AEG-Kanis, John Brown, and Nuovo Pignone had contracted to sell 125 turbines to the Soviet Union that depended on rotors and other key parts from GE or GE licensees. Alsthom-Atlantique produced rotors under license from GE, and many considered this firm's decision on U.S. sanctions pivotal. Without Alsthom-Atlantique rotors, the Soviets could not use Western turbines and would be forced to search for alternatives.

As the summer went on, European governments clarified their intention to defy the United States. Since contracts did not call for any deliveries until late July, officials and firms had some time to think about their response. Clear signs of defiance came at the beginning of July, as Prime Minister Thatcher openly criticized the United States. Previously, Thatcher had been restrained in her comments, afraid to jeopardize U.S. support in the Falklands War. However, as it became clear that there was no way Reagan would compromise in the face of private pleas, she decided that British interests demanded an open confrontation. In the House of Commons, she argued that "the question is whether one very powerful nation can prevent existing contracts being fulfilled; I think it is wrong to do that."[66] The British Board of Trade warned companies that they might be prohibited from complying with the American embargo, invoking the 1980 Protection of Trading Interests Act passed after the Afghanistan sanctions.[67]

In West Germany, Chancellor Schmidt declared that his government intended to go ahead with the pipeline deal regardless of the delays introduced by restrictions on U.S. technology. Spokesmen warned that they might take the United States to the International Court of Justice on this issue. The EC also warned of international legal action, calling the U.S. moves an unjustified "extraterritorial extension of U.S. jurisdiction."[68] The EC threatened other retaliation, such as withdrawal of support for American proposals in various international arenas, including GATT.[69] Perhaps most importantly, Alsthom-Atlantique announced that it would begin deliveries on time if the French government ordered it to do so.

In Italy, Prime Minister Giovanni Spadolini held a joint news conference with Thatcher on 8 July and announced that his government would allow Nuovo Pignone to go ahead with deliveries in spite of U.S. orders.[70] The Japanese government showed some confusion over how to react, caught between a desire to comply with U.S. wishes and a desire to act in concert with the Europeans. Major Japanese contracts were at stake, including sales of pipelayers by Komatsu and an energy-development project on Sakhalin Island.[71] The Japanese foreign minister denied that his government had decided to defy the U.S. regulations and insisted that Japan would not consider a joint response with the EC, since the Sakhalin project was separate from the pipeline. The director-general of economic planning, however, argued that Japan should "keep in step" with the EC.[72] As usual, Japan was using a bandwagoning strategy; the problem now was whose wagon to jump on.

On 22 July, the French government started a process of negative bandwagoning, or buck-passing, in which European governments followed one another in formally ordering their firms to ignore the American sanctions. Other cases in this study have shown instances of positive bandwagoning, or chain-ganging, where one state's decision to impose sanctions increases the probability that others will as well. However, if states' decisions are contingent in this manner—if bandwagoning is a general phenomenon—we should expect sometimes to see a mirror image of this process, in which a refusal to impose sanctions leads to a cascade of similar decisions. The pipeline case provides the clearest example of negative bandwagoning.

French foreign minister Claude Cheysson began the process by talking about a "progressive divorce" developing between the United States and its allies.[73] Prime Minister Pierre Mauroy announced that the members of the EC had decided that they could not accept the United States' decision and that the French government was ordering its firms to go ahead with their contracts. Cheysson described the distress that this situation was causing in Europe: "There is a remarkable incomprehension, and that is grave. The United States seems totally indifferent to our problems. It is the major ally and the world's biggest country and we don't even talk anymore."[74] French foreign trade minister Michel Jobert gave a further explanation of his government's decision: "If the United States wants to respect its embargo, let it start by not delivering eight million tons of grain. Let it make its own effort first."[75]

After the French decision, other Western European states "quickly fell in line."[76] Chancellor Schmidt said that his government could not accept measures that effectively extended U.S. sovereignty to Europe and that he expected other countries to follow the French lead. While the West German government never formally ordered its firms to defy American orders, claiming that it had no legal authority to do so, it openly encouraged them to make deliveries on time. Italy also declared that its contracts would be respected, without issuing a formal order to defy the United States.[78]

The British waited a few days before responding but saw no point in holding out once West German and French firms committed to making deliveries. On 2 August, Secretary of State for Trade Lord Cockfield invoked the Protection of Trading Interests Act, forbidding particular British companies from complying with the U.S. embargo.[78] John Brown, one of the four companies subject to Cockfield's order, was reportedly unhappy about the government's action; it preferred to avoid reprisals from the United States.[79]

The Europeans had decided to call Reagan's bluff.[80] A formal EC protest against unacceptable U.S. interference in members' internal affairs appeared on 12 August. This statement declared that American actions were contrary to international law and that the sanctions would not "delay materially the construction of the pipeline or delivery of the gas."[81] Soviet technology could meet the challenge of building the pipeline on time if Western technology was denied, by diverting resources from the other five pipelines being built simultaneously. In addition, the EC argued, these sanctions would give the Soviets a strong incentive to improve their own capacity to build turbines and compressors.

On 27 August, Dresser-France shipped three compressors to the Soviet Union, three days after the shipping date specified in their contracts. The decision to ship followed a direct order from the French government earlier in the week—accompanied by threats to requisition Dresser-France's facilities—and loss of a last-minute battle in U.S. federal court to block countersanctions. Immediately after the shipment, the Reagan administration banned Dresser-France from any commerce with the United States.[82] In the next few weeks, similar stories were played out with John Brown and AEG-Kanis, as they shipped components to the Soviet Union and were then barred from some trade with the United States. The administration quickly began to back down, however, reducing countersanctions to cover only oil and gas equipment rather than all commerce.[83]

Resistance to the administration's policies was building in the United States as well as abroad. Countersanctions would hurt American firms in addition to the intended targets. Officials concerned about the effects of an all-out trade war, including the new secretary of state George Shultz, Secretary of Commerce Baldrige, and Secretary of the Treasury Regan, had convinced Reagan to reduce the intensity of retaliatory measures against John Brown and other firms.[84]

In Congress, a movement was building to remove all U.S. gas- and oil-equipment sanctions, including domestic as well as extraterritorial ones. In hearings, representatives of U.S. firms harmed by the sanctions, such as Caterpillar, testified about the exports and jobs they were losing in a period of high unemployment.[85] Unfortunately for the administration, two of the American firms most directly affected by the sanctions, Caterpillar and Fiat-Allis, were headquartered in Illinois, in the district of House minority leader Bob Michel. Michel, along with fellow Republican Senator Charles Percy, mounted a campaign to end unilateral sanctions. In July, Representatives Paul Findley of Illinois and Don Bonker of Washington introduced a bill calling for the repeal of the 30 December and 18 June regulations. Arguments in the House stressed that unilateral sanctions hurt only the United States, not the Soviet Union. While Findley supported joint measures to restrict credit, he argued that "the pipeline sanctions represent a foreign policy travesty and an economic injustice."[86]

Other members of Congress took up the theme of making U.S. sanctions contingent on approval and joint action from the allies. Thus, a significant faction in the government had preferences more like those of a coadjustment than a coercion game. On 10 August, the House Foreign Affairs Committee approved Findley's bill. While passage by both houses was considered unlikely, and signature by Reagan an impossibility, supporters argued that Reagan had backed himself into an untenable position and needed their help to extricate himself.[87] The administration, however, did not appreciate these attempts to "help," and it lobbied aggressively against the bill. The dissent in Congress was sending troubling signals to Europeans already skeptical of American willingness to carry out countersanctions. If Congress was willing to repeal all U.S. trade-sanctions measures, it was unlikely to stand for an expensive trade war. As Shultz said in a letter to Foreign Affairs Committee members, the proposed legislation "would severely cripple the president's ability" to pursue his sanctions policy, by undermining the credibility of his countersanctions threat.[88]

On 13 August, Senator Paul Tsongas introduced a bill similar to that under consideration in the House. However, with the Senate controlled by Republicans reluctant to hand their president a major foreign-policy defeat, senators never acted on this bill.[89] On 29 September, the House debated its end-to-sanctions bill. Representative Michel argued that this legislation would not reduce pressure on the Soviet Union, since there was no pressure on Moscow anyway. He said that the allies had made their decision and that "their decision must . . . influence our own decision."[90] Representative Clement Zablocki noted the high costs borne by some American firms because of the sanctions, and he claimed that it was the "height of hypocrisy" for the president to extend the grain agreement while pressuring the Europeans to impose sanctions.[91] After debate, the House voted 206–203 in favor of an amendment that effectively gutted the bill, which then passed on a vote of 209–197.[92] Although Congress did not veto U.S. sanctions, these numbers showed the depth of opposition.

On top of disagreement in the legislative branch, dissent from the sanctions policy continued to build within the administration. An internal State Department study came out showing that deep cuts in Western exports to the Soviet bloc would hurt the West more than Moscow, as the newly industrialized countries (NICs) could make up most of the shortfall.[93] At the same time, a Defense Intelligence Agency report undermined one of the administration's arguments by concluding that imports of technology were so important to the Soviets that they would inevitably find ways to overcome hard-currency constraints. Given these voices in the United States, the Europeans quite rightly suspected that the administration would be forced to look for compromise rather than continuing to challenge them with countersanctions.

On 8 September, Treasury Secretary Regan suggested publicly that at a meeting of the NATO allies later that week, the United States might be willing to lift its sanctions if the Europeans would agree to alternative economic measures.[94] While no deal emerged from this meeting, the administration began searching for ways to get itself out of an increasingly uncomfortable position. Shultz, who favored finding some kind of compromise, had a series of bilateral talks with European officials in New York. At a meeting of NATO foreign ministers in Canada in early October, the allies agreed to undertake studies on East-West economic relations within a number of institutions, including the OECD, the International Energy Agency (IEA), and CoCom.[95] Soon after, a successful high-level meeting of CoCom officials reached consensus on general national-security controls.[96]

With congressional elections scheduled for the beginning of November and Republicans such as Michel being hurt on the sanctions issue, the pressure to compromise was turned up a notch. Assistant Secretary Eagleburger met with European and Japanese officials in Washington at the end of October looking for a solution, but he could not find a face-saving way to back down.[97] Shultz suggested that an agreement to increase controls on high-technology exports, end government-subsidized credits, and hold off on new gas agreements pending studies could allow the United States to drop the sanctions.[98] This arrangement, very close to that proposed by Haig in June, now looked to the Europeans like an unnecessary compromise. They put off State's proposals by insisting that they needed to discuss them within the EC.

Finally, on 13 November, President Reagan announced that he was dropping both the 18 June *and* the 30 December oil- and gas-equipment sanctions.[99] He claimed that that morning, the allies had agreed on a new strategy for East-West trade, so sanctions were no longer necessary. Two facts about Reagan's speech are worthy of note: it did not mention Poland at all, and it freed U.S. firms to compete for contracts as well as dropping countersanctions against European firms. Thus, in the long run, the coadjustment faction seems to have prevailed over the coercion school by forcing recognition of the futility of unilateral American sanctions.

The agreement to which Reagan referred consisted of no new gas contracts until a study of alternative energy sources was completed, tightened controls on strategic goods, and better monitoring procedures for export-credit policies. Work on the strategic-goods and credit issues had been proceeding quietly in CoCom and the OECD all summer, so these agreements represented no new concessions by the Europeans. In addition, projections for gas demand were down sharply because of the recession, so the agreement to hold off for a few months on new gas deals was hardly a sacrifice. The administration clearly found itself forced to back down with a barely face-saving agreement to cover its retreat. The following day, Foreign Minister Cheysson objected to Reagan's insinuation that France had made any kind of deal; Cheysson insisted that he knew of no new agreement.[100] British Foreign Secretary Francis Pym also called the lifting of sanctions a "unilateral decision by the Americans," with no concessions from the Europeans.[101]

Thus, the pipeline crisis ended with a whimper rather than a bang. The Europeans called the Americans' bluff, and the administration was not able to rally support behind a policy that might have led to a costly trade war with its allies. While we should not overlook the cooperation achieved on sanctions against Poland, nor the significance of EC import restrictions against the Soviet Union, the U.S. government failed in its effort to extend these sanctions to include the Siberian pipeline. The rest of this chapter is devoted to exploring the reasons for this failure. The next section examines one common explanation—the decline of U.S. hegemony. Later sections look at the European economic interest in the gas pipeline and the importance of the U.S. "no-grain-embargo" stance during the Polish crisis.

## The Effect of Declining Hegemony

In the early 1980s, U.S. foreign-policy fiascoes such as the pipeline crisis contributed to the growth of a literature on the decline of American power relative to that of other states. Since 1982, articles and books chronicling or questioning the extent of American decline and offering various explanations for the continuation or termination of cooperation, given the systemic condition of declining hegemony, have gained a prominent place in the literature of international-relations theory. Within this framework, the 1982 pipeline episode presented tantalizing anecdotal evidence for the purported reduction of American influence over its allies. In this section, I ask whether declining American hegemony provides an adequate explanation of the failure of cooperation in this particular case.

Various authors have postulated a link between reduced U.S. power and the outcome of the pipeline case, offering different interpretations of the complex connection between the United States' overall power and its actual influence in this particular case. Stephen Kobrin, for example, argues that "there is little question American power has declined relative to host countries, and that decline is manifest in diminished control over outcomes. The American government no longer is able to enforce export sanctions extraterritorially."[102] Kobrin examines the preferences of American allies and finds that they have changed as American power has declined. Because of this decline, he argues, other states have become less dependent on American technology and other resources and so less willing to accept American demands to cooperate in sanctions policies.

Bruce Jentleson also accepts the declining-hegemony hypothesis and proposes a more-complex link between power and outcomes. He contrasts East-West energy sanctions in the 1960s and 1980s and finds that U.S. ability to exert leverage was lower in the 1980s.[103] Because of the United States' declining overall power, the American government's ability to offer concessions or carry through with threats was diminished, thus reducing its influence over other states' policies.[104] In the pipeline case, reduced leverage was the result when various domestic interest groups were able to prevent Reagan from implementing threats to keep the Europeans in line. Jentleson finds both changed European preferences in the 1980s and decreased American ability to override differences of interest.

More generally, Gunnar Adler-Karlsson's classic study of Western trade controls finds that once European dependence on American aid had declined, the United States could no longer enforce a strategic trade embargo.[105] For Adler-Karlsson, reduced American power led to a failure of cooperation, as the U.S. government's ability to inflict pain lessened. Changed European preferences play a smaller role in his interpretation.

In chapter 4, I presented the aggregate results of a simple test of the hegemonic-decline hypothesis. These results are shown in tables 4.13 and 4.14 and in figures 4.6 and 4.7. As explained earlier, if this hypothesis holds, the coefficient of the variable US should be positive, reflecting generally greater American coercive power, while the coefficient of US*YEAR should be negative, reflecting a decline in coercive power between 1945 and 1989. (US is a dummy variable that indicates whether the United States took the lead in imposing sanctions; YEAR indicates the year in which sanctions were first imposed.)

In both the probit and regression estimations, the signs of the coefficients of US and US*YEAR are the opposite of those that would be predicted by the declining-hegemony thesis. US has a negative coefficient, showing that on average the United States manages to attract *less* cooperation than other leading senders, all else held constant. This effect is statistically significant in the regression estimation. The coefficient for the interaction term US*YEAR is positive, suggesting that the United States has, if anything, done better in getting cooperation in recent years than it did in the immediate postwar period.

As discussed in chapter 4, a number of explanations could account for continuing cooperation in the face of declining hegemony. However, most of these suffer from the problem of overpredicting the amount of cooperation found in the early years of the data set. Michael Mastanduno provides an explanation that perhaps comes closest to fitting the aggregate data, suggesting that the conventional wisdom overestimates the actual level of cooperation during the 1950s and 1960s. He describes the establishment of CoCom as a temporary blip of intense cooperative activity, explained by the Korean War's impact on European preferences and threat perceptions.[106]

Regardless of which is the correct explanation of the observed pattern, these aggregate results should lead us to question the declining-hegemony explanation of the pipeline incident. When put in the context of contemporaneous sanctions cases, the pipeline episode looks like an aberration; it shows an unusually low level of cooperation in a period when the United States tended to receive significant cooperation from others, as U.S.-led sanctions approached the level achieved by other states in the 1980s. However, from the perspective of the explanatory variables used in this study, the pipeline incident is not such an anomaly. They pointed to the importance of the costs borne by the major sender, the role of international institutions, and bandwagoning behavior in explaining the level of cooperation. The history of the pipeline case shows that the United States bore low costs relative to those of its alliance partners, that the pipeline issue was excluded from discussion in CoCom, and that a process of negative bandwagoning shaped European decisions.[107] Declining American power may have contributed indirectly to these more proximate causes of failed cooperation. As Jentleson argues, opposition from domestic groups was important. However, given the lack of empirical support for the declining-hegemony hypothesis, simpler explanations for unilateral U.S. action seem appropriate.

In addition to the aggregate data, evidence presented in the cases in this study also calls the declining-hegemony hypothesis into question. As the previous chapter showed, in 1980 the United States achieved a significant degree of cooperation in tightening controls on strategic goods in response to the Soviet invasion of Afghanistan. While the pipeline debacle was proceeding in 1982, the allies managed to continue coordinated action on strategic goods, holding the first high-level CoCom meeting in twenty-five years; moved closer to a joint policy on export credits for the Soviet Union through the OECD Consensus; and took similar steps directed at the Polish government. While the pipeline dispute dominated the headlines, it was notable primarily for its singularity. On most East-West issues, the allies were able to overcome their differences and achieve a respectable level of cooperation. However, when it came to Siberian gas, the policies of the United States and Europe diverged irreconcilably, and the United States was forced to back down.

Declining American hegemony cannot, in the context of continuing cooperation on other East-West trade issues, explain the Reagan administration's failure to stop the Europeans from fulfilling their contracts for equipment to build the Siberian natural-gas pipeline. While declining power may have contributed to American refusal to bear high costs, the aggregate evidence has to call any direct link into question. To explain the pipeline case, we need to look for more proximate, contextual factors. The next section explores an alternative explanation, one based on European energy demands and the nature of the natural-gas market.

## Siberian Gas and European Preferences

One plausible explanation of U.S. failure in the pipeline incident is that Europeans simply could not do without the gas pipeline. If they absolutely needed Siberian gas during the mid-1980s, the United States was facing an impossible task in convincing its allies to impose sanctions. Even if such sanctions did not prevent the Soviet Union from building the pipeline, they would have delayed its construction and raised the price of gas supplies. The costs of reimbursing Europe for these losses would have been beyond the capacity of any U.S. government, even at the height of American power. In this section I examine the reasons that Western Europe wanted to import gas from the Soviet Union. What were the alternatives to Soviet gas? How costly were they? Could they have been available in time to meet projected energy demand? Did the United States take steps to make such alternatives more attractive? The answers to these questions could hold the answer to the failure in the pipeline case, by showing that any attempt to move Europe away from Soviet energy was futile.

Natural gas is a unique commodity. There is no "natural-gas market" in the usual sense. Consumers receive gas through dedicated pipelines that require high initial capital investment. For this reason, contracts to build a pipeline and sell gas usually constitute long-term package deals, designed to spread risk across both consumers and suppliers. The quantity and price of gas to be delivered in these pipelines are negotiated far in advance, with the price of gas tied to that of other energy sources. Because there are only a few suppliers of gas and because the number of consumers is limited by the destinations of the pipelines, the supply of natural gas is determined by strategic interaction among buyers and sellers rather than by the functioning of a normal market. In Western Europe, governments control the purchase of natural gas. Analyses have shown that they collaborate quite closely, while the suppliers of gas have

**TABLE 8.1**
Western European Gas Imports from the Soviet Union

| | Total Soviet Sources (bcm) | | Siberian Pipeline (bcm)[a] | Percent of Total Supply from Soviet Sources | |
|---|---|---|---|---|---|
| | 1970 | 1980 | | 1980 | 1990 |
| West Germany | 0 | 10.7 | 10.5 | 15.0 | >30 |
| France | 0 | 4.0 | 8.0 | 11.7 | 30 |
| Italy | 0 | 7.0 | 8.5 | 27.6 | 40 |
| Austria | 1.0 | 2.9 | | | |
| Finland | 0 | 0.9 | | | |

*Source:* Jentleson, table 6.1, p. 186; Jonathan P. Stern, 1986, p. 65. Statistics from Jentleson used with the permission of Cornell University Press.

[a] Projected imports as of mid-1981. The actual amounts imported were significantly less than these projected figures. For example, Italy's 1984 contract with the Soviet Union provided for only 4.5–6.0 bcm per year.

difficulty overcoming their political divisions. Thus, some economists have modeled the Western European gas "market" as an oligopoly selling to a monopsony.[108]

To provide a simple overview of the gas supplies, tables 8.1 and 8.2 present figures on Western European imports of Soviet gas and on world gas reserves. The Soviet Union controls a huge share of the world's estimated natural-gas reserves—nearly one-third. Since exports of gas from North America to Western Europe are not practical given current technology, the Soviet Union, Northern Africa, and Iran constitute the major potential exporters of gas to the Continent. Britain has a policy of conserving its reserves in the North Sea for home use and is even considering imports from Norway in the future.

During the 1970s, the huge Groningen field in the Netherlands was the major source of imported gas for the rest of Western Europe. However, exporting at the current rate would exhaust the Groningen field by about 2020.[109] After the 1973 oil crisis, the Dutch government adopted a policy of conserving reserves for home consumption and planned to increase its imports of gas, including those from the Soviet Union, in the 1980s. However, in 1981 the Netherlands decided not to participate in the Siberian pipeline for economic reasons. Dutch policy did not allow for increasing exports in the mid-1980s, as this would too quickly draw down reserves. In the long run, the Netherlands may best be able to serve as a "surge supplier," providing increased exports to Western Europe for short periods in case of shortages.[110]

**TABLE 8.2**
World Natural-Gas Reserves

|  | Proven Reserves (bcm)[a] | Ultimately Recoverable (bcm)[b] | Percent of World Total |
|---|---|---|---|
| North America | 8,015 | 66,400 | 22.7 |
| U.S. | 5,519 |  |  |
| Latin America | 4,047 | 16,500 | 5.6 |
| Middle East | 16,839 | 51,600 | 17.6 |
| Iran | 10,700 |  |  |
| Africa | 5,136 | 33,400 | 11.4 |
| Algeria |  | 2,700 |  |
| Nigeria |  | 1,455 |  |
| Western Europe | 3,742 | 11,400 | 3.9 |
| Netherlands | 1,685 |  |  |
| Norway |  | 714 |  |
| U.K. |  | 708 |  |
| Far East | 4,924 | 13,500 | 4.6 |
| Socialist Countries | 31,145 | 96,100 | 32.8 |
| USSR | 30,600 |  |  |

Source: Maull, table 2, p. 20. Statistics used with the permission of The Atlantic Papers.
[a] Established as of 1980.
[b] Proven reserves plus estimated additional resources.

Algeria is a potentially large exporter to Europe. In fact, because of political ties, France has commitments to import at least one-third of its gas from its former colony.[111] However, as one of the more-radical members of OPEC (Organization of Petroleum Exporting Countries), Algeria has proven to be an unreliable supplier. Demanding price parity with crude oil, Algeria abrogated gas contracts repeatedly during the 1970s and 1980s.[112] A major deal to transport liquefied natural gas (LNG) from Algeria to the Continent and the United States fell through in 1980. Thus, although Algeria has the reserves to supply Western Europe, its customers question the reliability of supplies. A similar situation holds in Nigeria, where development of natural gas is just beginning. Iran also has large reserves, and a major deal was being negotiated for a pipeline to Western Europe and the southern Soviet Union in the 1970s. This arrangement, however, came to an abrupt halt with the Iranian revolution in 1979.[113]

Thus, the Soviet Union and Norway looked like two of the most-promising prospects for increased exports to Western Europe. After the oil shocks of 1973 and 1979, governments on the Continent decided to substitute consumption of gas for oil and to diversify sources of supply away from OPEC. These considerations pointed toward the Soviet Union and

Norway, but the Soviets had one crucial advantage: their gas was much cheaper to produce and could be available by the mid-1980s, while Norwegian production would probably not come on-line until the 1990s.

Siberian gas is buried in the permafrost, which means there are technical problems in getting it out of the ground, especially in winter. However, these problems pale in comparison to those involved in getting gas out of the huge new Norwegian fields in the North Sea. More than half of these reserves, in the Troll field and others, are more than three hundred meters below the sea floor and therefore almost beyond the reach of today's technology.[114] In addition, the gas lies below a layer of oil, which would be wasted if companies did not extract it first. These factors mean that Norway needs a price of almost $4.00 per million cubic feet (mcf) to make a profit, while Soviet gas makes a profit at a price of only $1.50/mcf.[115] Clearly, the Western Europeans had strong economic reasons to prefer Soviet gas. If they were to pay Norway a "security price premium" for gas, they would be forced to pay higher prices for imports from all sources, since prices are set by strategic interaction rather than production costs.[116] As an example of this kind of interaction, contracts for cheap Siberian gas allowed France to negotiate prices on a contract with Algeria in 1982 that were 15 to 20 percent below those set in 1981.[117]

Regardless of the incentives for Europeans to buy Norwegian gas, the Norwegian government's policy was to undertake development of its reserves at a cautious pace. It learned from the "Dutch disease," in which rapid development of the Netherlands' gas industry led to increased wages throughout the economy and therefore hurt exports of all other commodities. The Norwegian government was anxious to avoid this kind of structural dislocation. In addition, some Europeans questioned the reliability of Norwegian supplies, since the oil industry there had been plagued with strikes. Norway's proximity to the Soviet Union on its northern border and the security implications of energy development there added yet another complication.[118] Given these factors, increased exports of Norwegian gas to Western Europe by the mid-1980s appeared quite unlikely in 1981—although in the longer term, as technology improved, West Germany and others did plan to import significant amounts from Norway.

U.S. opponents of the Siberian gas pipeline nevertheless looked to Norway as a possible alternative supplier. During 1981, a U.S. delegation traveled to Norway and the Netherlands, trying to persuade these governments to increase exports rapidly to other European countries.[119] The Netherlands argued that its reserves were inadequate to meet Europe's needs. The Norwegians conceded that they had adequate reserves but refused to rush ahead with development, for economic reasons. Besides, they argued, they could not possibly get gas flowing from new fields for ten to fifteen years. Western European governments told American officials that even if Norway could provide some gas, they would consider it a supplement to Soviet supplies, not a substitute.

When Richard Perle traveled to Oslo in June 1982, he met with the same "polite but brusque" response.[120] His arguments that cheap Soviet gas would drive Norway out of the market fell on deaf ears. Norwegian energy minister Vidkunn Hveding stated, "We have said repeatedly that it is not technically feasible for us to become the major supplier until the mid 1990s and I am a bit puzzled that the U.S. insists on seeing us as an alternative. The Europeans need their gas now and cannot wait until the mid 1990s."[121] Although many forecasters in the United States and Europe were beginning to question whether the Europeans "needed their gas now," the Norwegian government's refusal to give in to U.S. demands blocked off one route by which the United States could compensate Europe for joining in pipeline sanctions. Although Washington demanded Norwegian cooperation, it apparently offered no economic assistance for a rapid gas-development plan.

The United States searched for other alternatives, such as increasing its own coal exports.[122] However, this plan fell through because such an increase would require major expenditures on port modernization, which the administration was unwilling to fund. To the amazement of Europeans, the administration suggested that they should increase imports of oil from OPEC and gas from Algeria—precisely the troublesome suppliers that had driven the Continent to the Soviet Union in the first place.

With all these factors in mind, the Western Europeans turned to the Soviet Union as an important supplier of gas for the mid-1980s. Soviet exports of oil would be decreasing during this period, so Moscow looked forward to gas exports to keep up its hard-currency earnings.[123] Because of the decrease in oil imports, Siberian gas imports would not change net energy purchases from the Soviet Union to any large degree—although the lack of a natural-gas market made oil imports preferable, according to arguments about dependence.[124] In 1980 and 1981, European firms competed eagerly for contracts to build two Siberian pipelines. As mentioned above, governments helped their firms in this competition by offering to subsidize export credits, resulting in interest rates approximately eight points below the market rate.[125]

By mid-1981, European governments were beginning to have second thoughts about this frenzy of contracts. Because of an economic recession, estimates of gas demand for the mid-1980s were scaled down significantly. In July 1981, *The Economist* reported that some analysts were admitting that Soviet gas was not needed in the near future.[126] The

Siberian project was scaled back from two pipelines to one, and only fields where gas was most accessible would be developed. The Dutch government revised its strategy of conserving reserves, extending contracts for another decade.[127] Falling oil prices led to predictions of an energy glut in the next few years. As one analyst noted, "Western European importers might be facing an embarrassment of choice over the next two decades."[128]

Arguments that the Europeans had no alternative to building the pipeline began to ring hollow. There was little doubt that even if the Europeans stopped all sales of pipeline equipment, the Soviets could build the pipeline within a couple of years of the scheduled completion date. An internal U.S. government report, prepared by the Central Intelligence Agency in August 1982, concluded that the Soviets would make gas deliveries, in spite of U.S. actions, by using existing pipe and alternative suppliers and by diverting goods from domestic construction.[129] Thus, although cheap Siberian gas provided strong incentives to go ahead with the pipeline contracts, the argument that these contracts were vital to European energy security is not tenable. Although it would have been costly, the Europeans could have gotten by without Siberian gas for a couple of years, until the Soviets completed the pipeline on their own.

Economic justification for the pipeline thus changed from energy needs to a Keynesian argument that equipment exports provided desperately needed jobs during the recession. Clearly, British firms were driven by this consideration, since Britain had no plans to import any Siberian gas. According to an official in the German economics ministry, West German pipeline deals were motivated by the same factor: "We would have been able to survive very comfortably without the Soviet natural gas. The pipeline contract was dictated by pure misery—jobs were the main consideration."[130] Pitt Treumann of the Amsterdam-Rotterdam Bank concurred: "The whole point of the pipeline was to give work to European exporters, and the gas itself was less important."[131]

Could this need for jobs explain the intensity of Europeans' resistance to U.S. demands? Clearly, the jobs created by the pipeline deal influenced European preferences. Yet one factor seems to undercut the explanatory power of this variable. As discussed above, European firms had reluctantly decided that they would rather comply with American demands than lose the American market. John Brown, for example, would have complied with the U.S. sanctions if the British government had not directly ordered it to fulfill its contracts. Dresser-France defied U.S. orders only after the French government threatened to requisition its facilities. These companies needed American commerce more than they needed the Soviet market. European firms were the entities directly affected by loss of business from the pipeline. Because they were prepared to comply with U.S. sanctions, however reluctantly, the argument that their need for Soviet exports tipped the scales loses its persuasive power. Europeans did, unquestionably, want the jobs generated by the pipeline contracts. However, U.S. countersanctions would have been even more costly in terms of jobs.

In addition, by 1982 Siberian gas no longer seemed essential to the European energy picture; and even a complete embargo on European exports would have only delayed, not stopped, the pipeline. Such an embargo certainly would have entailed high costs—perhaps driving up the price of Soviet gas in the future, after the Soviets had built their own pipeline. These costs explain why the United States found itself in a coercion game on this issue. However, at least from the firms' perspective, the costs of threatened U.S. countersanctions were even higher. Thus, the American failure resulted not from a lack of coercive tools, but from an unwillingness to use these tools. U.S. threats were potentially costly enough to push Europeans into sanctions—but, as I argue in the next section, they were not credible. The American government's unwillingness to bear the costs of sanctions, reflected in its refusal to impose a grain embargo, generated fatal questions about the intentions and credibility of the administration.

## The Grain Embargo: Why It Mattered

Many analysts have recognized the American refusal to impose a grain embargo against the Soviet Union as an irritant in the pipeline dispute, but few have credited it with a pivotal role. One exception is Jonathan Stern, who argued that "even those Europeans who were prepared to go along with sanctions after Afghanistan have had this view shaken by the Reagan administration's action in ending the grain embargo. With hindsight, this may prove to be the act which has fatally undermined US policy on commercial sanctions against the Soviet Union."[132]

As was shown in the analysis of the aggregate data on sanctions, the costs borne by the major sender play an important role in explaining cooperation. The event-count model showed that the major sender's willingness to bear significant costs could raise the number of countries participating in sanctions by as much as nine. In this section, I explore the link between American unwillingness to bear the costs of a grain embargo and European resistance to pipeline sanctions. I argue that American action had two effects. First, it added to European suspicions that the administration was actually interested in extending the scope of permanent export controls, not in responding to the crisis in Poland. Second, U.S. unwillingness to bear high costs convinced Europe that the administration was bluffing in its countersanctions threats. This behavior reinforced other actions that sent signals about lack of credibility to the Europeans.

Throughout the pipeline-sanctions crisis, Europeans demanded that the United States demonstrate its commitment to sanctions by cutting sales of its major export to the Soviet Union, grain. While Western European sales to the Soviets consisted primarily of industrial and manufactured goods, agricultural products accounted for 63 percent of American exports to the Soviet Union in 1979.[133] In this situation, if the United States exempted grain exports from the Western embargo, the price paid by the United States as a whole would be much smaller than that paid by Western Europe. As Stern noted, "if the U.S. was unwilling to sustain the financial loss of the grain embargo, it is difficult for Europeans to understand why they should be expected to bear what would certainly be the much larger adverse effect of abstaining from energy trade."[134] Refusal to consider a grain embargo came to symbolize the extent to which Washington wanted to avoid paying for its foreign policy.

Early reports suggested that the American delegations sent to Europe would meet with more success if they were allowed to discuss agricultural sales. One report noted that "to persuade the Europeans to impose significant sanctions of their own, President Reagan may have to take the politically painful step of curbing grain shipments."[135] In February, while the administration was declaring its intention to stop the pipeline, it sold half a million metric tons of corn to the Soviet Union in one week.[136]

European outcries about grain sales intensified after the administration extended sanctions to cover U.S. subsidiaries in June. French foreign trade minister Jobert said that the United States should make "its own effort first," by blocking delivery of grain.[137] However, two weeks later Agriculture Secretary John Block forecasted record Soviet grain purchases from the United States for the next year. His department had even suggested raising the ceiling on grain sales; but the idea was opposed by the State Department, which anticipated European outrage.[138] One French analyst who claimed to support the Reagan administration's sanctions policy said that these sales had directly undercut the U.S. government's aims in Western Europe.[139]

By August, Reagan was under attack at home and abroad for his refusal to impose restrictions on grain sales. Members of Congress called the decision hypocritical.[140] West German chancellor Helmut Kohl, in his first news conference after taking office, stressed the continuation of the previous government's policies on East-West trade. Referring to the

United States, he said that "one should not demand of the other what one would not like to have demanded of oneself."[141] In mid-October, the administration exacerbated the situation by announcing that it would resume negotiations on a grain agreement with the Soviet Union.[142] *The Economist* responded to this action by pointing out that a Wharton Econometrics study had shown that the Soviet Union saved about $32 billion by buying U.S. grain rather than growing its own, thus undercutting the administration's arguments that grain sales drained Soviet hard-currency reserves.[143]

Understandably, grain sales angered Europeans, leading them to argue that the United States was not bearing its fair share of the costs of sanctions. Yet the link between this anger and the intense defiance of sanctions remains fuzzy. Uncertainty about two aspects of the administration's stance—its real intentions and the credibility of its countersanctions threats—provides the link between rhetoric and action.

Analysts of sanctions and other foreign-policy actions have noted the importance of self-imposed costs for demonstrating resolve. Words are cheap, but costly actions provide other states with clues about a government's intentions and sincerity in carrying out a particular policy. As Hans Morgenthau argued, "the character of a foreign policy can be ascertained only through the examination of the political acts performed."[144] Deborah Larson finds that costly behavior is taken seriously precisely because it surprises other states: "Because it is unexpected and cannot easily be attributed to situational pressures, costly behavior is regarded as evidence of intentionality."[145] For example, a hegemonic power could demonstrate its commitment to norms and rules by incurring costs. Conversely, refusal to bear costs raises questions about a state's commitment and real intentions. A state that refuses to take costly actions will be suspected of acting opportunistically, attempting to fool others into accepting the "sucker's payoff."

In any East-West trade issue, Europeans find themselves suspicious of American intentions. Frequently, they wonder whether the United States is asking Europe to restrain trade just so American exporters can increase their profits. In the pipeline case, a different version of this suspicion arose. Reagan came into office talking about the Soviet Union as an "evil empire" and taking steps to limit East-West industrial trade. Europeans began to worry that the United States wanted to extend the scope of permanent Western export controls to include all industrial goods and to prevent energy imports, resulting in drastic reductions in trade between Western Europe and the Soviet bloc. Europeans and most Americans had rejected such restrictions, as discussed in the previous chapter. Such controls would differ from a coordinated response to events in Poland in that they would not be lifted if the situation in Poland improved.

While many Western Europeans were reluctant to take economic measures in response to the Polish crisis, they were even more strongly opposed to returning to the broad controls of the early 1950s on a permanent basis. Thus, they suspected that the Reagan administration was using the Polish situation as a cover for an attempt to trick them into a completely different game, one they were not willing to play. When the administration escalated its rhetoric and its restrictions on European trade during the summer of 1982 with only vague references to Poland, these fears were amplified. If the intent of sanctions was to punish the Soviet Union for its role in Poland, Europeans reasoned, the administration could inflict the most pain by cutting off grain exports. Unwillingness to do this inevitably added to suspicions that the administration had entirely different goals in mind. The U.S. refusal to accept the costs of a grain embargo helped convince European leaders that the United States was not sincere in its declarations that sanctions were intended to help the Polish people and would be lifted when the crisis was over.

Besides demonstrating intentionality, costs can help establish a government's credibility. Thomas Schelling alluded to this dynamic when he argued that the "right to be sued" would help convince other players of the credibility of one's threats.[146] David Baldwin has applied this insight to the problem of economic sanctions. According to Baldwin, a state might choose to impose sanctions that are more costly to itself than to the target precisely to demonstrate resolve and credibility of commitments.[147] He notes that "the ability to incur costs is inextricably linked with the ability to make binding commitments. In a cost-free world, no one could ever demonstrate resolve."[148] Thus, Baldwin argues, Reagan's choice of a cheap form of sanctions should have led the Soviet Union to question the credibility of his commitment to help the Poles.

If the refusal to embargo grain raised questions in Moscow, it did the same in London, Paris, and Bonn. These governments, besides asking questions about the real motivation for U.S. actions, wondered whether the United States would actually carry through with its threatened countersanctions. As mentioned above, these countersanctions would have been very costly for the United States, especially since they raised the possibility of an all-out trade war. Would a government unwilling to compensate its farmers for lost sales of eight million tons of grain really run the risk of a severe disruption of trade with the EC and possibly Japan? It seemed unlikely.

The grain-embargo question provided an important clue to U.S. domestic political constraints. If the administration could not put through a grain embargo, it would probably lose on countersanctions as well. Thus, the administration's unwillingness to push for a grain embargo in Congress angered U.S. allies but also helped them assess the likely outcome of any attempt to carry out measures with drastically higher domestic costs. Without a grain embargo, threats of countersanctions simply were not credible. Thus, European governments decided to take their chances and jointly call the administration's bluff. They proved correct in their assessment. Not only did the administration back down on its countersanctions threats, it lifted controls on American firms at the same time that it dropped its extraterritorial measures. In the long run, the administration was not willing to bear the costs of a grain embargo, countersanctions, or even unilateral pipeline controls.

This analysis of the U.S. threat raises one question: why did European governments call the American bluff while European firms, as mentioned above, preferred to back down? Without assuming that firms and governments had different preferences or degrees of risk aversion, but allowing for some uncertainty about the credibility of the U.S. threat, we find one possible answer in the different strategic positions of the firms and governments. With respect to the dozens of European firms with pipeline contracts, the U.S. government was playing a classic reputation game.[149] By hitting Dresser-France with stiff penalties, it hoped to deter further entry into the market by convincing other firms they would have to pay the same price.

However, there is no reason to expect that this divide-and-conquer strategy would work against the French government, for example. Here, the United States was dealing not with a series of independent firms, but with one government. The situation was analogous to that of duopolists, with one trying to force the other to exit.[150] Even if the French government had the same beliefs about U.S. preferences as its firms had, there is no reason to expect these two games to have the same equilibria. A U.S. strategy of strict punishment of the first few firms might convince the others to back down, while the French government would find it worthwhile to continue playing the game, deriving benefits from future rounds. Thus, threats could work against the firms but not the government, since firms were not in a position to derive benefits from future plays—they could make only one entry decision each.

Analysis of the pipeline crisis adds depth to the observation that the costs borne by the major sender are closely correlated with the level of cooperation. In the pipeline case, the American refusal to impose a grain embargo meant U.S. costs were low. The unwillingness of the Reagan administration to take costly measures while demanding that its allies do so infuriated the Europeans. More fundamentally, however, it sent signals about the administration's intentions and credibility. Refusal to take the one step that would actually cost the United States much added to suspicions that the Reagan administration was using the Polish crisis simply as a cover for a more-disturbing return to wide-ranging export controls and restrictions on energy imports. In addition, U.S. actions on the grain embargo and other issues told the Europeans that threats of reprisals that could have led to a trade war were not credible. Thus, as the aggregate data suggested, the costs borne by the United States are the missing piece in the puzzle of tenacious European resistance to pipeline sanctions. American refusal to impose a grain embargo reinforced other signals, tipping the scales toward defiance of the Reagan administration's demands.

## Conclusion

The 1982 sanctions against the Soviet Union and Poland constitute one of the classic cases of failure to cooperate. In this chapter, I argue that this failure actually involved only one aspect of the total sanctions effort—attempts to halt the construction of a natural-gas pipeline from Siberia to Western Europe. With respect to Poland itself, both the United States and Europe imposed some relatively innocuous sanctions. Britain, West Germany, and France also took mild measures against the Soviet Union, including an EC-approved reduction in imports of luxury goods. None of these measures involved much economic sacrifice from those imposing sanctions, nor did they inflict high costs on the Soviet Union. However, American and European policies were basically in accord on these sanctions.

The real divergence of policies occurred on the pipeline issue. Here, the United States unquestionably failed to gain European or Japanese cooperation and eventually had to back down even from its own gas- and oil-equipment embargo. In a typical bandwagoning pattern, European governments followed one another in forcing their firms to go ahead with pipeline contracts in spite of American regulations and threats of counter-sanctions. The explanatory variables used in this study, particularly the level of costs borne by the leading sender, give us insight into the intensity of European resistance to American demands. Alternative explanations of the failure involve the decline of American hegemony and the economics of the Western European gas market. Neither anecdotal nor aggregate data provide support for the hegemonic-decline argument. The pipeline incident cannot be seen as part of a pattern of decreased American ability to achieve cooperation, since the level of cooperation when the United States plays a leadership role increased overall between 1945 and 1989.

The structure of the European gas market did directly influence European preferences. The pipeline deal was driven by anxiety about energy supplies in the 1980s, an anxiety spawned by the oil crises of the 1970s. However, by 1982 the urgency of the energy situation had decreased considerably. Although Soviet gas remained a cheap source of energy,

European economies could have gotten along without it for a few years. Thus, while economic incentives go far toward explaining the European response, they do not appear to be adequate to account for the intense level of conflict seen in 1982.

I argue that the pivotal factor in explaining the failure of cooperation in this episode is the U.S. government's unwillingness to bear the costs of a grain embargo. This reticence led European governments to question both the intentions of the Reagan administration and the credibility of its threats. A government unwilling or unable to pay for a grain embargo would probably not carry through with costly countersanctions. In the end, Europe decided to call the U.S. bluff—and it won. This case suggests that the correlation between costs borne by the leading sender and the level of cooperation is due to the importance of self-imposed costs in demonstrating resolve and credibility, a suggestion that brings us back to the theoretical framework developed at the beginning of this book. In this coercion game, the United States linked pipeline sanctions to access to American technology in an attempt to gain cooperation. However, because the government did not take the necessary steps to make its threats credible, the sanctions failed.

# 9

# Conclusion

THIS CHAPTER summarizes the results of this study's investigation of when states cooperate and the implications of these results for future research on economic sanctions and on cooperation among states. First, I address the status of the hypotheses developed in chapter 2 about the conditions under which states will cooperate to impose sanctions. The cases and data in this book have given significant support to some, while others have not held up as well. Second, I outline new questions raised by the case studies, questions that deserve further research. Finally, I turn to an evaluation of how this project fits into broader research programs on international cooperation and economic sanctions. What substantive or methodological implications does this work have for these research programs? The combination of approaches utilized in this study allowed both hypothesis testing and insight into specific cases. By putting these cases in the broader framework of aggregate results on cooperation, we are led to more-plausible and more-generalizable explanations for the failure or success of international cooperation, suggesting the utility of this methodology in studies of international politics.

## Explaining International Cooperation on Economic Sanctions

This work began with a game-theoretic model of the decision about whether to impose economic sanctions. The range of different games that resulted from this model suggested that the three dominant approaches to explaining international cooperation—liberalism, realism, and neoliberal institutionalism—are too narrowly focused, each dealing with only one type of cooperation problem. Games that characterize sanctions decisions can be divided into three categories: coincidence, coercion, and coadjustment, each with a specific equilibrium. Coincidence games result in bilateral sanctions in equilibrium, while coercion games result in unilateral sanctions. In coadjustment games, neither state imposes sanctions at full capacity, but this is a suboptimal outcome. These games characterize, respectively, the liberal, realist, and neoliberal institutionalist approaches to explaining cooperation.

This simple model, which considered only two players and one period, obviously fails to capture many of the complexities of real-world cases of economic sanctions. Because actual cases involve more than two potential sanctioners, we frequently see in a single episode the dynamics of more than one type of game. For example, high-technology sanctions against the Soviet Union are characterized by a coercion game between the United States and European countries and, simultaneously, by a coadjustment game among the European states. In addition, the single-play model cannot capture the credibility effects that were so important in the data and the cases. Nevertheless, this exercise in game theory did lead to a typology of cooperation problems that was useful for suggesting factors that would tend to encourage or inhibit cooperation.

The empirical work in this study focused on seven hypotheses about factors that would influence the level of cooperation in post-1945 cases of economic sanctions. These hypotheses concerned the economic and political condition of the target; whether the case crossed East-West boundaries; whether the target received assistance; whether the leading sender bore high costs; declining U.S. hegemony; whether an international institution called for sanctions; and bandwagoning. They received varying degrees of empirical support.

First, the evidence here quite decisively refutes one hypothesis—that declining hegemony affects the level of cooperation. If the implications of hegemonic-stability theory held, the United States should have been, over time, decreasingly able to gain the cooperation of others. Instead, we find in the aggregate results that the United States has, on average, received less cooperation than other states but that its record has improved over time. Hegemonic-stability theory would lead us to expect the opposite pattern. In addition to these aggregate results, the two East-West cases in this study further undermine hypotheses about the role of hegemony. In 1980, the United States did persuade its allies to cut high-technology sales to the Soviet Union in spite of decreased U.S. control over resources in this area. In 1982, Washington failed to gain similar cooperation, but changes in relative power are not central to the explanation of this failure. Instead, American unwillingness to bear significant costs convinced its allies that they could afford to challenge the United States. Because incentives to cooperate increase as the distribution of power becomes less concentrated, and because institutions exist to facilitate such cooperation, hegemonic-stability theory tells us little about the level of cooperation in cases of economic sanctions.

Two hypotheses received little support in the statistical analysis—those involving the economic and political condition of the target and whether sanctions crossed East-West boundaries. Because sanctions are less likely to succeed against stable, economically well-off countries, we should expect a greater coincidence of interests when sanctions are directed against weak, poor states. While the coefficient of the variable measuring the target's condition was negative, as predicted, in most analyses it was not statistically significant. Thus, we cannot conclude anything specific about the impact of the target's condition on cooperation.

A similar situation holds for the impact of the Cold War. While the results showed a slight tendency toward more cooperation in East-West cases, this effect was not statistically significant. The case studies lend support to the conclusion that states have no more difficulty cooperating in North-South than in East-West cases, as questions of colonialism rather than the Cold War dominated the instance of greatest cooperation in this study—the Falklands episode. In general, the dynamics of cooperation in the two cases of sanctions directed against the Soviet Union seemed quite similar to those in the two North-South cases. Thus, surprisingly, similar models and factors seem to explain cooperation whether or not the issue was part of the East-West conflict. Issues of credibility and the role of institutions have far more explanatory power than, as a neorealist might expect, whether sanctions crossed Cold War boundaries. In general, strategic variables outperform alternative explanations.

One hypothesis—that assistance to the target would tend to increase the level of cooperation—received moderately strong support in the aggregate data but did not figure in the case studies. This discrepancy is due simply to case selection. If potential sanctioners and states sympathetic to the target tend to balance one another, we should find more cooperation when the target receives assistance. This effect does show up in the data. However, in the four cases examined more closely, the target never received significant assistance. Getting variation along this dimension would require additional case studies and may be a promising avenue for future research. The need for further work on balancing assistance to the target is particularly compelling, given the finding that potential sanctioners bandwagon among themselves. Such research may allow us to begin to specify the conditions under which bandwagoning or balancing occurs.

Three hypotheses received strong support in both the aggregate results and the case studies—the hypotheses about the costs borne by the leading sender, the effect of international institutions, and bandwagoning among potential sanctioners. The aggregate results showed a strong correlation of costs and institutions with the level of cooperation. The case studies provided evidence that these correlations reflect underlying causal processes and are not simply an artifact. They suggest that problems of credibility and the need to signal intentions explain these relationships.

In most cases of economic sanctions, one state has a strong interest in seeing sanctions imposed and in making them multilateral. Frequently, this situation puts that state in a coercion game, where other potential sanctioners are happy to free-ride on the leading sender's actions. Thus, the leading sender has to link other issues to the sanctions, making credible threats or promises in order to gain cooperation. The incentives to make such linkages and the credibility of such linkages are closely tied to the costs of sanctions for the leading sender and to international institutions. If the sender faces high costs, it will be under greater pressure to gain cooperation in order to make sanctions more effective. In addition, a willingness to bear high costs will help to convince others that the sender is serious about sanctions and will thus help make threats or promises more credible. Bearing high costs demonstrates that the proponent of sanctions can overcome domestic opposition, and it puts force behind the rhetoric of promises and threats. Refusal to bear costs has the opposite effect, leading other potential sanctioners to call the major sender's bluff. Even in the relatively congenial conditions of an assurance or coadjustment game, the leading sender must establish a credible commitment to sanctions if it hopes to gain others' cooperation. Thus, we should see that high costs lead to greater cooperation.

In the aggregate, we find that costs have a substantively and statistically significant impact on the level of cooperation. The case studies show that they do have a causal role in sanctions cases. In U.S. sanctions against Latin America, the United States bore very low or negative costs, and it received no cooperation from other states. In this case, low costs coincided with low incentives to gain cooperation—Washington paid lip service to the need for multilateral action but made only nominal efforts to convince others to impose sanctions. The positive role of costs is highlighted in the 1982 pipeline sanctions. Here, because the U.S. government refused to bear the costs of another grain embargo, Europeans did not believe American threats of countersanctions and refused to delay construction of the Siberian pipeline. This case shows the importance of self-imposed costs in demonstrating credibility and thus gaining cooperation. It contrasts to the situation in CoCom in 1980, where the United States bore a significant share of the costs of sanctions and did get cooperation on high-technology sanctions.

International institutions had a larger impact on cooperation than any other variable in this study. In the statistical analysis, we found a much-higher level of cooperation when a formal international organization called for sanctions. However, without the evidence found in the case studies, a skeptic could argue that this result was an artifact—that states used institutions merely to ratify their decisions and that institutions had no direct impact on state actions. The case studies in this book refute that criticism by showing direct links between institutional and state decisions. The case of British sanctions against Argentina and the case of high-technology controls, in particular, show how institutions constrain state decisions. In the sanctions against Argentina, the European Community played a central role. EC members did not impose sanctions on their own, but only through joint EC decisions. Even a non-EC member, Japan, appeared to base its actions on this institution's decisions. Ireland's decisions on sanctions provide additional evidence. After hostilities began in the Falklands, the Irish government developed a strong distaste for supporting the British through economic measures. However, it maintained sanctions through their original term because the EC would not agree to lifting them. Afraid of jeopardizing other EC benefits, such as farm subsidies, Ireland reluctantly abided by its obligations.

In the case of high-technology sanctions, the United States would have faced a much more difficult time in gaining any cooperation from its allies if the CoCom mechanism had not existed in 1980. The Europeans and Japanese agreed to a "no-exceptions" policy that tightened controls on exports of high-technology goods to the Soviet Union. None of these governments imposed additional restrictions on such exports prior to the institutional decision; they cooperated in this instance because they valued the other benefits CoCom provided. In the pipeline case two years later, Washington was prevented from using the CoCom mechanism because pipeline materials were not on the list of goods covered by CoCom. Thus, the U.S. government could find no analogue to the no-exceptions policy. CoCom provided an especially useful institutional environment, as it gave the United States veto power over exceptions requests. In instances where the United States attempted to use institutions in which it did not have veto power—such as the MDBs in the human-rights case—it had less success.

How did the EC and CoCom influence state decisions? In general terms, states complied with institutional decisions in order to avoid jeopardizing the broad functional benefits these organizations provided. In the EC case, Ireland valued Community participation highly for a wide range of reasons, including the benefits the Common Agricultural Policy provided to Irish farmers. Ireland's defection from sanctions would have called into question its reliability on other institutional agreements, jeopardizing its gains in other issue areas. The EC also facilitated cooperation by providing a framework for a side payment—British concessions on the EC budget. This issue linkage allowed the renewal of sanctions after fighting began in the Falklands.

In CoCom, a similar issue linkage within the institution explains compliance. CoCom deals, for the most part, with the assurance game of export controls on goods with significant military relevance. States value this function highly—first, because they see large costs if they control such exports while their allies do not; and second, because the boundary between militarily significant goods and those with less military relevance is not obvious, but subject to agreement within the institution. Thus, CoCom, although a weak institution, provides valuable information on the preferences and activities of its members. If members evaded the no-exceptions rule, others would question their reliability on the issues that CoCom more frequently manages—and the entire institution would be put in jeopardy. Thus, CoCom effectively coordinated foreign-policy sanctions in 1980 because it allowed the United States to link the issue of these sanctions to the assurance game of permanent export controls.

Overall, Britain and the United States used the EC and CoCom, respectively, to pursue economic-sanctions policies. I should note that while institutions were good for sanctions, the converse does not hold. In both the Falklands and CoCom cases, the leading sender pushed the limits of the institutions slightly beyond the issue areas that other members wanted them to cover. In the human rights cases, the United States made some feeble attempts to expand the functions of international financial institutions to cover human rights, without success. In the EC and CoCom situations, however, the sanctions were close enough to the day-to-day practices of the organizations to allow a plausible argument for linkage. However, continued use of these institutions for such "peripheral" purposes could threaten their existence, as other members begin to recalculate the costs and benefits of compliance. Continued American use of CoCom for foreign-policy goals, for example, could undermine its effectiveness on national-security controls, as some critics of U.S. policy have argued. Institutions can strengthen cooperation on sanctions, but the practice of sanctions can weaken institutions.

This finding about institutions fits well with the final major conclusion of this study—that potential sanctioners bandwagon. Their decisions are positively related to one another, and the result is either buck-passing or chain-ganging behavior. The aggregate results suggest that potential sanctioners did not make their decisions independently and did not appear to balance one another; instead, they bandwagoned, creating a situation of positive contagion. One state's decision to impose sanctions increased the probability that others would sanction as well. The contingent nature of decisions also shows up in most of the case studies, as governments declared that they would impose sanctions only as part of a joint effort. States show a strong aversion to being isolated in imposing sanctions, and the involvement of institutions increases the size of this effect. The degree of bandwagoning increases when international institutions are involved. These are precisely the results we expect in the kinds of games that characterize economic sanctions, and they show the importance of considering the strategic incentives facing states. Alternative explanations, such as one linking cooperation in a straightforward way to the goals of sanctions, do not hold up in the data. Cooperation increases not as the goals of sanctions become more ambitious, but as the leading sender establishes credible commitments.

The most strongly supported and substantively significant findings of this study are that the costs borne by the major sender and the involvement of international institutions have strong, significant impacts on cooperation; and that potential sanctioners bandwagon. All are consistent with an emphasis on the strategic problems facing states considering sanctions. I also find some evidence that assistance to the target state has a positive impact on cooperation. The economic and political condition of the target, whether the case crosses East-West boundaries, and the goals of sanctions appear to have negligible effects. I find no support for the hypothesis that cooperation declines along with U.S. hegemony. Thus, credibility and issue linkage provide the best answers to questions about what furthers cooperation.

## Additional Findings

While the statistical analysis and selection of case studies were designed to test the hypotheses discussed above, some unexpected patterns arose that deserve further attention. Since few authors have examined the question of cooperation on economic sanctions, except to note that it is necessary but difficult to achieve, this study cannot be considered the final word on the subject. Instead, it presents a framework for analyzing issues of cooperation, discusses some empirical results, and opens some questions for further study.

The case of British and EC sanctions against Argentina during the Falklands War suggests a direction for future research. We saw that the Europeans' willingness to join Britain in sanctions decreased significantly once actual hostilities broke out. This attitude reflects early-twentieth-century understandings of the role of economic sanctions in international politics, when many saw them as potential substitutes for military action. Analysts have discredited this belief in recent years, arguing that sanctions are not effective enough to substitute for military action. However, the Falklands case suggests that the idea of substituting economic for military responses may not have fallen completely out of favor. This case also has intriguing analogies with the sanctions and military action against Iraq in 1990–91. In general, the question of when states choose to use economic sanctions as opposed to other foreign-policy tools deserves more study.

The cases of U.S. human-rights sanctions against Latin America suggest another relevant dimension of sanctions: whether they are imposed in response to specific events in the target country, or in response to domestic politics in the sending country. In these human-rights cases, the impetus for sanctions came largely from American domestic politics rather than specific actions of the targets; the targets were guilty of human-rights abuses long before the United States considered imposing sanctions. In this situation, the issue of gaining international cooperation did not receive much attention within the U.S. government, and little cooperation emerged. The exception that proves the rule is the case of Chile, where states did impose sanctions in response to a specific event—a coup d'état—and where a significant level of cooperation resulted. Future research should differentiate between sanctions imposed for domestic reasons and those imposed in response to specific events in the target.

Finally, further work on the problem of cooperation in economic sanctions should expand the universe of cases to include those where no state imposed sanctions. In this study, at least one state imposed sanctions in every case. This truncation, however, leads to selection bias, which some of the statistical models took into account. However, inclusion of cases where states failed to overcome their collective-action problem would improve our understanding of coadjustment problems. The issue here is how to define this universe of cases—what do we mean by a "case" where no state imposed sanctions? Answering this question may require taking seriously the issue just raised—whether states impose sanctions for domestic or foreign-policy reasons.

## Implications for Theories of International Cooperation and Economic Sanctions

An interest in the literatures on economic sanctions and international cooperation motivated this study. This final section returns to these broader issues, discussing what implications this work might have for theories of international cooperation and of economic sanctions.

A first set of questions has to do with the methodology used in this study, which drew on game theory, statistical analysis, and case studies. How did each of these approaches contribute to the overall analysis? How did they complement one another?

The game-theoretic model introduced at the beginning of chapter 2 proved useful in developing a typology but did not lead directly to predictions about cooperation. Analysis of strategic interaction between states suggested that three types of cooperation problems—coincidence, coercion, and coadjustment—could characterize sanctions situations. Each of these types of problems fit into a particular theoretical approach to international relations, allowing me to draw on these literatures to develop specific hypotheses.

However, the models themselves could not generate hypotheses without this intermediate step. For game theory to directly generate predictions about behavior, we have to assume that equilibrium concepts constrain actual outcomes. However, in situations of coercion and coadjustment, the analytical problem is to explain how states *move away* from an equilibrium of either unilateral or no sanctions to multilateral sanctions. While the models can show why states find it difficult to maintain cooperation under such conditions, they do not specify factors that will facilitate cooperation. Because multilateral sanctions often seem to be a non-equilibrium outcome, the simple models used here are useful devices, but not sufficient unless embedded within bodies of theory on international politics.

We might be able to solve this dilemma by using more-sophisticated models that allow for uncertainty, repeated play, and different types of linkage. However, this approach has its own pitfalls. First, as many game theorists have noted, once we allow for these kinds of complications the number of equilibria escalates rapidly. Thus, these sophisticated models, while coming closer to reality, might leave us just as confused about precisely what outcomes to expect under what conditions. Second, once we add factors such as repeated play and uncertainty to the model, the range of cases to which it may apply shrinks. The simple model used here has the advantage that it should have some relevance to almost all situations of economic sanctions. In particular cases, such as the pipeline sanctions, we can make a strong argument for expanding on this model to include the effects of reputation and credibility. While looking at more-complicated games would probably improve our understanding of specific subsets of cases with common characteristics, simple models proved an extremely useful analytical device for developing hypotheses applicable to the universe of economic-sanctions cases. One path for further research might involve breaking down this universe into manageable subsets to allow use of models with greater predictive power.

A second methodological question has to do with the statistical analysis used in this study. I would argue strongly in favor of more use of these techniques in studies of both international cooperation and economic sanctions. When grounded in a theoretical framework, statistical approaches in international relations can be much more than inductive fishing expeditions, as some critics have charged they are. In this study, the aggregate analysis allowed me to identify patterns missed by studies that looked at only a few cases. For example, the conventional wisdom that sanctions are very costly to the sending countries did not hold up. We also saw how the emphasis put on the Rhodesian and South African cases could skew our understanding of the typical case of economic sanctions. Attempting to develop measures of cooperation applicable to all ninety-nine cases in the data set forced me to confront the question of defining clearly the concept of cooperation; the distinction between coadjustment and cooperation was the result. Because I could not find any fully acceptable measure of cooperation, I relied on three proxies and used statistical models appropriate for each. With an unobservable variable such as cooperation, this kind of technique helps solve some methodological problems. Finally, the aggregate analysis provided support for some hypotheses and not others, showing the generalizability of these explanations of cooperation.

However, this statistical work would be somewhat shaky if not bolstered by detailed case studies. Skeptics could argue that the aggregate results did not show any causal pattern—for example, that institutional approval only reflected state decisions without constraining them. By looking carefully at state preferences and decision making, the case studies provided support for the causal hypotheses underlying the aggregate results. The case studies and statistical work thus complemented one another, providing different types of support for the seven hypotheses examined here. Further complementarity resulted from the new insights that the typology of cooperation problems and quantitative results generated into cases that have already received substantial academic attention.

With respect to substantive issues, this work has some implications for research on economic sanctions. First, it shows that the role of self-imposed costs needs further attention. Sanctions can be a useful foreign-policy tool precisely because they force the sender to bear costs, costs that demonstrate resolve. But how can we distinguish a skillful strategy of using high-cost sanctions from a merely incompetent one? At what point does "demonstrating resolve" become simply an excuse for foreign-policy failure? More empirical work on the domestic politics of economic sanctions might begin answering some of these questions. Second, this study shows that states *can* achieve cooperation to impose sanctions, although it is difficult. Thus, we should question arguments that sanctions never work because alternative sources or markets always exist for sanctioned goods. Instead, we should frame this question positively: how can states increase the probability that targets will have a hard time circumventing sanctions?

This work also contributes to the growing literature on international cooperation. From a theoretical standpoint, it suggests that theorists of international cooperation have to expand the models they use beyond those that assume symmetrical interests. In the cases in this study, states seldom had symmetrical interests, a situation that changed the dynamics of cooperation. The typology of coincidence, coercion, and coadjustment games might be a first cut at dealing with problems of asymmetry. Some of the cases in this study also point to the central role of credibility and reputation in facilitating cooperation, suggesting that theories of international cooperation would benefit by considering these factors more carefully.

Finally, this study adds to the growing literature on the role of international institutions. It lends empirical support to the neoliberal institutionalist view that institutions constrain state behavior and have a significant impact on international outcomes, though this study uses a model in which interests are more asymmetric than in the models usually adopted by neoliberal approaches. It suggests that work on cooperation should continue to take the role of institutions seriously, and it adds one twist to this literature by showing that institutions tend to increase the level of bandwagoning behavior among states. States seem extremely reluctant to be isolated either in imposing sanctions or in refusing to impose them, and this effect becomes more pronounced when an institution gets involved. I have suggested that this fear of isolation results from the issue linkages that institutions create, so that defection on one issue can undermine cooperation on more highly valued ones. However, the question of the relationship between institutions and bandwagoning deserves further attention. The appearance of bandwagoning behavior suggests the need for investigation of the conditions under which states will balance or bandwagon, since bandwagoning challenges the conventional realist belief that states always practice balancing behavior.

From a methodological perspective, game theory as a method of generating hypotheses and the combination of quantitative and qualitative empirical research provided a great deal of explanatory leverage in this study and should prove useful in other studies of international cooperation. From a substantive viewpoint, the findings presented here should encourage further work on problems of credibility, asymmetrical interests, and the role of institutions in international relations.

# Notes

In the notes, works listed in the Bibliography are referred to by the author's name alone. The year of publication is given only where the Bibliography includes more than one work by the same author.

## Chapter 1
## Introduction

1. Some examples of this type of study include Jack; Wu; Knorr and Trager; Doxey, 1980; Wallensteen.

2. For an influential early explanation of the failure of sanctions, see Galtung.

3. See Doxey, 1980; Highley.

4. On Rhodesia, see Doxey, 1980; Losman; Renwick; Porter, 1978; Strack. On South Africa, see Doxey, 1972; Porter, 1979; Barber and Spicer.

5. See Galtung.

6. See Gilmore; Ghoshal; Paarlberg, 1980.

7. See also Wallensteen; Barber; Doxey, 1982; Fredrik Hoffmann; Mayall.

8. See Kobrin.

9. For example, see Kaempfer and Lowenberg, 1988, 1989; Kaempfer, Lehman, and Lowenberg.

10. Klaus Knorr, "International Economic Leverage and Its Uses," in Knorr and Trager, p. 104; von Amerongen; O'Leary; Paarlberg, 1978.

11. For one of the earliest statements of hegemonic-stability theory, see Kindleberger. See also Keohane, 1980; Krasner, 1976.

12. See Susan Strange; Russett; Mastanduno, 1988.

13. Snidal; Alt, Calvert, and Humes.

14. Axelrod, 1984.

15. Krasner, 1983. For discussion of the distinction between international institutions and organizations, see Oran R. Young, pp. 31–57.

16. Keohane, 1984.

17. See Oye.

18. For examples, see Patinkin; Stigler; Osborne.

19. See George.

## Chapter 2
## Model and Hypotheses

1. An equilibrium outcome in these games is defined as one from which neither player has an incentive to deviate unilaterally, i.e., a Nash equilibrium. At equilibrium, no unilateral change in behavior would increase the payoff to the player making the change.

2. An outcome is suboptimal, or Pareto-inferior, if there exists another outcome at which at least one player would receive a higher payoff and neither player

would receive a lower payoff. A Pareto-superior outcome is one in which both players cannot simultaneously improve their payoffs by moving to a different outcome.

3. See Ordeshook, pp. 130–31.

4. For the following argument, we need to assume only that at least one state prefers that the other impose unilateral sanctions. To simplify the argument, however, I use this restriction for both states.

5. A player has a dominant strategy if a particular pure strategy (i.e., either no sanctions or full sanctions) gives her the best possible payoff, regardless of how the other player chooses. If Player 1, for example, maximizes her payoff by imposing sanctions whether or not Player 2 does, Player 1 has a dominant strategy to sanction.

6. A Prisoners' Dilemma is defined by the preference ordering just described. The name comes from a description of the dilemma confronting two prisoners charged with a felony who are not allowed to communicate with one another or make binding commitments. Each has an incentive to confess to the crime in order to receive a lighter sentence; however, if both confess, they are worse off than if both admit nothing. See Ordeshook, pp. 206–7.

7. $X^*$ and $y^*$ are mixed strategies but can be interpreted in a slightly different manner than that in which we usually understand mixed strategies. Rather than specifying a probabilistic choice of $x = 0$ or $x = 1$, we could interpret $x^*$ as a point between $x = 0$ and $x = 1$. Equilibrium strategies thus take on the following meaning: by choosing strategy $y^*$, Player 2 holds Player 1 to a particular payoff regardless of the level of sanctions Player 1 imposes. Thus, Player 1 has no incentive to change $x$. The same situation holds for Player 2 when Player 1 chooses $x^*$. If either player moves away from $x^*$ or $y^*$, the other immediately has an incentive to change her chosen level of sanctions. Only at the point $x^*$, $y^*$, in a game without a dominant strategy, will neither player gain by changing the intensity of sanctions she has chosen.

8. Keohane, 1984, p. 51.

9. In an assurance game, both players' most-preferred outcome is mutual cooperation, so mutual cooperation is an equilibrium. However, each player is injured if the other defects, so mutual defection is a second, Pareto-inferior equilibrium. Jervis discusses the Stag Hunt as an assurance game in "Cooperation under the Security Dilemma." The name Stag Hunt refers to Jean-Jacques Rousseau's story about a group of hunters who need to cooperate to catch a stag but who could each capture a rabbit if they refused to cooperate. Although all prefer stag to rabbit, fears that the others could defect may lead to mutual defection to prevent the worst possible outcome—going hungry.

10. Putnam, p. 439.

11. Because either threats or inducements can be used, it is possible to argue that *coercion* is too harsh a term for this cooperation problem. However, regardless of the means used, the reluctant player is being manipulated into taking actions she would prefer to avoid. Thus, *coercion* seems an appropriate term, even though side payments rather than threats may be used to reduce the pain felt by the reluctant player. The dynamics of credible commitment are similar regardless of the linkage tactic adopted.

12. This definition of coadjustment is identical to Robert Keohane's definition of cooperation as mutual adjustment of policies (1984, pp. 51–52). My definition of cooperation encompasses a broader range of activity; it is closer to that used by Kenneth A. Oye in "Explaining Cooperation under Anarchy: Hypotheses and Strategies," in Oye, pp. 1–24.

13. See Grieco.

14. Gilpin, pp. 9–10.

15. Schelling, pp. 35–43.

16. For a classic example of such an argument, see Mitrany.

17. Baldwin, pp. 51–69.

18. See Axelrod, 1970.

19. Keohane, 1989, pp. 1–20.

20. Hufbauer, Schott, and Elliott, p. 9.

21. Baldwin, pp. 130–34.

22. Ibid., pp. 261–76.

23. Oye, p. 7.

24. Hufbauer, Schott, and Elliott, pp. 36–37.

25. For example, see Paarlberg, 1980.

26. Hufbauer and Schott, p. 82.

27. Miller; Hufbauer and Schott, pp. 455–60.

28. Waltz, pp. 176–83. One of the major debates in the field of international relations at the beginning of the 1990s was whether bipolarity still adequately described the international system, given the collapse of the Warsaw Pact.

29. Ibid., pp. 102–28.

30. Walt, 1987, 1988.

31. Conversely, assistance may decrease any probability of success, thus reducing overall interest in sanctions. These two motivations—balance and success—play against one another. Through data analysis and case studies, we will examine how states weigh these contending considerations.

32. See Arthur A. Stein.

33. See Schelling, pp. 123–24.

34. See Milgrom and Roberts; Kreps and Wilson; Selten.

35. Robert O. Keohane, "The Demand for International Regimes," in Krasner, 1983, p. 156.

36. Kobrin; see also Rodman.

37. See Jentleson.

38. Kindleberger; Keohane, 1980.

39. Axelrod, 1984; Oye, "Explaining Cooperation under Anarchy."

40. Keohane, 1988, p. 383.

41. Ibid.; Keohane, 1984, pp. 85–109.

42. See Tollison and Willett.

43. Even in this case, if other states use tactical issue linkage to change the nature of the game, decisions will become contingent on the credibility and costs of the issue linkage.

44. See Waltz, pp. 125–28; Walt, 1987, 1988; Snyder; Christensen and Snyder.

45. Waltz, p. 126.

46. Walt, 1987, 1988.
47. Snyder, pp. 130–31.
48. Walt, 1987, p. 17. See also Christensen and Snyder, pp. 140–41.
49. Snyder, p. 128.

## Chapter 3
## Measuring Cooperation and Explanatory Variables

1. See, for example, Keohane, 1988.
2. Hufbauer and Schott, p. 35.
3. Note that this is different than saying that 8 percent of non-major-sender trade is sanctioned. Generally, senders do not cut all economic ties with the target. Thus, the percent of trade actually sanctioned would be well below the value of NONMAJ. The low average value of NONMAJ is partially accounted for by the fact that in nearly half of the cases in this data set, only one country imposes sanctions and NONMAJ thus is 0. If these cases are eliminated from the data set, so that we are looking only at cases where there is some minimal level of cooperation, the mean of NONMAJ rises to approximately 22 percent.
4. Hufbauer and Schott, p. 37.
5. As discussed in chapter 2, assistance may have a second, offsetting effect, by decreasing the chance that sanctions will succeed in forcing the target to change its policies.
6. Hufbauer and Schott, pp. 103–6.
7. Ibid., pp. 38–39.
8. Ibid., pp. 666–70.
9. Ibid., pp. 655–65.
10. Ibid., pp. 180–86.
11. Weintraub, p. 11.
12. Hufbauer, Schott, and Elliott, p. 45.
13. Ibid., pp. 49–62.

## Chapter 4
## Estimating Models of Cooperation

1. The maximum value of NONMAJ in this sample is 75.25; the minimum is 0, reflecting cases where only one state imposed sanctions and no cooperation took place. See chapter 3 for a discussion of each variable used in the following analyses.
2. Different temperature scales (Fahrenheit, Celsius, etc.) are examples of interval-level measurement, because the difference between 20 and 30 degrees on such a scale can be compared to the difference between 40 and 45 degrees. This sort of comparison is not possible for an ordinal-level variable such as COOP.
3. See McKelvey and Zavoina.
4. We might choose an alternative assumption for the distribution of the underlying variable, such as an exponential distribution. If we conceive of cooperation as a quantity that can take on only positive values, the exponential distribution might seem more reasonable. I have estimated a model using this assumption; the results are very close to those from the probit analysis. The only major differ-

ence occurred with the variable COLDWAR. While the estimated coefficient for COLDWAR is positive for both models, it is statistically significant only in the exponential-distribution model. However, the log-likelihood for the exponential distribution is slightly lower than for the normal distribution, and the predictive power of the probit model is also somewhat higher (probit correctly places 63 percent of the cases, while the exponential model correctly predicts 59 percent). In addition, the probit model can be manipulated to yield coefficients that are directly comparable to those estimated in the preceding ordinary-least-squares analysis. Thus, I have chosen to concentrate the discussion in this chapter on the probit model.

5. The analysis in this section uses statistical models and programs by Gary King (1989a).

6. See, for example, McGowan and Rood.

7. See King, 1989a, 1989b, 1989c.

8. See King, 1989a.

9. The results in this section show robust standard errors rather than the usual measure of the standard errors of the coefficients. Robust standard errors allow for the possibility that the variance function has been misspecified.

10. See King, 1989b, pp. 126–29.

11. I should note that there are other potential explanations of the large value of gamma, such as omitted variables or heterogeneity among potential sanction-ers. Heterogeneity—differences across states in the probability that they will impose sanctions—could, however, result from a process of contagion. The GEC model shows apparent contagion. In the case studies, I will look for further support for the conclusion that positive contagion actually occurs.

12. See Walt, 1987.

13. Susan Strange; Russett.

14. Mastanduno, 1988.

15. Rodman.

16. Keohane, 1984.

17. Snidal.

18. Selection bias in the data set could have contributed to the upward slope of cooperation in cases of sanctions where the United States was the major sender. This data set contains only cases where at least one country imposed sanctions, none where no state acted. Thus, it eliminates those coadjustment cases where states were unable to overcome their cooperation dilemma to reach a Pareto-superior outcome. If coadjustment cases are more common in recent years, the level of cooperation during this period could be exaggerated in the data set, since it eliminates those situations where the no-sanctions equilibrium prevailed. However, the greater annual incidence of sanctions during the latter part of the period covered by the data set argues against this type of selection bias.

## Chapter 5
### Human Rights in Latin America: Explaining Unilateral U.S. Sanctions

1. See Forsythe, 1988, p. ix.

2. Lars Schoultz, "U.S. Economic Aid as an Instrument of Foreign Policy: The Case of Human Rights in Latin America," in Nelson and Green, p. 321.

3. U.S. House, Committee on Foreign Affairs, Subcommittee on International Organizations and Movements, *Human Rights in the World Community: A Call for U.S. Leadership,* 93d Cong., 2d sess., 27 March 1974. See also Salzberg and Young, p. 253.

4. See Schoultz, p. 195; Weissbrodt, p. 241.

5. Congressional Research Service, report by Vita Bite, "The Legislative Mandate" (hereafter cited as CRS report), p. 17.

6. U.S. House, Committee on Foreign Affairs, *Fiscal Year 1975 Foreign Assistance Request,* 93d Cong., 2d sess., 1974, pp. 280–81.

7. Stephen B. Cohen, p. 251.

8. Weissbrodt, p. 243.

9. Breslin, p. C4.

10. Vogelgesang, p. 129.

11. *New York Times,* 27 September 1974, p. 18.

12. Ibid.

13. See Henry Kissinger, *Years of Upheaval* (London: Weidenfeld and Nicolson and Michael Joseph, 1982), pp. 412–13.

14. Kommers and Loescher, p. 214; Morrell, p. 4.

15. Stephen B. Cohen, p. 253.

16. Weissbrodt, pp. 247–48.

17. Ibid.; Ernest W. Lefever, "The Trivialization of Human Rights," *Policy Review* 3 (Winter 1978), p. 13.

18. Bryce Wood, "Human Rights Issues in Latin America," in Dominguez, Rodley, Wood, and Falk, p. 182.

19. See Arnold.

20. CRS report, p. 105.

21. Weissbrodt, p. 261.

22. Ibid., p. 262; Stephen B. Cohen, p. 255.

23. For an expression of the theory underlying this argument, see Jeane Kirkpatrick, "Dictatorships and Double Standards," *Commentary* (November 1979), p. 34.

24. James Mayall, "The United States," in Vincent, pp. 165–87.

25. See, for example, Muravchik, p. 2.

26. Farer, 1983, p. 149.

27. Zbigniew Brzezinski, *Power and Principle: Memoirs of the National Security Adviser, 1977–1981* (New York: Farrar, Straus & Giroux, 1983), p. 49.

28. Muravchik, p. 2.

29. Carter's inaugural speech, 20 January 1977.

30. See Jimmy Carter, *Keeping Faith: Memoirs of a President* (New York: Bantam Books, 1982), p. 145; Cyrus Vance, *Hard Choices: Critical Years in America's Foreign Policy* (New York: Simon and Schuster, 1983), p. 33; Brzezinski, p. 38.

31. Interview with Robert Pastor, 28 June 1990. Pastor notes that the administration preferred a multilateral policy—for example, working through the OAS—but does not recall that the administration's decisions were dependent on the reactions of other potential sanctioners.

32. *Washington Post,* 29 October 1978, p. C1.

33. Stephen B. Cohen, p. 254.

34. CRS report, p. 26.

35. Ibid., p. 21.

36. Ibid., p. 22.

37. U.S. Senate, Committee on Foreign Relations, Subcommittee on Foreign Assistance, p. 49.

38. *Washington Post,* 29 October 1978, p. C2.

39. Ibid.; Patrick J. Flood, "U.S. Human Rights Initiatives concerning Argentina," in Newsom, p. 133; Pastor interview; Lisa L. Martin and Kathryn Sikkink, "U.S. Human Rights Policy toward Argentina and Guatemala," in Peter Evans, Harold K. Jacobson, and Robert D. Putnam, eds., *International Bargaining and Domestic Politics: An Interactive Approach* (Berkeley: University of California Press, forthcoming).

40. Breslin, p. C4.

41. Schoultz, pp. 124–25. The Reagan administration managed, however, to leave this position unfilled for over a year, until it was occupied by Elliott Abrams.

42. Breslin, p. C4.

43. See Roberta Cohen, "Human Rights Decision-making in the Executive Branch: Some Proposals for a Coordinated Strategy," in Kommers and Loescher, p. 233.

44. *Washington Post,* 31 March 1977, p. 17.

45. Ibid.; Maynard.

46. Stephen B. Cohen, p. 255.

47. CRS report, pp. 105–7. For lists of human-rights legislation, see Newsom, appendix D, pp. 223–34; U.S. House, Committee on Foreign Affairs, *Human Rights Documents: Compilation of Documents Pertaining to Human Rights,* 97th Cong., 1st sess., September 1983, pp. 24–27.

48. *New York Times,* 25 February 1977, p. 1.

49. The Ford administration had explicitly used the "extraordinary-circumstances" loophole to continue military assistance to Argentina. See U.S. Department of State report to the House Committee on International Relations, *Human Rights and U.S. Policy: Argentina, Haiti, Indonesia, Iran, Peru, and the Philippines,* p. 6.

50. Breslin, p. C1.

51. CRS report, p. 57; Loescher, p. 460.

52. International lawyers have cited this language as evidence of the impact of international law on U.S. domestic legislation. See, for example, Buergenthal, 1987, pp. 303–10.

53. Schoultz, p. 281.

54. See Sanford, p. 1.

55. Ibid., p. 293; *Washington Post,* 9 July 1976, p. 2.

56. Sanford, pp. 284–85.

57. U.S. Senate, Committee on Foreign Relations, Subcommittee on Foreign Assistance, p. 91.

58. Ibid., p. 286.

59. *New York Times,* 29 April 1977, p. 5.

60. U.S. Senate, Committee on Foreign Relations, Subcommittee on Foreign Assistance, p. 287.

61. Ibid., p. 288.

62. *Washington Post,* 20 February 1978, reprinted in *Congressional Record,* 23 February 1978, pp. 4455–56; *American Banker,* 25 September 1978, p. 21.

63. *Congressional Record,* 23 February 1978, p. 4451.

64. See Sidney Weintraub, "Human Rights and Basic Needs in United States Foreign Aid Policy," in Newberg, p. 236.

65. For example, see Department of State memorandum from Stephen A. Oxman, Special Assistant to the Deputy Secretary, to the members of the Christopher Committee, 1 May 1978, declassified under Freedom of Information Act Request No. 8903755. This memorandum records a strategy of shifting from voting "no" on non–basic human needs IFI loan requests from Argentina to voting "yes" in response to improving human-rights conditions. Participants in this process recall that this careful calibration of signals resulted in messages that were far too complex to be deciphered by target governments (Pastor interview).

66. See U.S. House, Committee on Banking, Finance, and Urban Affairs, Subcommittee on International Development Institutions and Finance, p. 294.

67. Rossiter, 1984b, p. 18.

68. *Washington Post,* 9 July 1976, p. 2.

69. Ibid.

70. Ibid.

71. Sanford, p. 8.

72. Richard A. Falk, "Ideological Patterns in the United States Human Rights Debate: 1945–1978," in Hevener, p. 30.

73. U.S. State Department, *Human Rights and U.S. Foreign Policy,* Publication 8959, December 1978, pp. 16–17.

74. U.S. Senate, Committee on Foreign Relations, Subcommittee on Foreign Assistance, p. 76.

75. Ibid., p. 71.

76. Ibid.

77. *Congressional Record,* 22 March 1978, p. 7967.

78. U.S. House, Committee on Foreign Affairs, 1980, p. 17.

79. See Sanford, pp. 3–5.

80. See Mower, 1979, p. 204.

81. U.S. House, Committee on Foreign Affairs, p. 18.

82. U.S. House, Committee on Banking, Finance, and Urban Affairs, Subcommittee on International Development Institutions and Finance, p. 292.

83. Ibid., p. 301.

84. Weintraub, p. 233.

85. Ibid., pp. 295–96.

86. Flood, p. 137.

87. Weintraub, p. 237.

88. Richard P. Claude, "Western European Public Opinion on American Human Rights Advocacy," in Nelson and Green, p. 105. The United States Information Agency and International Communication Agency funded this survey, in which 959 Germans, 944 Italians, 970 French, and 1,716 British were interviewed. See also Morrell, p. 6.

89. Luard, 1981, p. 11.
90. Luard, 1980, p. 580.
91. Luard, 1981, p. 22.
92. Owen, p. 2.
93. Putnam and Bayne, p. 76.
94. Stewart, pp. 2, 6, 40.
95. Ibid., p. 39.
96. Ibid., pp. 49–50.
97. Christopher Brewin, "Europe," in Vincent, p. 190.
98. See Alston, 1982, pp. 162–64.
99. Brewin, p. 200.
100. See J. E. S. Fawcett, "Human Rights: The Applicability of International Instruments," in Dowrick, p. 86.
101. See Kaufman and Whiteman. The Genocide Convention, which is different in character than the essential human-rights treaties, was finally ratified in 1986, although with important reservations that eliminated much of its power. See *Congressional Record*, 19 February 1986, pp. S1355–77; Lillich.
102. Ministry of Foreign Affairs of the Kingdom of the Netherlands, *Human Rights and Foreign Policy* (The Hague, December 1979), pp. 10–12.
103. Ibid., p. 85.
104. See Baehr.
105. See Matthews and Pratt.
106. Doxey, 1979, p. 19.
107. See Nolan.
108. Hufbauer and Schott, pp. 479–84.
109. See Cassese.
110. Sanford, pp. 19–22.
111. See Kissinger, pp. 374–413.
112. Hufbauer and Schott, p. 479.
113. See Heraldo Muñoz, "Chile's External Relations under the Military Government," in Valenzuela and Valenzuela, p. 307.
114. London *Times,* 5 January 1974, p. 18.
115. London *Times,* 8 November 1973, p. 10.
116. United Nations Secretary-General, pp. 9–13.
117. United Nations Economic and Social Council, Committee on Human Rights, Subcommittee on Prevention of Discrimination and Protection of Minorities, vol. 3, pp. 17–18, 84–87. See also *New York Times,* 22 December 1976, p. 2.
118. London *Times,* 1 October 1973, p. 2.
119. London *Times,* 8 November 1973, p. 18.
120. London *Times,* 29 November 1973, p. 16.
121. London *Times,* 27 March 1974, p. 6.
122. London *Times,* 30 March 1974, p. 5.
123. London *Times,* 22 March 1974, p. 9.
124. London *Times,* 9 April 1974, p. 1; 11 April, p. 9; 15 April, p. 1; 16 April, p. 13; 2 May, p. 2; 6 May, p. 5; 14 May, p. 1; 15 May, p. 5; 16 May, p. 1; 17 May, p. 11; 22 May, p. 10.

125. London *Times,* 17 May 1974, p. 11; 22 May, p. 10.

126. See Cusack, p. 121.

127. U.S. House, Committee on International Relations, Subcommittee on International Organizations, *Chile: The Status of Human Rights and Its Relationship to U.S. Economic Assistance Programs,* 1976, p. 1.

128. Ibid., p. 16.

129. Cusack, p. 121.

130. *Congressional Record,* 4 May 1978, pp. 12715–16.

131. United Nations Economic and Social Council, Committee on Human Rights, Subcommittee on Prevention of Discrimination and Protection of Minorities, vol. 3, p. 16.

132. Ibid., p. 29.

133. Ibid., p. 7; *Congressional Record,* 4 May 1978, pp. 12714–15; Charles Meynell, "How Chile Reappeared on the Tombstones," *Euromoney,* June 1977, pp. 101–5.

134. See U.S. House, Committee on Foreign Affairs, Subcommittees on International Economic Policy and Trade and on Inter-American Affairs, *U.S. Economic Sanctions against Chile,* 1981, pp. 10–14.

135. Ibid., pp. 27–29.

## Chapter 6
## The Falkland Islands Conflict

1. For histories of the Falkland Islands, see Goebel; Ian J. Strange; Kratochwil, Rohrlich, and Mahajan.

2. See Haig, p. 263.

3. See Ian J. Strange, pp. 247–54.

4. These costs had prevented the British from stationing forces in the Falklands capable of defending the islands. After June 1982, the population of the islands tripled, as the number of military personnel stationed there far exceeded the original eighteen hundred inhabitants. All in all, Britain achieved an expensive victory in 1982.

5. For a discussion of the positions of various parts of the British government on the Falklands, see *The Economist,* 27 November 1982, pp. 19–26.

6. For a history of these negotiations, see Hastings and Jenkins, pp. 15–44.

7. The British government had decided recently to decommission the *Endurance,* one of many moves that convinced the Argentine junta that the British were not seriously committed to defending the Falklands.

8. Hastings and Jenkins, pp. 54–60.

9. *UN Chronicle* 19, no. 5 (May 1982), p. 3.

10. See Parsons, pp. 169–72; *UN Chronicle* 19, no. 5 (May 1982), pp. 3, 5–10.

11. *Financial Times,* 28 April 1982, p. 4.

12. *Financial Times,* 7 April 1982, p. 1.

13. Great Britain, Parliament, House of Commons (hereafter cited as House of Commons), p. 4.

14. *Financial Times,* 10 April 1982, p. 2.

15. *Financial Times,* 14 April 1982, p. 1.

16. Hufbauer and Schott, p. 717.

17. *Financial Times,* 7 April 1982, p. 1; Reuters North European Service, 6 April 1982.

18. After EC sanctions were lifted, West Germany went ahead with delivery of four frigates to Argentina in spite of British objections. See *Financial Times,* 27 September 1982, p. 3.

19. Reuters North European Service, 5 April 1982.

20. Janis A. Kreslins, "Chronology: The Falklands War," *Foreign Affairs: America and the World 1982,* p. 740; *Financial Times,* 7 April 1982, pp. 1, 4; House of Commons, p. 75.

21. *The Economist,* 3 March 1984, p. 29; Haig, p. 266.

22. Worcester and Jenkins; Norpoth.

23. See House of Commons, p. 1.

24. *Irish Times,* 4 May 1982, p. 1.

25. See Dabat and Lorenzano.

26. Daoudi and Dajani, 1983a, p. 119.

27. *Time,* 26 April 1982, p. 31.

28. House of Commons, p. 23.

29. Eberhard Rein, "The Community and the Falklands: A Stand against Aggression," *Europe 82,* no. 5/6 (May/June 1982), p. 15; Reuters North European Service, 6 April 1982.

30. Reuters North European Service, 6 April 1982.

31. Reuters North European Service, 5 April 1982.

32. Cawl Cosgrove Twitchett, "The Falklands: Community Diplomacy at Work," *Europe 82,* no. 7 (July 1982), p. 11; *Irish Times,* 12 April 1982, p. 6.

33. Reuters North European Service, 9 April 1982.

34. *Irish Times,* 7 April 1982, p. 1.

35. *Irish Times,* 8 April 1982, p. 8.

36. Reuters North European Service, 9 April 1982, AM cycle.

37. *Financial Times,* 10 April 1982, p. 2.

38. "Statement of the Ten on the Falklands (Brussels, 10 April 1982)," reprinted in *European Political Co-operation (EPC),* 5th ed. (Federal Republic of Germany: Clausen & Bosse, 1988), pp. 150–51.

39. Reuters North European Service, 10 April 1982; *New York Times,* 11 April 1982, p. 1; *Christian Science Monitor,* 12 April 1982, p. 12.

40. House of Commons, pp. 74–75.

41. *Irish Times,* 12 April 1982, p. 6.

42. *Financial Times,* 27 April 1982, p. 2.

43. House of Commons, pp. 102–3.

44. *Christian Science Monitor,* 12 April 1982, p. 12.

45. House of Commons, p. 85.

46. See Clark, pp. xiii–xiv; Hindmarsh; Irving Fisher.

47. This could be considered a problem of non-overlapping win sets. See Putnam.

48. *Financial Times,* 14 April 1982, p. 1.

49. *Irish Times,* 15 April 1982, p. 4.

50. *Official Journal* of the European Communities, no. L 102 (16 April 1982), pp. 1–3.

51. *Financial Times,* 16 April 1982, p. 4.
52. Reuters North European Service, 22 April 1982.
53. *Irish Times,* 9/10 April 1982, p. 1.
54. Reuters North European Service, 20 April 1982.
55. *Christian Science Monitor,* 22 April 1982, p. 9.
56. *New York Times,* 29 April 1982, p. A1.
57. *Irish Times,* 27 April 1982, p. 6.
58. *Irish Times,* 28 April 1982, p. 8.
59. Reuters, 28 April 1982, AM cycle.
60. Twitchett, p. 11.
61. Reuters North European Service, 3 May 1982.
62. *Irish Times,* 4 May 1982, pp. 1, 6.
63. *New York Times,* 5 May 1982, p. A1.
64. *Irish Times,* 5 May 1982, p. 1.
65. *Irish Times,* 3 May 1982, p. 8.
66. *Irish Times,* 7 May 1982, p. 1.
67. Ibid., p. 9.
68. Reuters North European Service, 4 May 1982.
69. *Financial Times,* 6 May 1982, p. 4.
70. *Financial Times,* 5 May 1982, p. 1.
71. Edwards, p. 307.
72. *Financial Times,* 8 May 1982, p. 2.
73. *Irish Times,* 12 April 1982, p. 6.
74. *Financial Times,* 16 April 1982, p. 4.
75. *Financial Times,* 27 April 1982, p. 2.
76. *Irish Times,* 27 April 1982, pp. 6, 7.
77. *Irish Times,* 30 April 1982, p. 1.
78. *Financial Times,* 5 May 1982, p. 1.
79. *Irish Times,* 8 May 1982, p. 8.
80. Reuters North European Service, 8 May 1982.
81. *Irish Times,* 10 May 1982, pp. 1, 6.
82. *Financial Times,* 10 May 1982, p. 1.
83. *Irish Times,* 11 May 1982, p. 4.
84. *Financial Times,* 10 May 1982, p. 1.
85. *Irish Times,* 13 May 1982, p. 1.
86. *Irish Times,* 14 May 1982, p. 1.
87. Reuters North European Service, 14 May 1982; *Financial Times,* 15 May 1982, p. 2.
88. *New York Times,* 17 May 1982, p. A1.
89. Calvert, 1982, p. 125.
90. Pieter Jan Kuyper, "Community Sanctions against Argentina: Lawfulness under Community and International Law," in David O'Keeffe and Henry G. Schermers, eds., *Essays in European Law and Integration* (Deventer, the Netherlands: Kluwer B.V., 1982), p. 149; *Irish Times,* 18 May 1982, p. 1.
91. *Financial Times,* 19 May 1982, p. 4.
92. Reuters North European Service, 18 May 1982.
93. *New York Times,* 22 May 1982, p. 7.

94. H. Peter Dreyer, "EC Institutions: Agreeing to Disagree," *Europe,* no. 232 (July/August 1982), p. 29; Panayitois Ifestos, *European Political Cooperation: Towards a Framework of Supranational Diplomacy?* (Brookfield, Vt.: Gower Publishing Co., 1987), p. 316; *Irish Times,* 19 May 1982, p. 1.

95. Reuters, 20 May 1982, AM cycle.

96. *Christian Science Monitor,* 20 May 1982, p. 24.

97. *New York Times,* 22 May 1982, p. 7.

98. *New York Times,* 25 May 1982, p. A1.

99. *Financial Times,* 26 May 1982, p. 2.

100. *Irish Times,* 26 May 1982, p. 9.

101. *Bulletin EC,* May 1982, pp. 7–9.

102. Economist Intelligence Unit, pp. 1–2.

103. Heritage Foundation Reports, International Briefing no. 10, 21 June 1982; "UK Gets Budget Refund," *Europe,* no. 233 (September/October 1982), p. 51; Ifestos, p. 317; F. S. Northedge, "Britain and the EEC: Past and Present," in Roy Jenkins, ed., *Britain and the EEC* (London: Macmillan Press, 1983), p. 34.

104. Latin American Bureau, p. 112.

105. *New York Times,* 12 May 1982, p. A14.

106. Salmon, p. 207; *Irish Times,* 6 May 1982, p. 4.

107. Joyce and Murtagh, p. 145.

108. *Irish Times,* 3 May 1982, p. 8.

109. MacQueen, p. 42.

110. Joyce and Murtagh, p. 157.

111. MacQueen, p. 44.

112. Joyce and Murtagh, p. 154.

113. *Irish Times,* 7 April 1982, p. 1.

114. *Irish Times,* 8 April 1982, p. 8.

115. Ibid.

116. Joyce and Murtagh, p. 158.

117. Ibid., p. 159.

118. *Irish Times,* 12 April 1982, p. 6.

119. *Irish Times,* 13 April 1982, p. 6.

120. See Claude.

121. See Purcell.

122. See, for example, *The Economist,* 10 April 1982, p. 11.

123. David C. Gompert, "American Diplomacy and the Haig Mission: An Insider's Perspective," in Coll and Arend, p. 111.

124. *Christian Science Monitor,* 16 April 1982, p. 3; 22 April 1982, p. 9.

125. *Irish Times,* 8 April 1982, p. 6; 12 April 1982, p. 5.

126. *The Economist,* 12 November 1983, p. 32.

127. Ibid., p. 33.

128. *The Economist,* 3 March 1984, pp. 29–31.

129. *Christian Science Monitor,* 27 April 1982, p. 1.

130. Reuters, 30 April 1982, AM cycle.

131. U.S. Department of State press release, 30 April 1982.

132. United States, *Federal Register* 47, no. 89 (7 May 1982), p. 19842.

133. Acevedo, p. 326.

134. Reuters, 30 April 1982, AM cycle.

135. For discussions of the long-term impact on relations with Latin America, see U.S. House, Committee on Foreign Affairs, Subcommittee on Inter-American Affairs.

136. See, for example, statements made at the UN, in *UN Chronicle* 19, no. 5 (May 1982), p. 8.

137. Quoted in Inis L. Claude, "UN Efforts at Settlement of the Falkland Islands Crisis," in Coll and Arend, pp. 125–26.

138. *Irish Times,* 14 April 1982, p. 9.

139. Reuters, 17 April 1982, AM cycle.

140. *Financial Times,* 30 April 1982, p. 2.

141. Middlebrook, p. 63.

142. *Financial Times,* 1 June 1982, p. 4.

143. Kyodo News Service, 8 April 1982.

144. Kyodo News Service, 13 April 1982.

145. *Christian Science Monitor,* 22 April 1982, p. 9.

146. Reuters North European Service, 15 April 1982.

147. Reuters North European Service, 1 May 1982.

148. *New York Times,* 2 May 1982, p. 13.

149. Ibid.

150. Reuters North European Service, 2 May 1982.

151. See *UN Chronicle* 19, no. 5 (May 1982), pp. 7, 19; no. 7 (June 1982), pp. 10, 12.

152. *Platt's Oilgram News* 60, no. 74 (19 April 1982), p. 1.

153. *New York Times,* 26 April 1982, p. A8.

154. Reuters North European Service, 26 April 1982.

155. Reuters North European Service, 27 April 1982.

156. *New York Times,* 28 April 1982, p. A1.

157. *Christian Science Monitor,* 29 April 1982, p. 24.

158. Reuters North European Service, 29 May 1982.

159. Reuters, 30 April 1982, AM cycle.

160. *New York Times,* 1 May 1982, p. 7.

161. Reuters North European Service, 15 May 1982.

162. Reuters North European Service, 3 June 1982.

163. Xinhua General Overseas News Service, 8 June 1982.

164. Reuters North European Service, 30 June 1982.

165. *Christian Science Monitor,* 16 April 1982, p. 3.

166. Reuters North European Service, 23 April 1982.

167. Reuters North European Service, 12 June 1982.

## Chapter 7
## Western Technology-Export Controls

1. For studies of the grain embargo, see Paarlberg, 1980; Falkenheim; Robert L. Paarlberg, *Food Trade and Foreign Policy: India, the Soviet Union, and the United States* (Ithaca: Cornell University Press, 1985); Roger B. Porter, *The U.S.-U.S.S.R. Grain Agreement* (Cambridge: Cambridge University Press, 1984).

2. Neoclassical economists would quarrel with the concept of "strategic goods." Assuming that resources will be moved to the sector with the highest marginal benefits, any imports will allow the government to increase the amount it can spend on the military. Thus, all goods could be considered "strategic." This argument rests on stringent assumptions, including the assumption that every state has sufficient resources and know-how to produce any good. It implies that potential military adversaries should not engage in trade with one another. Since few states are willing to accept this conclusion, countries tend to examine the military relevance of a potential export. Discussions of the concept of strategic goods and of how this concept has been misused can be found in Thomas C. Schelling, *International Economics* (Boston: Allyn and Bacon, 1958), pp. 489–504; and Baldwin, pp. 214–24. As these authors point out, in economic terms there is no reason to believe that the strategic value of a good is necessarily related to its potential military applications. However, in practice, states have found military relevance a useful proxy for strategic value. Though recognizing the potential fallacy underlying this usage, I adopt it in this chapter because it gives the clearest insight into states' preferences.

3. For example, for years the issue of how stringently to control computers created severe strains in CoCom and within the U.S. government. See U.S. Senate, Permanent Subcommittee on Investigations, October 1984, p. 21.

4. See U.S. House, *Export Administration Act of 1979*.

5. U.S. Senate, Committee on Foreign Relations, *A Background Study on East-West Trade,* 89th Cong., 1st sess., February 1965, p. 7. This argument, as well as the following analysis, holds through the period covered in this study (1945 to 1989) but will have to be reexamined in light of the collapse of the Warsaw Pact.

6. See Falkenheim, p. 118; Statement of Philip M. Klutznick, Secretary of Commerce, in U.S. Senate, Committee on Banking, Housing, and Urban Affairs, Subcommittee on International Finance, 1980, pp. 29–30.

7. For example, see Lacorne.

8. Hirschman, pp. 14–17.

9. The classic work on this period is Adler-Karlsson.

10. See Dvorin.

11. H.R. Reports, no. 524, 91st Cong., 1st sess., 1969, p. 9.

12. See Barry Carter for an overview of export-control legislation; see also Robert Weissberg, *Public Opinion and Popular Government* (Englewood Cliffs, N.J.: Prentice-Hall, 1976), pp. 164–65; Bertsch, 1988, p. 5.

13. Dobson, p. 600.

14. U.S. State Department, *The Battle Act Report, 1971* (Twenty-Fourth Battle Act report), May 1972.

15. For example, see the testimony of Michael Blumenthal, then president of the Bendix International Corporation, in U.S. Senate, Committee on Banking and Currency, Subcommittee on International Finance, *Export Expansion and Regulation,* 91st Cong., 1st sess., 1969, p. 92.

16. See Joan Edelman Spero, *The Politics of International Economic Relations,* 2d ed. (New York: St. Martin's Press, 1981), pp. 305–6.

17. William J. Long, "The Executive, Congress, and Interest Groups in U.S.

Export Control Policy: The National Organization of Power," in Bertsch, 1988, p. 38.

18. Soviet trade statistics, from Spero, p. 311.

19. U.S. Congress, Office of Technology Assessment (hereafter cited as OTA), p. 12.

20. Paula Stern, *Water's Edge* (Westport, Conn.: Greenwood Press, 1979); Gasiorowski and Polachek, pp. 709–29.

21. U.S. Department of Defense, *An Analysis of Export Control of U.S. Technology—A DoD Perspective*, 1976; Bucy, pp. 135–38; Gustafson.

22. See Huntington.

23. See Hufbauer and Schott, pp. 603–6; U.S. Senate, Committee on Governmental Affairs, Permanent Subcommittee on Investigations, 1980, p. 62.

24. For a description of the U.S. export-licensing system, see National Academy of Sciences, esp. pp. 94–95.

25. Stent, 1983.

26. John R. McIntyre, "The Distribution of Power and the Inter-agency Politics of Licensing East-West High-Technology Trade," in Bertsch, 1988, p. 123.

27. OTA, p. 127.

28. Ibid., p. 118.

29. U.S. Congress, Joint Economic Committee, 1984, p. 1.

30. Yergin, p. 51.

31. Gary Bertsch and Steven Elliott, "Controlling East-West Trade in Britain: Power, Politics, and Policy," in Bertsch, 1988, pp. 204–5.

32. Ibid., pp. 206–7.

33. OTA, p. 190.

34. Woolcock, 1982, p. 59.

35. OTA, p. 191; U.S. State Department, *The Strategic Trade Control System, 1948–56* (Ninth Battle Act Report), 28 June 1957, p. 26.

36. Bertsch and Elliott, p. 210.

37. Stephen Woolcock, "Great Britain," in Rode and Jacobsen, p. 143.

38. Renata Fritsch-Bournazel, "France," in Rode and Jacobsen, p. 128.

39. OTA, p. 185.

40. Ibid.

41. Ibid., p. 186.

42. Since 1981, the French government has set up two additional systems for export control, under U.S. pressure and in response to large-scale and illegal Soviet acquisition of technology uncovered by the "Farewell Papers." A "national procedure" was established by a prime minister's directive in October 1981 to deal with the most-sensitive high-technology exports. In January 1986, the government established a system of distribution licenses; they work in a manner similar to that of U.S. distribution licenses, allowing multiple transactions under a single license.

43. OTA, p. 187.

44. See Hanns-Dieter Jacobsen, "The Special Case of Inter-German Relations," in Rode and Jacobsen, pp. 120–27.

45. For a discussion of the theory behind the use of such inducements, see

David A. Baldwin, "The Power of Positive Sanctions," *World Politics* 24, no. 1 (October 1971), pp. 19–38.

46. For a complete study, see Angela Stent, *From Embargo to Ostpolitik: The Political Economy of West German–Soviet Relations, 1955–1980* (Cambridge: Cambridge University Press, 1981).

47. Woolcock, 1982, pp. 53, 55.

48. Hanns-Dieter Jacobsen, "East-West Trade and Export Controls: The West German Perspective," in Rode and Jacobsen, p. 159.

49. OTA, p. 175.

50. Ibid., pp. 176, 180.

51. Ibid., p. 183.

52. Ibid.

53. Gordon B. Smith, "Controlling East-West Trade in Japan," in Bertsch, 1988, p. 137.

54. Ibid., pp. 138–39.

55. See Curtis.

56. OTA, p. 193.

57. Ibid., p. 197.

58. Ibid., p. 193.

59. Smith, in Bertsch, 1988, p. 144.

60. See U.S. Senate, Committee on Banking, Housing, and Urban Affairs, Subcommittee on International Finance and Monetary Policy, *Toshiba-Kongsberg Technology Diversion Case,* Hearings, 100th Cong., 1st sess., 17 June 1987, S. Hrg. 100–182.

61. Australia announced its intention to join CoCom on 14 April 1989 (*Reuter Library Report,* 15 April 1989, PM cycle).

62. See Adler-Karlsson, p. 45; OTA, p. 154.

63. Mastanduno, 1988.

64. U.S. State Department, *World-Wide Enforcement of Strategic Trade Controls* (Third Battle Act Report), 27 September 1953.

65. U.S. State Department, *Strategic Trade Control System.*

66. Ibid., p. 17.

67. Ibid.

68. Laurie C. Battle, *Progress in the Control of Strategic Exports to the Soviet Bloc,* Report to the U.S. Senate Committee on Foreign Relations, 29 January 1953.

69. Mastanduno, 1988, p. 148.

70. Battle.

71. Ibid.

72. For example, see U.S. Senate, Permanent Subcommittee on Investigations, October 1984, statements by William Root, p. 234 and William Schneider, p. 274; U.S. Senate, Committee on Foreign Relations, *A Background Study on East-West Trade,* 1965, p. 7.

73. OTA, p. 158; Mastanduno, 1988, p. 138.

74. U.S. State Department, *Strategic Trade Control System,* p. 26.

75. Ibid.

76. Ibid.; U.S. State Department, *Fourteenth Battle Act Report to the Congress,* December 1960.

77. U.S. House, Select Committee on Export Control, *Investigation and Study of the Administration, Operation, and Enforcement of the Export Control Act of 1949, and Related Acts,* 87th Cong., 2d sess., 1962, p. 78.

78. U.S. Senate, Committee on Banking and Currency, Subcommittee on International Finance.

79. "Special Report on Multilateral Export Controls by the President," *Report to the Congress,* 10 July 1978, p. 6.

80. McIntyre and Cupitt, p. 100; U.S. Senate, Committee on Governmental Affairs, Permanent Subcommittee on Investigations, 1980, p. 72.

81. U.S. Senate, Permanent Subcommittee on Investigations, October 1984, p. 7.

82. Richard Perle, in *East-West Trade and Technology Transfer: New Challenges for the United States,* Second Annual Forum sponsored by the Institute for Foreign Policy Analysis, Inc. and the International Security Studies Program, Fletcher School of International Law and Diplomacy, Tufts University, 23–24 September 1985, pp. 24–25.

83. Bertsch and Elliott, p. 210; Michael Mastanduno, "The Management of Alliance Export Control Policy: American Leadership and the Politics of CoCom," in Bertsch, 1988, p. 261.

84. See *New York Times,* 28 December 1979, p. A1.

85. Cyrus Vance, *Hard Choices: Critical Years in America's Foreign Policy* (New York: Simon and Schuster, 1983), p. 391.

86. Jimmy Carter, *Keeping Faith: Memoirs of a President* (New York: Bantam Books, 1982), p. 471.

87. Zbigniew Brzezinski, *Power and Principle: Memoirs of the National Security Adviser, 1977–1981* (New York: Farrar, Straus & Giroux, 1983), p. 430.

88. Moyer and Mabry, 1983, pp. 28–29.

89. Brzezinski, p. 433.

90. Jimmy Carter, pp. 475–76.

91. *New York Times,* 5 January 1980, p. 1.

92. *New York Times,* 6 January 1980, p. 12.

93. Ibid., pp. 1, 14.

94. *New York Times,* 10 January 1980, p. 16; *U.S. News and World Report,* 28 January 1980, p. 21.

95. Reuters, 9 January 1980, AM cycle.

96. *New York Times,* 10 January 1980, p. 18.

97. *New York Times,* 12 January 1980, p. 30.

98. U.S. House, Committee on Foreign Affairs, Subcommittee on Europe and the Middle East, 1981, p. 65.

99. Xinhua General Overseas News Service, 13 February 1980.

100. *New York Times,* 25 January 1980, p. 3.

101. Reuters, 29 January 1980, BC cycle.

102. U.S. Senate, Committee on Banking, Housing, and Urban Affairs, Subcommittee on International Finance, p. 119.

103. Ibid.

104. *New York Times,* 25 January 1980, p. 8.

105. *New York Times,* 6 February 1980, p. 1.

106. U.S. House, Committee on Foreign Affairs, Subcommittee on Europe and the Middle East, 1981, p. 104.

107. Reuters, 8 February 1980, PM cycle.

108. *New York Times,* 9 February 1980, p. 1.

109. *Christian Science Monitor,* 14 February 1980, p 3.

110. *Christian Science Monitor,* 19 February 1980; Reuters, 19 February 1980, AM cycle.

111. Vance, p. 393.

112. Reuters, 23 February 1980, PM cycle.

113. *Business Week,* 25 February 1980, p. 59.

114. Statement of William Root, U.S. Senate, Permanent Subcommittee on Investigations, October 1984, p. 241; statement of William Perry, in U.S. Senate, Committee on Banking, Housing, and Urban Affairs, Subcommittee on International Finance, p. 94.

115. U.S. House, Committee on Foreign Affairs, Subcommittee on Europe and the Middle East, 1981, p. 66.

116. McIntyre and Cupitt, p. 101.

117. Root, p. 73.

118. Reuters, 7 January 1980, BC cycle.

119. Reuters, 9 May 1980, AM cycle.

120. Eugene Kozicharow, "New Sanctions Sought against Soviets," *Aviation Week and Space Technology,* 7 April 1980, p. 53.

121. Reuters, 17 January 1980, PM cycle.

122. *Business Week,* 28 January 1980, p. 34.

123. U.S. Senate, Committee on Banking, Housing, and Urban Affairs, Subcommittee on International Finance, p. 29.

124. Root, p. 73.

125. Reuters, 10 April 1980, BC cycle.

126. European Parliament, p. 7.

127. U.S. Senate, Committee on Banking, Housing, and Urban Affairs, 1979, pt. 1, p. 224.

128. *New York Times,* 19 July 1978, p. 1.

129. OTA, p. 81.

130. U.S. Senate, Committee on Governmental Affairs, Permanent Subcommittee on Investigations, 1980, p. 65.

131. *New York Times,* 21 July 1978, sec. 4, p. 1.

132. *New York Times,* 20 July 1978, p. 4.

133. London *Times,* 20 July 1978, p. 5.

134. London *Times,* 21 July 1978, p. 5.

135. London *Times,* 20 July 1978, p. 7.

136. *New York Times,* 21 July 1978, p. 1.

137. U.S. Senate, Committee on Banking, Housing, and Urban Affairs, 1979, pt. 1, p. 56.

138. Ibid., p. 210.

139. Ibid.

140. Yergin, 1980, pp. 33, 67; U.S. Senate, Committee on Governmental Affairs, Permanent Subcommittee on Investigations, 1980, p. 62.

141. Yergin, 1980, p. 67; OTA, p. 187.

142. U.S. Senate, Committee on Banking, Housing, and Urban Affairs, 1979, pt. 3, pp. 27–28.

143. *New York Times,* 6 April 1979, sec. 4, p. 1.

144. U.S. Senate, Committee on Governmental Affairs, Permanent Subcommittee on Investigations, 1980, p. 62.

145. Ibid., pp. 68–69.

146. Ibid., p. 4.

147. Ibid., pp. 16–17; originally published in *Commentary* by Carl Gersham, April 1979.

## Chapter 8
## The Polish Crisis and Gas-Pipeline Sanctions

1. See in particular Jentleson; Blinken.

2. *Christian Science Monitor,* 26 December 1980, p. 23.

3. *The Economist,* 11 April 1981, pp. 47–48.

4. *New York Times,* 12 December 1980, p. A1.

5. Jonathan P. Stern, 1986, p. 52.

6. Jentleson, table 6.1, p. 186.

7. Jonathan P. Stern, 1982, p. 73; originally printed in the *Washington Star,* 28 June 1981.

8. U.S. Senate, Committee on Governmental Affairs, Subcommittee on Energy, Nuclear Proliferation, and Government Processes, p. 15.

9. *Manchester Guardian,* 26 May 1981, p. 16.

10. Putnam and Bayne, pp. 155–56.

11. Jentleson, pp. 183–84.

12. U.S. Senate, Committee on Governmental Affairs, Subcommittee on Energy, Nuclear Proliferation, and Government Processes, p. 43.

13. Haig, pp. 248–49.

14. Ibid., p. 252.

15. Ibid., p. 251.

16. *New York Times,* 16 December 1981, p. A1.

17. *New York Times,* 19 December 1981, pp. 6, 7; 20 December 1981, p. A22; 21 December 1981, p. A13.

18. *New York Times,* 23 December 1981, p. A1.

19. *New York Times,* 22 December 1981, p. A1.

20. *New York Times,* 23 December 1981, p. A1.

21. *Weekly Compilation of Presidential Documents,* 23 December 1981, pp. 1404–7.

22. Ibid., p. 1406.

23. Haig, p. 254.

24. *Weekly Compilation of Presidential Documents,* 29 December 1981, pp. 1429–30.

25. Reuters North European Service, 30 December 1981.

26. *New York Times,* 3 January 1982, p. A14.

27. *New York Times,* 7 January 1982, p. A1.

28. *New York Times,* 12 January 1982, p. A8.

29. U.S. House, Committee on Foreign Affairs, Subcommittee on Europe and the Middle East, 1982, p. 40.

30. *Business Week,* 25 January 1982, p. 26.

31. DeSouza, p. 101.

32. *Bulletin EC,* December 1981, p. 12.

33. *Bulletin EC,* January 1982, p. 44.

34. *Bulletin EC,* February 1982, p. 49.

35. *U.S. Export Weekly,* 2 March 1982, p. 597.

36. *Bulletin EC,* March 1982, p. 66.

37. *U.S. Export Weekly,* 16 March 1982, pp. 672–73; *New York Times,* 12 March 1982, p. A6.

38. Haig, p. 256.

39. See U.S. House, Committee on Foreign Affairs, Subcommittee on Europe and the Middle East, 1982, p. 6; Crawford, pp. 443–44.

40. *U.S. Export Weekly,* 9 February 1982, p. 509.

41. U.S. House, Committee on Foreign Affairs, Subcommittee on Europe and the Middle East, 1982, p. 41.

42. *U.S. Export Weekly,* 23 March 1982, p. 717.

43. Ibid.

44. See Crovitz, pp. 12–13.

45. *The Economist,* 20 March 1982, p. 70.

46. See U.S. House, Committee on Foreign Affairs, Subcommittee on Europe and the Middle East, 1982, p. 33. For a discussion of the OECD Consensus, see Moravcsik.

47. *U.S. Export Weekly,* 23 March 1982, p. 717.

48. Crawford, p. 446.

49. *New York Times,* 16 March 1982, p. A9.

50. Haig, pp. 305–6.

51. Quoted in Putnam and Bayne, p. 165.

52. *Financial Times,* 7 June 1982, p. 2.

53. *New York Times,* 7 June 1982, p. D7.

54. *Washington Post,* 15 June 1982, pp. A1, A13.

55. *Washington Post,* 24 June 1982, p. A33.

56. *New York Times,* 26 June 1982, p. 6.

57. U.S. Senate, Committee on Governmental Affairs, Subcommittee on Energy, Nuclear Proliferation, and Government Processes, p. 15.

58. *New York Times,* 22 June 1982, p. A18; Haig, p. 312.

59. *Weekly Compilation of Presidential Documents,* 18 June 1982, p. 820.

60. *New York Times,* 26 June 1982, p. 6.

61. *Daily Report for Executives,* no. 123, 25 June 1982, p. L-3.

62. *The Economist,* 26 June 1982, p. 18.

63. Ibid.

64. *Washington Post,* 25 June 1982, p. A21, quoting from *Frankfurter Rundschau.*

65. *New York Times,* 29 June 1982, p. A10.
66. *New York Times,* 2 July 1982, p. A1.
67. *Financial Times,* 1 July 1982, p. 1.
68. *New York Times,* 2 July 1982, p. A4.
69. *Business Week,* 19 July 1982, p. 51.
70. *Financial Times,* 8 July 1982, p. 1.
71. See *Far Eastern Economic Review,* 23 July 1982, pp. 43–50.
72. *Financial Times,* 9 July 1982, p. 4.
73. *New York Times,* 23 July 1982, p. A1.
74. Ibid., p. A6.
75. Ibid.
76. *Newsweek,* 2 August 1982, p. 37.
77. *Wall Street Journal,* 26 July 1982, p. 21.
78. See *International Legal Materials,* 1982, pp. 851–52.
79. *Wall Street Journal,* 3 August 1982, p. 37.
80. *The Economist,* 2 August 1982, p. 37.
81. *New York Times,* 13 August 1982, p. A4.
82. *New York Times,* 27 August 1982, p. D1.
83. *New York Times,* 1 September 1982, pp. A1, D5; *Washington Post,* 1 September 1982, pp. A1, A17.
84. *New York Times,* 1 September 1982, p. A1.
85. See U.S. Senate, Committee on Foreign Relations, Subcommittee on International Economic Policy, *Soviet-European Gas Pipeline,* 1982.
86. *Congressional Record,* 22 July 1982, p. E3429.
87. *Congressional Quarterly,* 14 August 1982, p. 1961.
88. Ibid.
89. *Congressional Record,* 13 August 1982, pp. S10514–15.
90. *Congressional Record,* 29 September 1982, p. H7915.
91. Ibid., pp. H7917–18.
92. Ibid., pp. H7927–30; *Congressional Quarterly,* 2 October 1982, p. 2467.
93. *Washington Post,* 24 July 1982, p. A10.
94. *Washington Post,* 8 September 1982, p. A4.
95. *Washington Post,* 4 October 1982, p. A22.
96. *Washington Post,* 10 October 1982, p. A23.
97. *Washington Post,* 30 October 1982, p. A1; *New York Times,* 30 October 1982, p. 1.
98. *New York Times,* 30 October 1982, p. 48.
99. *Weekly Compilation of Presidential Documents,* 13 November 1982, pp. 1475–76.
100. *New York Times,* 15 November 1982, p. A10.
101. *Washington Post,* 15 November 1982, p. A15.
102. Kobrin, p. 47.
103. Jentleson, p. 23.
104. Ibid., p. 41.
105. See Adler-Karlsson.
106. Mastanduno, 1988.

107. The United States attempted to put the pipeline on the agenda of a high-level CoCom meeting in January 1982. However, since gas and oil equipment had been taken off the list of controlled goods decades before and had little direct military relevance, French and other officials successfully argued that this issue was outside the boundaries of acceptable CoCom discussion. See Crawford and Lenway, p. 391; Reuters North European Service, 20 January 1982; *Financial Times,* 19 January 1982, p. 4.

108. See Austvik.

109. Jonathan P. Stern, 1986, pp. 105–22.

110. International Energy Agency, *Energy Policies and Programmes of IEA Countries, 1983 Review* (Paris: Organization for Economic Cooperation and Development, 1984), pp. 286–87.

111. Janne Haaland Matlary, "Perspectives on the Role of Norwegian Gas," in Conant, p. 129.

112. Jonathan P. Stern, 1986, pp. 72–104.

113. Jonathan P. Stern, 1982, p. 69.

114. Jonathan P. Stern, 1986, pp. 4–41.

115. See Alt and Eichengreen.

116. Austvik, p. 25.

117. *Daily Report for Executives,* no. 123, 25 June 1982, p. L-3.

118. Holst, p. 88.

119. *Manchester Guardian,* 26 May 1981, p. 16.

120. *New York Times,* 3 June 1982, p. A1.

121. *Financial Times,* 26 June 1982, p. 2.

122. U.S. Senate, Committee on Governmental Affairs, Subcommittee on Energy, Nuclear Proliferation, and Government Processes, p. 37.

123. See U.S. Central Intelligence Agency, pp. 12–13. This report predicted that oil shortages in the Soviet Union would force it to begin importing more OPEC oil. The report had a strong impact on the thinking of the Reagan administration but underestimated the Soviet Union's ability to develop its natural-gas reserves rapidly.

124. Jonathan P. Stern, 1980, p. 140.

125. *Wall Street Journal,* 2 November 1982, p. 27.

126. *The Economist,* 25 July 1981, p. 65.

127. *Financial Times,* 15 July 1982, p. 3.

128. Jonathan P. Stern, "International Gas Trade: The Three Major Markets," in Conant, p. 19.

129. *Washington Post,* 1 September 1982, p. A1.

130. *Wall Street Journal,* 2 November 1982, p. 1.

131. Ibid.

132. Jonathan P. Stern, 1982, p. 78.

133. Ibid., p. 79; U.S. Senate, Committee on Banking, Housing, and Urban Affairs, 1981, p. 97.

134. Jonathan P. Stern, 1982, p. 79.

135. *Business Week,* 25 January 1982, p. 26.

136. *New York Times,* 14 February 1982, p. E5.

137. *New York Times,* 23 July 1982, p. A6.

138. *New York Times,* 31 July 1982, pp. 33–34.

139. *Wall Street Journal,* 26 July 1982, p. 21.

140. *Congressional Quarterly,* 14 August 1982, p. 1961.

141. *New York Times,* 5 October 1982, p. A1.

142. *Weekly Compilation of Presidential Documents,* 15 October 1982, p. 1318; *Chicago Tribune,* 16 October 1982, p. 1.

143. *The Economist,* 23 October 1982, p. 25.

144. Hans J. Morgenthau, *Politics among Nations: The Struggle for Power and Peace,* 2d ed. (New York: Alfred A. Knopf, 1954), p. 5.

145. Deborah Welch Larson, "Order under Anarchy: The Emergence of Convention in U.S.-Soviet Relations" (Paper delivered at the 1989 annual meeting of the American Political Science Association, Atlanta, Georgia, 31 August–3 September), p. 6.

146. Schelling, pp. 35–43.

147. Baldwin, p. 107.

148. Ibid., p. 283.

149. Kreps and Wilson; David M. Kreps and Robert Wilson, "Sequential Equilibria," *Econometrica* 50, no. 4 (July 1982), pp. 863–94; Alt, Calvert, and Humes.

150. Drew Fudenberg and Jean Tirole, "A Theory of Exit in Duopoly," *Econometrica* 54, no. 4 (July 1986), pp. 943–60.

# Bibliography

Acevedo, Domingo E. 1984. "The U.S. Measures against Argentina Resulting from the Malvinas Conflict." *American Journal of International Law* 78, no. 2 (April): 323–44.

Adler-Karlsson, Gunnar. 1968. *Western Economic Warfare, 1947–1967.* Stockholm: Almquist & Wiksell.

Aeppel, Timothy. 1985. "The Evolution of Multilateral Export Controls: A Critical Study of the CoCom Regime." *The Fletcher Forum* 9, no. 1 (Winter): 105–24.

Agnelli, Giovanni. 1980. "East-West Trade: A European View." *Foreign Affairs* 58, no. 4 (Summer): 1016–33.

Alston, Philip. 1982. "International Trade as an Instrument of Positive Human Rights Policy." *Human Rights Quarterly* 4, no. 2 (Spring): 155–83.

Alston, Philip, and Maria Rodriguez-Bustelo. 1988. *Taking Stock of United Nations Human Rights Procedures.* Report of a Fletcher School of International Law and Diplomacy workshop, Lake Mohonk, N.Y., January.

Alt, James E., Randall L. Calvert, and Brian D. Humes. 1988. "Reputation and Hegemonic Stability: A Game-Theoretic Analysis." *American Political Science Review* 82, no. 2 (June): 445–66.

Alt, James E., and Barry Eichengreen. 1989. "Parallel and Overlapping Games: Theory and an Application to the European Gas Trade." *Economics and Politics* 1, no. 2 (July): 119–44.

American Association for the International Commission of Jurists. 1985. *Human Rights and Foreign Policy: The Role of Government.* New York: American Association for the International Commission of Jurists.

Amine, James L. 1983. "Economic Sanctions: Falkland Islands (Malvinas)." *Harvard International Law Journal* 23, no. 2 (Winter): 404–9.

Arnold, Hugh M. 1980. "Henry Kissinger and Human Rights." *Universal Human Rights* 2, no. 4 (October–December): 57–71.

Austvik, Ole Gunnar. 1987. *The Western European Gas Market: A Security Price Premium for Norwegian Gas?* Norwegian Institute of International Affairs, no. 110 (July).

Avery, William, and David P. Forsythe. 1979. "Human Rights, National Security, and the U.S. Senate: Who Votes for What, and Why." *International Studies Quarterly* 23, no. 2 (June): 303–20.

Axelrod, Robert. 1970. *Conflict of Interest: A Theory of Divergent Goals with Applications to Politics.* Chicago: Markham Publishing Co.

———. 1984. *The Evolution of Cooperation.* New York: Basic Books.

Baehr, Peter R. 1982. "Concern for Development Aid and Fundamental Human Rights: The Dilemma as Faced by the Netherlands." *Human Rights Quarterly* 4, no. 1 (Spring): 39–52.

Baldwin, David A. 1985. *Economic Statecraft.* Princeton: Princeton University Press.

Barber, James. 1979. "Economic Sanctions as a Policy Instrument." *International Affairs* 55, no. 3 (July): 367–84.

Barber, James, and Michael Spicer. 1979. "Sanctions against South Africa—Options for the West." *International Affairs* 55, no. 3 (July): 385–401.

Bayard, Thomas O., Joseph Pelzman, and Jorge Perez-Lopez. 1983. "Stakes and Risks in Economic Sanctions." *World Economy* 6, no. 1 (March): 73–87.

Becker, Abraham S. 1986. "U.S.-Soviet Trade and East-West Trade Policy." In Arnold L. Horelick, ed., *U.S.-Soviet Relations: The Next Phase* (Ithaca: Cornell University Press), pp. 175–97.

Benson, Sumner. 1986. "The Defense Department and the Politics of Economic Security." Paper prepared for the Economics and Security Seminar, Center for International Affairs, Harvard University, 11 March.

Berman, Harold J., and John R. Garson. 1967. "United States Export Controls: Past, Present, and Future." *Columbia Law Review* 67, no. 5 (May): 791–890.

Bertsch, Gary. 1980. "US-Soviet Trade: The Question of Leverage." *Survey: A Journal of East and West Studies* 25, no. 2 (Spring): 66–80.

Bertsch, Gary K., ed. 1988. *Controlling East-West Trade and Technology Transfer: Power, Politics, and Policies.* Durham: Duke University Press.

Bertsch, Gary K., and John R. McIntyre, eds. 1983. *National Security and Technology Transfer: The Strategic Dimensions of East-West Trade.* Boulder: Westview Press.

Bingham, Jonathan B., and Victor C. Johnson. 1979. "A Rational Approach to Export Controls." *Foreign Affairs* 57, no. 3 (Spring): 894–920.

Blinken, Antony J. 1987. *Ally versus Ally: America, Europe, and the Siberian Pipeline Crisis.* New York: Praeger.

Bonker, Don. 1986. "Protecting Economic Interests." *Issues in Science and Technology* 3, no. 1 (Fall): 96–104.

Breslin, Patrick. 1977. "Human Rights: Rhetoric or Action?" *Washington Post*, 27 February, p. C1–4.

British Institutes' Joint Energy Policy Programme. 1983. *Energy—Two Decades of Crisis.* Aldershot, Hampshire: Gower.

Brown, Cynthia, ed. 1985. *With Friends Like These.* New York: Pantheon Books.

Buchan, David. 1984a. "Technology Transfer to the Soviet Bloc." *Washington Quarterly* 7, no. 4 (Autumn): 130–35.

———. 1984b. *Western Security and Economic Strategy towards the East.* Adelphi Papers, no. 192 (Autumn).

Bucy, J. Fred. 1980–81. "Technology Transfer and East-West Trade: A Reappraisal." *International Security* 5, no. 3 (Winter): 132–51.

Buergenthal, Thomas. 1987. "Human Rights in the Americas: View from the Inter-American Court." *Connecticut Journal of International Law* 2, no. 2 (Spring): 303–10.

———. 1988. *International Human Rights in a Nutshell.* St. Paul, Minn.: West Publishing Co.

Buergenthal, Thomas, Robert Norris, and Dinah Shelton. 1986. *Protecting Human Rights in the Americas: Selected Problems.* 2d ed. Kehl, West Germany: N.P. Engel.

Buncher, Judith F., ed. 1977. *Human Rights and American Diplomacy: 1975–1977.* New York: Facts on File.

Burns, Jimmy. 1987. *The Land That Lost Its Heroes: The Falklands, the Post-War, and Alfonsin.* London: Bloomsbury.

Burns, Robert Andrew. 1985. *Diplomacy, War, and Parliamentary Democracy: Further Lessons from the Falklands or Advice from Academe.* Lanham, Md.: University Press of America.

Calvert, Peter. 1982. *The Falklands Crisis: The Rights and the Wrongs.* New York: St. Martin's Press.

————. 1983. "Latin America and the United States during and after the Falklands Crisis." *Millennium: Journal of International Studies* 12, no. 1: 69–96.

Campbell, Robert. 1981. *Soviet Technology Imports: The Gas Pipeline Case.* California Seminar on International Security and Foreign Policy, Discussion Paper No. 91. Santa Monica: California Seminar, February.

Carrick, R. J. 1978. "East-West Technology Transfer in Perspective." *Policy Papers in International Affairs,* no. 9.

Carter, Barry E. 1988. *International Economic Sanctions: Improving the Haphazard U.S. Legal Regime.* Cambridge: Cambridge University Press.

Cassese, Antonio. 1979. "Foreign Economic Assistance and Respect for Civil and Political Rights: Chile—A Case Study." *Texas International Law Journal* 14: 251–63.

*The Center Magazine* 17, nos. 1–4 (January–August 1984), "Human Rights and American Foreign Policy."

Christensen, Thomas J., and Jack Snyder. 1990. "Chain Gangs and Passed Bucks: Predicting Alliance Patterns in Multipolarity." *International Organization* 44, no. 2 (Spring): 137–68.

Clark, Evans, ed. 1932. *Boycotts and Peace: A Report by the Committee of Economic Sanctions.* New York: Harper & Brothers.

Claude, Inis L., Jr. 1983. "The Use of the United Nations in the Falklands Crisis." *Global Perspectives* 1, no. 1 (Spring): 64–71.

Cohen, Roberta. 1982. "Human Rights Diplomacy: The Carter Administration and the Southern Cone." *Human Rights Quarterly* 4, no. 2 (Spring): 212–41.

Cohen, Stephen B. 1982. "Conditioning U.S. Security Assistance on Human Rights Practices." *American Journal of International Law* 76, no. 2 (April): 246–79.

Coll, Alberto R., and Anthony C. Arend, eds. 1985. *The Falklands War: Lessons for Strategy, Diplomacy, and International Law.* Boston: George Allen & Unwin.

*Columbia Human Rights Law Review* 14, no. 2 (Fall–Winter 1982–83), "Symposium: The Influence of the United States on Human Rights in Central America."

Commission of the European Communities. 1981. *Natural Gas Supplies and Prospects in the Community.* Luxembourg: European Community.

Conant, Melvin A., ed. 1986. *The World Gas Trade: A Resource for the Future.* Boulder: Westview Press.

Congressional Research Service. Foreign Affairs and National Defense Division. 1979. *Human Rights and U.S. Foreign Assistance: Experiences and Issues in Policy Implementation (1977–1978).* Senate Committee on Foreign Relations (November).

Connell-Smith, Gordon. 1982. "The OAS and the Falklands Conflict." *The World Today* 38, no. 9 (September): 340–47.

Crawford, Beverly. 1987. "How Regimes Matter: Western Control of East-West Trade Finance." *Millennium: Journal of International Studies* 16, no. 3:431–52.

Crawford, Beverly, and Stefanie Lenway. 1985. "Decision Modes and International Regime Change: Western Collaboration on East-West Trade." *World Politics* 37, no. 3 (April): 375–402.

Crovitz, Gordon. 1983. *Europe's Siberian Gas Pipeline: Economic Lessons and Strategic Implications*. Institute for European Defence and Strategic Studies, Occasional Paper No. 6. London: Alliance Publishers.

Curtis, Gerald L. 1977. "The Tyumen Oil Development Project and Japanese Foreign Policy Decision-Making." In Robert A. Scalapino, ed., *The Foreign Policy of Modern Japan* (Berkeley: University of California Press), pp. 147–73.

Cusack, David F. 1977. *Revolution and Reaction: The Internal Dynamics of Conflict and Confrontation in Chile*. Denver: University of Denver.

Dabat, Alejandro, and Luis Lorenzano. 1984. *Argentina: The Malvinas and the End of Military Rule*, Trans. Ralph Johnstone. London: Verso Editions.

Daoudi, M. S., and M. S. Dajani. 1983a. *Economic Sanctions: Ideals and Experience*. London: Routledge & Kegan Paul.

———. 1983b. "Sanctions: The Falklands Episode." *The World Today* 39, no. 4 (April): 150–60.

Derian, Patricia M. 1979. "Human Rights in American Foreign Policy." *Notre Dame Lawyer* 55 (December): 264–80.

DeSouza, Patrick J. 1984. "The Soviet Gas Pipeline Incident: Extension of Collective Security Responsibilities to Peacetime Commercial Trade." *Yale Journal of International Law* 10, no. 1 (Fall): 92–120.

Dilloway, James. 1986. *Is World Order Evolving? An Adventure into Human Potential*. New York: Pergamon Press.

Dobrovolny, Jiri. 1983. "East-West Trade in a Transition Period." *East European Quarterly* 27, no. 3 (September): 331–41.

Dobson, Alan P. 1988. "The Kennedy Administration and Economic Warfare against Communism." *International Affairs* (Autumn): 599–616.

Dominguez, Jorge I., Nigel S. Rodley, Bryce Wood, and Richard Falk. 1979. *Enhancing Global Human Rights*. New York: McGraw-Hill.

Dowrick, F. E., ed. 1979. *Human Rights: Problems, Perspectives, and Texts*. Westmead, Great Britain: Saxon House.

Doxey, Margaret. 1972. "International Sanctions: A Framework for Analysis with Special Reference to the UN and Southern Africa." *International Organization* 26, no. 3 (Summer): 527–51.

———. 1979. "Human Rights and Canadian Foreign Policy." *Behind the Headlines* 37, no. 4.

———. 1980. *Economic Sanctions and International Enforcement*. London: Macmillan.

———. 1982. "Do Sanctions Work?" *International Perspectives* (July–August): 13–15.

Dvorin, Shirley Miller. 1980. "The Export Administration Act of 1979: An Examination of Foreign Availability of Controlled Goods and Technologies." *Northwestern Journal of International Law and Business* 2: 179–99.

Economist Intelligence Unit. 1982. "European Political Cooperation Shows Results." *European Trends* 71 (May): 1–4.

Edwards, Geoffrey. 1984. "Europe and the Falkland Islands Crisis, 1982." *Journal of Common Market Studies* 22, no. 4 (June): 295–313.

European Parliament. 1982. *Working Documents, 1982–83*. Document 1–83/82 (8 April), "On the Significance of Economic Sanctions."

Falkenheim, Peggy L. 1987. "Post-Afghanistan Sanctions." In David Leyton-Brown, ed., *The Utility of Economic Sanctions* (New York: St. Martin's Press), pp. 105–30.

Farer, Tom J. 1983. "Human Rights and Human Welfare in Latin America." *Daedalus* 112, no. 4 (Fall): 139–70.

———. 1988. *The Grand Strategy of the United States in Latin America*. New Brunswick, N.J.: Transaction Books.

Feinberg, Richard E. 1980. "U.S. Human Rights Policy: Latin America." *International Policy Report* 6, no. 1 (October).

Fisher, Irving. 1923. *League or War?* New York: Harper & Brothers.

Fisher, Stewart W. 1982. "Human Rights in El Salvador and U.S. Foreign Policy." *Human Rights Quarterly* 4, no. 1 (Spring): 1–38.

Fishlow, Albert. 1982. "The United States and Brazil: The Case of the Missing Relationship." *Foreign Affairs* 60, no. 4 (Spring): 904–23.

Forsythe, David P. 1980. "American Foreign Policy and Human Rights: Rhetoric and Reality." *Universal Human Rights* 2, no. 3 (July–September): 35–53.

———. 1988. *Human Rights and U.S. Foreign Policy: Congress Reconsidered*. Gainesville: University of Florida Press.

Fowler, Michael Ross. 1987. *Contending Approaches to Human Rights in U.S. Foreign Policy*. Lanham, Md.: University Press of America.

Freedman, Lawrence. 1982. "The War of the Falkland Islands, 1982." *Foreign Affairs* 61, no. 1 (Fall): 196–210.

Galtung, Johan. 1967. "On the Effects of International Economic Sanctions: With Examples from the Case of Rhodesia." *World Politics* 19, no. 3 (April): 378–416.

Gasiorowski, Mark, and Solomon W. Polachek. 1982. "Conflict and Interdependence: East-West Trade and Linkages in the Era of Detente." *Journal of Conflict Resolution* 26, no. 4 (December): 709–29.

George, Alexander L. 1979. "Case Studies and Theory Development: The Method of Structured, Focused Comparison." In Paul Gordon Lauren, ed., *Diplomacy: New Approaches in History, Theory, and Policy* (New York: The Free Press), pp. 43–68.

German, Robert K. 1982. "Norway and the Bear: Soviet Coercive Diplomacy and Norwegian Security Policy." *International Security* 7, no. 2 (Fall): 55–82.

Ghoshal, Animish. 1983. "Going against the Grain: Lessons of the 1980 Embargo." *World Economy* 6, no. 2 (June): 183–94.

Gibson, Geoffrey. 1983. "Falklands Postscript: An Anglo-Argentine View." *The World Today* 39, no. 2 (February): 75–79.

Gilmore, Richard. 1980. "Grain in the Bank." *Foreign Policy* 38 (Spring): 168–81.

Gilpin, Robert. 1981. *War and Change in World Politics*. Cambridge: Cambridge University Press.

Goebel, Julius. 1982. *The Struggle for the Falkland Islands: A Study in Legal and Diplomatic History*. New Haven: Yale University Press.

Gordon, Dennis R. 1987. "The Paralysis of Multilateral Peacekeeping: International Organizations and the Falklands/Malvinas War." *Peace and Change* 12, no. 1/2: 51–63.

Great Britain. Parliament. House of Commons. 1982. *The Falklands Campaign: A Digest of Debates in the House of Commons, 2 April to June 1982*. Her Majesty's Stationery Office.

Grieco, Joseph M. 1988. "Anarchy and the Limits of Cooperation: A Realist Critique of the Newest Liberal Institutionalism." *International Organization* 42, no. 3 (Summer): 485–507.

Gustafson, Thane. 1981. *Selling the Russians the Rope? Soviet Technology Policy and U.S. Export Controls*. Santa Monica: Rand, April.

Haig, Alexander M., Jr. 1984. *Caveat: Reagan, Realism, and Foreign Policy*. New York: Macmillan Publishing Co.

Hastings, Max, and Simon Jenkins. 1983. *The Battle for the Falklands*. New York: W. W. Norton & Co.

Hawk, David. 1979. "Human Rights at Half-Time." *The New Republic*, 7 April, pp. 21–23.

Hevener, Natalie Kaufman, ed. 1981. *The Dynamics of Human Rights in U.S. Foreign Policy*. New Brunswick, N.J.: Transaction Books.

Hevener, Natalie Kaufman, and David Whiteman. 1988. "Opposition to Human Rights Treaties in the United States Senate: The Legacy of the Bricker Amendment." *Human Rights Quarterly* 10, no. 3 (August): 309–37.

Hewett, Ed A. 1984. *Energy, Economics, and Foreign Policy in the Soviet Union*. Washington, D.C.: Brookings Institution.

Highley, Albert E. 1938. *The First Sanctions Experiment*. Geneva: Geneva Research Centre, July.

Hindmarsh, Albert E. 1933. *Force in Peace: Force Short of War in International Relations*. Cambridge: Harvard University Press.

Hipel, Keith W., Muhong Wang, and Niall M. Fraser. 1988. "Hypergame Analysis of the Falklands/Malvinas Conflict." *International Studies Quarterly* 32, no. 3 (September): 335–58.

Hirschman, Albert O. 1980. *National Power and the Structure of Foreign Trade*. Expanded edition. Berkeley: University of California Press.

Hoffmann, Fredrik. 1967. "The Functions of Economic Sanctions: A Comparative Analysis." *Journal of Peace Research* 2: 140–60.

Hoffmann, Stanley. 1983. "Reaching for the Most Difficult: Human Rights as a Foreign Policy Goal." *Daedalus* 112, no. 4 (Fall): 19–49.

Holst, Johan Jergen. 1986. "The Effect on Norway: Increased Precaution." In Sverre Jervell and Kare Nyblom, eds., *The Military Buildup in the High North: American and Nordic Perspectives* (Lanham, Md.: University Press of America), pp. 77–89.

Hufbauer, Gary Clyde, and Jeffrey J. Schott, assisted by Kimberly Ann Elliott. 1985. *Economic Sanctions Reconsidered.* Washington, D.C.: Institute for International Economics.

Hufbauer, Gary Clyde, Jeffrey J. Schott, and Kimberly Ann Elliott. 1990. *Economic Sanctions Reconsidered: History and Current Policy.* 2d ed. Washington, D.C.: Institute for International Economics.

Huntington, Samuel P. 1978. "Trade, Technology, and Leverage: Economic Diplomacy." *Foreign Policy* 32 (Fall): 63–80.

Institute for Foreign Policy Analysis and The International Security Studies Program, The Fletcher School of International Law and Diplomacy, Tufts University. 1985. *East-West Trade and Technology Transfer: New Challenges for the United States.* Conference Report, Second Annual Forum, 23–24 September.

International Energy Agency. 1982. *Natural Gas: Prospects to 2000.* Paris: Organization for Economic Cooperation and Development.

Jack, D. T. 1940. *Studies in Economic Warfare.* London: P. S. King & Son.

Jentleson, Bruce W. 1986. *Pipeline Politics: The Complex Political Economy of East-West Energy Trade.* Ithaca: Cornell University Press.

Jervis, Robert. 1978. "Cooperation under the Security Dilemma." *World Politics* 30, no. 2 (January): 167–214.

Joyce, Joe, and Peter Murtagh. 1983. *The Boss: Charles J. Haughey in Government.* Dublin: Poolbeg Press.

Kaempfer, William H., James A. Lehman, and Anton D. Lowenberg. 1987. "Divestment, Investment Sanctions, and Disinvestment: An Evaluation of Anti-Apartheid Policy Instruments." *International Organization* 41, no. 3 (Summer): 457–73.

Kaempfer, William H., and Anton D. Lowenberg. 1988. "The Theory of International Sanctions: A Public Policy Approach." *American Economic Review* 78, no. 4 (September): 786–93.

———. 1989. "Sanctioning South Africa: The Politics behind the Policies." *Cato Journal* 8, no. 3 (Winter): 713–27.

Keohane, Robert O. 1980. "The Theory of Hegemonic Stability and Changes in International Economic Regimes, 1967–1977." In Ole Holsti et al., *Change in the International System* (Boulder: Westview Press), pp. 131–62.

———. 1984. *After Hegemony: Cooperation and Discord in the World Political Economy.* Princeton: Princeton University Press.

———. 1988. "International Institutions: Two Approaches." *International Studies Quarterly* 32, no. 4 (December): 379–96.

———. 1989. *International Institutions and State Power.* Boulder: Westview Press.

Kindleberger, Charles P. 1973. *The World in Depression, 1929–1939.* Berkeley: University of California Press.

King, Gary. 1989a. "Event Count Models for International Relations: Generalizations and Applications." *International Studies Quarterly* 33, no. 2 (June): 123–47.

———. 1989b. *Unifying Political Methodology: The Likelihood Theory of Statistical Inference.* New York: Cambridge University Press.

————. 1989c. "Variance Specification in Event Count Models: From Restrictive Assumptions to a Generalized Estimator." *American Journal of Political Science* 33, no. 3 (August): 762–84.

Knorr, Klaus, and Frank N. Trager, eds. 1977. *Economic Issues and National Security*. Lawrence: University Press of Kansas.

Kobrin, Stephen J. 1988. "Hegemony, American Multinationals, and the Extraterritorial Enforcement of Export Embargoes." Paper presented at the annual meeting of the American Political Science Association, Washington, D.C., 1–4 September.

Kommers, Donald P., and Gilburt D. Loescher, eds. 1979. *Human Rights and American Foreign Policy*. Notre Dame: University of Notre Dame Press.

Krasner, Stephen D. 1976. "State Power and the Structure of International Trade." *World Politics* 28, no. 3 (April): 317–43.

————, ed. 1983. *International Regimes*. Ithaca: Cornell University Press.

Kratochwil, Friedrich, Paul Rohrlich, and Harpreet Mahajan. 1985. *Peace and Disputed Sovereignty: Reflections on Conflict over Territory*. Lanham, Md.: University Press of America.

Kreps, David M., and Robert Wilson. 1982. "Reputation and Imperfect Information." *Journal of Economic Theory* 27: 253–79.

Lacorne, Denis. 1986. "The Management of Multilateral Embargoes: A European Perspective." Paper presented at the annual meeting of the American Political Science Association, Washington, D.C., 28–31 August.

Latin American Bureau. 1982. *Falklands/Malvinas: Whose Crisis?* London: Latin American Bureau.

Latin American Newsletters. 1983. *The Falklands War: The Official History*. London: Latin American Newsletters.

Lawyers' Committee for Human Rights. 1986. *The Reagan Administration's Record on Human Rights in 1985*. New York: The Watch Committees, January.

Lebahn, Axel. 1983. "The Yamal Gas Pipeline from the USSR to Western Europe in the East-West Conflict." *Aussenpolitik* 34 (Third Quarter): 257–80.

Lieber, Robert J., ed. 1983. *Will Europe Fight for Oil? Energy Relations in the Atlantic Area*. New York: Praeger.

Lillich, Richard B., ed. 1981. *U.S. Ratification of the Human Rights Treaties: With or without Reservations?* Charlottesville: University Press of Virginia.

Little, Walter. 1984. "The Falklands Affair: A Review of the Literature." *Political Studies* 32: 296–310.

Loescher, G. D. 1977. "U.S. Human Rights Policy and International Financial Institutions." *The World Today* 33, no. 12 (December): 453–63.

Lorentsen, Lorents, and Kjell Roland. 1985. "Norway's Export of Natural Gas to the European Gas Market: Policy Issues and Model Tools." In Olav Bjerkholt and Eric Offerdal, eds., *Macroeconomic Prospects for a Small Oil Exporting Country* (Dordrecht: Martinus Nijhoff), pp. 173–90.

Losman, Donald L. 1979. *International Economic Sanctions: The Cases of Cuba, Israel, and Rhodesia*. Albuquerque: University of New Mexico Press.

Luard, Evan. 1980. "Human Rights and Foreign Policy." *International Affairs* 56, no. 4 (Autumn): 579–606.

————. 1981. *Human Rights and Foreign Policy*. New York: Pergamon Press.

McGowan, Patrick J., and Robert M. Rood. 1975. "Alliance Behavior in Balance of Power Systems: Applying a Poisson Model to Nineteenth-Century Europe." *American Political Science Review* 69, no. 3 (September): 859–70.

McIntyre, John R., and Richard T. Cupitt. 1980. "East-West Strategic Trade Control: Crumbling Consensus?" *Survey: A Journal of East and West Studies* 25, no. 2 (Spring): 81–108.

McKelvey, R., and W. Zavoina. 1975. "A Statistical Model for the Analysis of Ordinal Dependent Variables." *Journal of Mathematical Sociology* 4: 103–20.

MacQueen, Norman. 1985. "The Expedience of Tradition: Ireland, International Organization and the Falklands Crisis." *Political Studies* 33: 38–55.

Marantz, Paul. 1987. "Economic Sanctions in the Polish Crisis." In David Leyton-Brown, ed., *The Utility of Economic Sanctions* (New York: St. Martin's Press), pp. 131–46.

Marie, Jean-Bernard. 1985. *Human Rights or a Way of Life in a Democracy.* Strasbourg: Council of Europe.

Mastanduno, Michael. 1985. "Between Economics and Security: The Western Politics of East-West Trade." Ph.D. thesis, Princeton University.

———. 1988. "Trade as a Strategic Weapon: American and Alliance Export Control Policy in the Early Postwar Period." *International Organization* 42, no. 1 (Winter): 121–50.

Matthews, Robert, and Cranford Pratt. 1985. "Human Rights and Foreign Policy: Principles and Canadian Practice." *Human Rights Quarterly* 7, no. 2 (May): 159–88.

Maull, Hanns W. 1981. *Natural Gas and Economic Security.* The Atlantic Papers, no. 43. Paris: The Atlantic Institute for International Affairs.

Mayall, James. 1984. "The Sanctions Problem in International Economic Relations: Reflections in Light of Recent Economic Experience." *International Affairs* 60, no. 4 (Autumn): 631–42.

Maynard, Edwin S. 1989. "The Bureaucracy and Implementation of US Human Rights Policy." *Human Rights Quarterly* 11, no. 2 (May): 175–248.

Melendez, Federico. 1984. *The Falklands: A Study in International Confrontation.* Carlsbad, Calif.: Arcadia Publications.

Merrill, Andrea T. 1982. *Chile: A Country Study.* Washington, D.C.: Secretary of the Army.

Middlebrook, Kevin J., and Carlos Ricos, eds. 1986. *The United States and Latin America in the 1980s: Contending Perspectives on a Decade of Crisis.* Pittsburgh: University of Pittsburgh Press.

Middlebrook, Martin. 1985. *Operation Corporate: The Falklands War, 1982.* London: Viking.

Milgrom, Paul, and John Roberts. 1982. "Predation, Reputation, and Entry Deterrence." *Journal of Economic Theory* 27: 280–312.

Miller, Judith. 1980. "When Sanctions Worked." *Foreign Policy* 39 (Summer): 118–29.

Mitrany, David. 1975. *The Functional Theory of Politics.* London: St. Martin's Press for the London School of Economics and Political Science.

Molineau, Harold. 1986. *U.S. Policy toward Latin America: From Regionalism to Globalism.* Boulder: Westview Press.

Moore, John Norton. 1982. "The Inter-American System Snarls in Falklands War." *American Journal of International Law* 76, no. 4 (October): 830–31.

Moravcsik, Andrew M. 1989. "Disciplining Trade Finance: The OECD Export Credit Arrangement." *International Organization* 43, no. 1 (Winter): 173–205.

Morrell, Jim. 1981. "Achievement of the 1970s: U.S. Human Rights Law and Policy." *International Policy Report* (November).

Mossavar-Rahmani, Bijan, Oystein Noreng, and Gregory F. Treverton. 1987. *Natural Gas in Western Europe: Structure, Strategies, and Politics.* Harvard International Energy Studies, no. 3. Cambridge: Energy and Environmental Policy Center, Harvard University.

Mower, A. Glenn, Jr. 1979. *The United States, the United Nations, and Human Rights.* Westport, Conn.: Greenwood Press.

———. 1985. *International Cooperation for Social Justice: Global and Regional Protection of Economic/Social Rights.* Westport, Conn.: Greenwood Press.

Moyer, Homer E., Jr., and Linda A. Mabry. 1983. "Export Controls as Instruments of Foreign Policy: The History, Legal Issues, and Policy Lessons of Three Recent Cases." *Law and Policy in International Business* 15, no. 1: 1–170.

Muller, Harald. "U.S. Energy Policy." In Rode and Jacobsen, pp. 200–12.

Muravchik, Joshua. 1986. *The Uncertain Crusade: Jimmy Carter and the Dilemmas of Human Rights Policy.* Lanham, Md.: Hamilton Press.

National Academy of Sciences. 1987. *Balancing the National Interest: U.S National Security Export Controls and Global Economic Competition.* Washington, D.C.: National Academy Press.

Nelson, Jack L., and Vera M. Green, eds. 1980. *International Human Rights: Contemporary Issues.* Stanfordville, N.Y.: Human Rights Publishing Group.

Netherlands. Ministry of Foreign Affairs. 1979. *Human Rights and Foreign Policy.* The Hague, December.

Newberg, Paula R., ed. 1980. *The Politics of Human Rights.* New York: New York University Press.

Newsom, David D., ed. 1986. *The Diplomacy of Human Rights.* Lanham, Md.: University Press of America.

Nincic, Miroslav, and Peter Wallensteen, eds. 1983. *Dilemmas of Economic Coercion.* New York: Praeger.

Nolan, Cathal J. 1985. "The Influence of Parliament on Human Rights in Canadian Foreign Policy." *Human Rights Quarterly* 7, no. 3 (August): 373–90.

Noreng, Oystein. 1982. "Friends or Fellow Travelers? The Relationship of Non-OPEC Exporters with OPEC." In Ragaei El Mallakh, ed., *OPEC: Twenty Years and Beyond.* (Boulder: Westview Press), pp. 193–215.

Norman, Albert. 1988. *The Falkland Islands, Their Kinship Isles, the Antarctic Hemisphere, and the Freedom of the Two Great Oceans: Discovery and Diplomacy, Law and War.* Vol. 2. Northfield, Vt.: Albert Norman.

Norpoth, Helmut. 1987. "Guns and Butter and Government Popularity in Britain." *American Political Science Review* 81, no. 3 (September): 949–59.

Nossal, Kim Richard. 1989. "International Sanctions as International Punishment." *International Organization* 43, no. 2 (Spring): 301–22.

European Communities. *Official Journal*, no. L 102 (16 April 1982): 1–3; no. L 136 (18 May 1982): 1–2.

O'Leary, James P. 1981. "The Utility of Economic Sanctions." *Parameters: Journal of the U.S. Army War College* 11, no. 3 (September): 48–53.

Ordeshook, Peter C. 1986. *Game Theory and Political Theory.* Cambridge: Cambridge University Press.

Organization for Economic Cooperation and Development. 1984. *East-West Technology Transfer.* Paris: OECD.

Osborne, D. K. 1976. "Cartel Problems." *American Economic Review* 66, no. 5 (December): 835–44.

Owen, David. 1978. *Human Rights.* New York: W.W. Norton & Co.

Oye, Kenneth A., ed. 1986. *Cooperation under Anarchy.* Princeton: Princeton University Press.

Oye, Kenneth A., Robert J. Lieber, and Donald Rothchild, eds. 1983. *Eagle Defiant: United States Foreign Policy in the 1980s.* Boston: Little, Brown.

Paarlberg, Robert L. 1978. "Food, Oil, and Coercive Resource Power." *International Security* 3, no. 2 (Fall): 3–19.

———. 1980. "Lessons of the Grain Embargo." *Foreign Affairs* 59, no. 1 (Fall): 144–62.

Parmelee, Maurice. 1924. *Blockade and Sea Power.* New York: Thomas Y. Crowell Co.

Parrott, Bruce, ed. 1985. *Trade, Technology, and Soviet-American Relations.* Bloomington: Indiana University Press.

Parsons, Anthony. 1983. "The Falklands Crisis in the United Nations, 31 March–14 June 1982." *International Affairs* 59, no. 2 (Spring): 169–78.

Patinkin, Don. 1947. "Multiple-Plant Firms, Cartels, and Imperfect Competition." *Quarterly Journal of Economics* 61 (February): 173–205.

Pearce, Joan. 1982. "The Falkland Islands Dispute." *The World Today* 38, no. 5 (May): 161–65.

Porter, Richard C. 1978. "Economic Sanctions: The Theory and the Evidence from Rhodesia." *Journal of Peace Science* 3, no. 2 (Fall): 93–110.

———. 1979. "International Trade and Investment Sanctions: Potential Impact on the South African Economy." *Journal of Conflict Resolution* 23, no. 4 (December): 579–612.

President's Commission on Industrial Competitiveness. 1985. *Global Competition: The New Reality.* January.

Purcell, Susan Kaufman. 1982. "War and Debt in South America." *Foreign Affairs* 61, no. 3, *America and the World, 1982,* pp. 660–74.

Putnam, Robert D. 1988. "Diplomacy and Domestic Politics: The Logic of Two-Level Games." *International Organization* 42, no. 3 (Summer): 427–60.

Putnam, Robert D., and Nicholas Bayne. 1984. *Hanging Together: The Seven-Power Summits.* Cambridge: Harvard University Press.

Quiroga, Cecilia Medina. 1988. *The Battle of Human Rights: Gross, Systematic Violations and the Inter-American System.* Dordrecht: Martinus Nijhoff.

Renwick, Robin. 1981. *Economic Sanctions.* Harvard Studies in International Affairs No. 45. Cambridge: Center for International Affairs, Harvard University.

Rode, Reinhard, and Hanns-D. Jacobsen, eds. 1985. *Economic Warfare or Detente: An Assessment of East-West Economic Relations in the 1980s.* Boulder: Westview Press.

Rodman, Kenneth A. 1988. "Hegemonic Decline, Multinational Corporations, and U.S. Economic Sanctions since the Pipeline Case." Paper presented at the annual meeting of the American Political Science Association, Washington, D.C., 1–4 September.

Root, William A. 1984. "Trade Controls That Work." *Foreign Policy* 56 (Fall): 61–80.

Rossiter, Caleb. 1984a. "The Financial Hit List." *International Policy Report* (February).

———. 1984b. "Human Rights: The Carter Record, the Reagan Reaction." *International Policy Report* (September).

Rubin, Seymour J. 1982. "The Falklands (Malvinas), International Law, and the OAS." *American Journal of International Law* 76, no. 3 (July): 594–95.

Russell, Jeremy. 1983. *Geopolitics of Natural Gas.* Cambridge: Ballinger Publishing.

Russett, Bruce. 1985. "The Mysterious Case of Vanishing Hegemony: Or, Is Mark Twain Really Dead?" *International Organization* 39, no. 2 (Spring): 207–31.

Salmon, Trevor C. 1982. "Ireland: A Neutral in the Community?" *Journal of Common Market Studies* 20, no. 3 (March): 205–27.

Salzberg, John, and Donald D. Young. 1977. "The Parliamentary Role in Implementing International Human Rights: A U.S. Example." *Texas International Law Journal* 12: 251–78.

Sanford, Jonathan E. 1977. *U.S. Policy and the Multilateral Banks: Politicization and Effectiveness.* Staff Report to the Subcommittee on Foreign Assistance, Senate Committee on Foreign Relations (May).

Schelling, Thomas C. 1980. *The Strategy of Conflict.* Cambridge: Harvard University Press.

Schoultz, Lars. 1981. *Human Rights and United States Policy toward Latin America.* Princeton: Princeton University Press.

Selten, Reinhard. 1978. "The Chain-Store Paradox." *Theory and Decision* 9: 127–59.

Smith, Gordon B., ed. 1984. *The Politics of East-West Trade.* Boulder: Westview Press.

Snidal, Duncan. 1985. "The Limits of Hegemonic Stability Theory." *International Organization* 39, no. 4 (Autumn): 579–614.

Snyder, Glenn H. 1991. "Alliances, Balance, and Stability." *International Organization* 45, no. 1 (Winter): 121–42.

Social Sciences Today Editorial Board, USSR Academy of Sciences. 1984. *The Malvinas (Falkland) Crisis: The Causes and Consequences.* Latin America: Studies by Soviet Scholars, no. 3. Moscow: Social Sciences Today.

Spulber, Nicolas. 1968. "East-West Trade and the Paradoxes of the Strategic Embargo." In Alan A. Brown and Egon Neuberger, eds., *International Trade and Central Planning.* (Berkeley: University of California Press), pp. 104–26.

Stein, Arthur A. 1980. "The Politics of Linkage." *World Politics* 33, no. 1 (October): 62–81.

Stein, Jonathan B. 1982. "U.S. Controls and the Soviet Pipeline." *Washington Quarterly* 5, no. 4 (Autumn): 52–59.

Stent, Angela E. 1983. "Technology Transfer to the Soviet Union." *Arbeitspapiere zur Internationalen Politik* 24 (April).

―――. 1987. "Economic Containment." In Terry L. Deibel and John Lewis Gaddis, eds., *Containing the Soviet Union: A Critique of US Policy*. (Washington, D.C.: Pergamon-Brassey's International Defense Publishers), pp. 59–77.

Stern, Jonathan P. 1980. *Soviet Natural Gas Development to 1990*. Lexington, Mass.: Lexington Books.

―――. 1982. *East European Energy and East-West Trade in Energy*. British Institutes' Joint Energy Policy Programme, Energy Paper No. 1. London: Policy Studies Institute.

―――. 1986. *International Gas Trade in Europe: The Policies of Exporting and Importing Countries*. British Institutes' Joint Energy Policy Programme, Energy Paper No. 8. Aldershot, Hampshire: Gower.

Stewart, Shirley, ed. 1979. *Human Rights in United States and United Kingdom Foreign Policy: A Colloquium*. (Palace of Westminster, 27–28 November 1978). American Association for the International Commission of Jurists.

Stigler, George J. 1964. "A Theory of Oligopoly." *Journal of Political Economy* 72: 44–61.

Strack, Harry R. 1978. *Sanctions: The Case of Rhodesia*. Syracuse, N.Y.: Syracuse University Press.

Strange, Ian J. 1983. *The Falkland Islands*. 3d ed. Newton Abbot, London: David & Charles.

Strange, Susan. 1987. "The Persistent Myth of Lost Hegemony." *International Organization* 41, no. 4 (Autumn): 551–74.

Taylor, Michael. 1976. *Anarchy and Cooperation*. New York: John Wiley & Sons.

Tolley, Howard, Jr. 1987. *The U.N. Commission on Human Rights*. Boulder: Westview Press.

Tollison, Robert D., and Thomas D. Willett. 1979. "An Economic Theory of Mutually Advantageous Issue Linkage in International Negotiations." *International Organization* 33, no. 4 (Autumn): 425–49.

Tonelson, Alan. 1982–83. "Human Rights: The Bias We Need." *Foreign Policy* 49 (Winter): 52–74.

Trindade, A. A. Cancado. 1982. "The Evolution of the Organisation of American States (OAS) System of Human Rights Protection: An Appraisal." *German Yearbook of International Law* 25: 498–514.

United Nations Economic and Social Council. Committee on Human Rights, Subcommittee on Prevention of Discrimination and Protection of Minorities. 1978. *Study of the Impact of Foreign Economic Aid and Assistance on Respect for Human Rights in Chile*. UN Doc. E/CN.4/Sub.2/412, vols. 3, 4 (21 August).

United Nations Secretary-General. 1977. *Protection of Human Rights in Chile*. UN Doc. A/32/234 (11 October).

United Nations Security Council. 1982. Resolution 502, UN Doc. S/RES/502 (3 April). Resolution 505, UN Doc. S/RES/505 (26 May).

U.S. Central Intelligence Agency. 1977. *The International Energy Situation: Outlook to 1985*. (April).

U.S. Congress. Joint Economic Committee. 1982a. *East-West Commercial Pol-icy: A Congressional Dialogue with the Reagan Administration.* 97th Cong., 2d sess., 16 February.
————. 1982b. *Soviet Pipeline Sanctions: The European Perspective.* Hearing, 97th Cong., 2d sess., 22 September.
————. 1984. *East-West Technology Transfer: A Congressional Dialog with the Reagan Administration.* 98th Cong., 2d sess., 19 December. S. Prt. 98–277.
U.S. Congress. Office of Technology Assessment. 1979. *Technology and East-West Trade.* November.
U.S. Defense Department. 1986. *The Technology Security Program.* A Report to the 99th Congress, 2d sess.
U.S. House. 1979. *Export Administration Act of 1979.* 96th Cong., 1st sess., 26 September. Conference Report No. 96–482.
U.S. House. Committee on Banking, Finance, and Urban Affairs, Subcommittee on International Development Institutions and Finance. 1978. *U.S. Participa-tion in Multilateral Development Institutions.* Hearings, 95th Cong., 2d sess., 28 February, 14–15 March, 5 April, 18 May.
U.S. House. Committee on Foreign Affairs. 1980. *Resolution of Inquiry concern-ing Human Rights Policies.* Hearing, 96th Cong., 2d sess., 6 February.
————, Subcommittees on International Economic Policy and Trade and on Inter-American Affairs. 1981. *U.S. Economic Sanctions against Chile.* Hearing, 97th Cong., 1st sess., 10 March.
U.S. House. Committee on Foreign Affairs, Subcommittee on Europe and the Middle East. 1981. *An Assessment of the Afghanistan Sanctions: Implications for Trade and Diplomacy in the 1980's.* 97th Cong., 1st sess., April.
————. 1982. *Developments in Europe, February 1982.* Hearing, 97th Cong., 2d sess., 9 February.
U.S. House. Committee on Foreign Affairs, Subcommittees on Europe and the Middle East and on International Economic Policy and Trade. 1984. *East-West Economic Issues, Sanctions Policy, and the Formulation of International Economic Policy.* Hearing, 98th Cong., 2d sess., 29 March.
U.S. House. Committee on Foreign Affairs, Subcommittee on Human Rights and International Organizations. 1981. *Implementation of Congressionally Man-dated Human Rights Provisions.* 97th Cong., 1st sess.
U.S. House. Committee on Foreign Affairs, Subcommittee on Inter-American Affairs. 1982. *Latin America and the United States after the Falklands/Mal-vinas Crisis.* Hearings, 97th Cong., 2d sess., 20 July, 5 August.
U.S. House. Committee on Foreign Affairs, Subcommittee on International Rela-tions. 1979. *Human Rights and U.S. Foreign Policy.* Hearings, 96th Cong., 1st sess., 2 May, 2 August.
U.S. House. Committee on International Relations, Subcommittee on Interna-tional Economic Policy and Trade. 1978. *Export Licensing: CoCom List Re-view Proposals of the United States.* 95th Cong., 2d sess., June.
U.S. House. Committee on International Relations, Subcommittee on Interna-tional Organizations. 1976. *Chile: The Status of Human Rights and Its Rela-tionship to U.S. Economic Assistance Programs.* Hearings, 94th Cong., 2d sess., 29 April, 5 May.

————. 1976. *Human Rights Issues at the Sixth Regular Session of the Organization of American States General Assembly.* 94th Cong., 2d sess.

U.S. House. Committee on Science, Space, and Technology. 1987. *National Academy of Sciences Report on International Technology Transfer.* Hearings, 100th Cong., 1st sess., 4 February, 23 April.

U.S. House. Committee on Ways and Means, Subcommittee on Trade. 1984. *Report on Trade Mission to Central and Eastern Europe.* 98th Cong., 2d sess., 29 March.

U.S. Senate. Committee on Banking and Currency, Subcommittee on International Finance. 1968. *East-West Trade.* Hearings, 90th Cong., 2d sess., June.

U.S. Senate. Committee on Banking, Housing, and Urban Affairs. 1979. *U.S. Export Control Policy and Extension of the Export Administration Act.* Hearings, 96th Cong., 1st sess., pt. 1, 5 and 6 March; pt. 3, 3 May.

————. 1981. *Proposed Trans-Siberian Natural Gas Pipeline.* Hearing, 97th Cong., 1st sess., 12 November.

————, Subcommittee on International Finance. 1980. *U.S. Embargo of Food and Technology to the Soviet Union.* Hearings, 96th Cong., 2d sess., 22 January, 24 March.

U.S. Senate. Committee on Banking, Housing, and Urban Affairs, Subcommittee on International Finance and Monetary Policy. 1987. "Statement by Secretary of Commerce Malcolm Baldrige," 12 March.

U.S. Senate. Committee on Foreign Relations. 1983. *Human Rights Documents.* 98th Cong., 1st sess., September.

U.S. Senate. Committee on Foreign Relations, Subcommittee on Foreign Assistance. 1977. *Human Rights.* Hearings, 95th Cong., 1st sess., 4, 7 March.

U.S. Senate. Committee on Foreign Relations, Subcommittee on International Economic Policy. 1981. *East/West Economic Relations.* Hearing, 97th Cong., 1st sess., 16 September.

————. 1982a. *Soviet-European Gas Pipeline.* Hearing, 97th Cong., 2d sess., 3 March.

————. 1982b. *Economic Relations with the Soviet Union.* Hearings, 97th Cong., 2d sess., 30 July, 12–13 August.

U.S. Senate. Committee on Governmental Affairs, Permanent Subcommittee on Investigations. 1980. *Transfer of Technology to the Soviet Bloc.* Hearing, 96th Cong., 2d sess., 20 February.

————. 1982. *Transfer of United States High Technology to the Soviet Union and Soviet Bloc Nations.* 97th Cong., 2d sess., 15 November. Report 97–664.

————. 1984. *Transfer of Technology.* Hearings, 98th Cong., 2d sess., 2, 3, 11, 12 April.

U.S. Senate. Committee on Governmental Affairs, Subcommittee on Energy, Nuclear Proliferation, and Government Processes. 1981. *Soviet Energy Exports and Western European Energy Security.* Hearing, 97th Cong., 1st sess., 14 October.

U.S. Senate. Permanent Subcommittee on Investigations. 1984. *Transfer of Technology.* 98th Cong., 2d sess., 5 October. Report 98–664.

U.S. State Department. Battle Act reports, various dates.

————. 1978. *Human Rights and U.S. Policy: Argentina, Haiti, Indonesia, Iran, Peru, and the Philippines.* 31 December.

Valenzuela, J. Samuel, and Arturo Valenzuela, eds. 1986. *Military Rule in Chile: Dictatorship and Oppositions.* Baltimore: Johns Hopkins University Press.

Vincent, R. J., ed. 1986. *Foreign Policy and Human Rights: Issues and Responses.* Cambridge: Cambridge University Press.

*Virginia Journal of International Law* 14, no. 4 (Summer 1974), "Symposium: Human Rights, the National Interest, and U.S. Foreign Policy."

Vogelgesang, Sandy. 1980. *American Dream, Global Nightmare: The Dilemma of U.S. Human Rights Policy.* New York: W. W. Norton & Co.

von Amerongen, Otto Wolff. 1980. "Economic Sanctions as a Foreign Policy Tool?" *International Security* 5, no. 2 (Fall): 159–67.

Wallensteen, Peter. 1968. "Characteristics of Economic Sanctions." *Journal of Peace Research* 3: 248–67.

Walt, Stephen M. 1987. *The Origins of Alliances.* Ithaca: Cornell University Press.

————. 1988. "Testing Theories of Alliance Formation: The Case of Southwest Asia." *International Organization* 42, no. 2 (Spring): 275–316.

Waltz, Kenneth N. 1979. *Theory of International Politics.* New York: Random House.

Weintraub, Sidney, ed. 1982. *Economic Coercion and U.S. Foreign Policy: Implications of Case Studies from the Johnson Administration.* Boulder: Westview Press.

Weiss, Arnold H. 1978. "Human Rights in World Bank–IMF Lending." *American Banker*, 25 September, p. 21.

Weissbrodt, David. 1977. "Human Rights Legislation and U.S. Foreign Policy." *Georgia Journal of International and Comparative Law* 7: 231–87.

Wienert, Helgard, and John Slater. 1986. *East-West Technology Transfer: The Trade and Economic Aspects.* Paris: Organization for Economic Cooperation and Development.

Williams, Phil. 1983. "Miscalculation, Crisis Management, and the Falklands Conflict." *The World Today* 39, no. 4 (April): 144–49.

Woolcock, Stephen. 1982. *Western Policies on East-West Trade.* London: Routledge & Kegan Paul.

Worcester, Robert, and Simon Jenkins. 1982. "Britain Rallies 'Round the Prime Minister." *Public Opinion* 5 (June/July): 53–55.

Wu, Yuan-Li. 1952. *Economic Warfare.* New York: Prentice-Hall.

Yergin, Angela Stent. 1980. *East-West Technology Transfer: European Perspectives.* The Washington Papers, vol. 8, no. 75. Beverly Hills: SAGE Publications.

Young, Amy. 1985. "Human Rights Policies of the Carter and Reagan Administrations: An Overview." *Whittier Law Review* 7: 689–96.

Young, Elizabeth. 1982. "Falklands Fall-out." *The World Today* 38, no. 9 (September): 327–30.

Young, Oran R. 1989. *International Cooperation: Building Regimes for Natural Resources and the Environment.* Ithaca: Cornell University Press.

Zaleski, Eugene, and Helgard Wienert. 1980. *Technology Transfer between East and West.* Paris: Organization for Economic Cooperation and Development.

# Index